Sustainable Value Creation in Hospitality:
Guests on Earth

Edited by

Elena Cavagnaro

(G) **Goodfellow Publishers Ltd**

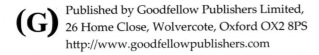

Published by Goodfellow Publishers Limited,
26 Home Close, Wolvercote, Oxford OX2 8PS
http://www.goodfellowpublishers.com

British Library Cataloguing in Publication Data: a catalogue record for this title is available from the British Library.

Library of Congress Catalog Card Number: on file.

ISBN: 978-1-911396-38-3

 Design and typesetting by P.K. McBride, www.macbride.org.uk

Cover design by Cylinder

Printed and bound in Great Britain by Marston Book Services Ltd, Oxfordshire

Contents

Acknowledgements   vi

The Authors   vii

1   Guests on Earth: An introduction to sustainability in hospitality   1
Elena Cavagnaro

2   The Sustainable Hospitality Value Chain   11
Elena Cavagnaro

Part I: Distribution   27

3   Tourist Mobility: Is transport a necessary evil?   29
Matthias Olthaar

4   Distribution at the Destination: An underestimated force to improve hospitality services and enhance sustainable development   50
Sarah Seidel

5   Are You Aware of What You Share With a Third-Party Internet Site? Sustainability challenges concerning privacy in the sharing of information   62
Marit de Vries, Niels van Felius, Elena Cavagnaro

6   The Impact of Third-Party Internet Sites on the Hotel Guest Journey   84
Niels van Felius, Elena Cavagnaro and Marit de Vries

Part II: Buildings   105

7   Technology: A Double Edged Sword   107
Elena Cavagnaro

8   Equipping Better Buildings   118
Thulani Xhali and Philipp Kanthack

Part III: Purchasing   145

9   Purchasing Local for Sustainable Development   147
Sarah Seidel and Elena Cavagnaro

10 Sustainable Purchasing in an International Context: A relational perspective **169**
Ko Koens and Harry Reinders

**11 Sustainable Transport of Goods: Tackling backstage challenges
        of the hospitality industry**   **186**
Jörn Fricke

Part IV: Operations   **205**

12 Social Responsibility – Your Employees   **207**
Frans Melissen and Nadia Teunissen

13 The Changing Role of Work: Staff outsourcing in the 'gig economy'   **221**
Bill Rowson and Elena Cavagnaro

14 The Rooms Division   **247**
Femke Vrenegoor

15 The Food & Beverage Department: At the heart of a sustainable hotel   **274**
Elena Cavagnaro

16 Conclusion   **300**
Elena Cavagnaro

Index   **305**

Best Cases

Case 3.1: Alpine Pearls — 35

Case 3.2: BlaBlaCar — 36

Case 3.3: Holidays by rail — 36

Case 4.1: Alpine Pearls — 56

Case 4.2: Association of Christian hotels — 57

Case 5.1: 'A Random Hotel' and safeguarding guest data — 72

Case 5.2: 'Just a hotel' and a TPI — 75

Case 6.1: Online Travel Agency BookDifferent — 97

Case 7.1: Philips and the Service of Light — 111

Case 7.2: Bakeys' edible cutlery — 112

Case 7.3: Dancing and walking generate energy — 112

Case 8.1: Accreditation Systems: Van der Valk and BREEAM: Deliberate Sustainability — 124

Case 8.2: Materials and Energy: Materials Passport: The Madaster Foundation — 125

Case 8.3: Financing: The Hilton Universal City and PACE — 126

Case 9.1: Fogo Island Inn — 157

Case 9.2: Healthy Kansas Hospitals — 158

Case 10.1: Fairmont Hotels – sustainable development as a core value — 175

Case 10.2: How a horse became a cow — 176

Case 10.3: Eurostar – creating long-term supplier relationships — 177

Case 11.1: Economic challenge — 193

Case 11.2: Environmental challenge — 194

Case 11.3: Social challenge — 194

Case 12.1: The inclusive project 'Hotel with 6 stars' of the Meliá Roma Aurelia Antica — 211

Case 12.2: Design your employees' customer journey — 212

Case 12.3: Travellers café Viavia Jogja — 212

Case 13.1: NH Hotel Group's commitment to labour rights — 233

Case 13.2: Bilderberg, a careful approach to outsourcing — 234

Case 13.3: Creating value for employees and the local community at Costa Navarino — 235

Case 14.1: Please Disturb — 254

Case 14.2: Cradle-to-cradle mattresses – Royal Auping — 256

Case 15.1: Fair Trade — 282

Case 15.2: Food of the future — 285

Case 15.3: Feldmilla and a sustainable food supply chain — 286

Acknowledgments

A project of this scope can never be brought to a good end without the help of many people. I would like to take the opportunity to thank them all.

In particular, also on behalf of all authors of the book, I wish to thank all professionals from the hospitality and tourism industry who shared with us examples of best practices. All these examples clearly illustrate that it is possible to create value on the environmental, social and economic dimensions in the hospitality industry.

Without the support of the members of NHL Stenden Research Group Sustainability in Hospitality and Tourism, and in particular of David Casey, I would never have embarked in this project. Not only are several Research Group members authors of chapters in this book, but they also provided extensive and sensible feedback on each others' and my own chapters.

This book has been envisioned thinking of the needs of managers in the hospitality industry, as they have been expressed or become clear to me and to the colleagues collaborating on this book. Our students have also been a source of information and inspiration. In particular I wish to thank the students of the Hospitality Excellence Program, introduced by the Dutch Hotels Schools in collaboration with the Koninklijke Horeca Nederland (Royal Association of Businesses in the Catering and Related Industry, 'Hospitality Netherlands'). One of the challenges presented to the students participating in this program was connected to sustainability. I thank them not only for sharing their doubts and insights with me, but also for their enthusiasm for sustainability. On a similar line, I wish to thank all bachelor and master students at Stenden Hotel Management School who in the past years collaborated in my research. This book is dedicated to you all in my heart.

A word of thank is due to all authors who, sometimes under severe personal circumstances, have contributed to this work. I wish also to thank all colleagues from Stenden Hotel Management School, and particularly its dean Dr. Craig Thompson, for their understanding and support. They covered for me when I had to dedicate several days on a row to editing the book.

Last but not least I wish to thank Tim Goodfellow and Sally North, from Goodfellow Publishing. I shared the first idea for this book with Tim Goodfellow during the 'Guests on Earth' conference organized by my professorship at Stenden (now NHL Stenden) in 2015. Tim Goodfellow saw the potential of a book on sustainability in hospitality structured around the Sustainable Hospitality Value Chain. His early support for this idea was essential to the success of the project. Sally North, editorial director at Goodfellow Publishing, has been invaluable during the whole editing process. I thank her particularly for her patience and good advice.

Elena Cavagnaro, Leeuwarden, 1 March 2018

The authors

Dr Elena Cavagnaro, UAS Professor of Sustainability in Hospitality and Tourism, NHL Stenden University of Applied Sciences, Stenden Hotel Management School, Academy of International Hospitality Research, Leeuwarden, The Netherlands

Lennart Buchholz, BA student at Stenden Hotel Management School, Leeuwarden, The Netherlands

Niels van Felius, MA, NHL Stenden University of Applied Sciences, Stenden Hotel Management School, Academy of International Hospitality Research, Leeuwarden, The Netherlands

Dr Jörn Fricke, Breda University of Applied Sciences, Academy of Hotel and Facility Management, Breda, The Netherlands

Philipp Kanthack, Purchasing Manager Stenden Hotel, NHL Stenden University of Applied Sciences, Leeuwarden, The Netherlands

Dr Ko Koens, NHTV Breda University of Applied Sciences, Academy of Hotel and Facility Management, Breda, The Netherlands

Dr Matthias Olthaar, UAS Professor of Green Logistics, NHL Stenden University of Applied Sciences, Emmen, The Netherlands

Frans Melissen, NHTV Breda University of Applied Sciences, Academy of Hotel and Facility Management, Breda, The Netherlands

Harry Reinders, NHTV Breda University of Applied Sciences, Academy of Hotel and Facility Management, Breda, The Netherlands

Dr Bill Rowson, NHL Stenden University of Applied Sciences, Stenden Hotel Management School, Academy of International Hospitality Research, Leeuwarden, The Netherlands

Sarah Seidel, MA, NHL Stenden University of Applied Sciences, School of Leisure and Tourism, Academy of International Hospitality Research, Leeuwarden, The Netherlands.

Dr Silvana Signori, Professor of Accounting and Governing Sustainability, University of Bergamo, Italy

Nadia Teunissen, NHTV Breda University of Applied Sciences, Academy of Hotel and Facility Management, Breda, The Netherlands

Femke Vrenegoor, MA, NHL Stenden University of Applied Sciences, Stenden Hotel Management School, Academy of International Hospitality Research, Leeuwarden, The Netherlands

Marit de Vries, MA, NHL Stenden University of Applied Sciences, Stenden Hotel Management School, Leeuwarden, The Netherlands

Thulani Xhali, General Manager, Stenden Hotel, NHL Stenden University of Applied Sciences, Leeuwarden, The Netherlands

1 Guests on Earth:
An introduction to sustainability in hospitality

Elena Cavagnaro

This book is titled *Sustainable Value Creation in Hospitality, Guests on Earth,* and you are probably wondering what exactly these words imply. In this introduction we briefly explain what we mean by hospitality and by sustainability. We also clarify why we believe that sustainability matters to hospitality, and why all those who work in this fascinating sector should behave like 'guests on Earth'.

Hospitality is generally understood to be the art of making people feel welcome. Hospitality is demonstrated in private settings, as when we invite a friend to dine with us; in social settings; when we relate to foreigners; and in commercial settings. Restaurants, cafes, caterers, hotels and other forms of accommodation such as those offered by Airbnb, are all part of commercial hospitality. This book focuses specifically on commercial hospitality and, within this setting, on hotels and other forms of accommodation, even though several of its chapters will also prove useful to the food and beverage sector, including restaurants, cafes and caterers. Before addressing why it is important for hospitality to engage in sustainability and why therefore this book is useful for people wishing to join or already working in the hospitality industry, I would add that I hope this book will also be interesting for professionals working in the broader tourism industry for at least three reasons. First, because it discusses themes such as tourism transportation that are of immediate interest to the tourism industry in general. Second, because hotels and accommodations are essential components in any tourism package, and thus getting to know their operations better may be useful for all tourism professionals. And third, because of the so-called multiplier effect of hotels, or in other words the capacity of this industry to generate returns for a broader area and not only for the hotel premises itself. Take, for example, the labour and all goods, such as food and furniture, needed in a hotel. If labour and goods are sourced locally, this will have a positive socio-economic effect on the community surrounding the hotel. A vibrant community, in its turn, is attractive from a tourism perspective. Therefore, also in this respect, hotels are of interest to tourism developers and professionals.

The core activity of hotels is to provide lodgings, food and drink to their guests. Many hotels also provide leisure, conference and banqueting facilities and business services. Obviously, the mix of services and facilities provided depends on the market they serve and on new developments. One of the most exciting developments the hospitality industry is facing is the increasing attention that several social actors are paying to sustainability.

Sustainability requires that organisations create value not only in the economic but also in the social and environmental dimensions. Consider, for example, a hotel that makes a profit but at the same time pollutes the environment with its waste and sets the health of its employees at risk by regularly putting them on overtime. That hotel does not contribute to a better, more sustainable world because it does not create value along all three economic, social and environmental dimensions. On the contrary, in the process of creating economic value for itself, it takes value from society because it generates costs that have to be met by the community in which the hotel is located, such as costs involved in handling the waste and in restoring the health of overworked staff. Conversely, hotels can contribute to a more sustainable world by investing, for example, in renewable energy and employee development, as we will see more in depth in Chapter 2, *The Sustainable Hospitality Value Chain*.

Between the 1970s and the 1990s sustainability advocates focused mainly on the role that national and regional governments can play in bringing about sustainability. The necessity of involving businesses in achieving a more equitable and environmentally friendly world started to be recognised in the mid-1990s. The first targets were large corporations in the oil and chemical industries, such as Shell and ExxonMobil, because they are highly visible and have a largely negative impact on the natural environment. Companies whose products are closely linked with people's health, such as the food giant Unilever, were targeted next. Industries that comprise a few major chains and a large number of smaller independent chains or establishments, such as hospitality and tourism, are less visible and escaped attention for a while. However, since the start of the new millennium those industries have also been under increasing scrutiny.

In this context, 2016 and 2017 were two especially intense years. In 2016, the Paris climate agreement called upon all industries, and particularly the tourism and hospitality industry, to take responsibility for climate change. Tourism currently accounts for almost 5% of worldwide carbon emissions, while accommodations account for approximately 20% of the emissions from tourism (UNWTO and UNEP, 2008). The tourism and hospitality industry's contribution to global warming is therefore significant, and the Paris climate agreement rightly requested that it take measures to reduce its negative impact on the natural environment. Moreover, the United Nations designated 2017 as the International Year of Sustainable Tourism for Development. The aim of the UN is to utilise the transformative force of tourism, not only as an ally in lowering carbon emissions, but also as an opportunity to celebrate cultural diversity, foster social inclusiveness, reduce poverty, promote peace and stimulate sustainable economic growth (UN, 2016). Finally, the role that hotels may, knowingly or unknowingly, play in modern forms of workers' exploitation is also increasingly under scrutiny (Lashley, 2017).

Several hotels responded to the increasing pressure to behave more sustainably with eco-efficiency programmes that not only reduced their impact on the natural environment but also improved their economic bottom line. To improve in the social dimension of sustainability, some hotels have started to scrutinise working conditions on their own properties and in the supply chain, as well as other social challenges, as we will see for example in the case dedicated to the Accor hotel chain in Chapter 18, *Rooms Division*. In short, hotels are starting to take responsibility not only for profit, but also for people and the planet all along the value chain (see more on these concepts in Chapter 2, *The Sustainable Hospitality Value Chain*). However, and notwithstanding some excellent examples, hospitality is still lagging behind other industries in setting sustainability at the centre of its strategy and seriously implementing it in its operations (Melissen *et al.*, 2016). During interviews with hotel managers on sustainability, I have learnt that the first question that needs to be addressed is why they should focus on sustainability. Therefore, before introducing the role that this book hopes to play in helping hotels to become more sustainable, I wish to first discuss why hotels should engage in sustainability.

Basically, the question as to why hotels should engage in sustainability has already been answered, namely to respond to pressures from institutions that increasingly hold the hospitality industry accountable for its negative impact on people and the planet. In fact, if the hospitality industry does not respond properly, society might start questioning its right to continue operating. This right is called the *social licence to operate* and refers to society's acceptance of business activities. A social licence to operate is lost when society concludes that the economic value created by a business is outweighed by its negative impact in other areas, such as the water pollution caused by a hotel's operations or the annoying behaviour of tourists. Society may well conclude that a business has lost its social licence to operate even before the social or environmental base of a destination is completely worn out. Consider, for example, the protests by citizens of cities such as Barcelona and Amsterdam against all-invasive tourists. These protests may be interpreted as a signal that the social acceptance of the tourism and hospitality industry is eroding. Building on this and similar trends, futurist Ian Yeomen predicts that by 2030 people might forego the pleasure of tourism due to the negative impact that it has on other values they treasure, such as a healthy natural environment and strong social ties. Though a ban on tourism might seem far-fetched, society is definitely aware of the negative social and environmental impacts of tourism (Yeoman, 2011). Tourism and hospitality may therefore rightly choose to embrace sustainability to respond to social pressure and keep their social licence to operate.

What all the above-mentioned examples show is that one reason why hotels engage in sustainability is to respond to external pressure and avoid the potentially huge costs of non-compliance with societal expectations. Although responding to societal pressure is better than denying it and rejecting any responsibility to act sustainably, businesses that are externally motivated more often than not only seek to conform with the minimum requirements of relevant laws and regulations on, for example, environmental impacts, health and safety. Compliance brings its rewards, such as risk minimisation and improved reputation (Benn *et al.*, 2014). Yet, although this is an important first step, compliance is a reactive stance and fails to recognise the unique potential that the hospitality industry has in addressing social and environmental issues, and to reap the fruit of a more pro-active, intrinsically motivated approach to sustainability. Hotels, in fact, are in a unique position to address sustainability issues because they maintain strong relations with social, economic and environmental systems at all levels, i.e., global, national, regional and local. Consider a major hotel chain, such as Hilton. It is a globally operating company, with properties at 570 locations in 6 continents (see: http://www3.hilton.com/en/about/hilton/index.html, accessed on 06 February 2018). Compare this with Unilever, the global food giant. Besides its headquarters in Rotterdam (the Netherlands) and London (UK), Unilever has just over 500 subsidiaries of which most are in West Europe and North America (see the summary spreadsheet available at: https://www.unilever.com/search.html?se arch=production+facilities&contenttype=xls, accessed on 06 February 2018). The diffuse, worldwide presence of Hilton – and of many other global hotel chains – places it in a perfect position to make a significant contribution to sustainable development on a global and local scale. Smaller chains and independent hotels enjoy a similar opportunity at the local level, because they are or could become profoundly linked to specific communities and (tourism) destinations. For this reason, hotels may and should go beyond giving minimal responses to external pressures and embrace sustainability as an opportunity to extend hospitableness beyond their guests, towards their own employees and the employees of their business partners along the chain, the local community and the entire planet.

As noted, intrinsically motivated hotels seize the unique opportunity inherent to their situation to make our world a better one and consider sustainability as part and parcel of their corporate promise to provide guests with an authentic, hospitable experience. This is in fact the main answer that hotel managers who are forerunners in sustainability usually give when I question them as to why they engage in it. There are, however, differences in the more specific reasons they voice, in the measures they take and in the benefits they reap. Generally speaking, we can distinguish three specific reasons why intrinsically motivated companies engage in sustainability, and they are because they consider themselves as stewards of the social and environmental base on which their future depends; because sustainability is a huge business opportunity; and because sustainability is transformational and innovative by nature.

Let us consider these answers one by one, starting with sustainability as stewardship and a guarantee for the survival of the hospitality industry. The sustainability policy of Meliá Hotels International illustrates this view exceptionally well. Meliá Hotels is a Spanish family-owned business and, with more than 370 hotels in 43 countries in 4 continents, is one of the largest hotel companies in the world. In its sustainability policy Meliá Hotels International openly states that it aims to contribute to a better, more sustainable world. In explaining why it opts for sustainability, Meliá Hotels International states the following:

"… We believe that sustainability is the key factor which will allow tourism to continue to be the driver of economic development in many countries. …Tourism is a business which is extremely sensitive to the environment in which it takes place. Extreme climate and weather events such as hurricanes and floods, drought or lack of snow, have an effect on tourism. The loss of a cultural identity in a destination may make it less attractive for tourism as it implies the disappearance of something that made it unique. The existence of poverty in certain communities in which we operate is also a reality to be faced. Seeking improvements in such situations are an obligation which we must satisfy before our staff, our customers and society in general" (Meliá Hotels International, 2018).

In the quote taken from its Sustainability Policy, Meliá Hotels International makes a clear case for sustainability as stewardship and as a necessity for the survival of all organisations, such as hotels, that depend for their success on a healthy natural environment and on a lively, attractive community at the destination. Unfortunately, there are many examples of the negative impact of the hospitality and tourism industry on the natural and social environment of destinations. As already mentioned, the hospitality and tourism industry is responsible for 5% of all CO_2 emissions worldwide. CO_2 is a greenhouse gas that contributes to global warming. Global warming is not only a major threat to human life on earth in the medium-long term, but is already a risk for many communities such as the ones living on river deltas and on islands. For example, atoll islands such as the Polynesian Tuvalu and the Fiji Islands in the Pacific might disappear due to coral bleaching and rising sea levels – both consequences of climate change (Nunn, 2012). If these islands have to be abandoned, their inhabitants will need to relocate, with all the consequent difficulties, pain and suffering. From a hospitality and tourism point of view the islands' disappearance will mean the loss of a destination and a culture that attract tourists. As Meliá Hotels International states, if the hotel industry does not address its contribution to climate change it will in the end erode the environmental and social base on which it feeds and thus destroy itself. Opting for sustainability is therefore a necessity for the continuity of hospitality as a commercial undertaking.

Hotels that opt for a stewardship approach usually focus on reducing their negative impact on the natural environment, as this quote from the Corporate Social Responsibility policy of a Dutch small hotel chain, Bilderberg, shows:

Bilderberg uses a system of sustainable operational management in all its hotels. For example, we are taking steps to reduce our water and energy consumption and are drastically reducing the amount of waste we produce (www.bilderberg.nl/en/about-us/, accessed 06 February 2018).

Bilderberg's choice is a sensible one, because the benefits of the stewardship approach lie largely in efficiency gains, and thus in costs reduction and productivity increase. Following Bilderberg's example, companies may reduce costs and at the same time positively affect the natural environment by lowering the consumption of scarce natural resources, like fresh water, while increasing the amount of goods and services produced (Benn *et al.*, 2014). This strategy is known as eco-efficiency. One of the most impressive examples of eco-efficiency in hotels that has been shared with me, is the energy reduction achieved in a period of three years at Radisson Blu Hotel Amsterdam Airport (The Netherlands). Radisson Blu, now a brand of the Carlson Redizor Hotel Group, is renowned for its attention to environmental sustainability. Harriet Koopman (GM at Radisson Blu Amsterdam Airport till 2015) told me that by introducing several energy saving measures she was able to save 80% on energy costs at this four star property. The two measures that helped to reduce energy consumption the most were the new climate control system and blinds for the windows. Both reduced the use of energy-hungry air conditioning. Among other measures, Harriet Koopman mentioned light sensors and key-cards that switch room lights on and off. The savings achieved surprised not only her, but also all colleagues whom she mentioned it to. And, most importantly, guests' experience was not affected (personal communication, 28 October 2017).

Eco-efficiency is an important stage in the process towards more sustainable hotel operations because eco-efficiency gains can only be reaped if resource stewardship is carefully implemented in processes all along the supply chain. Moreover, eco-efficiency is here to stay. Consider, for example, that in 1992 the European Union introduced a label to measure the energy efficiency of white goods, cars and houses. In its 2010 revised form, the Energy Label ranges from A+++ for the most efficient to G for the least efficient goods (EU, 2017). Finally, if employees are involved in devising efficiency measures, stewardship can also lead to employee involvement and pride.

Eco-efficiency, though, has its limits. A well-known example of the limits of eco-efficiency is provided by developments in the car industry. Contemporary cars have a much better fuel per kilometre ratio than a few years ago, and therefore they emit fewer noxious gasses per driven kilometre. Unfortunately, this efficiency gain has been largely counteracted by car owners driving more than they used to. Something similar happens with energy-saving light bulbs: consumers seem to leave energy-saving bulbs on more often than non-energy saving bulbs so that the hoped-for energy reduction is not fully achieved. As we will see throughout this book, people's behaviour is surely a force to reckon with when introducing sustainability measures. Moreover, and most importantly, from a sustainability perspective, eco-efficiency is limited to the environmental dimension of sustainability and – within this dimension – it is only concerned with reducing negative impacts. As Chapter 2, *Sustainable Hospitality Value Chain*, will show, while reduction is needed, environmental sustainability is also aimed on the one hand at eliminating all harmful gaseous, fluid and solid waste and on the other hand at restoring environmental damage. Surprisingly, intrinsically motivated hotels move quite quickly beyond a stewardship and eco-efficiency approach to sustainability.

In fact, several hotel chains, including Bilderberg, Radisson Blu and Meliá Hotels International, have already moved beyond environmental stewardship and eco-efficiency and view sustainability as a huge business opportunity, the second of the three afore-mentioned reasons why intrinsically motivated hotels engage in sustainability. More specifically, these hotels see sustainability as an opportunity to gain competitive advantage not only by reducing costs (as in the eco-efficiency approach) but also by differentiating themselves from competitors and opening up new markets. Differentiation is badly needed in the hotel sector because mainstream hotels largely look similar and are therefore interchangeable in the minds of the guests. The success of Airbnb has acutely shown that travellers are looking for authentic, unique experiences, and has underlined the need for differentiation. Sustainability may offer an opportunity to stand out. To better understand this approach let me introduce the example of a small Dutch hotel chain that has been intentionally designed to appeal to all guests, but particularly to guests who do not wish to compromise sustainability when enjoying the comfort of a good hotel. This chain is called Conscious Hotels. As the owners state on their website, Conscious Hotels wishes to be 'fully sustainable'. By that they mean going beyond eco-efficiency by, for example, using renewable energy, building a green roof hosting bees and designing furniture from recycled yoghurt pots, refrigerators and coffee cup holders. To achieve these objectives Conscious Hotels has teamed up with universities, artists and the communities around the hotels. Since its establishment Conscious Hotels has been very successful, also in financial terms, and in 2017 the owners opened their third hotel in the highly competitive city of Amsterdam and announced plans for a fourth (Conscious Hotels, n.d.).

The benefits of seeing sustainability as a business opportunity are increased market share, market leadership and stakeholders' commitment (Benn *et al.*, 2014). In fact, a master's student whose research on online guest reviews I supervised, found Conscious Hotels was mentioned by a surprising number of guests as an example of what a sustainable hotel should look like. Its market leadership was broadly recognised. The downside of engaging in sustainability, based on growth opportunity, is that hotels might disengage when market growth slackens off for whatever reason. The second risk of linking sustainability to differentiation and market opportunities is to forget that sustainability is not only about enlarging the consumers' base, but also about a more equitable world where even people who will never enjoy the comfort of a hotel can enjoy a decent life.

To overcome the limitations of the eco-efficiency and the business opportunity approach to sustainability, an approach is needed where sustainability is chosen for its power to transform and innovate and thus to bring to life a more ecologically sound and equitable society. The third reason for why intrinsically motivated hotels opt for sustainability is indeed its transformative and innovative power. Conscious Hotels can also be used as an example here, as they fully embrace sustainability and – in their new property developments – push for innovation. Yet, the most striking example, I know of in this industry, of a company designed to innovate in order to fully achieve social and environmental sustainability is G Adventures. G Adventures was founded in 1990 by Bruce Poon Tip and is the fastest growing adventure-tourism company in the world. Bruce Poon Tip started the company almost singlehandedly, and with a dream, namely to offer authentic, sustainable travel experiences. G Adventures states that:

> Our role as a company is to ensure that we're giving back more to the communities and the natural surroundings that we help you to visit than what is being taken away in our travels. Preserving cultural heritage and conserving and replenishing the natural environment, while improving the lives of local people, is the essence of our way of travelling and is integrated into every decision and action we take at G Adventures. (familytravel.org/member/g-adventures/ accessed 06 February 2018).

This statement is not a lofty promise, and has been operationalised in all the choices G Adventures has made, from environmental protection and animal welfare, via employee engagement to partnering with remote and poor communities, to develop tourism experiences. For G Adventures, partnering with local communities means developing local entrepreneurship whenever it cannot find it. For example, in San Juan La Laguna (Guatemala), in Ometepe (Nicaragua) and in the jungle of Bolivia, G Adventures developed homestay programmes together with the local community. The latter example is particularly telling, because by helping locals to build a new stream of income, unsustainable tree felling and drug trade were effectively stopped. In Cambodia, G Adventures developed a restaurant and training centre run entirely by local street youth and women who were previously employed in the sex industry. As a training centre, the restaurant plays a role in teaching marginalised people new skills and helping them join the food and beverage business (Poon Tip, 2013). When G Adventures does find entrepreneurs who are already operating at one of its destinations, it will choose them as its suppliers in the belief that 'supporting local entrepreneurs and small businesses strengthens communities, raises the overall quality of life, and ensures that the places you love will continue to be loved'. (G Adventures, n.d.). In other words G Adventures sees its business as the result of a process of co-creation with stakeholders such as guests, employees and the local community that increases instead of diminishes the quality of life of present and future generations.

G Adventures illustrates the central aim of companies that opt for sustainability beyond eco-efficiency and market leadership reasons, namely to leverage the transformative and innovative force of sustainability in order to redefine the business environment in the interests of a more sustainable world (Benn *et al.*, 2014). The benefits to the company are similar to the benefits listed for the above-mentioned strategy, i.e., market leadership, enhanced reputation, and stakeholders' commitment. Yet besides these benefits, companies like G Adventures achieve a much higher goal and that is to leave the world in a better condition than they found it.

What conclusion can we draw from discussing reasons why businesses engage in sustainability? I think the main conclusion is that the hospitality and tourism industry in general, and hotels in particular, are in a perfect position to engage resolutely in sustainability: considering the tremendous use of natural resources and the amount of waste produced by hotels, there is enough scope for eco-efficiency; considering that hotels nowadays are quite interchangeable, sustainability can offer an opportunity for diversification; and since hotels have (or can develop) strong ties with the community at destination and since guests are on their premises, they can engage more easily than other businesses in conversations with their stakeholders and co-create truly sustainable solutions with them.

The purpose of this book is to support the efforts of organisations in the hospitality and tourism industry, specifically of hotels, that wish to go beyond mere compliance with sustainability-related laws and regulations. It will offer advice for hotels that see themselves as stewards of natural resources and plan to engage in eco-efficiency measures, and it will prove useful for those hotels that see a major business opportunity in sustainability. Our aim, though, is to show that by considering sustainability as an innovative and transformative force and by connecting with all the stakeholders of a hotel, new business models can be created that, while incorporating eco-efficiency gains and developing a distinctive guest proposition, go beyond the two approaches and deliver long-lasting value on a social, environmental and financial bottom line. To underline this aim we chose 'Guests on Earth' as the subtitle for our book. This aims to convey the notion that planet Earth is a hospitable place for life and that we should reciprocate by acting as good guests. Consider, for example, that Earth is the only planet in the solar system that has developed into a hospitable place for life. Planets nearer to the sun are too hot to sustain life; those further from it are too cold. Moreover, and even more astonishingly, if one takes a moment to reflect on it, Earth has evolved in the course of its history into a place that is increasingly hospitable to all forms of life. At the start, some 4.5 billion years ago, Earth was too inhospitable for any life form. Nowadays, and notwithstanding periods of mass extinction, planet Earth counts an estimated 8.7 million life forms (Mora *et al.*, 2011). Moreover, planet Earth provides us with goods and services that we need to survive but cannot produce. A very simple and effective example is oxygen. You and I need oxygen to live; yet we do not produce it. Plants do. Therefore, we depend on plants for our life, and consequently on the fertile soil in which they grow and on the rain that waters them. If we wish to survive and to pass on our planet as a place fit for life to our children and grandchildren, we need to respect Earth and not abuse its hospitableness. In short, we need to behave as guests on Earth. By seeing ourselves as such, we cannot but conclude that showing true hospitableness as a host does not end at the doors of the hotel but extends to care and compassion to all people and Earth as a whole.

References

Benn, S., Dunphy, D. and Griffiths, A. (2014) *Organizational Change for Corporate Sustainability*, 3rd edition, New York: Routledge.

Conscious Hotels (n.d.) *About us*, www.conscioushotels.com/about-us/. Accessed 6 February 2018.

EU (2017) *Energy Labels*, https://europa.eu/youreurope/business/environment/energy-labels/index_en.htm. Accessed 6 February 2018.

G Adventures (n.d.) *Responsible Travel*, G Local, https://www.gadventures.com/about-us/responsible-travel/. Accessed 6 February 2018.

Lashley, C. (2017) Liberating wage slaves: towards sustainable employment practices, in C. Lashley (ed.), *The Routledge Handbook of Hospitality Studies*, London and New York: Routledge, pp. 389-400.

Melia Hotel (2018) *Sustainability Policy*. www.meliahotelsinternational.com/en/corporate-responsibility/positioning/sustainability-policy.

Melissen, F., Cavagnaro, E., Damen, M. and Düweke, A. (2016) Is the hotel industry prepared to face the challenge of sustainable development, *Journal of Vacation Marketing*, **22** (3) 227-238, DOI: 10.1177/1356766715618997.

Mora, C., Tittensor, D.P., Adl S., Simpson, A.G.B. and Worm, B. (2011) How many species are there on Earth and in the ocean?, *Journal of PLOS Biology*, **9** (8), e1001127, DOI:org/10.1371/journal.pbio.1001127.

Nunn, P.D. (2012) *Climate Change and Pacific Island Countries, Asia-Pacific Human Development Report Background Papers Series 2012/07,sp.*: UNDP.www.uncclearn.org/sites/default/files/inventory/undp303.pdf. Accessed 29 August 2017.

Poon Tip, B. (2013) *Looptail: How One Company Changed the World by Reinventing Business*, New York: Business Plus.

UN (2016) *Resolution adopted at the General Assembly on 22 December 2015, 70/193. International Year of Sustainable Tourism for Development, 2017*, http://www.un.org/en/ga/search/view_doc.asp?symbol=A/RES/70/193. Accessed 7 June 2017.

UNWTO and UNEP (2008) *Climate Change and Tourism: Responding to Global Challenges*, Madrid: UNWTO.

Yeoman, I. (2011) *Tomorrow's Tourist, Scenarios and Trends*, Abingdon: Routledge.

Websites

Bilderberg Hotel: www.bilderberg.nl/en/about-us/. Accessed 6 February 2018.

Conscious Hotels: www.conscioushotels.com/home. Accessed 6 February 2018.

Hilton: www3.hilton.com. Accessed 6 February 2018.

Meliá Hotels International: www.meliahotelsinternational.com. Accessed 6 February 2018.

Unilever: www.unilever.com. Accessed 6 February 2018

2 The Sustainable Hospitality Value Chain

Elena Cavagnaro

Learning goals

After studying this chapter, readers will have the ability to:

1 Define sustainability as value creation in an environmental, social and economic dimension at the level of societies, organizations and individuals;

2 Explain the fundamental principles for the environmental, social and economic dimension of sustainability;

3 Compare and contrast the concepts of shared value and sustainability;

4 Describe the four quadrants of the Sustainable Hospitality Value Chain;

5 Compare and contrast the Sustainable Hospitality Value Chain with Porter's value chain.

This book is based on three main overarching concepts: sustainable value creation; the principles underlining the environmental, social and economic dimension of sustainability; and the Sustainable Hospitality Value Chain. This chapter explains these three concepts in dedicated sections.

Sustainable value creation

In the introduction to this book, sustainability was briefly defined as value creation in the economic, social and environmental dimensions. The introduction also illustrated why the hospitality industry is in a perfect position to engage in sustainability. In this section we explain the concept of sustainable value creation in more depth on the basis of Cavagnaro and Curiel (2012) and Cavagnaro (2016). For more information or further sources please refer to these two books.

An organisation creates value when the costs of producing and delivering a good or service are lower than the benefits gained by selling it. In this definition of value creation, costs and benefits are broadly understood. In other words, value is not only considered in economic terms but may include social costs, such as health problems caused by unsafe working conditions, and social benefits, such as the creation of jobs. The definition also includes environmental costs, such as water pollution, and environmental benefits, such as renewable energy. Yet, in contemporary business management thought the concept of value is largely explained with an exclusive reference to the financial bottom line of a company. Value is considered to be the same as profit and is realised when the *economic* costs of producing and distributing a good or service are less than the *economic* benefits obtained by selling it. From this perspective there are two main strategies to increase profit, i.e., increasing revenues or reducing costs. To understand the limits of a purely economic understanding of the concept of value creation, let us briefly but critically assess both strategies by looking at their merits and demerits.

Let us first consider increasing revenues. For the sake of the argument, we look at increasing revenues under very positive conditions, which is when a market is growing. In a growing market an increasing number of people ask for a specific product and service; it is therefore easy to increase revenues by expanding the market base. Yet even when a market is growing, an expansion strategy has its downsides both in general, and in the specific context of sustainability. To illustrate these downsides let us consider the example of tourism growth in the city of Amsterdam in The Netherlands. Nowadays, Amsterdam is one of the most appealing European cities for tourists. Yet this has not always been the case. Around the 1980s Amsterdam's position on the tourism market was rather weak. Its image had suffered from various incidents and a weakening economic climate, whilst the competition of other European cities was increasing. Amsterdam was increasingly considered a city of problems rather than opportunities. To change the tide and re-establish Amsterdam as a tourism and business destination, in September 2004 Amsterdam Partners, an organisation established a year earlier to manage the marketing efforts of Amsterdam, launched a campaign to re-brand the city. The campaign had great success and its slogan, '**I Am**sterdam', is still in use today (Kavaratzis and Ashworth 2006). Building upon the success of the '**I Am**sterdam' campaign, in 2009 the Municipality of Amsterdam issued a new plan to expand tourism by focusing on the so-called MICE industry (Meetings; Incentives; Congresses and Events). Tourist numbers increased sharply, from 4,192,000 in 2004 to 7,435,000 in 2016. Overnight stays in Amsterdam also increased from 8,000,000 in 2004 to more than 14,000,000 in 2016. The hotel business boomed; in 2004 Amsterdam counted 341 hotels with 17,728 rooms and 37,763 beds; in 2016 it boasted 458 hotels with 30,645 rooms and 67,095 beds (Municipality of Amsterdam, n.d.). Room occupancy also increased, except in the years immediately after the 2008 financial crisis.

Amsterdam has an old city centre, nestled around its canals. Cars, trams, bikes and people living in the city know how to manage the narrow streets. As long as the number of tourists remained limited, they were of no inconvenience to day-to-day life in the city. On the contrary, they helped to make Amsterdam the lively destination that everyone wished to visit. With their increasing numbers, and in some cases odd behaviour, tourists become a nuisance in the streets of Amsterdam. Residents first tried to accommodate them by taking a different route to work, for instance, or by getting up earlier than the tourists. Residents then started protesting against their city being taken over by tourists, as they saw it. The Municipality of Amsterdam announced in 2016 that they would reconsider their strategy, regulate the offer of Airbnb, and put a halt to further hotel developments. The case of Amsterdam is not unique. Other European cities, such as Florence in Italy, Barcelona in Spain and Berlin in Germany, are wrestling with the same issue, namely the rapid growth and saturation of a market. A market saturates because there are limits to the selling of a product even when a market is growing. In the case of Amsterdam the product is the city itself and the limits are its narrow streets and the forbearance of its residents confronted with an increasing number of tourists. The conclusion that we can draw from this and similar examples is that strategies exclusively or largely focused on (economic) growth are not sustainable in the long term because they fail to consider the impact of growth on the surrounding community and the natural (or man-made as in the case of cities) environment.

Let us consider whether the same applies to the second strategy, i.e., cost reduction. Are there limits to cost reduction?

In general, businesses always keep a keen eye on costs, because even in a booming market they tend to grow faster than the revenues. When growth slows down though, attention to costs increases and businesses tend to shift their focus from increasing revenues to cutting costs. From a purely economic perspective, costs should indeed be avoided as best as possible and therefore managers tend to cut costs as far as the law and the continuity of operations permit. In some cases, businesses look for ways to avoid overly strict laws and regulations. They might relocate to countries with more lenient laws and, if they cannot relocate, they might interpret laws and regulations in ways that are the most advantageous for themselves. Typical places where managers in hospitality look for 'avoidable costs' are maintenance, purchasing and personnel.

Though costs should always be managed properly, a purely economic perspective could induce a company to shift costs to the future or to other people rather than to cut costs. Consider, for example, the case of purchasing bed linen. In order to get the lowest price possible, a purchasing manager might not consider the conditions under which that linen is produced. It could turn out that the bed linen was produced under very unsafe working conditions in a workshop in Bangladesh; that children were employed in harvesting cotton in India; and that chemicals in the water used in the bleaching process has contaminated the drinking facilities of a village nearby the plant. This could result in bad publicity for the business that purchases the bed linen. However, that is not the point that we wish to make here. The point is that businesses that pursue value creation only on the economic bottom line, might put people and our planet at risk. In other words, the costs that the business has avoided to pay, have not ceased to exist but have been passed on to other people and to the natural environment. These costs might not appear in the business financial accounts, yet they have still to be met – by the people who work under unsafe conditions; by the children working in the fields and by the inhabitants of the village nearby the cotton bleaching plant. In the long term, the country where these people live will be confronted with social issues such as young men and women with no education and no work (the children who used to work but were dismissed when they reached adulthood) and environmental issues such as water pollution that could lead to illness and crop failures (in and around the village). What this example teaches us is that cutting costs can go too far and damage people and our planet. This conclusion is similar to the one we reached when considering a market expansion strategy. There are limits to both strategies, and a situation that brings in profit for a business but generates higher costs for society is not sustainable. In other words, value creation is sustainable only if it creates value along economic, social and environmental dimensions all at the same time. In the case of business organisations we speak of value creation along the three dimensions of profit, people and the planet (see Figure 2.1 below).

Figure 2.1: Sustainable value creation at the level of organisations

Business organisations are not the only ones that are asked to create value on a triple bottom line. Governments too should look further than economic growth alone. Let us think back a moment to the case of Amsterdam. The 2004 and 2009 policies of the Municipality of Amsterdam were mainly orientated towards growth of the number of tourists and thus of revenues for Amsterdam's businesses and the city. This policy could not be sustained in the long run because it did not address its social and environmental impacts. Even for governments, value creation is sustainable only if value is created along the economic, social and environmental dimensions. Governments can be local governments, such as the Municipality of Amsterdam, regional governments, such as of a province, national governments, such as of a whole country, and supranational governments such as the European Union. Figure 2.2 shows that the three dimensions where value can be created at the level of society are in line with the three dimensions of value creation at the level of business organisations. Profit in fact contributes to the economic development of a society; care for people at the level of organisations contributes to social development at society level because, for example, working conditions are safe and the health of workers is not jeopardised; care for the planet at the level of organisations contributes to environmental value at society level because, for example, water and soil are not polluted in the production of goods and services.

Figure 2.2: Sustainable value creation at the level of organisations and societies

To complete the picture we need to also consider the role of individuals in the process of value creation. As management guru Peter Ducker is credited to have said, societies consist of organisations and organisations of individual human beings. We human beings, alone or in groups, are the ones who take decisions in organisations and societies. We are therefore the ones who may decide to pursue only profit at the expense of people and planet. We may also decide to design processes inside the organisation we work for in such a way that value is created simultaneously along the economic, social and environmental dimensions. When considering how decisions are made, the main question that needs to be answered is "which motives guide the decision making process?". Several disciplines, such as sociology, motivational studies and neurobiology, have studied this question. Interestingly, the conclusion that these disciplines reach is similar, namely, that we human beings are moved by three main sets of motives. Let us look at these three sets one by one.

The first set is constituted by our desire to meet our immediate and less immediate needs, such as the need for food and drink; the need for warm clothes and shelter; and the desire to enjoy life. These are strong motives because they are linked to our individual survival. Without food we can only survive for a few weeks, without water only a few days. If we enjoy life, our chance of survival is higher than if we are stressed or in pain. This set of motives has been labelled 'care for me' (Cavagnaro and Curiel, 2012).

The second set of motives derives from our need to bond and build meaningful relationships with others. This set is based on our ability to feel what other people feel, in short to empathise with others. By feeling what other people feel we can rejoice with them or be compassionate towards them. Altruism (our capacity of selfless and disinterested concern for the well-being of others), solidarity and striving for a world at peace are values linked to the second set of motives. 'Care for me & you' is the label of this set (Cavagnaro and Curiel, 2012).

The third set of motives reflects the deep understanding that our life is part of a larger web of life. To explain this point, let us concentrate a moment on breathing. Most people breath unconsciously and effortlessly. Yet we all know that without breathing we could only survive a few minutes. We breathe in oxygen to sustain our life; yet we – human beings – do not produce oxygen. Plants produce oxygen. Our life is inextricably linked with the life of plants, and if we destroy plants in the end we destroy ourselves. The example of oxygen is only one of a long series of examples showing that all life on our planet is linked together, and that we therefore need to extend care and compassion to all life on earth, and not only to other human beings. Acting on this understanding is called 'care for all' (Cavagnaro and Curiel, 2012).

Figure 2.3: Sustainable value creation at the level of societies, organisations and individuals (adapted from Cavagnaro and Curiel, 2012).

Before concluding the discussion on human motives, it is necessary to note that the three sets of motives explained above are not equally strong. All of us, unless we are particularly ill, wish to survive. As a consequence, the 'care for me' motive is more salient to individuals than the 'care for me & you' and the 'care for all' motives, and, under particular circumstances, it can crowd out these other two motives. Yet, as Figure 2.3 illustrates, it is thanks to our ability to care for others and not only for ourselves that we can promote value creation along the people dimension at the level of organisations and along the social dimension at the level of societies. It is thanks to our capacity for 'caring for all' that we can create value along the planet dimension at the level of organisations and along the environmental dimension at the level of societies. Hence the necessity for keeping all three care dimensions equally strong by developing them in ourselves and helping others, such as our team members and our guests, to develop theirs.

To conclude, sustainable value creation means to simultaneously create value along the economic, social and environmental dimensions at the level of societies, organisations and individuals. Sustainable value creation is not a given, but a purposeful process that needs to be carefully designed and managed at each level. Out of the three levels of sustainability illustrated in Figure 2.3, this book focuses on the middle level, i.e., the level of organisations. When appropriate we will also show how individual motives can be leveraged to create sustainable value.

Principles of sustainable value creation

In the previous section we defined sustainability as value creation along the economic, social and environmental dimensions at the level of societies, organisations and individuals. We also concluded that sustainable value creation is not a given, but a purposeful process that needs to be carefully designed and managed at each level. As general management theories teach, processes should be aligned with a company's strategy and the strategy should be based on principles. Principles are therefore the starting point of organisational design. To design an organisation that creates sustainable values, we need to know and understand the general principles of sustainability. By principles we mean basic, universal guidelines that inform specific strategies and actions. This definition will hopefully become clearer in the following discussion in which we explain the general principles of each dimension of sustainability.

Achieving prosperity and a healthy financial position is the basic principle of the economic dimension of sustainability. This principle differs from the usual understanding of economic growth and profit because it does not require unlimited expansion or growth. It does require continuity and therefore a situation in which costs do not exceed revenues. As stated previously, in the context of sustainability we consider all costs that are incurred when making a product or offering a service, including social and environmental costs. There should be no unmet costs or costs left to be paid by future generations.

The basic principles of the social dimension of sustainability are derived from ethics. Ethics is the study of what is fair, just and good in human relationships. Ethics states that two universal principles guide the interaction between people.

Those principles are to avoid harm and to do good. Universal here means that a community based on the contrary principles, i.e., a society where people harm each other and avoid helping each other, will not be able to survive on the long term. To better understand this point, let us consider both principles in general and in the context of sustainable value creation in particular.

We will start with 'avoiding harm' because of the two, this one is considered the most fundamental principle of human interaction. To form and keep a community together it is essential that people refrain from harming each other. To paraphrase a well-known saying, people 'should not do unto others what they do not want others to do unto them'. If people start harming each other, a conflict arises. If this conflict is not quickly resolved, it can escalate and in the end destroy a community. A most striking recent example is the so-called Islamic State (IS). Founded through violence in a part of Iraq and Syria, and based on the exclusion of people who are not 'true Muslims', IS survived only three years from its inception in 2014. It caused thousands of deaths, mass destruction in cities and major loss of cultural heritage. Without considering other societal and political challenges, it will take the affected region in Iraq and Syria years to recover from this destruction. Some communities will likely not recover at all.

Avoiding harm is the most basic of the two principles that guide social interaction precisely because, as the case of IS shows, a community can only survive if people refrain from harming each other. In the context of sustainability, avoiding harm is not restricted to the community to which a person belongs. The principle extends to communities that are further away but that are still touched by decisions made in one's own community. To exemplify, let us consider again the example of hotel linen. A manager might be guided by his or her desire not to harm guests, and therefore opt for linen that is not impregnated with chemicals that can be detrimental to the health of the hotel's guests. The manager might also look beyond the guests and consider the impact of his or her choice on the people who grow the cotton out of which the material is made and the people who work in the factory where the linen is produced. The manager might then look for an alternative that provides the best guarantee that those people are not harmed either.

To do good is the second principle that guides interaction among people. This principle demands that we not only refrain from harming other people but that we also reach out to them and try to influence their life in a positive way. In the case of the afore-mentioned manager, this could imply that he or she decides to explain to the hotel guests why that type of linen was chosen in the hope that this will lead to a higher demand for material that is produced without people being harmed.

As noted previously, avoiding harm is considered to be the most fundamental of these two principles. Whilst we have a moral duty not to leave a person or a community less well off than we found them, we are not under an equal obligation to improve their lives. This point is recognised by the Brundtland commission in its 1987 definition of sustainability, which is considered the classic definition of this term. Sustainability is defined by the Brundtland commission as a form of development that meets the needs of the present generation without compromising the ability of future generations to meet their own needs (WCED, 1987). The definition is clearly about not harming, while its aim (a better quality of life for present and future generations) is about doing good.

The hotel linen example shows the implication of the 'do not harm' principle for the social dimension of sustainability. Yet, 'do not harm' also underpins the basic principle of the environmental dimension of sustainability. This basic principle is generally known as no-waste or zero waste. The principle of no-waste means that the leftovers of human activities should not poison the natural environment. Let us explain this statement by starting with an observation, namely that all living creatures on planet Earth generate leftovers. A cow eats grass, ruminates it, grows and produces milk thanks to the nutrients in the grass, and expels what it cannot use in the form of urine and manure. The manure fertilises the land, so that grass can grow anew and provide the cow with fresh pasture. In this example the leftovers (manure) of one process (milk production) are used as food in another process (grass growing). The leftovers are not wasted, but are the input for a new cycle of production. In this example of a healthy environmental cycle, milk production can go on indefinitely. In nature there are thousands of examples of circular processes where the 'waste' of one process is the 'food' of another process. In fact circular processes are the mechanisms that makes planet Earth a place fit for life. Yet a circular process can get out of balance. Let us consider intensive farming. In intensive farming so many cows are kept in one place that the manure they produce is too much to be fed back into the surrounding land. If it were fed back, the soil would receive too much fertiliser and that abundance, instead of increasing productivity, will ultimately result in uncultivable land and polluted ground water. Manure therefore becomes 'waste' that has to be disposed of somehow. Today, there are thousands of examples of processes that generate 'waste'. CO_2 emission is just another example. CO_2 is produced by humans and other animals in the process of breathing, and is also generated when fossil fuels such as oil and coal are burnt. CO_2 is also needed by plants to grow. Here, too, there is an optimum balance when as much CO_2 is produced as plants can process. Yet nowadays we use so much fossil fuel that this cycle is broken. That we fell forests to harvest timber and to clear land for farming does not help to restore the balance. As a consequence, CO_2 accumulates in the atmosphere with global warming as a consequence. CO_2 has become 'waste'.

The principle of zero waste calls on us to re-design all processes where leftovers cannot be fed back into the natural cycle or disposed of without harming nature. Zero waste is based on the principle of not doing harm, but it may go beyond not harming by also embracing the ethical principle of doing good. As we have seen above, to achieve zero waste processes should be redesigned so that leftovers are the input for a new cycle of production. In doing so, broken circular processes are healed and zero waste does good because it helps preserving the Earth as a place fit for life. The environmental version of the 'doing good' principle is therefore restoring and if possible even improving planet Earth's capacity to support life.

The end goal of zero waste is a circular or cradle-to-cradle economy. In a circular or cradle-to-cradle economy everything that is used can be broken down into components that can either be fed back to nature or be reused to make new products and services. An example of these new types of products is the floor tiles produced by Interface. Interface floor tiles have been designed so that all materials can be extracted without loss of quality and reused to make new tiles (Anderson, 2009). It is an ingenious product that helps Interface to cut costs because it does not need to buy new materials. With its innovative floor tile Interface therefore creates value not only along an environmental but also along a financial dimension.

As a conclusion to our discussion of the principles of sustainable value creation, Table 2.1 summarises these principles for each dimension of sustainability.

Table 2.1: Sustainability dimensions and principles

Sustainability dimension	Principle
Economic value, profit	Prosperity or financial health and continuity
Social value, people	Do not harm Do good
Environmental value, planet	Do not harm: zero waste Do good: restore planet Earth capacity to support life

The sustainable hospitality value chain

The final section of this chapter is dedicated to the concept of the value chain. A value chain is defined as the activities through which organisations create value for their customers. As we have noted in the section above, one of the main principles of sustainability is that human activities should do no harm to people or planet. Human activities include by definition the activities deployed inside organisations to create value for their customers and therefore sustainability principles apply all along a value chain. The more precisely we understand which activities a company undertakes to create value, the better we can appreciate where this company may create sustainable value by avoiding harm and doing good. The concept of value chain is therefore very important in the context of sustainability.

Michael Porter is credited for having introduced the value chain concept in his very influential book entitled *Competitive Advantage* (1985). In this book Porter defines a value chain as the set of activities involved in creating, producing, selling, delivering and supporting a company's products and services. Porter outlined a general-purpose value chain that companies can use to examine their activities, to understand how these activities are connected with each other and with the value chains of suppliers and customers, and to improve on those activities in order to create competitive advantage. In his general-purpose value chain Porter distinguishes between primary activities and support activities. Primary activities, such as operations and marketing, are involved in the creation of the product or service sold to the customer. As their name suggests, support activities support the primary activities by providing materials, human resources and technology needed in the primary process and by performing other company-wide functions. Procurement and HRM are examples of support activities.

The idea behind Porter's value chain is that managers should define and then analyse both primary and support activities in the light of their contribution to value creation and competitive advantage. Porter defines value narrowly as the amount of money that buyers are willing to pay for the products and services provided by an organisation. Consequently, value is measured as revenues minus costs – in short, as profit.

When first introduced, Porter's value chain caused a revolution in strategic management. In assessing its merits from a sustainability perspective it should first of all be stressed that Porter recognises the interrelation of an organisation's value chain with the value chains of its suppliers, of the channels – such as retail stores – through which its goods are sold, and of its customers. In this sense Porter's value chain offers a positive contribution to sustainability because it signals to managers that the organisation for which they are working does not operate in isolation. However, the primary focus of a value chain analysis is internal to the company under scrutiny. As a consequence, the impacts of a company in the chain are seldom considered in value chain analyses. A sustainability approach, on the other hand, requires that an intra-firm perspective be relinquished and that the impact of an organisation's operations beyond its own walls be examined. Sustainability involves both looking back and looking ahead in the supply chain. Moreover, from a sustainability point of view, Porter's concept of value is too narrow because it focuses exclusively on financial revenues. Consequently, value chain analyses have focused mainly on economic viability and have paid insufficient attention to the social and environmental impacts of a company's operations and to the (re)allocation of resources within and between actors in the chain. As we have seen previously, sustainability is only achieved when value is created simultaneously along an economic, a social and an environmental dimension. To be applicable in a sustainability context, Porter's value chain needs to be broadened to include social and environmental benefits and costs. Otherwise, as Fearne, Garcia Martinez and Dent noted, a value chain analysis "risks producing recommendations which either ignore the competitive advantage offered from improving environmental management and social welfare, or have such detrimental external consequences as to render any proposals unsustainable when exposed to government or broader (public) scrutiny" (2012:575).

In a recent article for the *Harvard Business Review* co-authored with Mark Kramer, Michael Porter recognises the negative consequences of defining value creation in strictly financial terms. In their own words companies "[...] view value creation narrowly, optimising short term financial profit in a bubble while missing the most important customer needs and ignoring the broader influences that determine their longer-term success" (Porter and Kramer, 2011:4). As a way out of this impasse Porter and Kramer propose the concept of shared value, i.e., creating economic value in a way that also creates value for society by addressing societal needs and challenges. Value is here redefined as benefit (including social benefits) minus costs – whether hereby also social costs are included is less clear from Porter and Kramer's *Harvard Business Review* article. Also unclear is whether shared value looks at people not only as buyers – and thus as new markets to be exploited – but also as employees and citizens, a critique that has been levelled at the 'Bottom of the Pyramid' concept introduced by Prahalad, and that Porter and Kramer subscribe as an example of shared value creation (Cavagnaro and Curiel, 2012). Porter and Kramer maintain that shared value solutions are able to minimise social impacts by, for example, cutting energy and raw material use. Whether they are able to extend beyond the identification of opportunities for increasing efficiency, is doubtful (Fearne *et al.*, 2012). On a more abstract level, it is remarkable that Porter and Kramer fail to see that creating social and environmental value does not always generate economic value in a time frame that is acceptable to businesses competing in a market economy. Similarly, focusing on customer value as the driver of shared value creation in the chain (as do Fearne *et al.*, 2012) fails to see that not all customers are interested in sustainable goods and services. This notwithstanding, the appeal by Porter and Kramer to consider the local cluster formed by other companies, local institutions and the surrounding community as key to a firm's economic success reinforces the notion already present in the concept of value chain that a firm should look beyond its own walls in order to survive and thrive. What still needs to be done to adapt Porter's value chain concept to sustainability, is to develop a value chain analysis instrument that incorporates all three dimensions of sustainability.

The *Sustainable Hospitality Value Chain* (SHVC) was designed by Elena Cavagnaro in collaboration with the research group Sustainability in Hospitality and Tourism of Stenden Hotel Management School with the intention of overcoming the weaknesses of Porter's value chain analysis described above. To this end, Porter's value chain has been broadened by borrowing concepts from life-cycle assessment and sustainable value creation. The SHVC thus provides a more holistic approach to sustainability than those focusing only on quality improvements and on reducing the use of resources (Hart, 2010).

The initial idea for the SHVC came from the keynote address held by Professor Guido Palazzao during the 2012 EuroCHRIE conference in Lausanne. Palazzo's scheme was reworked and connected with the Three Levels of Sustainability framework (Cavagnaro and Curiel, 2012) to form the SHVC (see Figure 2.4).

The triangle at the centre of the SHVC represents the organisational level of sustainability as outlined in the Three Levels of Sustainability framework (Cavagnaro and Curiel, 2012). This triangle stresses that the aim of the SHVC is the creation of value along an economic, a social and an environmental dimension.

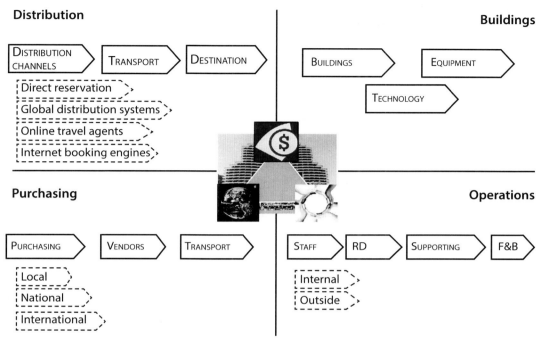

Figure 2.4: The sustainable hospitality value chain (Cavagnaro, 2015)

The SHVC itself is constituted by four quadrants. Each quadrant highlights an area in which a hospitality organisation can create triple bottom line value. The 'boxes' within the quadrants illustrate the main activities of each specific quadrant. We will briefly describe starting from the top left quadrant, Distribution.

Distribution covers the movement of guests, employees, information (such as reservations) and products, to and from a lodging facility. In this quadrant, therefore, you will find 'boxes' such as distribution channels, transport and the destination itself. All these boxes present specific sustainability challenges that should be addressed to create sustainable value. Consider, for example, that tourism-related transportation is responsible for 3.75% of worldwide CO2 emissions (UNWTO and UNEP, 2008). The question is then how people and goods can reach a tourism destination without contributing to global warming.

The next quadrant, Buildings, refers to the physical structures needed to host guests. As it could be expected, it contains boxes for buildings and equipment. Technology is added here because hospitality businesses can add sustainable value to buildings and equipment using sustainable technology. Take, for example, cradle-to-cradle, a concept that has been briefly presented in the section above. Cradle-to-cradle technology not only reduces the amount of resources used but also avoids generating waste by redesigning products so that their components can be feed back in the production cycle. Life-cycle assessment, where the social and environmental benefits and costs of a product throughout its economic life are calculated, is also an essential tool in this quadrant.

The bottom left quadrant, Purchasing, focuses on the support activities needed to provide a hotel with the goods that are needed to serve its guests, such as linen, food, beverages and amenities. In this quadrant we distinguish three boxes: purchasing, (contacts with) vendors and transportation (from and to suppliers).

As Porter remarks, purchasing refers to the *purchasing* of goods and services that are used as input in a hotel value chain and not to the *purchased* inputs themselves. In this quadrant, though, we will refer both to the processes followed by a purchasing department and to the items purchased. From a sustainability perspective, purchased inputs may be local, fair-trade and organic food; eco-labelled cleaning materials and paper; energy-saving light bulbs and so on. Purchasing departments usually make use of procedures for dealing with vendors. From a sustainability perspective it is essential to consider not only the economic but also the social and environmental impact of these procedures. For example, is the agreed price for certain commodities such that the suppliers – and ultimately the producers – can support themselves and their family sufficiently? In other words, a sustainable relationship with vendors implies not only long-term collaboration but also a keen consideration of the distribution of costs and benefits along the supply chain (Fearne *et al.*, 2012). Purchasing, moreover, can occur locally, nationally and internationally – each presenting specific challenges and opportunities. Considering that even locally purchased goods have to be moved, transportation and green logistics are an integral part of this quadrant.

The last quadrant, on the bottom right, is labelled Operations, and is comparable with the primary activity Operations and the supporting activity Human Resource Management (HRM) in Porter's value chain.

Regarding hotel operations, in this book we focus on the Rooms Division (RD) and on the Food & Beverages (F&B) department for two main reasons. Firstly, because RD and F&B are pivotal in a hotel's value proposition to its guests. Hospitality, in fact, is often defined as the provision of accommodation and food and beverages to guests in a safe environment. Secondly, because both RD and F&B present several sustainability challenges that require a narrow notion of value to be purposefully trespassed to create sustainable value to all involved stakeholders. Consider, for example, restaurant menus. Generally speaking in most so-called Western countries, restaurant dishes are high on animal proteins. Guests, chef says, ask for it. Yet, dishes low on animal proteins are better both for the guests' and for our planet's health. Being still rather uncommon they have to be introduced by design (Cavagnaro, 2015).

Among the support processes identified by Porter, the focus in this book is set on staff (HRM). The reason for our choice is twofold. On the one hand, hospitality is defined as a people business where well-trained and hospitable staff are paramount to create value for the guests. On the other hand, we focus on HRM issues because, paradoxically considering the highlighted importance of staff, hospitality is one of the industries where (often unskilled) staff have to work long days for relatively low pay. Other support processes (such as finance) will be touched upon only indirectly in this book.

Conclusion

The book uses the SHVC as an ordering tool to present and discuss the several sustainability challenges that confront hotels. The book is therefore divided into four sections, one for each quadrant. The contributions in each section address the 'boxes' or activities specific to a quadrant. Each contribution has been written by one or more authors, each expert in a particular area and all possessing a deep understanding of sustainability and hospitality. Each contribution considers the main sustainability challenges in its specific 'box', presents two to three best cases and finally shares tools to address these challenges.

References

Anderson, R.C. (2009) *Confessions of a Radical Industrialist, Profits, People, Purpose: Doing business by respecting the Earth*, New York: St Martin's Press.

Cavagnaro, E. (2015) Sustainable restaurant concepts, in Sloan, P. and Legrand, W. (eds.), *Handbook of Sustainable Food, Beverages and Gastronomy*, London: Routledge, pp. 245-252.

Cavagnaro, E. (2015) Introduction of the Sustainable Hospitality Value Chain (SHVC), in Cavagnaro, E., van Felius, N. and Vrenegoor, F., *Minor Future Proof Hospitality - The CSR challenge, Module book 2015-2016*, Leeuwarden: Stenden University of Applied Sciences, pp.18-20

Cavagnaro, E. (2016) *Being Human, Sustainability from the inside out*, Leeuwarden: Stenden.

Cavagnaro, E. and Curiel, G.H. (2012) *The Three Levels of Sustainability*, Sheffield: Greenleaf.

Fearne, A., Garcia Martinez, M. and Dent, B. (2012) Dimensions of sustainable value chains: implications for value chain analysis, *Supply Chain Management: An International Journal*, **17** (6), 575-581

Hart, S.L. (2010) *Capitalism at the Crossroads: Next generation business strategies for a post-crisis world*, 3rd edn, Prentice Hall (New Jersey): Pearson Education

Kavaratzis, M. and Ashworth, G.J. (2006) Changing the tide: the campaign to rebrand Amsterdam, paper presented at the ERSA 2006 Conference, 30 August-3 September 2006, Volos, Greece.

Municipality of Amsterdam (n.d.) *Visualisatie dashboard toerisme* (Visualisation Dashboard Tourism), http://www.ois.amsterdam.nl/visualisatie/dashboard_toerisme.html. Accessed 29 September 2016

Porter, M.E. (1985) *Competitive Advantage: Creating and sustaining superior performance*, New York: The Free Press.

Porter M.E. and Kramer, M.R. (2011) Creating shared value, How to reinvent capitalism – and unleash a wave of innovation and growth, *Harvard Business Review*, January-February, pp. 1-17

UNWTO and UNEP (2008) *Climate Change and Tourism: Responding to global challenges*, Madrid: UNWTO.

WCED (World Commission on Environment and Development) (1987) *Our Common Future*, Oxford: Oxford University Press.

Part I: Distribution

Introduction

Elena Cavagnaro and Sarah Seidel

This book uses the Sustainable Hospitality Value Chain (SHVC) as an ordering tool to present and discuss the several sustainability challenges that confront hotels (Cavagnaro, 2018). The SHVC consists of four quadrants, and the book is therefore divided into four parts, one for each. Distribution is a SHVC quadrant and covers the movement of guests, employees, information (such as reservations) and products, to and from a lodging facility. All these activities present specific sustainability challenges that should be addressed to create sustainable value.

At first sight it may be surprising to find distribution addressed in a book dedicated to hospitality. Distribution is commonly considered to consist of activities that are external and thus not under the control of a hotel. In hospitality value chain analysis, operations, such as food and beverages (discussed in Part IV); purchasing (discussed in Part III) and equipping building (discussed in Part II) are considered to be links in the chain. Distribution is usually neglected.

This book, however, is dedicated to sustainability in hospitality and is built on the premise that hotels should also take responsibility for those links in the chain that may seem external and out of their control. Consider, for example, transportation. CO_2 emissions due to transportation have already reached unsustainable levels. On their way to their hotel, guests use transportation, sometimes travelling distances literally half way around the world. Even though it is the guest who made the decision to travel and even though it is the transportation company that causes the emissions, we maintain that a hotel has the duty to consider and act upon its own responsibility by, for example, encouraging its guests to 'take a vacation from their own car' as in the case of the Apline Pearl destinations discussed by Olthaar.

From this perspective Part I is thus dedicated to analysing the sustainability challenges encountered in distribution and offering tools to address these challenges. It consists of four chapters. The first, authored by Matthias Olthaar, is dedicated to tourist mobility. It is indented to support managers from the tourism and hospitality industry in the transition to a global carbon-neutral society with a focus on transport. Olthaar approaches this task from three inter-related perspectives: technological innovations, behavioural change of tourists, and institutional innovations. He concludes that only orchestrated efforts incorporating all three approaches will lead to more sustainable tourist mobility.

The second chapter, by Sarah Seidel, looks at distribution at the destination. It may appear that when tourists finally reach their destination, distribution is completed. However, tourists usually do not linger inside the perimeters of their hotel. It is therefore legitimate to ask how does the movement of tourists takes place at the destination; what kind of challenges it represents; and which means can be deployed to reach a more sustainable form of travelling at the destination. These questions are asked and answered in this chapter.

The last two chapters introduce challenges and opportunities for distribution in an era where communication between hosts and guests is largely mediated by the Internet. Generally speaking e-commerce and online marketing are presented in the literature as a means to enlarge an organisation's customer base and to ease the access of customers to the company's products and services. While concurring with this view, here we also consider the ethical and sustainability challenges connected to this development. The chapter by Marit de Vries, Niels van Felius and Elena Cavagnaro on Third Party Internet sites (TPIs) illustrates that data collection and data handling by TPIs do not only open up opportunities to understand guests better, but have also implications for the guests' privacy and the hotel's profitability that have to be addressed. The fourth and last chapter, by Niels Van Felius, Elena Cavagnaro and Marit de Vries, focuses on the increased influence of TPIs on the guest journey. It raises the question of whether guests are not gently pushed and then kept in a 'bubble' impeding them from seeing the whole picture when searching for a new travel experience or booking a hotel, and to fully reap the benefits of the experience itself when travelling.

All four chapters show how the challenges connected to distribution can be addressed by illustrating best practices and by sharing tools designed to support managers in handling these challenges sustainably.

3   Tourist Mobility:
Is transport a necessary evil?

Matthias Olthaar

Learning goals

This chapter helps readers to understand and critically evaluate different measures to address sustainability issues in tourist mobility. It covers:

1   The environmental impact of tourist mobility;

2   Suggested solutions for mitigating problems and accompanying challenges and dynamics in practical situations;

3   Solutions from three different perspectives: 1) technological, 2) human behaviour, and 3) policy.

Introduction

Tourism and hospitality create value for both consumers and providers of tourism and hospitality-related activities. Though current consumers and providers of tourist activities can appropriate this value in terms of respite, renewal, and happiness for consumers, and economic development, income and job generation for providers, future generations may well be prevented from being able to appropriate the same value (Becken, 2006; McKercher *et al.*, 2010; Nawijn and Peeters, 2010; Jones, 2014). Climate change makes tourism and hospitality, as we currently know them, victims since global warming and loss of biodiversity threaten the attractiveness of many currently popular tourist locations. However, tourism and hospitality simultaneously contribute a relatively large extent to global greenhouse gas (GHG) emissions (Ram *et al.*, 2013). A rough 5% of global GHG emissions were attributed to tourist activities, in a 2008 report by the United Nations World Tourism Organization (UNWTO). A large part of the tourism sector's share in global GHG emissions comes as a result of tourist transport activities. Tourism and transport are inextricably linked. In the past few decades tourist mobility increased significantly for all transport modalities (airplane, coach, automobile, cruise ship, etc.) and this trend is predicted to continue even further. This poses serious threats for the global climate. Consequently an increasing number of both practitioners and scholars ponder on opportunities to provide tourists with the same value yet through different means. This chapter explores opportunities to engage tourism and hospitality in the transition to a global carbon-neutral society, with a focus on transport.

Tourist mobility has various effects on the natural environment other than climate change, such as loss of biodiversity, soil erosion, and water, air, and soil toxicity. This is a consequence of both the *use* and *production* of transport modalities and related infrastructure. The focus in this chapter is on GHG emissions and climate change. Though transport is not directly in the sphere of influence of hotels and other providers of tourism and hospitality-related activities, it is in their sphere of concern due to their dependency on tourist flows. It is therefore of great importance to include a discussion on tourist mobility in a book dedicated to sustainable value creation in hospitality. In exploring opportunities to make tourist mobility carbon-neutral, three pathways to achieving this are being discussed: 1) technological innovations, 2) behavioural change of tourists, and 3) institutional innovations (i.e. policy making). We find that technological innovations 1) will likely fall short in solving the sustainability issues. In order to address these challenges behavioural change 2) is needed. Yet, since large-scale behavioural change is unlikely to come voluntarily, 3) institutions need to be designed that prescribe people's behaviour in more sustainable terms.

The chapter continues as follows: first, as a concluding part of this introduction, we define our concept of transportation. The major sustainability challenges are being addressed next. There is then a selection of best-practice cases, followed by a discussion of tools to address these challenges. The chapter then concludes and provides references for further reading.

Let us now define transportation and its relationship with the academic discipline logistics. Logistics distinguishes various sub-disciplines, including distribution logistics, production logistics, service logistics, and reverse logistics. Logistics is pre-dominantly concerned with the optimization of the flows of goods, information, and money. These can be flows between organizations, but also within organizations. Distinctions are made between flows of goods in which goods undergo a physical transition, and flows of goods in which the goods do not undergo any physical transition. Transportation concerns the latter and is part of the sub-discipline distribution logistics (Visser and Van Goor, 2015). In the current chapter, transportation does not relate to the flow of goods, information, and money, but only the transportation of tourists. In other words, transport in this chapter is not about transport activities to supply goods to tourist accommodations, but instead concerns tourist mobility. The term 'mobility' covers transport modalities, and also the number of trips, travel distance, time, speed, and cost (Ram *et al.*, 2013). The term 'tourist' should be read as all kinds of travellers that consume tourism and hospitality services and includes businessmen, visitors of events, day trippers, other recreational travellers, etc.. For the ease of reading we refer only to tourists, but the discussions relate to other travellers as well.

Sustainability issues related to transportation of tourists are similar to sustainability issues related to the transportation of goods. In both cases emissions of greenhouse gases, use of transport modalities, and the construction and maintenance of infrastructure are important issues from an ecological perspective. From the social perspective, global trade facilitated by global transportation supports economic development of poor areas and job generation for people. This is an argument to stimulate global trade, despite the needed transportation. Solutions, however, require a different approach for the transportation of tourists than for the transportation of goods. The differences are rooted in various causes:

- Tourists have different mobility needs than goods (e.g. moving from road to marine transportation is not as doable for tourists as it is for goods),

- Shortening transportation routes by means of, for example, bringing production and consumption sites closer to one another is often not possible as major tourist attractions such as the Niagara Falls or the Colosseum in Rome cannot be replaced, and

- Tourists do not have the same incentives as logistics professionals to work on transportation efficiency. This is predominantly relevant when tourists use their own transport modalities.

Main sustainability challenges

Tourism and hospitality brings major benefits to both consumers and providers of tourist activities. Tourists enjoy respite and renewal, happiness, experiences different from daily life (novelty), escape, and enhanced relationships resulting in positive emotions (Nawijn and Peeters, 2010; Ram *et al.* 2013; Jones, 2014). Providers of tourism and hospitality such as regions, individuals and organizations, including hotels and restaurants, enjoy job and income generation as well as tax and foreign exchange revenues (Becken, 2006; McKercher *et al.*, 2010). The size of the global travel and tourism economy was US$ 5,869 billion in 2016 (i.e. over 8% of global GDP), and the industry is responsible for 1 out of 13 jobs on the planet (WTTC, 2017). A note is due here: the World Travel and Tourism Council (WTTC) distinguishes between direct, indirect, and induced contributions of travel and tourism. The figures provided here are the direct and indirect contributions combined. Next to direct contributions, indirect contributions are important to the industry. They include things such as expenses on new aircraft, investments in hotels, governmental tourism and marketing agencies. The induced contributions concern the economic effect resulting from the spending of people directly and indirectly employed by the travel and tourism industry. For a full explanation of these concepts you are advised to read the report (WTTC, 2017).

The sector continues to be the largest and fastest growing sector worldwide (McKercher *et al.*, 2010; May, 2012). Benefitting economically from this is of great interest to policy makers, entrepreneurs, corporations, and workers. Nonetheless, tourism is generally not a sustainable sector. As it has been explained in the Introduction (page 2) and in the chapter on the Sustainable Hospitality Value Chain (pages 12-13), sustainability is a multi-faceted term. It has been defined in terms of economic sustainability, environmental sustainability, and social sustainability (Cavagnaro and Curiel, 2012). Ideally these three come together. In the case of tourism, despite concepts such as 'eco-tourism', this is rarely the case due to tourism's consumptive, i.e. resource-intensive, nature (Snyman, 2012). Destination ecosystems and the global climate risk being irreversibly damaged (Jones, 2014). The share of tourism to global CO_2 emissions is estimated at 5% with a range of 3.9-6%. Of all tourist activities, mobility has the largest environmental impact. A 2008 report by the UNWTO estimated transport to comprise 75% of all CO_2 emissions in the tourism sector, and aviation 40%, even though the share of air transport in tourist movements is relatively small. In particular air travel is detrimental to the environment since GHG emitted at high altitudes are much more harmful than those emitted at surface level. If these effects are included, the shares would increase to 89% and 74% respectively (UNWTO, 2008). The table summarizes the estimated shares of CO_2 emissions for different tourism activities.

Table 3.1: Estimated share of tourism activities to tourism CO_2 emissions (including same-day visitors) per tourism activity - Source: UNWTO, 2008: 133

	Global CO_2 emissions for tourism		
	Basic	Corrected for high altitude emissions; likely estimate	Corrected for high altitude emissions; maximum estimate
Air transport	40%	54%	74%
Car transport	32%	24%	14%
Other transport	3%	3%	1%
Accommodation	21%	16%	9%
Activities	4%	3%	2%
Tourism total	100%	100%	100%

A challenge is that tourism and tourist mobility continue to grow, with Airbus predicting annual traffic volume growth at 4.7% and Boeing at 5.5% for the aviation industry alone. This will lead to a tripling of air travel between 2005 and 2050 (Gössling and Cohen, 2014). Despite many initiatives to reduce GHG emissions and successes in various other economic sectors, the global tourism sector's GHG emissions continue to grow. This growth according to the UNWTO (2008) is estimated at 130% between 2005 and 2035 including expected technological efficiency gains. Gössling and Peeters (2015) estimate an increase of 169% between 2010 and 2050, excluding day trips. These figures stand in stark contrast to the needed substantive reductions in GHG emitted of 40-70% by 2050 as prescribed by the Intergovernmental Panel on Climate Change (Scott *et al.*, 2015).

Dilemmas

Improved education, increasing incomes and more leisure time enable more people to travel more frequently and over larger distances (Gössling and Peeters, 2007; Ram *et al.* 2013; Scott *et al.,* 2010; Scott *et al.,* 2015). Though each of these three enablers is an indicator of growing welfare, this growing welfare is unsustainable if consumed on polluting activities such as flying. Though it is clear that tourism and hospitality, and particularly tourist mobility, have a high impact on the natural environment, the promises of distance, escape, and economic development are still too attractive to tourists, entrepreneurs, and policy makers alike not to pursue them. Several dilemmas occur consequently. First, perceived distance allows tourists "to express unconscious needs through unusual experiences" (Ram *et al.,* 2013: 1023). These experiences are attractive to tourists, yet travelling large distances is not environmentally-friendly. Also tourists believe that travelling large distances makes them happier, though there is no empirical proof for this effect (Ram *et al.,* 2013). Second, though distance does not affect happiness, tourism and hospitality in general (irrespective of distance) does contribute to happiness, and tourists tend to worry less while on holiday (Nawijn and Peeters, 2010). If tourism is to change, the question is how this affects tourists' (perceived) happiness. Third, tourism contributes to economic and social development in both industrialized and developing countries. Changing tourism patterns will affect the economies of tourist regions (Becken, 2006; Snyman, 2012). Fourth, a characteristic of transportation is that it is not considered to be a value-adding activity. It is a necessary means to get somewhere, but not of value to tourists in itself. Simultaneously transportation will always impact the environment. If it is not due to the use of transport modalities, such as in the case of electric vehicles powered with renewable energy, it is due to the production of these modalities and the creation of infrastructure. The paradox therefore is that the best transportation is no transportation at all. Less tourist mobility, for example by means of domestic vacationing and fewer but longer holidays, is suggested by many authors as one of the solutions to the tourism sector's sustainability issues. A note is due here: the term 'domestic' is a confusing one as, when considering the impact of transport, it means something entirely different for the United States than for a country such as Luxembourg. In this chapter, 'domestic' should be read as a regional holiday destination that can be reached with surface transport.

In sum, to achieve a more sustainable form of tourism, tourism mobility should decrease, either by convincing tourists to forego travelling or to choose nearby (dometic) destinations. However, transportation, or logistics, is an important economic sector to many societies. Think of airlines such as Emirates and Ethiopian, both reporting year-on-year growing and impressive turnovers and staff numbers, as well as stable profits with a growing long-term trend. Limiting the need for transportation activities may have strong impacts on societies' economies. Shortening value chains may be at the expense of jobs and tax revenues. At the same time it is uncertain whether these jobs will be replaced by others.

Similarly, several regions depend for their economies to a large extent on the tourism and hospitality sector and hence need tourist inflows. A dilemma results for policy makers: perhaps the same vacationing value can be created for tourists with domestic holidays or fewer trips, yet less consumption on transportation may hit economies and individuals relatively hard. A question arises as to how sustainable consumption can be stimulated.

Nonetheless, the severity of the dilemmas is subject to increased scrutiny. Environmental activists may claim that dilemmas one and two are a result of the pursuit of "narrow personal benefits" (McKercher et al., 2010: 298) and cannot legitimately be considered as dilemmas. Others argue that positive emotions are indeed attached to tourism and distance, yet these emotions can also result from domestic or short-haul trips. In addition, Ram et al. (2013) distinguish between emotions and moods. While emotions last only a short time, moods last longer. Though emotions are indeed positively associated with tourism and can also be recalled some time after a tourist trip, moods do not change as a consequence of tourist activities. The third dilemma, however, is less easy to play down, particularly for developing countries. For high-income countries, domestic tourism may substitute foreign tourists' economic activity, yet for low-income countries this is much more challenging since tourism is a luxury expense (Dubois and Ceron, 2006). Nonetheless, if no action is undertaken, many vulnerable tourist areas will become victims of global climate change and hence lose incomes from tourism eventually anyway. This is both a threat to tropical destinations in developing countries as well as, for example, to ski resorts and low-lying tourist islands in industrialized countries, since these sites become unattractive to tourists if temperatures rise too much. Australia is one country that may be hit severely by continuing climate change and changing tourist behaviour (McKercher et al., 2010). As it has already been observed in the Introduction to this book (page 6), according to certain studies "climate change could lead to a gradual shift of tourist destinations towards higher latitudes and altitudes, resulting in the decline of many traditional resorts" (McKercher et al., 2010: 298). The fourth dilemma arguably is not one that receives much attention from policy makers as yet. Ships are still allowed to make use of highly polluting 'bunker oil' and huge (state-led) investments in airports continue, such as the new multi-billion project in Istanbul with its ambition to become the world's largest airport with a capacity of 150-200 million passengers annually. In fact, growth in arrivals is celebrated by politicians and media alike, and nation-states have financial stakes in major airplane manufacturers, as France, Germany, and other countries do in Airbus. Another challenge is that when neighbouring countries or states do not adopt the same policy measures intended to reduce air transportation, customers may easily cross the border in order to depart from a neighbouring country's airport.

Concluding this discussion, we may state that better education, higher incomes and more leisure time are outcomes of improved welfare. These sources of the environmental problems related to tourism should not be changed. However, these sources are distinctive of the current global economy in which problems such as low education, low income, little leisure time are (being) solved while simultaneously new ones are created such as environmental degradation. The question for today's economy is how problems can be solved through growing welfare without creating new ones. In the case of tourist mobility we discuss three means below: technology, behavioural change, and institutional innovations. This discussion is introduced by best cases showing that there are ways in which some of the above-illustrated dilemmas may be successfully tackled.

3

Best cases

Case 3.1: Alpine Pearls

The organization Alpine Pearls offers holidays with full mobility but without customers' use of their own car. In their own words this means "car- and carefree holidays". The so-called 'pearls' are twenty-five villages in the Alpine area in six countries: Germany, France, Austria, Italy, Slovenia, and Switzerland. The villages form part of a network, the Alpine Pearls, that offers green mobility within and between the villages, as each of the villages can easily be reached by train or bus. To ensure the guaranteed full mobility in the pearls, shuttle services, hikers' and ski buses, taxicab services, e-cars, bicycles, and e-bikes are available. Guest and Mobility Cards ensure free use of public transportation. Active, pleasurable and relaxing holidays are all offered.

According to Alpine Pearls the trips to the holiday destination can even become an unforgettable adventure as they lead tourists on spectacular routes. Alpine Pearls plans the entire car-free trips for its customers. Holidays like these are not only sustainable but offer many other benefits to tourists including 1) no stress of driving to the holiday destination, 2) no problems with finding parking places, 3) a stay in in a low-traffic zone and hence little exhaust and noise, 4) safe transportation, 5) possibility to meet new people, and 6) being able to enjoy a drink without having to drive.

There are also benefits to the tourism and hospitality industry. Many of the pearls are old villages that had farming as a major economic activity. Farms located far from the village centre started hospitality activities such as restaurants. The availability of full mobility makes it easy and convenient for tourists to visit these restaurants. Since tourists do not drive themselves it is possible for them to enjoy alcoholic beverages.

On a critical note it should be mentioned that also airport transport services are offered to tourists arriving by airplane, though they only recommend air travel to tourists coming from far away. When exactly to speak of 'far' is not mentioned (Alpine Pearls, 2017; personal communication).

Case 3.2: BlaBlaCar

Car occupancy rates in Europe average 1.6 persons, despite much larger car capacities. The higher the car occupancy rate, the lower the greenhouse gas emissions per person. Through smart online applications BlaBlaCar facilitates car sharing in an innovative way. Car drivers that have excess capacity can connect with people in search of transportation. When routing overlaps and sufficient capacity is available people can share their car mobility. BlaBlaCar is currently active in twenty countries, has more than 30 million members and transports over ten million people every three months. This saves money for users, reduces congestion, and reduces emissions of greenhouse gases. In addition it can be fun to travel with others and meet new people. Given the vast number of members, the large number of countries BlaBlaCar is active in, and the ease of online communication it is possible to travel to many tourist destinations with other BlaBlaCar members. Travelling this way may reduce the stress of driving for tourists and can contribute to making the journey a tourist attraction as well. BlaBlaCar takes several measures to ensure safe travelling, such as verifying the users, rating schemes for users, and in case women still feel uncomfortable travelling with others it is possible to opt for 'ladies only' trips (BlaBlaCar, 2017).

The tourism and hospitality industry may use this tool for its environmentally-conscious customers. Customers sharing routes can be connected using the tool. This may be particularly interesting for people going on holiday, business trip or to a restaurant alone or in small groups, wishing to meet or network with other people.

Case 3.3: Holidays by rail

Passenger-kilometre carbon dioxide emission for rail transportation are as low as 0.026. The rate is much higher for other means of transportation such as air plane (0.378 for mid-haul flights and 0.432 for long-haul flights) and car (0.18). It is slightly higher for buses (0.019; Dubois and Ceron, 2006). Vast railway networks exist in Europe, North-America and many Asian countries. Travelling by train offers many benefits as compared to travelling by other means of transportation: boarding involves far less hassle than boarding an air plane; train stations are typically located much nearer to travellers' homes than airports; there is no stress of driving; many trains offer catering on board; travelling by train offers opportunities to play family games or read books; it is safe; the holiday starts with the journey; and opportunities exist to meet new people. Nonetheless travelling by train is not highly popular. Several reasons exist: for long-haul trips the travelling time is much greater than travelling by airplane; not all destinations can be reached (easily) by train or public transport; travelling by train involves more hassle with carrying luggage than travelling by car; it is often more expensive than travelling by car or airplane; and it reduces mobility at the destination as compared to travelling by car. Different companies try to make going on holiday by train as attractive as possible. These include the international firm holidaysbyrail.com and the Dutch spoordeelwinkel.nl. The latter is a business unit of the Dutch Railways (in Dutch: Nederlandse Spoorwegen). Spoordeelwinkel.nl offers day trips and short stay city trips including train tickets. The package deals include tickets for excursions, lunch, dinner and coffee vouchers and in the case of short stay city trips also hotel reservations. The packages are lower in price than the sum of the separate items sold independently, but moreover are interesting because the mode of travel adds to the comfort level of tourists (Spoordeelwinkel, 2017). The trips offered also serve for promotional purposes for the Dutch Railways.

Holidaysbyrail.com focuses on long stay holiday trips and offers holidays by rail all over the world. The emphasis is on Canada, the United States of America, and Europe. Each of these geographical areas have well developed railway networks. The company clearly makes the transportation itself part of the journey rather than just a means to get to the destination. One way of doing so is to offer rail holidays with a certain theme, including lakes and mountains, scenic tours, river cruise, national parks, family holiday, and culinary and wine. Such holidays allow tourists to travel while minimizing environmental impact (Holidaysbyrail, 2017). On a critical note it must be mentioned that holidaysbyrail.com also offers fly-rail combinations for tourists who wish to travel part of their journey by airplane. If this is done then a holiday by rail is no longer sustainable. In other words, opportunities exist for tourists to travel environmentally friendly, but opportunities to do the opposite exist simultaneously as well. Remarkably holidaysbyrail.com does not mention anything on their website about sustainability. This is different, for example, for a Dutch competitor named treinreiswinkel.nl.

Treinreiswinkel.nl provides tourists with information about the share of tourist mobility in total greenhouse gases emitted in the tourism industry and the savings that can be made when travelling by train. It also offers customers the opportunity to bring their bicycle on the train. Treinreiswinkel.nl is furthermore Travelife certified. Travelife is a tourism industry body that certifies sustainable accommodations, tour operators, and travel agents. Treinreiswinkel.nl, finally, compensates for all greenhouse gases emitted while travelling by train for every holiday booked. They do so via 'GreenSeat' (Treinreiswinkel, 2017; Travelife, 2017). Travelling by train makes tourism much more sustainable as it addresses many of the suggested solutions for greening tourist mobility, including:

- Making use of surface transport rather than air transport;
- Making use of collective transport modalities (train, coach, etc.) rather than individual transport modalities (car);
- Making (surface) travel a value-adding activity, particularly when this is chosen as alternative to air travel;
- Voluntarily participating in carbon offsetting schemes.

For hotels, restaurants, and other providers of accommodation and hospitality activities, opportunities exist to be part of packages offered by holidaysbyrail.com, treinreiswinkel. nl, or similar companies. Even when a hotel is not located nearby a train station, mobility solutions exist to arrange transportation to and from the train station as, for example, the Alpine Pearls case demonstrates.

Tools to address the challenges

The question how to design an economy that solves problems without creating new ones is not one that can easily be answered. Scholars and practitioners tend to propose various possibilities from their own specific disciplines. In this chapter we aim to demonstrate that these disciplines, whether technological, behavioural, or institutional, are all intertwined, and that a multidisciplinary approach is needed to tackle complex problems such as keeping socio-economic growth while protecting the natural environment. We start with the technological means to mitigate unsustainable tourist mobility, followed by behavioural change, and finally discusses institutional means.

Technology to mitigate unsustainable tourist mobility

Technology as a means to mitigate unsustainable tourist mobility can be divided into two different aspects: technology related to the *use* of transport modalities and infrastructure, and technology related to the *production of* transport modalities and infrastructure. Both are explained below.

Let us start with the use of transport modalities. Technological improvements to make tourist mobility more sustainable predominantly need to be found in increased fuel efficiency of different transport modalities and alternative fuels (Gössling *et al.*, 2007). Several technological innovations succeeded in reducing transportation's environmental impact per kilometre travelled for almost all modalities. However, progress made is currently insufficient to meet the previously stated goals of the Intergovernmental Panel on Climate Change (Gössling *et al.*, 2012). Additionally, increasing trip numbers and distances travelled, and consumer choices for more polluting modalities (e.g. air travel versus surface travel) all result in net increases of GHG emissions caused by tourist mobility (Peeters, 2013; Ram *et al.*, 2013). In order to reduce GHG emissions by 80% of the 1990 levels by 2050, as agreed in Paris climate agreement in 2015, "overall travel efficiency must improve by a factor of 16, or almost 94%" (Ram *et al.*, 2013: 1018), in a 'business-as-usual' scenario incorporating a predicted growth of 400% in this same period (Ram *et al.*, 2013). Though the aviation industry may claim expected future efficiency gains, scholars are less optimistic, since historic data demonstrate that annual efficiency gains decrease over time (Gössling and Peeters, 2007; Scott *et al.*, 2010). Another challenge is that technological improvements may not reduce total GHG emissions. For example, studies have found that increases in the speed of transport systems do not make tourists spend less time on travelling, but rather encourage them travel further (Ram *et al.*, 2013). Increasing fuel efficiency may additionally reduce the costs of flying and therefore encourage people to fly more often or for longer distances, as has been observed in the Introduction using the example of car driving (page 7).

Efficiency gains seem not to be able to reduce GHG emissions sufficiently. The industry therefore speaks of alternative fuels, such as biofuel or hydrogen for airplanes and electric vehicles for surface transport. However, the creation of hydrogen and electricity requires a lot of energy that is not necessarily green. Biofuel requires vast areas of land, which is not good for the environment either and may compete with land needed for food production. Scott *et al.* (2010) calculated that the total land size needed to produce biomass for biofuels at 2005 levels would be 1 million km², equal to the size of Germany, France, the Netherlands and Belgium combined. Of course advances can be made in biofuels such as biofuels made from organic waste or algae (Scott *et al.*, 2010; SkyNRG, 2016). Nevertheless, it may be clear that producing biofuels requires a lot of resources and it remains questionable whether this is realistically feasible, particularly in the light of growing demand for aviation services. Expectations over the role of alternative fuels may therefore be too high. Consider, for example, that Airbus does not expect to be able to use hydrogen in the next couple of decades, meaning that reducing GHG emissions by using biofuel may come too late (Gössling and Peeters, 2007). According to Scott *et al.* (2010: 400) "Technology change, air traffic management and sustainable fuels (i.e. 'biofuels') will help to avoid about one third of this growth, and emissions from aviation would consequently grow by just over 100% by 2035". In other words "[no] workable alternatives to kerosene have yet been identified for the short to medium-term" (Becken, 2006: 113).

Other technological improvements that could be made to mitigate unsustainable tourist mobility are to: 1) improve routing (more direct routes); 2) increase the seatlng capacity of public transport modalities; and 3) use vehicle-monitoring technology and eco-driver training in order to change driving behaviours (Rutty *et al.*, 2014; Scott *et al.*, 2015). Though these improvements may reduce GHG emissions per person per kilometre, they fall short of preventing an increase of total GHG emissions and do not structurally solve the problem.

Having discussed the use of transport modalities, it is time to turn to their production.

The use of fossil fuels is one of the main problems in transportation (Rutty *et al.*, 2014; Scott *et al.*, 2015). Nonetheless not only the environmental impact of the *use* of transport modalities should be considered when discussing sustainable tourist mobility, but equally so the *production* of transport modalities and their required infrastructural networks. Producing means of transportation and infrastructure also affects the natural environment due to, among other things, the extraction of raw materials, energy usage in the supply chain, and waste streams in the supply chain both during production as well as at *end-of-use* or *end-of-life* of transport modalities. Filimonau *et al.* (2011) and Scott *et al.* (2015) are among the few to mention this. To produce a car, for example, requires, amongst many other materials, the toxic metal lead. Of all lead used globally, 60% is for car manufacturing. By 2030 lead reserves will run out according to some studies (Ellen MacArthur Foundation, 2013). To mitigate the effects of producing transport modalities it is important to adopt the principles of the circular economy. In a circular economy, material resources maintain their value in production chains so that no waste occurs. This means that at the end of their economic life products will return to their production chains and the material resources in them will be used again for new products. In this way not only waste is reduced but also no, or less, virgin materials are needed. A report by the Ellen MacArthur Foundation, Sun, and McKinsey (2015) identifies four loops in the circular economy: 1) repair and maintain; 2) reuse; 3) refurbish; and 4) recycle. If these steps are followed in the proposed order, product lives are extended, and materials can be used repeatedly in production chains. This does, however, require that products are designed for disassembly such that original materials can be recovered without loss of quality of these materials. Circular economy practices are still in a stage of infancy.

In short, making tourist mobility sustainable with technological innovations does not seem to be a very promising way to go. Even though technological solutions exist, they are unlikely to be available in the short term, sufficient and scalable. Nevertheless, they should be pursued in order to contribute to greening tourist mobility. In addition to technological improvements behavioural changes are needed. The next section discusses behavioural change as a means to mitigate unsustainable tourist mobility. The suggested solutions for technological improvements are summarized here:

- Greening the fuels of transport modalities (i.e. green electricity, biofuels, green hydrogen);
- Increasing seating capacity of public transport modalities;
- Making modalities more energy-efficient;
- Improving routing (more direct routes);
- Using vehicle-monitoring technology and eco-driver trainings;
- Investing in circular production chains for transport modalities and circular infrastructure.

Behavioural change to mitigate unsustainable tourist mobility

Tourist travel behaviour evolved over the past decades in a highly and increasingly unsustainable manner. As mentioned above, tourists nowadays make more use of air transportation, travel longer distances, and travel more often. Preferably this behaviour will be reversed soon in order to minimize the environmental impact of travelling. A more sustainable transport behaviour would mean that tourists choose surface and public transport modalities, travel less frequently with longer stays, rather than more frequently with short stays, and reduce the distances travelled (Dubois and Ceron, 2006; Peeters and Schouten, 2006; Guiver *et al.*, 2007; Scott *et al.*, 2010; Filimonau *et al.*, 2011; Hergesell and Dickinger, 2013; Ram *et al.*, 2013; Jones, 2014). Even though "Approximately 80% of trips in the world are domestic and involve surface transportation" (Ram *et al.*, 2013: 1018) and changes will hence not affect most trips, this change of behaviour is very difficult to realize for several reasons. First, though consumers are increasingly aware of sustainability issues, there is a gap between awareness and action

(Nawijn and Peeters, 2010; Ram *et al.*, 2013). This can, among other things, be attributed to lacking a sense of urgency, the perception that the responsibility to act lies elsewhere, low regard held for alternatives such as public transport, belief in technological solutions, tourist uncertainty about the seriousness of sustainability issues, and hedonic behaviour that is inherent to tourism and makes tourists unwilling to think about sustainability issues while on holiday, even if they are environmentally-conscious consumers in daily life (Dickinson and Dickinson, 2006; Gössling and Peeters, 2007; McKercher *et al.*, 2010; Ram *et al.*, 2013). Second, tourism is now considered a right, and air travel is no longer a luxury form of mobility (Dubois and Ceron, 2006). Third, tourists' identities have changed towards cosmopolitan ones (Gössling and Peeters, 2007), meaning it has become normal to travel globally. Fourth, possibly as a consequence of the previous two reasons, imposed restrictions on travel distance and frequency, and transport modality may compromise tourist happiness since they feel that they are being limited in their choices. This decreasing level of happiness is likely to be only small and temporary, but may meet resistance from tourists (Nawijn and Peeters, 2010). The way in which current tourists' minds have been trained, makes it very difficult to change their behaviour from unsustainable practices and move it towards more sustainable practices (Rutty *et al.* 2014). Theoretically travelling less frequently and shorter distances may appeal, but in practice it is not possible to shorten the value chain between tourists' residential areas and 'must see' destinations such as the Colosseum in Rome, the Great Wall of China or the Niagara Falls. In other words, if to be able to visit these locations is perceived not only as a right but also more and more as a common activity, it will become very difficult to change tourist behaviour and consequently lower the environmental impact of tourists' transportation. Those tourists wishing not to alter their travel behaviour could alternatively choose to voluntarily offset their GHG emissions through so-called carbon-offsetting schemes. Through such schemes, for example, tourists can pay for the planting of trees, which will absorb GHGs from the air and thus compensate for GHGs emitted while travelling. Such schemes, however, are subject to increased criticism because there is no single standard. A variety of organizations offer carbon offsetting schemes, each using their own price levels and their own calculations for GHG compensations. These differences affect the effectiveness and credibility of these schemes, which may explain their limited popularity (Gössling *et al.*, 2007; Scott *et al.*, 2015).

The behaviour of tourist providers could also be changed. This could, for example, be done by making sustainable tourist activities more attractive. One way of doing so is by making tourist mobility a value adding activity. In this case then, transportation will no longer be a necessary means or cost to get somewhere, but a valuable activity in itself. Schieffelbusch *et al.* (2007) suggest viewing tourist trips as 'chains of services' in which the various aspects of a trip are integrated. This could, for example, be done by means of integrating visits to tourist attractions and sights along the travel route, preferably while travelling by means of public transport. According to Guiver *et al.* (2007) public transport could also be made more appealing by adding a novelty component such as steam trains and vintage buses. However, the extent to which these modalities are sustainable is debatable because, for example, vintage buses are less fuel efficient than modern ones. Finally, tour operators could train their drivers to drive more eco-friendly (Rutty *et al.*, 2014). For business travellers and students, virtual mobility may provide a solution. Using advanced information and communication technologies, the hospitality industry may provide opportunities for business people to do business with limited travelling. Students may study from home without having to travel to the home country of a university (Aguado *et al.*, 2014). Finally, hotels may offer transportation services to their customers such as offering transport from airports in busses, providing bicycles or bicycle tours to guests, and stimulate the use of local public transport. The 'Alpine Pearls' case demonstrates an interesting example of how to create value for both consumers as well as providers of tourism and hospitality activities by means of offering sustainable mobility solutions.

In short, various theoretical solutions exist by which changed tourist behaviour could have positive impacts on the natural environment. Eventually changing tourism consumption patterns will not change tourist happiness (Ram *et al.*, 2013). However, the majority of tourists most likely will neither change their behaviour voluntarily, nor participate in voluntary carbon offsetting schemes (Rutty *et al.*, 2014; Scott *et al.*, 2010). Policies affecting behaviours of both tourists and providers of tourist activities are therefore needed in order to realize changing behaviours of tourists. The next section discusses the policy-side of sustainable tourist mobility. The suggested solutions for making tourist behaviour more sustainable are summarized below:

- Making use of surface transport rather than air transport;
- Making use of collective transport modalities (train, coach, etc.) rather than individual transport modalities (car);
- Travelling less frequently with longer stays, rather than more frequently with short stays;
- Reducing distances travelled;
- Making (surface) travel a value-adding activity, particularly when this is chosen as alternative to air travel;
- Voluntarily participating in carbon offsetting schemes;
- Offering virtual mobility;
- Stimulating the use of environmentally friendly modalities by hotels.

Policy to mitigate unsustainable tourist mobility

Behaviour of both providers of tourism and tourists alike needs to change. Though minority groups may actually change their behaviour, significant impact is only achieved through large-scale collective action (Dickinson and Dickinson,

2006). Since large-scale collective action is unlikely to come voluntarily, policies are needed to prescribe the behaviour of individuals and organisations. The challenge in policy making lays not so much in defining policies that make transportation more sustainable. After all, these are mostly known and include: carbon taxes on fossil fuels; "the development of a vision for a fundamentally different global tourism economy" (Scott *et al.*, 2010: 403); incentives for low-carbon technologies; making carbon trading/offsetting mandatory; developing public transport, for example by investing in rail infrastructure; and many others (Guiver *et al.*, 2007; Scott *et al.*, 2010, 2015; McKercher *et al.*, 2010; Nawijn and Peeters, 2010; Ram *et al.*, 2013; Gössling and Cohen, 2014). The challenge lays in the extent to which the goal of greening the economy conflicts with the goal of economic growth. Policy makers are attracted by the economic potential that infrastructure for tourist mobility seems to offer. Investments in infrastructure are common across many countries and should improve mobility, yet typically result in tourists travelling larger distances (Ram *et al.*, 2013; Schieffelbusch *et al.*, 2014). Such investments therefore create jobs when infrastructure is developed and maintained, but they also indirectly increase employment in the transportation and tourism sector. The perceived importance of tourism and transportation to the global and regional economies is one of the factors that led to the exclusion of agreements on aviation and other forms of transport in the 2015 Paris climate agreement. To date, except for local initiatives with limited impact, greening the transportation industry is exempted from policy making. Policy making will in the near future therefore have little impact on making tourist mobility more sustainable. There are, however, some signs that indicate a change in the status quo. The government of The Netherlands that was installed late 2017, for example, states that it aims to introduce CO_2-taxes, including taxes on fuel for airplanes. If indeed new regulation on this matter is being introduced and enforced, traveling by airplane will become more expensive. Box 3.1 below further details the complexities of and dynamics behind policy making.

Box 3.1

It goes without saying that the absence of effective policies is not satisfactory in the light of the lack of technological possibilities and behavioural change of tourists, for those interested in making tourism and hospitality more sustainable. To provide some perspective, this box explains some of the complexities and dynamics behind policy making. It starts with self-regulation by the industry and continues with governmental regulation.

The aviation industry has been trusted to develop policies for self-regulation. Though recently the industry made a new agreement to reduce GHG emissions, the question is whether this self-regulation is effective.

First, based on the logic of self-interest, it is unrealistic to assume that the aviation industry will develop regulation that results in tourists opting less often for the airplane as mode of transportation, even though this is required in order to meet the climate goals of the Paris climate agreement, including a maximum increase in global temperatures of 1.5° Celsius. Indeed, when studying the agreement it is clear that the industry relies on technological solutions. Remarkably, Boeing and Airbus both already produce airplanes that meet future standards agreed upon at Paris. Environmental organizations therefore argue that the Paris agreements fall significantly short to engage the industry in serious change (ANP, 2016; Lampert and Volcovici, 2016).

Second, the past demonstrates that previous declarations and agreements made by the industry where high in ambitions, but fell short in developing achievable, measurable and realistic goals for actually realizing these ambitions. In addition, the transport industry has been said to be neither responsible nor credible. This is not only true for the aviation industry, but holds true for the marine industry as well (Scott *et al.* 2010, 2015). Governments therefore cannot rely solely on self-regulation and should develop policies in which the goals of greening the economy and economic growth are aligned as much as possible, without compromising sustainability goals to the extent that the outcomes of these compromises are detrimental in the future. To a certain extent such policies are already developed. The European Commission Directive2009/29/EC and legislation Decision406/2009/EC are well-known examples. "The first is a trade scheme [...] imposing caps on CO_2 emissions of large emitters [...]. The second is legislation assigning targets for non-emissions trading sectors on a national level, covering transport, residential, services and some industry" (Gössling and Cohen, 2014: 197). However, the European Commission simultaneously argues that "curbing mobility is not an option" (EC, 2011:5, as cited in Gössling and Cohen, 2014: 198) and many aspects of transportation remain ignored on the EU policy agenda. This is not due to lack of knowledge, but to the fact that scientific knowledge does not sufficiently translate into policies. In the words of Banister and Hickman (2013: 292, as cited in Gösssling and Cohen, 2014: 198) this is a major "implementation gap". Explanations for this gap vary from philosophical stances on market-based measures, belief in technological innovations and voluntary change of behaviour, and taboos (Gössling and Cohen, 2014).

Hence the need for policy makers to accept scientific wisdom and act upon it is high, but this need is challenged by major obstacles. Interestingly, though policy is intended to change behaviour of market actors including consumers, Ram *et al.* (2013: 1029) argue that "behavioral change by policy makers is probably the main issue." A vicious circle results when policy makers need the approval of the public in order to change their behaviour, while the public needs policies to change theirs. Environmental organizations and visionary leaders both in politics and industry may have a role in disrupting this circle.

As is clear, policy making is needed to tackle sustainability issues related to tourist mobility, yet policy making is confronted with its own complexities. The suggested solutions to use policy making as a means to mitigate unsustainable tourist mobility are summarized here:

■ The development of a vision for a fundamentally different global tourism economy;

- Carbon taxes on fossil fuels;
- Incentives for low-carbon technologies;
- Developing public transport;
- Making carbon trading/offsetting mandatory;
- Finding new or upscaling existing local solutions to align the goals of greening the economy and economic growth as much as possible;
- Not relying on self-regulation by the industry;
- Overcoming challenges that prevent needed policies from being developed and implemented;
- Disrupt the 'policy maker behaviour – public behaviour' paradox (e.g. by engaging environmental organizations).

Conclusion

The tourism sector faces a major problem. Few scholars, if any, argue that tourism is sustainable, except for some positive economic and social developments in low-income countries generating income from (eco-)tourism. Tourist mobility is to a large extent responsible for the sector's current unsustainable practices. In order to make tourist mobility more sustainable, not only the modalities, or actual transportation, need to become greener, but tourist behaviour needs to change as well. Transport is not a value-adding activity and it is difficult to make it one. Most tourists use transportation as a means to arrive somewhere, and hardly consider it an end or a goal in itself. A challenge is to reduce the number of kilometres travelled per tourist while simultaneously greening transportation. This should *preferably* be done in such a way that it does not compromise tourists' value obtained from travelling, in the form of respite, renewal, happiness, novelty, change and enhanced relationships. Neither technological improvements, nor behavioural change, nor policy change alone can sufficientlyeduce tourist mobility's impact on the natural environment. Only orchestrated efforts incorporating all three aspects will lead to more sustainable tourist mobility. This will be a major challenge given the current interests of various stakeholders in the tourism and hospitality industry. These interests can be perceived to conflict with sustainability goals and need to change in the next few decades. Nonetheless, there may be as much to gain as there is to lose: "The result would be an altered competitive marketplace where changes in destination choice, transport modes and accommodation would create very large opportunities for companies offering railway and coach travel and for domestic / short-haul international tourism" (Scott *et al.*, 2010: 403). Or to put it even stronger, if nothing changes there is much to lose, but little to gain, since climate change, loss of biodiversity, sea level rise, reduced water availability and quality, and related effects will damage tourist regions (McKercher *et al.*, 2010; Scott *et al.*, 2010; Schieffelbusch *et al.*, 2014).

The cases demonstrate that providers of tourism and hospitality activities can be innovative and competitive by means of providing sustainable tourist mobility, even in the absence of policies. When orchestrated efforts result in technological, behavioural and institutional innovations being realized simultaneously, firms such as those exemplified in the cases, may improve their competitiveness through a first-mover advantage. Nonetheless, though changing consumer mobility may be good for the natural environment and innovative businesses, it may be harmful to economic and social development. In particular regions that are difficult to access by other modalities than airplanes, such as many developing countries or remote and peripheral areas such as Australia, New Zealand, parts of Sweden and Pacific islands, are vulnerable with respect to these changes (McKercher *et al.*, 2010; Schieffelbusch *et al.*, 2014; Snyman, 2012). For these regions it is important to develop other sustainable economic sectors if tourism is no longer a viable option due to its harmful nature, or to offer tourist trips with time-consuming yet entertaining (i.e. value-adding) surface-level travels.

In the case of tourism, however, there is a paradox in logistics. Whereas logistics in production chains can be shortened 'simply' by changing manufacturing locations, certain things are not possible with tourism. The Colosseum in Rome, the Grand Canyon, the Niagara Falls and the Chinese Wall cannot be relocated. Possibly the development of virtual reality for tourism provides a venue for a less transport-dependent tourism. This is worthwhile following, though currently still too fragile to discuss in depth.

Furthermore, though discussions on sustainable tourist mobility emphasize the effects of aviation, the greening of surface and marine transportation should not be neglected. Greening surface transportation is less a challenge than greening air and marine transportation due to increasing opportunities to electrify surface transportation and generating wind, solar and hydro energy, but actually stimulating this greening should not be neglected despite its relative easiness.

In conclusion, action is need from a wide range of stakeholders in order to both maintain less damaging tourist activities and reduce more damaging tourist activities, to avoid those changes in the natural environment will make tourist places deteriorate due to loss of coral, desertification, loss of biodiversity, rising temperatures and sea levels, less snow, etc. It is time to redefine near-future tourism. The redefining for transportation comes in terms of short-distance, less frequent but long-stay travels, using value-adding public transport modalities produced in circular supply chains, while transport modalities become greener. In this way tourists can continue to enjoy respite, renewal, happiness, novelty, change, and enhanced relationships, providers may still capture revenues from tourists' activities, and economies continue to enjoy the monetary and employment benefits of tourism and hospitality as an important economic service sector.

Further readings

McKinnon A., Browne, M., Piecyk, M. and Whiteing, A., eds. (2016) *Green Logistics: Improving the environmental sustainability of logistics*, 3rd ed., London: KoganPage.

Black, W.R. (2010) *Sustainable Transportation*, New York: The Guilford Press.

References

Aguado, T., Monge, F. and Del Olmo, A. (2014) Virtual mobility in higher education. The UNED Campus Net Program. *Open Praxis*, **6** (3), 287-293.

Alpine Pears (2017) *Alpine Pearls*. http://www.alpine-pearls.com. Accessed 7 December 2016.

ANP (2016) *Ook klimaatakkoord voor burgerluchtvaart*. http://www.trouw.nl/tr/nl/39681/nbsp/article/detail/4390781/2016/10/06/Ook-klimaatakkoord-voor-burgerluchtvaart.dhtml. Accessed: 8 December 2016.

Becken, S. (2006) Editorial – tourism and transport: the sustainability dilemma, *Journal of Sustainable Tourism*, **14** (2), 113-115.

BlaBlaCar (2017) *BlaBlaCar*. http://www.blablacar.com. Accessed: 7 December 2016.

Cavagnaro, E. and Curiel, G. H. (2012) *The Three Levels of Sustainability*, Sheffield: Greenleaf Publishing.

Dickinson, J. E. and Dickinson, J. A. (2006) Local transport and social representations: challenging the assumptions for sustainable tourism, *Journal of Sustainable Tourism*, **14** (2), 192-208.

Dubois, G. and Ceron, J. P. (2006) Tourism/leisure greenhouse gas emissions forecasts for 2050: factors for change in France, *Journal of Sustainable Tourism*, **14** (2), 172-191.

Ellen MacArthur Foundation, Sun, and McKinsey (2015) Growth within: a circular economy vision for a competitive Europe, report. https://www.mckinsey.de/files/growth_within_report_circular_economy_in_europe.pdf. Accessed: 24 March 2018.

Ellen MacArthur Foundation (2013) *The circular economy applied to the automotive industry*. https://www.ellenmacarthurfoundation.org/circular-economy/interactive-diagram/the-circular-economy-applied-to-the-automotive-industry. Accessed: 6 December 2017.

Filimonau, V., Dickinson, J.E., Robbins, D. and Reddy, M.V. (2011) A critical review of methods for tourism climate change appraisal: life cycle assessment as a new approach, *Journal of Sustainable Tourism*, **19** (3), 301-324.

Gössling, S. and Cohen, S. (2014) Why sustainable transport policies will fail: EU climate policy in the light of transport taboos, *Journal of Transport Geography*, **39**, 197-207.

Gössling, S. and Peeters, P. (2007) It does not harm the environment! An analysis of industry discourses on tourism, air travel, and the environment, *Journal of Sustainable Tourism*, **15** (4), 402-417.

Gössling, S. and Peeters, P. (2015) Assessing tourism's global environmental impact 1950-2050, *Journal of Sustainable Tourism*, **23** (5), 639-659.

Gössling, S., Broderick, J., Upham, P., Ceron, J.P., Dubois, G., Peeters, P. and Strasdas, W. (2007) Voluntary carbon offsetting schemes for aviation: efficiency, credibility and sustainable tourism, *Journal of Sustainable Tourism*, **15** (3), 223-248.

Gössling, S., Hall, C.M., Ekström, F., Engeset, A.B. and Aall, C. (2012) Transition management: a tool for implementing sustainable tourism scenarios?, *Journal of Sustainable Tourism*, **20** (6), 899-916.

Guiver, J., Lumsdon, L., Weston, R. and Ferguson, M. (2007) Do buses help meet tourism objectives? The contribution and potential of scheduled buses in rural destination areas, *Transport Policy*, **14**, 275-282.

Hergesell, A. and Dickinger, A. (2013) Environmentally friendly holiday transport mode choices among students: the role of price, time and convenience, *Journal of Sustainable Tourism*, **21** (4), 596-613.

Holidaysbyrail (2017) *Holidays By Rail*. http://www.holidaysbyrail.com Accessed: 15 December 2016.

Jones, C. (2014) Scenarios for greenhouse gas emissions reduction from tourism: an extended tourism satellite account approach in a regional setting, *Journal of Sustainable Tourism*, **21** (3), 458-472.

Lampert, A. and Volcovici, V. (2016) *U.N. group agrees to first CO2 emission standards for aircraft*. http://www.reuters.com/article/climatechange-aviation-idUSL2N15N21M. Accessed: 8 December 2016.

May, M. (2002) The growth of tourism and air travel in relation to ecological sustainability, *International Journal of Tourism Research*, **4**, 145-150.

McKercher, B., Prideaux, B., Cheung, C. and Law, R. (2010) Achieving voluntary reductions in the carbon footprint of tourism and climate change, *Journal of Sustainable Tourism*, **18** (3), 297-317.

Nawijn, J. and Peeters, P.M. (2010) Travelling 'green': is tourists' happiness at stake?, *Current Issues in Tourism*, **13** (4), 381-392.

Peeters, P.M. (2013) Developing a long-term global tourism transport model using a behavioural approach: implications for sustainable tourism policy making, *Journal of Sustainable Tourism*, **21** (7), 1049-1069.

Peeters, P. and Schouten, F. (2006) Reducing the ecological footprint of inbound tourism and transport to Amsterdam, *Journal of Sustainable Tourism*, **14** (2), 157-171.

Ram, Y., Nawijn, J. and Peeters, P.M. (2013) Happiness and limits to sustainable tourism mobility: a new conceptual model, *Journal of Sustainable Tourism*, **21** (7), 1017-1035.

Rutty, M., Matthews, L., Scott, D. and Del Matto, T. (2014) Using vehicle monitoring technology and eco-driver training to reduce fuel use and emissions in tourism: a ski resort case study, *Journal of Sustainable Tourism*, **22** (5), 787-800.

Schieffelbusch, M., Jain, A., Schäfer, T., and Müller, D. (2007) Transport and tourism: roadmap to integrated planning developing and assessing integrated travel chains, *Journal of Transport Geography*, **15**, 94-103.

Scott, D., Peeters, P. and Gössling, S. (2010) Can tourism deliver its 'aspirational' greenhouse gas emission reduction targets?, *Journal of Sustainable Tourism*, **18** (3), 393-408.

Scott, D.C., Gössling, S., Hall, C.M., and Peeters, P. (2015) Can tourism be part of the decarbonized global economy? The costs and risks of alternate carbon reduction policy pathways, *Journal of Sustainable Tourism*, **24** (1), 52-72.

SkyNRG (2016) *SkyNRG*. http://skynrg.com/ Accessed: 8 December 2016.

Snyman, S.L. (2012) The role of tourism employment in poverty reduction and community perceptions of conservation and tourism in southern Africa, *Journal of Sustainable Tourism*, **20** (3), 395-416.

Spoordeelwinkel (2017) *Spoordeelwinkel*. http://www.spoordeelwinkel.nl. Accessed 15 December 2016.

Travelife (2017) *Sustainability in tourism*. http://www.travelife.org. Accessed 15 December 2016.

Treinreiswinkel (2017) *Treinreiswinkel*. http://www.treinreiswinkel.nl. Accessed 15 December 2016.

UNWTO and UNEP (2008) *Climate Change and Tourism: Responding to Global Challenges*, report. http://sdt.unwto.org/sites/all/files/docpdf/climate2008.pdf. Accessed 24 March 2018.

Visser, H. and Van Goor, A. (2015) *Werken met logistiek*. Groningen: Noordhoff Uitgevers.

WTTC (2017) *Travel and Tourism Economic Impact 2017 World*, report. London: World Travel and Tourism Council.

3

4 Distribution at the Destination:

An underestimated force to improve hospitality services and enhance sustainable development

Sarah Seidel

Learning goals

This chapter should help readers to understand the issue of distribution in the destination from a hospitality perspective, and to reflect on possible means and techniques to distribute positive impacts and minimise negative impacts on all three sustainability dimensions. After reading this chapter the reader will:

1 Be aware of the opportunities and responsibilities of the hospitality providers for distributing at the destination;

2 Be able to critical evaluate the challenges and dilemmas hospitality providers might face in regards to spreading visitors;

3 Be acquainted with techniques that hospitality providers can use to distribute guests at the destination.

Introduction

Distribution at the destination is in itself a critical topic for hospitality businesses. One might argue straight away, that a hospitality company such as a hotel does not distribute and particularly not to any parts of destination beyond the facilities of the hotel itself. In addition, distribution is rather abstract: distribution of wealth, of risk, of commitment? This chapter is going to mainly focus on the distribution of people, as this is the factor that will positively (or negatively) influence the destination the most, and will also result in a distribution of benefits and reduce/spread negative impacts on all three dimensions of sustainability.

Hence, this chapter introduces the importance of this topic for a hospitality business and, indeed, shows that many hotels or accommodation businesses are already heavily involved in the distribution at the destination. It will show how hospitality businesses can enhance positive impacts and reduce negative effects on the economic, social and environmental dimensions. Finally, from a sustainability standpoint it is also argued more and more that hospitality businesses are responsible, both for their guests (which might include tourists coming from far away and who are not a all familiar with the destination), for the resources that their guests use, and for the people at the destination on whom the guests leave an impact.

The word *distribution* is often applied to goods being distributed in a region. However, in relation to the hospitality and tourism industry, distribution is a bit more complicated. You are certainly familiar with the fact that hospitality and tourism products are classified as service products, and that service products have different characteristics from goods in that they are intangible (cannot be touched), heterogeneous (different people will experience them differently), perishable (cannot be stored, e.g. an unoccupied hotel room is lost). In addition, services are directly delivered to people by people, so both the supplier and the guests are part of the product and the production process. There is one more characteristic of a service that is crucial to understand when linked to the concept of distribution at the destination, as services are also in most cases place-bound (a hotel can only deliver its services within its facilities).

The location where the service takes place cannot usually be moved; it is the customer that has to be moved. If you think of going to visit a city for a weekend that include a hotel stay, visits to restaurants and cafes, an evening at the theatre, a shopping tour and a guided tour; all of these services are bound to their place, and you are the one that moves.

If you now consider distribution at the destination from the perspective of a hospitality business, a major factor is the movement of the guests within the destination. One might now think two things: first, it is not the business of, for example, a hotel to be concerned with what its guests do during the day; and second, the hotel has no influence on where its guests go. The first has been a long-standing argument and has served as an excuse for denying responsibilities (further explanations and examples are below). The second argument is partly correct as, indeed, a hotel does not necessarily have a direct influence on choices where the guests go, as visitors will take their own decisions However, the moment a hotel distributes maps of the place, recommends certain sites or services to its guests or distributes discount vouchers for a free drink in their own restaurant, it is influencing the movement of its guests. Even small actions might have a significant contribution in relation to sustainability. Think of a hotel offering reduced price or even included tickets for public transportation, this will influence many guests to leave their car at the hotel and travel with public transport in the destination.

Hotels and other hospitality providers indeed have been involved in distributing the guests for a long time. However, this has been mostly done to enhance only one of the sustainability dimensions, namely the economic. The most common form here are loyalty cards or memberships, and package tours or special offers. A general issue for hospitality providers is the fact that hospitality is usually not the main feature of the tourism product, but is a secondary element (Jansen-Verbeke, 1986; Page and Connell, 2014). This means that the tourists who stay in a hotel, in most cases will not be there for the purpose of visiting that hotel. Their primary purpose for visiting the destination, for leisure tourists, may be to see its sites, or visit friends and relatives; whie business travellers will be there for meetings or conferences. These guests need accommodation or other hospitality, and will search for these having chosen the destination.

As a consequence, hotels and particularly hotel chains have developed loyalty/membership cards. Most major chains or even smaller ones have programmes where customers receive discounts or smaller special gifts when they book with the same hotels. This is particularly common for business travellers (Swarbrooke and Horner, 2016; Freyer, 2015) where companies make agreements with hotel chains and then, as a consequence, only book with that chain. Hence, guests will be more likely to visit a certain hospitality business. Similar loyalty programmes now also exist with other hospitality providers, e.g. restaurants, where you a customer might receive an incentive such as free drinks after having visited a certain number of times. From the perspective of the hospitality provider, these loyalty programs offer the possibility of attracting customers again. Otherwise, there are not many ways to ensure a long-term relationship with the customer, apart from delivering an extraordinary service or superb value for money so the customer would like to return again. A hotel has no possibilities for long-term contracts as there are in other industries.

Special offers or packages fall into a similar category of adding value, by offering additional services or experiences which should differentiate the hospitality provider in the eyes of the customers and offer them an outstanding value for money, while producing increased financial benefits for the provider. A lot of these special offers are focussed on keeping the customer in the facilities of the hospitality provider, and are especially common with hotels. On many hotel websites you will find special offers where, for example, a guest can book a 'wellness weekend' which includes not only the overnight stay but also meals, a couple of wellness treatments (often just one or two of each kind so a customer might book additional ones if they liked them) and access to the spa facilities. When these offers are not focussed on the facilities of the hospitality providers, they often focus on cooperation partners, with the hotel receiving a commission, if it is a major sight with limited carrying capacity (think of Madame Tussauds or the Alhambra), guests might receive special tickets, e.g. with no waiting time, that they can sell to their guests and therewith have a special added value in their offer. Of course, in examples, the main focus of this kind of visitor management is usually very much on the economic benefit for the hospitality provider, either by having a special product to offer or, in most cases, by receiving a commission.

Special offers that concentrate on other benefits and, in particular, are not only of value for the hospitality provider itself but mainly focus on saving natural resources or benefitting the local population are rather scarce. You can find some examples in the best cases below. However, while both of these cases show examples of how hospitality providers create benefits on the social and environmental dimension (or at least limit damage), both case studies still show also a focus on the economic dimension and were, indeed, hard to find. So, while writing this chapter it turned out that there were few cases where the social and environmental dimension of sustainability where a focus and where the actions were initiated by hospitality providers themselves in opposed to programmes that were initiated by local governments or nature organisations (who have a very different mission).

Now that we have explained that hospitality has a responsibility in the distribution of tourists, let us continue with the challenges related to sustainable distribution and then, after the best cases are presented, offer solutions to these challenges.

Sustainability challenges

The first challenge is that hospitality businesses have no direct influence on the movement of their customers outside of their own facilities. This issue has also been elaborated by Matthias Olthaar in Chapter 3, and to this chapter that you are referred to for further insights from a transportation perspective. Indeed, it has been argued that it should not be the purpose of a hospitality business to be involved in it, as it is not a part of the hospitality product. In fact, many books on Hospitality Management will only include internal factors and leave out external processes, such as the logistics of their guests. Others, however, start arguing in the opposite direction, that both tour operators and hospitality providers are responsible for their guests and for the impact that their guests have; as they have the benefits, they should also be held responsible for the negative impacts (Gordon and Nelke, 2016). Many negative impacts of tourism and inappropriate tourism distribution are not visible straight away or cannot be attributed to single players. Hence, it is difficult to pin down responsibility on a single stakeholder or would require significant cooperation of different stakeholders to take actions. In addition, many negative impacts such as high visitor pressure, disturbance of local inhabitants or damage of natural areas are not always easy to identify and often only become visible when the damage is significant. Hence, it also requires interest and attention as well as the will to cooperate from the side of the hospitality provider and other parties.

Indeed, many techniques of hospitality providers are focussed on not distributing people evenly through the destination so that other local stakeholders can benefit. Think of such offers as all-inclusive holidays. Often all-inclusive holidays take place in area that have some outstanding features (such as a warm climate and stunning scenery) but are not necessarily well equipped with other tourism facilities. From the point of view of the hospitality provider, an all-inclusive holiday is very profitable as basically all the money the tourists spend during their holiday stays within the facilities of the hotel, or at least will earn commissions, such as when tourists hire a guide via the hotel. Hence, it is tempting for hospitality providers to offer all-inclusive or similar offers. The above-mentioned incentives of offering guests a discount at the hotel's restaurant or special fees for meals follow very much the same principle of keeping as much of the customers' spending within their facilities instead of having it spent in 'competing' restaurants and facilities. The consequence of this is that other, less well-developed, players at the destination are excluded from the benefits that tourism may bring.

A point closely related to this might be the most significant challenge in tourism distribution, and an issue that has been discussed in many social studies on tourism, namely the gap between the attitude and behaviour of people at a tourism destination and their attitude and behaviour at home in their everyday life (Barr *et al.*, 2010). On holiday, the guests of the hospitality provider will often feel that they are the paying customer and should, hence, be allowed to do what they want to. Moreover, they are on holiday, and who would like to be restricted on holidays when you need to follow rules all the time during your daily life? In short, tourists would generally not like to think too much, but rather enjoy their holidays and relax. Consequently, many techniques that hospitality providers could use to distribute the positive impacts of the visitors and minimise the negative ones will not work, or at least not be very popular. A hotel that closes its golf courses during a period of aridness to save water will not only receive complaints but most likely lose customers to a competitor with an open golf course. In general, it has been researched that tourists do not like to be restricted, so an overabundance of rules or restrictions of access (for example to sensitive nature areas) will either result in dissatisfaction or in people not accepting them (Mason, 2008; Candrea and Ispas, 2009).

Indeed, there are many techniques that can be applied by hospitality providers and other parties at the destination, but that might not work well. For example, often visitor management in sensitive areas has been done by simply limiting access, or by strict rules and regulations in places where access cannot be limited because the area is too large or has too many access points, such as a nature reserve (Mason, 2008). There is ample evidence that tourists in particular will not always stick to rules, no matter how much these are actually in their favour. Open any newspaper and (in e.g. January 2016) you will find articles on ski tourists being killed by an avalanche as they left the official ski paths (which is strictly forbidden), or tourists dying of thirst in Australia's desert for leaving the official path (which is forbidden) and not walking with a tour guide (which is recommended).

The examples above may be waved away as extreme cases. However, researchers in tourism increasingly concentrate on tourists' behaviours in not only nature sensitive, but also potentially dangerous nature sites, such as phenomenon Trolltunga. A stunning rock 700 meters above Lake Ringedalsvatnet in Norway, Trolltunga is a favourite site among tourists for spectacular photographs. It will, however, take an expert climber 10-12 hours to reach it through dangerous terrain. During the last years (and in line with the trend of posting your most spectacular selfies on social media) there has been an enormous increase in accidents, mostly with tourists that were neither equipped nor experienced enough to take the hike to the Trolltunga, despite the fact that guest houses and hotels in the area not only distribute maps but also the safety instructions and warnings to guests (see for example: The Telegraph, 2015). You will probably know of other examples, such as unprepared tourists entering nature sensitive areas or regions that offers activities only for people highly skilled in the corresponding discipline, ignoring warning signs and any other form of well-intended advice. Considering these examples it should be concluded that, indeed, the power of hotels is often very limited, and that it will cost hotels additional resources to educate their visitors while the chance of success is doubtful. Hosts may feel caught in the dilemma of making the customers feel uncomfortable or even offended while trying to care for their safety. The question is whether, for example, the owner of a B&B should tell guests who seems to be going on a dangerous hike that they are neither equipped nor fit enough for it. Where exactly should hospitality providers draw the line between being responsible for their customers and the people/area around, to actually being hospitable and friendly to the guest?

It is a tricky business to find the right balance. Yet, the dilemma may become even more difficult to solve, as it might also involve sacrificing profit in order to protect not only the tourist's safety but also the wellbeing of the community and the natural environment. In fact, many activities that tourists want to do might be ethically questionable. Think for example of dolphin watching tours, elephant riding or a visit to a major tourism site such as the Seaworld in San Diego which has been criticised for holding killer whales in captivity (Independent, 2016). Imagine that, as a hotel, you try to minimise your impact on the environment. Yet, if guests ask for tickets at the reception, would you be able to deny these without upsetting them? In addition, if you do not sell these tickets your hotel might lose the commission, while the guest may buy the same ticket somewhere else. As a result, the hotel action has no positive impact, and a reckless provider receives the profits. To take a more common example: hotels often receive commissions on private car rentals if hotel guests book a car through them. Motivating customers to use public transport instead, therefore, would result in a loss of financial benefit. So, sometimes choices for the more sustainable option might result in not receiving some financial benefits, along with a potentially disappointed customer.

The distribution of people (the guests) in a destination is often believed to automatically result in a distribution of wealth as well, so that less privileged members of a community also enjoy revenues brought in by tourism. Unfortunately, this is not always true, especially as many of the visitor management techniques applied by hospitality providers are often aimed at enhancing the provider's economic benefits. Hence, it is instead a few selected stakeholders that will benefit financially – and, particularly in less developed countries or mass tourism destinations, these tend to be larger corporations and international organisations that financially benefit the most already anyway (Page and Connell, 2014). These organisations often do not invest the profits back into the destination but draw them to their home base, which results in money 'leaking' out of the destination, which is termed 'economic leakage'. Consequently, other parties such as locals at the destination, do not benefit financially. In other words, the multiplier effect, a concept explained in Chapter 9 on local purchasing, is prevented from occurring (Page and Connell, 2014).

Best cases

Case 4.1: Alpine Pearls

Already introduced in Chapter 3 (page 37), the Alpine Pearls are a cooperation of 25 small cities and villages located in six different countries in Europe. To understand the necessity of tourists' distribution for the Alpine region, it should be considered that the Alps was one of the first regions in the world where the negative impacts of mass tourism became evident; where limits to the carrying capacity of a destination started to be researched; and where the need for sustainable tourism was put into focus (Freyer, 2015; Widman, 2018). Therefore the need to spread visitors from popular places to smaller ones is keenly felt in the Alps. That the Alpine Pearls wish to contribute to this virtuous goal, is already evident from the opening page of its website where the Alpine Pearls are compared to a necklace of 25 pearls including 'known places' and 'insiders tip' (https://www.alpine-pearls.com/en/about-us/alpine-pearls/, Accessed on 6 February 2018). Hence tourists are lured from places where the carrying capacity is reached, to rather unknown places that have sufficient carrying capacity to cater for these tourists – on the website beautifully referred to as the 'insiders tip'. By buying a package tour offered via the website of the Alpine Pearls, tourists might visit places they would not visit otherwise and are led to spend money at these places. Hence, there are more locals who benefit. At the same time, the visitors' pressure on the main tourist regions might lower a bit and allow both the social protection of locals and tourists – who are less disturbed by (other) tourists – and the environmental protection of sensitive areas.

To reach its goal, the Alpine Pearls association is applying several techniques, including special package offers. Contrary to mainstream holiday packages, though, Alpine Pearls include in its packages features that are designed for a positive impact on the natural environment, such as sustainable transport (train, solar-powered car and so on) or guided access to certain areas. Interestingly, this offer is not presented as a restriction but as a service that will enhance the tourist experience. Therefore, Alpine Pearls avoid messages such as 'you must not drive an own vehicle, you must not access this track on your own', and uses instead messages that showcase the extra service or special feature of the product, such as 'take a vacation from your own car', to experience the surroundings of the area in a special way.

Finally, the Alpine Pearls use some nudging techniques that may be considered very tiny or rather traditional means but have actually a special impact on the tourist. A tourist that visits a certain number of local restaurants, for example, will receive a small gift in form of a cooking book with local recipes. The promise of the gift attracts the customer to visit several of the restaurants at the chosen location, while, once obtained, the customer has a special souvenir from the place (personal communication by Alpine Pearls visitor E. Cavagnaro, Leeuwarden, The Netherlands, June 2017).

4

Case 4.2: Association of Christian hotels

The German association of Christian hotels VCH (Verband Christlicher Hotels) was founded in 1904 with the purpose of offering a home away from home for guests by living and communicating Christian values. VCH collaborates with similar European associations in, for example, Austria and Switzerland, and with the international cooperation Christian Hotels/Hospitality International, which was formed on the example of the Swiss and German association. Part of the association is a registered society which, among other things, fosters an academy that trains and educates, with a focus on the disadvantaged (VCH Hotels, 2017).

From a quick look at the website of the VCH, one might argue that it is very much a website that sells packaged tours and promotes the hotels to tourists. Yet, when looking more closely, one will soon find several differences compared to mainstream websites. A significant numbers of the tours for example, either take place at or are connected to cultural or religious places, such a monastery; or have an educational element, such as in package tours following important Christian reformatory leaders (VCH Hotels, 2017).

In addition, upon visiting the hotel, one may observe that the information provided to the tourists is significantly more than the usual standard of major sites. The author visited one of the hotels in Berlin in August 2017, half a year after a so-called Islamic terrorist attack on the Christmas market of Berlin on 19th December 2016 had shocked the world. The author was offered information and brochures on activities related to the Christian-Islamic dialogue and joint activities of both churches. She was also offered information on other religious and/or cultural sites one would not necessarily claim to be the major tourist attractions in Berlin, such as several churches and mosques from different religions. This seems like a minor effort to take, however, it might have both an educative purpose and nudge tourists in behaving differently at the destination – that is by directing them to cultural/religious sites that are important for a cultural or religious minority but are not often visited. Hence, the hotel helps spreading tourists and potentially makes other places popular in a rather congested tourism destination as Berlin.

Tools to address the challenges

In general, there has been a shift in tourism industry stakeholders from hard to soft visitor management techniques. It depends a bit which tourism stakeholders we look at; some were always extremely involved in the distribution process at the destination (such as local governments forbidding access to a sensitive area); some already experimented with more organic techniques (such as nature park management distributing maps and instructions in nature sensitive areas); and some were not much involved at all. Unfortunately, the latter category contains many commercial organisations such as tour operators and hospitality providers. This is often the case because, as we have seen in the introduction to this chapter, they thought it was not their responsibility to better manage tourists as it mainly touched areas that were not in their core business.

Even though more initiatives have slowly been developed during recent years, the hospitality industry is still lagging behind. Unsurprisingly, most attention to tourism distribution has been given by organisations located in sensitive areas. In this context two main techniques are popular with tourism and hospitality providers, which is the spreading of information or offering an incentive such as special experiences (Mason, 2008). We will discuss them both below.

Providing information to guests is one of the most popular techniques, and most likely the easiest for hotels. In nature sensitive areas the provision of information has often an educational aim. This, though, does not need to be the case for a hospitality provider. The clerk at the reception can easily hand out information, recommend for example public transport, support the customer with maps and then recommend a nice local restaurant for dinner. This information will be highly appreciated by the customer as being supportive. In fact, the clerk does not give any mandatory rules nor will the guests perceive them as such – which might be very much the case when reading signs at the entrance of a site or being told by a nature guide upon entering a park what you are allowed to do and what you should avoid doing. Prerequisite here is that the hospitality provider has done enough research to provide this information, so that he for example knows which businesses belong to local owners, which businesses still produce local craft or which attractions take care of animal welfare. The hotel can also easily provide folders, brochures, or, as in some hotels, posters. It might even be possible to 'sneak in' educational information, which the customer will appreciate as local insider knowledge. This is an easy technique and one that the customer will directly appreciate, but requires the hospitality providers to do their research.

A popular technique that is already massively used by tour operators and also by many hotels is the incentive technique. Incentive here means offering some kind of (perceived) extra to the customer. Often these offers are marketed as the 'hidden treasure' for the customers. Think for example of offering insider trips to sites which are not known to tourists very well, instead of only selling sites whose carrying capacity is already reached. This is the approach that has been taken by the Alpine Pearls (see Case 4.1 above). If the carrying capacity is reached in major sites, a visit can be granted by special tickets. For example, the hotel may obtain tickets for a site at times when fewer visitors are there and sell these to its guests, often at a cheaper rate, and thereby lead them to the place at a non-critical time. To make this possible, the hotel needs to make some effort and cooperate, or start a partnership with other stakeholders such as theatres or sites in the destination.

Packages are still one of the easiest options for hospitality providers to spread visitors and at the same time add value for money to their product. Such a package can be the offering by a hotel of a weekend stay outside of the main season, including visits to sites and restaurants nearby. Thus other stakeholders who also suffer of the lack of tourists in the shoulder season can benefit and, potentially, some tourists may be lured away from a visit during high season. As in the example above, working out this solution requires partnership and cooperation of different stakeholders.

It seems a bit of an odd visitor management technique, but not offering something at all or not making guests aware of its existence might be highly effective. In December 2016 Tripadvisor announced that they will no longer be selling tickets to any tourist attraction which include physical contact with wild or endangered species and thereby banned hundreds of attractions from the direct reach of their customers (The Guardian, 2016). Hospitality providers have the same option: ban some items, promote others and/or provide incentives for a more sustainable activity. The same goals can also be reached the other way around, namely by making a sustainable option easily available for customers. A hotel selling tickets for public transport and offering a map with instructions on how to get to the city centre and back to the hotel might easily turn away customers from taking a cab due to simply not knowing where to go or not wanting to take the effort to go and buy a ticket first. Again, the customer might appreciate this as an additional service and not even notice the difference.

In general, an important thought the hospitality provider needs to hold on to is to keep the (financial) benefits the tourists leave in the destination and avoid or minimise the negative impacts. It might be that neither all possible benefits nor all possible negative impacts are actually visible to the hospitality provider himself. Hence, a close cooperation and dialogue with other stakeholders at the destination is important. The most important mechanism for spreading financial benefits, the tourism multiplier effect (Page and Connell, 2014), is elaborated in Chapter 9 on local purchasing. It basically means that when money is spent in the region and stays there, a multiplication effect is happening. To highlight an example may be helpful. Imagine a tourist who pays money to take part in a tour hosted by a local guide. Thanks to the tourist's choice, the tour guide earns an income and usually pays taxes. Consequently, not only the tour guide can spend his income but also the local authorities can spend the tax money, thus, contributing to the prosperity of the destination. Hence, local collaboration is important for the socio-economic benefit of the region. Even more important, this local collaboration can be a major feature in the tourism product offered to the customer. There is an increase in tourists looking for 'real' or 'authentic' experiences, and offering the guests tours by a local guide, selling special packages including dinner at a small local restaurant and promoting similar activities in the region can become a special feature of a hotel, and help to diversify it from the competition (Hall and Gössling, 2013; Hall, Mitchell and Sharples, 2003). However, to reach this outcome the hospitality provider needs to put effort into thinking along the value chain or potential value chain in the destination. He needs to analyse where the guests go when they are not inside the facilities of the hospitality provider, what kind of activities will be the most beneficial for the destination where the business is located, and how to start the dialogue and cooperation with the other stakeholders in the destination. Hence, the process is more complicated and some effort is needed to see with the eyes of the guest and of the other stakeholders in the destination. However, with these thought processes some of the soft techniques elaborated above, might be easily applied. It could be as easy as leaving folders in the hotel lobby on display for the guests, while many rewards await on the financial, social and environmental dimension of sustainability.

Conclusions

To conclude the issue of distribution at the destination: The topic has until now not been a major focus of hotels and other hospitality providers, unless there is a direct financial benefit in either gaining money or offering a better product involved. Indirect benefits have been mainly considered in sensitive areas (such as nature protection areas) or in situations where the negative impacts were so obvious that the hospitality providers faced a backlash, too.

However, a more sustainable hospitality industry means taking responsibility not only for the hospitality business itself but also for the destination where the business is situated. It means checking the entire value chain of a tourist's trip, and avoiding looking only at the small part of the trip when the tourist is on the premises of the hospitality provider. Hence, efforts need to be taken to analyse what positive benefits can be created in cooperation with other stakeholders in the destination and how negative impacts can be avoided or at least minimised.

A hospitality provider does not necessarily have a direct influence on its guests as to how they behave or to where they go outside his facilities. However, there are lots of possibilities for small interventions to guide the guests. During the last years, soft techniques for visitor management have proven to be more successful than hard, injunctive ones and are becoming more common. For hotels or other accommodations such simple practices as recommending certain facilities, sharing information brochures or selling tickets for public transport may be easily implemented. Hotel guests are often tourists not familiar with the region and will appreciate these recommendations as a good service by the hotel instead of understanding it as being forcibly educated.

References

Alpine Pearls (2017) *Alpine Pearls*. http://www.alpine-pearls.com. Accessed 7 December 2016.

Barr, S., Shaw, G., Coles, T. and Prillwitz, J. (2010) "A holiday is a holiday": practicing sustainability, home and away, *Journal of Transport Geography*, **18** (3) 474–481.

Candrea, A.N. and Ispas, A. (2009) Visitor management, A tool for sustainable touristm development in protected areas, *Bulletin of the Transilvania University of Braşov*, **2** (51), 131-136.

Freyer, W. (2015) *Tourismus*, 11th edn, München: De Gruyter Oldenbourg.

Gordon, G. and Nelke, A. (eds.)(2016) *CSR und Nachhaltige Innovation: Zukunftsfähigkeit durch soziale, ökonomische und ökologische Innovationen* [CSR and sustainable innovations: Being future proof through social, economical and ecological innovations], Wiesbaden: Springer Gabler.

Hall, C. M. and Gössling, S. (2013), *Sustainable Culinary Systems: Local foods, innovation, tourism and hospitality*, New York: Routledge

Hall, C. M., Mitchel. M. and Sharples, L. (2003) Consuming places: The role of food, wine and tourism in regional development, in Hall, C. M. (ed), *Food Tourism Around the World: Development, management and markets*, Oxford: Butterworth-Heinemann.

Jansen-Verbeke, M. (1986) Inner-city tourism: Resources, tourists and promoters, *Annals of Tourism Research*, **13** (1) 79-100.

Mason, P. (2008) Visitor management in protected areas: from "hard" to "soft" approaches?, *Current Issues in Tourism*, **2** (3) 181-194.

Page, S. and Connell, J. (2014) *Tourism: A Modern Synthesis*, 4th edition, Andover (UK): Cengage Learning EMEA.

Swarbrooke, J. and Horner, S. (2016) *Business Travel and Tourism*, Oxford: Butterworth, Heinemann.

The Guardian, (2016) *TripAdvisor bans ticket sales to attractions that allow contact with wild animals*. https://www.theguardian.com/travel/2016/oct/12/tripadvisor-no-touch-policy-wild-animals-holiday-attractions. Accessed 18 January 2018.

The Telegraph, (2015) *Trolltunga death an accident waiting to happen, says tour guide*. http://www.telegraph.co.uk/travel/news/Trolltunga-death-an-accident-waiting-to-happen-says-tour-guide/. Accessed 18 January 2018.

The Independent (2016) *SeaWorld San Diego to end its controversial killer whale show*. http://www.independent.co.uk/news/world/americas/seaworld-san-diego-to-end-its-controversial-killer-whale-show-a7515611.html. Accessed 18 January 2018.

Widman, E. (2008) *Nachhaltige Entwicklung im Tourismus in den Alpen: Ökotourismus als Chance für eine nachhaltige Entwicklung*. Thesis at University Mainz.

VCH-Hotels Deutschland (2017). https://www.vch.de/. Accessed 18 January 2018.

5 Are You Aware of What You Share With a Third-Party Internet Site?

Sustainability challenges concerning privacy in the sharing of information

Marit de Vries, Niels van Felius and Elena Cavagnaro

Learning goals

After studying this chapter, readers will have the ability to:

1 Describe the guest journey and identify the impact of Third-Party Internet sites (TPIs) on that journey;

2 Identify the elements in the process of information distribution when using TPIs;

3 Describe the business models of TPIs and their impact on hotels;

4 Explain the sustainability challenges linked to hotels using TPIs as a distribution channel; and

5 Provide examples of how hotels address these sustainability challenges.

Introduction

Suppose you book a hotel room in Amsterdam via Booking.com, for example, for the nights of 25 and 26 August. What happens to the information you send to Booking.com in this seemingly innocent process via the Internet? And what are the consequences for a hotel when you book a room through a so-called Third-Party Internet site (TPI), instead of the hotel's own website? These two questions are central to this chapter. The point we wish to make is that the relationship between TPIs and users on the one hand, and TPIs and hotels on the other, is gradually becoming more focused on the former. This situation leads to sustainability challenges that need to be addressed.

Chapter 6 contains an overview of the existing types of distribution channels, including offline channels and Internet Distribution Systems (IDS), and their associated definitions. This chapter focuses on TPIs. A TPI is defined as "an IDS operated by a variety of travel intermediaries not directly controlled by a hotel" (Hayes and Miller, 2011: 289).

To better understand the sustainability challenges that occur when using a TPI, throughout this chapter we will use the example of a guest who is looking for a hotel in Amsterdam for the nights of 25 and 26 August. In other words, to assess the impact of TPIs we will follow a guest journey. As Chibili indicates, in order to determine a proper digital marketing strategy, it is important to understand the guest journey from the moment the search starts until the moment guests receive a post-stay e-mail to write a review about their stay in the hotel (2016). A typical guest journey is illustrated in Figure 5.1. The arrows show how digital marketing and TPIs influence the guest journey. We will explain this in more detail below.

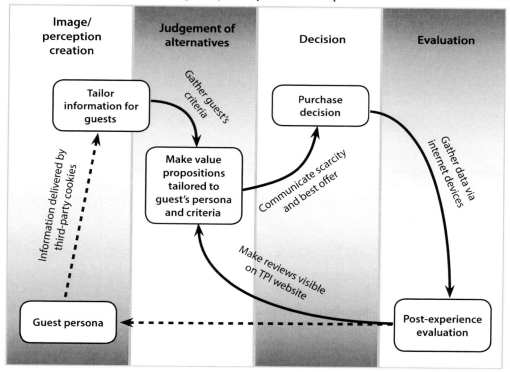

Figure 5.1: The guest journey from an organizational perspective (designed by the authors)

A typical guest journey begins on the left side of Figure 5.1, when someone starts dreaming about a destination – in our example, Amsterdam. Looking for inspiration, our fictitious person searches on the Internet using, for example, Google. This is probably not his first time using Google and cookies are probably already stored in the browser history. These cookies then initiate an algorithm and provide the searcher with information tailored to his profile and wishes.

Now it is up to him to assess the accommodation alternatives presented by the TPI and to make a decision. It is important here to note that the order in which alternatives are presented, as shown more clearly in the section, is not casual but is influenced by various factors, including previous choices the searcher has made and the marketing activities of a hotel. The presented overview of hotels includes some with the notification 'only three rooms left' or '2 other people are currently viewing this hotel'. Here, business intelligence (BI) and marketing are playing their part in creating a sense of scarcity, pushing the person to decide immediately in which hotel he wants to stay. After the decision is made and the hotel is booked, the TPI sends e-mails to inform the guest that, for example, his journey to Amsterdam will start in 2 days. Furthermore, suggestions are given as to what else to do during his stay in Amsterdam. All these marketing efforts are influenced by the big data stored on the TPI and by the data provided by the guest while searching for a hotel. One day after the check-out date, the TPI sends out an e-mail with the request to evaluate the hotel online. A few days or weeks later, big data from the TPI will be reused for marketing purposes, in order to send an e-mail or advertisement for a new travel experience. The inevitable conclusion is that TPIs have the power to control the entire guest journey, including the order in which hotels are presented to the person searching online. Moreover, TPIs collect and analyse data on both the guest and the hotel during each step of the guest journey. TPIs, therefore, not only have power over guests but also over hotels, and with power comes the responsibility of using it in an equitable and ethical manner. By equitable we mean that all stakeholders involved should profit from the transaction; and ethical refers to the responsibility of guaranteeing privacy.

In this chapter we will illustrate that equity and ethics are at risk in the relationship between TPIs and hotels, creating sustainability challenges that need to be addressed. We will first describe the sustainability challenges related to data collection and data handling, and thus to privacy and ethics. We will then address a specific challenge related to the business model of the TPIs and to equity. In doing so, we will also describe in more detail the steps in the guest journey and methods that the TPIs use to influence them. Two best case scenarios are then presented and we conclude by proposing sustainability solutions with regard to the challenges. We wish to stress that all the examples of companies have been freely chosen by the authors and without any prejudice to those companies.

Main sustainability challenges related to data collection and handling

When explaining the guest journey, we briefly noted that TPIs collect and handle data through the use of cookies and algorithms. Here we will provide a more specific explanation of both the process of collecting data using cookies, and the process of handling data using algorithms. We will point out the sustainability challenges related to both processes, i.e., privacy and security issues.

Cookies and algorithms

Let us start by looking at cookies and their use. "The cookie mechanism allows a web server to store a small amount of data on the computers of visiting users, which is then sent back to the web server upon subsequent requests" (Nikiforakis *et al.*, 2013: 541). Cookies are therefore used to store information. To illustrate how this mechanism works, we will return to the guest journey and the example of booking a hotel room. When someone enters a search with keywords such as 'hotel' and 'Amsterdam', a search results page is displayed, and the first cookies are set in the browser. When the searcher clicks on one of the search results, Booking.com for example, cookies are again set in the browser. When our fictitious person further specifies the search by, for example, adding a type of hotel, such as 4 or 5 stars, new cookies are stored. Now suppose he stops his search for a hotel and resumes his search two days later. The advertisements on the search results pages are related to all the cookies stored in his browser during the previous search.

In this way, a profile is created of the searcher's browsing habits and his so-called *digital fingerprint* is generated. This digital fingerprint is then used by organizations to provide him with (new) offers related to the needs indicated by the cookies (Nikiforakis *et al.*, 2013). Without cookies, a server does not learn what a guest's preferences are and no tailored offers, i.e., offers with a high probability of being chosen and purchased, can be made. Nowadays, it is even possible to log in to a TPI with your social media account. This means that the information shared on social media is directly accessible and can be used by a TPI, thereby refining the searcher's digital fingerprint. This phenomenon is described in more detail in Chapter 6.

Web servers create a guest profile by analyzing the cookies. Algorithms are used for this analysis. To understand the sustainability challenges related to data collection and handling, we therefore need at least some basic knowledge of what algorithms are and how they work. An algorithm is a process in which an entered value (the input) is converted into a new value (the output). For example, entering the key words '4-star hotel' in a search engine is the input. The output is then the list of all hotels that meet the criteria for a 4-star hotel. So basically, all that an algorithm does is find patterns in a vast amount of data. In our example of a guest who used '4-star hotel' as a search criterion and then stopped the search, it's the algorithms that cause ads for 4-star hotels to be displayed during his later, new search. Algorithms thus disclose hidden patterns in stored data and create the ability to predict the guest's future behaviour. This is possible thanks to predictive analytics. In our example, when the guest resumes his search two days later, predictive analytics combine the information of the first search with the information of the resumed search. Based on the vast amount of information stored in cookies and analysed by algorithms, a prediction can be made of what type of trip a guest wants to make, which type of hotel he prefers and which activities he likes so that a tailored offer can be presented to him (Xiang *et al.*, 2015; Agost, 2016). As Agost says: "Predictive analytics help to better understand user needs and match this knowledge to possible products and services" (2016: 2). This quote perfectly summarizes the relevance of predictive analytics to TPIs on the one hand and the hospitality and tourism industry on the other. At the same time, two important issues are not mentioned. The first issue is whether the data stored in the company's database for predictive analysis is handled correctly. The second issue is how the privacy of a guest is guaranteed when cookies are stored in the browser. These two issues are important for cyber ethics and security, and will be discussed in the next section.

Cyber ethics, cyber security and privacy

Cyber ethics is also referred to as internet, information, or computer ethics. It is the study of the legal, social and moral issues arising from the use of the Internet. Cyber ethics focuses on privacy issues such as sharing personal data with third parties and access to sensitive information by employees. One of the difficulties in applying cyber ethics lies in the fact that the Internet is an infrastructure where technology and resources are combined to provide a service to the user (Sohrabi and Khanlari, 2009; Agost, 2016). It is therefore not easy to draw the line between the handling and sharing of data needed to provide the service and the handling and sharing of data not needed to provide the service or benefit the end user. However, when this line is crossed, an ethical challenge arises in the cyber domain.

To better understand this challenge, let us use our example of a guest who is booking through a TPI to see how it develops. When potential guests visit a TPI, as we have seen, they leave a digital fingerprint behind that eventually becomes a privacy fingerprint because it contains information about the user that can be considered private, such as a personal phone number. More often than not, this is an unconscious rather than a conscious fingerprint. Zwitter (2015) highlights two important things, namely, the consequences of using the Internet of Things and the choice in what the user shares. Examples of unconscious use of the Internet of Things are wearing a smart watch or driving a car; both are equipped with GPS trackers and therefore collect data. The choice of sharing data is related to the use of Facebook or a mobile phone, for example, which impose practically no restrictions on what kind of user data is collected.

A digital fingerprint increases the more a guest searches. For example, when the same guest searches via the same TPI for multiple hotels, with different classifications, for different time periods and at other locations, his digital fingerprint increases. All this data is collected and analysed, and forms a large information bundle that contains private information regarding the preferences of the guests. As long as a TPI stores this information safely and only uses or shares the information for the benefit of the end user, i.e., the guest, that TPI behaves ethically and vigilantly. If this is not the case and the information is used or shared in a way that does not benefit the end user, that constitutes a privacy leak. In other words, a privacy matter becomes a privacy leak if the transfer of sensitive data is not intended by the user. This raises the question of how to prevent privacy leaks.

It should be noted that safeguarding the privacy of guests is not only related to how data is shared, but also to how it is stored. If data is not stored safely, it can be accessed by unauthorized persons or organisations and used for illegal purposes – cybercrime. Unfortunately, cybercrime such as ransom mails and hacking of databases of governmental agencies, is no longer an exception. It is estimated (Deloitte, 2017) that in a medium-sized country, such as the Netherlands, around 10 billion euros will be spent annually on cyber threats, of which 9 billion is spent by large organizations (including hotel chains) and 1 billion by small and medium sized enterprises, SMEs (including smaller and independent hotels).

At this stage, the risk of SMEs being attacked by hackers is four times lower than that of larger organisations. Still, all organisations that collect data, including TPIs and hotels, are responsible for storing this data securely. After a guest has booked a room via Booking.com, the hotel will receive the reservation. Depending on the situation at the hotel, the reservation might automatically end up in the Property Management System (PMS) or in the e-mail inbox of the responsible employee. For the sake of convenience, let us suppose here that the reservation ends up directly in the PMS. Once the reservation is included in the PMS, personal details passed on by the guest, like a phone number and credit card details, are displayed together with the reservation. Although the guest has shared this information, it is still private information. If the guest has used a TPI, such as Booking.com, to book then the e-mail address displayed in the hotel's PSM system is an e-mail address created by Booking.com. Booking.com in this case is responsible for safeguarding the data that the guest has provided to them. However, the hotel is always responsible for the data distributed by Booking.com to their PMS.

To conclude this section, we would like to stress that the main ethical challenges faced by TPIs are related to respecting privacy when collecting, analysing, using and storing data. If these challenges are not properly addressed, this could have negative consequences for the TPI's end-user, damage end-user's confidence in TPIs and thus threaten the long-term existence of TPIs. Solutions to the aforementioned challenges are proposed later in this chapter. Before considering these, we will address the second important sustainability challenge described in the introduction – the challenge related to the business models of TPIs.

Main sustainability challenges related to the business models of TPIs

To appreciate the impact of the business models of TPIs on hotels, we need to understand the role of TPIs as distribution channels and the influence that a hotel's marketing efforts has on how the hotel is displayed in search engines.

Over the past 10 years, TPIs have become important booking channels for hotels. Figure 5.2 shows how guests booked a hotel room in 2016: via a TPI (Online Travel Agency (OTA)) or via the brand website (from an online supplier direct).

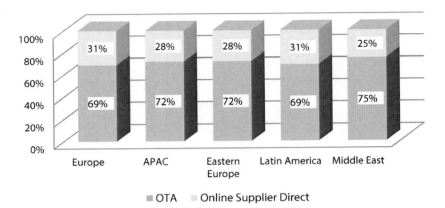

Figure 5.2: Online hotel room bookings 2016 based on Rauch, *et al.* (2017)

Figure 5.2 clearly shows that most online bookings worldwide reach hotels through a TPI and that therefore hotels cannot simply dismiss the services of TPIs. Of course, the services offered by TPIs come at a cost, namely commission. The amount of commission charged depends on the TPI's business model. By business model we mean the value proposition of a company and ultimately the way a company earns its money. An overview of the various business models that apply to TPIs is provided in the table below.

Table 5.1: TPI business models.

Subtype of TPI	Business model	Example
Referral site	"A cost-per-click advertising format, where the advertiser only pays when someone clicks on the listing and is then led deeper into the booking engine" (Lanz, 2015: 5)	TripAdvisor
Agency model (OTA)	"The hotels, as principal players, determine the commission fee for the agent websites; and then the websites determine how much effort will be done for each hotel, including but not limited to the ranking position of the webpage, picture views and video shows, etc." (Guo et al., 2013: 21)	Hotels.com
Merchant model	Holding rooms for online merchants on heavily discounted rates (30-50% off) with the risk for the hotel to end up with unsold inventory (Hayes and Miller, 2011)	Sabre
Opaque model	A pre-set amount per room is paid to the hotel. The difference between the price paid by the guest and the amount paid to the hotel is the earning for the Opaque model which mostly also include reservation costs. (Priceline.com, 2017)	Priceline.com

Table 5.1 shows that, despite some differences in the business models of TPIs, all TPIs have a financial impact on the companies that work with them. Of course, hotels always incur costs when they use a channel to reach potential guests,

whether it is offline or online. Still, hotels are not always fully aware of which costs, both monetary and non-monetary, are associated with the use of the various channels. We have therefore created the table below to clarify the costs that hotels incur when using offline and online channels. Here, a comparison is made between tools needed for offline bookings (via telephone or e-mail) and tools needed for online bookings (via a TPI). The left column contains the name of each tool, followed by its description and use. The third column lists the associated costs and the fourth and fifth columns show whether those costs are required for offline and/or online use.

Table 5.2 shows that in a very basic online situation, a hotel only needs a Property Management System (PMS) and a partnership with a TPI. In this situation the extra costs for a hotel are the commissions the hotel must pay to the TPI.

Table 5.2: Comparison of technological equipment needed for offline and online bookings.

Name	Description	Used to	Costs	Offline	Online
Property Management System (PMS)	"The hardware and software used to record reservations, guest stay information, and payments, as well as to record and store other relevant hotel operations data" (Hayes and Miller, 2011: 111)	Record reservation, guest information	Installation costs and annual fee	Yes	Yes
Third-party Internet site (TPI)	"Those operated by a variety of travel intermediaries not directly controlled by a hotel" (Hayes and Miller, 2011: 289)	Enable guests to book a hotel room via a TPI	Commission per room night sold		Yes
Brand website	"A web address whose content is 100 percent controlled by a hotel's own management team" (Hayes and Miller, 2011: 287)	Provide an online booking tool to make a reservation	Development costs and annual fee		Optional
Central Reservation System (CRS)	"The structure used to accept hotel guests' reservations and communicate them to an individual hotel's property management system (PMS)" (Hayes and Miller, 2011: 111)	Connect the TPI, the brand website, and the PMS	Installation costs and annual fee		Optional
Online Reservation System	A tool integrated in the brand website offering guests the opportunity to book a hotel room via the brand website	Enable guests to book a hotel room via the brand website	Installation costs and annual fee		Optional
Reputation Management System	A central system collecting ratings and comments (positive and negative) given by guests and converting them into a score	Enable hotels to monitor the guest reviews re their stay	Installation costs and annual fee		Optional

Rate Shopping Program	A program that compares real-time hotel room rates of TPIs based on the criteria specified by the user (e.g. competitive set, room type)	Provide an overview of rates of past, current and future competitors	Annual fee		Optional
Revenue Management System	A system used in deciding whether to accept or deny a reservation for a hotel room with a specific requirement (e.g. amount of guests, no. of nights, room) based on historical data in the system	Adjust room rates according to the strategy developed on all connected systems	Installation costs and annual fee		Optional

Taking figures from 2015 (Rabobank, 2016; Ali, 2015) and combining them with Booking.com as an example, we arrive at the following cost estimate for this basic situation.

Table 5.3: Estimation of commission costs for using a TPI.

Description	Figures related to the Netherlands (2015)
Average ADR (Average Daily Rate) per room night	€ 115.13
Average commission percentage charged per room night	15%
Total number of nights stayed in 2015	14,800,000
Total room revenue for nights stayed in 2015	€ 1,703,924,000
Total commission costs to be paid to TPI (based on 15%)	€ 255,588,600

The information in Table 5.3 can be applied to any hotel by adapting the following to the hotel's specific information: a) calculate the average of the ADR of bookings made via Booking.com; b) calculate the number of nights sold via Booking.com; and c) apply the commission percentage charged by Booking.com.

Whereas the elements that are to be calculated vary per hotel, the calculation presented in Table 5.3 only provides an estimate of the amount that hotels spend for a TPI's service. Seen from a TPI's perspective, this amount represents their income; from a hotel's perspective, it is a marketing expense. Clearly, as regards their marketing efforts, hotels are becoming increasingly dependent on TPIs throughout the guest journey. This dependence means higher costs for hotels than in the basic situation. To understand how high and threatening these costs can be for the economic sustainability of the hotel, we need to better understand how TPIs are interwoven with the guest journey. We will do this by returning to the example of the guest who is looking for a hotel in Amsterdam for the nights of 25 and 26 August.

As was shown in the previous section, algorithms are used to scrutinise all data provided by the guest immediately after the guest has entered the first key words in a search engine during the first phase of his guest journey – the Image/

Perception creation phase. In this process, algorithms search for a match between the guest's search data and the data provided by a hotel. The more information a hotel provides, the better a match can be found between the guest's wishes and the hotel's possibilities. The mechanism involved, Search Engine Marketing, and its specific technique, Search Engine Optimization, are discussed below (page 88). Training staff in the use of these techniques and purchasing tools to analyse relevant information for a guest, involve costs that need to be included in the marketing budget.

It should be taken into account that when a guest uses a search engine to find accommodation in Amsterdam, the resulting web page usually contains a combination of TPIs, brand websites that use a pay-per-click advertising system, and only very rarely a direct brand website. In a pay-per-click (PPC) system, a hotel must bid on specific key words that have been inserted in the search criteria. The payment connected to a key word is to the search engine and not to the TPI. When frequently used keywords are purchased and implemented on the hotel's website, the hotel might appear on the first page of search results. That this actually happens depends on how many other hotels bid for the same keyword. The advantage of using a PPC system lies in the fact that data shared by the guest is owned by the hotel. On the other hand, it involves costs that the hotel must pay. The hotel can set its own budget for this. Budgets vary anywhere between € 50 per month for small hotels and € 500,000 per month for international chains.

In the phase of assessing alternatives, our visitor will see a list of hotels in Amsterdam that are related to his search criteria. It is essential that the hotel name pops up as high as possible on the first search result page, because only 20% of searchers browse to the next page. In a search engine such as Google, several elements influence the ranking in the search results, such as content about the hotel, reviews left by guests, offered rates, a large inventory, preferred program partner and brand positioning in the market. If the search is done through a TPI, all these elements have less influence than the fee that a hotel pays to the TPI. Suppose our guest chooses Trivago for his hotel search. After clicking on the Trivago link, hotels are displayed that meet his search criteria. Once a hotel has been selected and the link to the hotel provided by Trivago has been clicked, the hotel must pay Trivago a certain fee. Canzoniere (2014) states that the sole opportunity for a hotel to directly influence a TPI's web algorithm, lies in the amount of commission paid; the higher the commission paid, the better the search results are.

After completing the decision phase and after visiting a hotel, the guest reaches the evaluation phase and is often given the opportunity to leave a review via the TPI. As mentioned, the number of reviews influences the hotel's position on the ranking page and therefore the hotel appreciates guests posting a review. No additional costs are associated with this.

This brief analysis of the impact of a TPI on the guest journey shows that if a hotel wishes to reap the full benefits of working with a TPI, then it needs to allocate a larger budget to its online marketing expenses than that calculated in the basic situation presented in Table 5.3. The exact amount to be allocated depends on several factors, including the amount of revenue obtained through online channels, the number of employees involved in marketing, and the number of online channels used.

The point that we wish to make here is that the costs incurred when using a TPI have to be added to the hotel's marketing budget and cannot be used to invest in other activities. From a sustainability perspective, these could be investments in training employees or in the community, or in developing other sustainable projects within the hotel such as in renewable energy, or in data security which, if lacking, can lead to serious privacy issues and unintentional leakage of private data. Moreover, the costs incurred by hotels for working with a TPI can become so high that they threaten the hotel's survival in general and its ability to invest in sustainability in particular. However, doing without TPIs is quite impossible, because TPIs, as we have seen, are interwoven with the marketing efforts of a hotel throughout the guest journey and hotels are increasingly dependent on TPIs as a distribution channel. So new sustainable solutions are needed. In fact, many hotels have already been faced with this challenge and some have already found a workable solution. In the next chapter, on best cases scenarios, we will present two of these solutions; one with regard to the sustainability challenges of safe data handling, and one with regard to a sustainable financial relationship with a TPI. Please note that the solutions given in these scenarios work for the specific companies that shared them with us, and may not be suitable in other situations.

Best cases

This section discusses two best cases. We will first describe how a hotel protects a guest's data when a reservation is made. We will then look at a hotel that, by offering its hotel rooms via other channels than a TPI, has reached new market segments, has restored the power balance with a TPI and has freed up financial resources for sustainable investments. In both cases, the hotel names are known to the authors but are not revealed considering both hotels wished to remain anonymous. The first hotel is referred to as 'A Random Hotel' (ARH) and the second hotel as 'Just a Hotel' (JAH).

Case 5.1: 'A Random Hotel' and safeguarding guest data

As shown in Table 5.2, different types of technological tools can be used to receive offline and online bookings. At A Random Hotel (ARH) hotel reservations are received both offline (by e-mail, phone, or at the front desk) and online. ARH has installed all the technological equipment listed in Table 5.2, except for the Reputation Management System. This choice enables ARH to receive hotel reservations in all possible ways, but it also implies that ARH must provide data storage. In this case, the data is all the guests' details that come in via the offline and online channels ARH uses. In order to protect the guests' data and safeguard the proper use of their details, all ARH's departments work closely with the hotel's Information and Communication Technology (ICT) department. We will now discuss which procedures ARH has in place to safeguard guest data, by examining which tools ARH uses and how they are linked to each other.

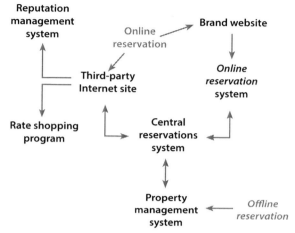

Figure 5.3: Linked technological tools at ARH (designed by the authors)

All technological tools that ARH uses to process bookings are shown in Figure 5.3. The arrows have a dual function: they indicate how ARH's technological tools are interlinked and show that all incoming information is collected in the Property Management System (PMS). For example, when a guest makes a reservation via the brand website, i.e., the ARH website, the Online Reservation System is used. The reservation is then forwarded to the Central Reservation System, which in turn shares the information with the PMS.

As this example shows, information on guests' bookings flows from one tool to the next. The flow of guest data takes a slightly different route.

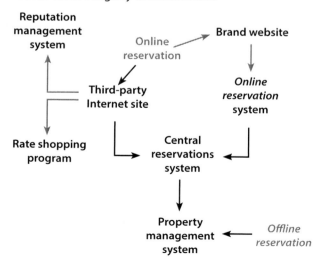

Figure 5.4: Flow of guest data at ARH (designed by the authors)

Figure 5.4 shows where guest data is involved in the process. The grey arrows indicate the interconnection of the tools as shown in Figure 5.3, whilst the black arrows indicate the flow of guest data. Figure 5.4 shows that the PMS is not only the central point of information flows, but also the tool where guest data is collected and stored. To safeguard guest data, processes had to be designed for the responsible use of the data stored in the PMS. How did ARH deal with this?

The first step was to evaluate which departments have access to the PMS, and for what purpose. This information was then used to decide which departments have access to which data. The PMS is used by the following departments within ARH: Reservations, Revenue, Front Office, Housekeeping, Restaurant, Kitchen, Marketing and the General Manager. These departments do not all use the PMS for the same purpose; they need different kinds of information from the system. The Reservations department, the main user, is responsible for the entire process involved in making a hotel reservation, adapting to the guest's wishes and to company standards, confirming the booking to the guest, and if necessary providing the other departments with information about the reservation. In order to be able to make such extensive use of the system, employees in the Reservations department have the highest user rights. User rights are settings in the system data of the PMS that determine each user's level for accessing certain data. Guest data is sensitive and therefore specific attention was paid to setting the user rights at the appropriate level. Consequently, the extent of each employee's access to guest data is related to their role and position. The following example will clarify this point. When a guest makes a reservation and confirms this with credit card details, this information is stored in the Central Reservation System and in the PMS. Only the Reservations and Front Office departments can see the credit card information. The former needs this information in order to charge the credit card when the reservation is made, if applicable to the type of reservation. The latter needs this information in order to settle the bill upon the guest's arrival and/or departure. The Housekeeping and Restaurant departments do not need credit card details. To prevent abuse, employees in those departments therefore do not have access to these details. The user rights of all departments have been specifically set by first identifying what type of information they need to perform their duties.

To further ensure the proper use of guest data, ARH has designed three layers of protection in relation to user rights. The first layer is focused on transparency and consistency in the allocation of user rights by allowing only the system administrator to allocate rights to employees. The second layer focuses on the right to change information in the system, the so-called change level. Employees are assigned a change level in line with their position and role. The last level relates to access to information. By information here we mean all information regarding a reservation, such as the number of rooms booked. However, special attention is paid to guest data such as credit card details.

Since 2015, it has been agreed worldwide that credit card details should not be stored in a PMS unless the data has been tokenized and the system is PCI DDS certified. PCI DSS stands for Payment Card Industry Data Security Standard. This security measure is designed to create guidelines for safeguarding payment card data and to provide a secure environment for transactions with payment cards. Tokenizing means that only the last four digits of the 16 digits of a payment card, are visible and the rest are replaced by a series of 'Xs'. ARH's PMS system meets these requirements.

In addition to developing these processes to ensure the safe handling of data stored in the system, ARH requires each employee to sign a confidentiality agreement stating that the employee may not disclose personal data of guests. The agreement also states that the consequences of non-compliance range from receiving an official warning to termination of the employment contract.

Lastly, the PMS itself has to be protected against the risk of the system being hacked. ARH has minimised this risk by organising their software location in a specific way. By software location we mean where the software is installed: on servers at ARH, or via SAAS. SAAS stands for Software as a Service, which means that data is stored in the cloud. Working in the cloud has several advantages, such as cost savings (not having your own servers) and reliability (24/7 helpdesk and support) as well as some disadvantages, such as downtime (when the server needs updating) and limited control (when it comes to the backend of the server). As far as installing software at the location is concerned, the main advantage is that the control lies directly with ARH's ICT department. The main drawbacks are the high costs of installing a server and managing updates to ensure data security. ARH has therefore opted for a cloud-based solution and checked for certifications such as GDPR, PCI DSS and of the data centre when selecting the SAAS. . We will briefly discuss General Data Protection Regulation later (page 86). PCI DSS has already been discussed previously. By choosing a certified data centre, one is assured that the organisation that provides the data centre guarantees that the data that is collected and handled is protected. Consequently, the provider and not ARH is responsible if any data is leaked or hacked in the data centre.

Case 5.2: 'Just a hotel' and a TPI

Since 2014, 'Just a hotel' (JAH) has seen a huge growth in online bookings throughout the year. In January 2016, after reviewing 2015, JAH management concluded that the main cause of the large increase in occupancy was the number of reservations received via TPIs. After closing 2015 with an occupancy rate of 96.5%, JAH management also concluded that the impact of TPIs on this growth was disproportionately large and threatened the hotel's financial sustainability and its ability to reach a healthy balance between different market segments. On a financial level, the high occupancy rate and the growth of the TPI market segment led to high commission costs. As to market segments, a decrease in corporate business was observed that was directly related to the increase in bookings through TPIs and JAH's aim to achieve a high occupancy rate. The reason for this is the booking window, i.e., the number of days between the time a booking is made and the actual arrival date. The market segment served by TPIs has a different booking window than corporate clients. On average, the booking window for the TPI market segment is 26.45 days versus 7.21 days for the corporate market segment. As a consequence, all JAH rooms are already reserved by the TPI market segment before the corporate market segment starts to book. The TPI market segment is therefore taking over the corporate market share. In order to maintain a healthy balance between market segments, in the knowledge that there will be much last-minute demand from the corporate market segment, and in order to restore the balance of power between hotel and TPI, JAH decided to slow down the bookings made via the TPI market segment.

Since one of the TPIs, here called TPI A, is the largest driving force behind growth and has the largest market share in the TPI market segment, it was clear to JAH that taking action in this direction would be the most effective measure. The hotel currently enjoys the 'Desired status' at TPI A, which means that JAH is displayed above all 'Normal status' hotels. This generates more bookings for the hotel, although it comes at a price, namely 17% commission instead of the relative standard of 14%. The plan that JAH devised to slow down bookings was to switch to 'Normal status'. This would save 3% in commission costs and would hopefully restore the balance between the TPI market segment and the corporate market segment.

Switching to 'Normal status' had immediate effect, as can be seen in Figures 5.5 to 5.7.

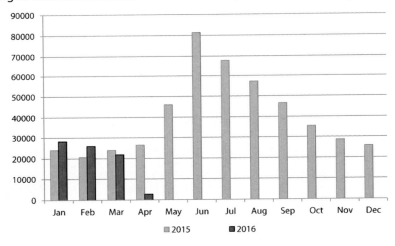

Figure 5.5: Difference in visitors booking via TPI A (by kind permission of JAH)

Figure 5.5 shows that, after introducing the new strategy, the number of visitors from the TPI market segment who booked via TPI A in March 2016 dropped (by 8%) compared to March 2015. In January and February 2016, however, JAH had witnessed a growth in visitors from the TPI market segment of 17% and 25% respectively.

Figure 5.6 shows that once JAH switched from 'Desired status' (17% commission) to 'Normal status' (14% commission) the number of reservations in all market segments increased in January and February as compared to the previous year.

Lastly, Figure 5.7 shows that the number of room nights booked by all market segments in March 2016 dropped by 8%. What is not shown here is the hotel's revenue, which grew by 2% due to the improvement in the average daily rate (ADR).

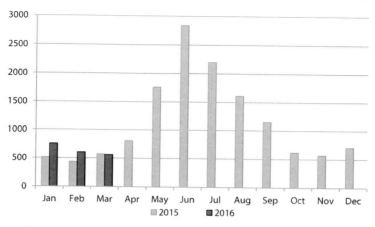

Figure 5.6: Difference in reservations made after switching to 'Normal status' (by kind permission of JAH)

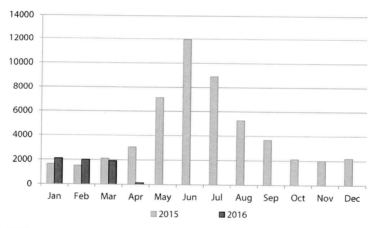

Figure 5.7: Difference in booked room nights (by kind permission of JAH)

Some other side effects were also observed when JAH switched to 'Normal status'. First, the number of rooms reserved via TPI A decreased. Second, and surprisingly, the number of rooms booked via the brand website decreased. Third, a remarkable change was seen in the number of bookings coming in via the second largest TPI, namely TPI B. TPI B immediately picked up TPI A's lost business, causing a negative effect on the commission as TPI B charges 23% commission per booked room night. The smaller agents also benefited from the business that was not captured by TPI A. It can therefore be concluded that switching to 'Normal status' had a widespread impact within the TPI market segment itself and that the desired effect within this market segment was not achieved in the first month. However, a more positive picture emerged when comparing the total TPI market segment to the total corporate market segment: the number of rooms booked via the corporate market segment fell in January and February 2016, but rose in March 2016. The total number of reservations continued to rise in March 2016, albeit at a slower pace compared to the average growth in the first two months of 2016, namely 1.77% versus 9.2%.

To summarise, slowing down bookings via TPI A has had a positive effect on the shift from the TPI market segment to the corporate market segment. The shift within the TPI market segment itself, though, did not have the expected results and definitely not the desired results. Also given the total number of reservations made, JAH witnessed a weaker growth compared to previous months. This was also a negative effect, which can be linked directly to the decreasing number of visitors via the TPI.

From this case it can be concluded that the balance between the corporate market segment and the TPI market segment as a whole can be controlled. However, the impact on the total number of bookings and the bookings made within the TPI market segment should be carefully considered before making the final decision to switch to 'Normal status' with the TPI which provides the highest number of guests. The brand website should also be improved before such a measure is taken.

Having presented these two best case scenarios, it is now time to look at the sustainability solutions that relate to the sustainability challenges as discussed earlier.

Tools to address the challenges

Given the afore-mentioned challenges and the best case scenarios, this section contains ideas for sustainability solutions. We will first consider solutions for safeguarding data during collection and handling, and then we will look into rebalancing the balance of power between hotels and TPIs with specific attention to TPIs' business model and marketing possibilities. By offering these suggestions we hope to pave the way for hotels towards a more sustainable approach to working with TPIs.

Data collection and handling

Much attention is currently focused on measures to secure guest or personal data. As mentioned above, this attention is related to the increase in cybercrime and the costs associated with protecting companies and solving security issues. When it comes to handling guest data in general and from a sustainability perspective in particular, the first step is to comply with laws and regulations. Legislation around data privacy is becoming a priority for many countries and regions. For example, strict regulations regarding privacy are already in place in the European Union (EU) and on 27 April 2016 a new version of the General Data Protection Regulation (GDPR) was adopted which must be fully implemented by 25 May 2018. The modified regulations apply when the data controller (the organisation that collects the data), the data processor (the company that handles the data and supports the data controller, e.g., a cloud service), and/or the data subject (e.g., information shared by the hotel guest) resides in the EU. The European Commission states that "personal data is any information relating to an individual, whether it relates to his or her private, professional or public life. It can be anything from a name, a home address, a photo, an e-mail address, bank details, posts on social networking websites, medical information, or a computer's IP address" (European Commission, 2017). Companies that do not comply with the new regulations are subject to fines of up to 4% of the annual worldwide revenue in the case of an enterprise or otherwise up to 20 million euros. The effect of these regulations is already apparent in European countries. In the Netherlands, for instance, an increase has been observed in the number of cyber security systems which is also related to the implementation of the 'Personal Data Protection Act'. This is a specific Dutch law that was enforced as a result of the GDPR. Moreover, in June 2017, the Dutch parliament requested that a Digital Trust Centre (DTC) be set up for the purpose of improving cyber security (Deloitte, 2017).

In line with these regulations, there is a recent development that is visible to users and mandatory for companies, namely the Transport Layer Security (TLS) protocol in combination with the Public Key Infrastructure (PKI). When correctly implemented, they are rewarded with a certificate that is cryptographically signed by Certificate Authorities (CAs). In practice, this means that the URL of the website starts with 'https' and a symbol of a lock is displayed. If a website does not have the correct certification or is attacked, the certificate is revoked and the user receives an error message. The owner of the website must then withdraw the compromised certificate in order to prevent attackers from gaining access to the website or using the website for phishing purposes (Larisch, 2017).

The examples above show that the regulations for secure storage and handling of data are being tightened up and that companies, including hotels, must comply with the regulations. Indeed, all organisations are expected to comply with laws and regulations but organisations that aim for sustainability even more so. Consider for example that in the classic definition of Corporate Social Responsibility given by A.B. Carroll, abiding by the law is the second responsibility of an organisation after its economic, and before its ethical and philanthropic responsibility (Carroll, 1991). Carroll's definition also indicates that sustainable companies are expected to do more than just comply and that they adopt a proactive, ethical attitude with respect to handling guest data.

An example of a company that does more than the law requires is best case ARH. Asking employees to sign a confidentiality agreement goes a step further than the required level of legal responsibility. Carroll's approach also calls for an analysis of responsibilities. If we look at TPIs and hotels, TPIs such as Booking.com are responsible for securing the data that guests provide them. Hotels are in turn responsible for the data sent by Booking.com to their PMS. To meet this responsibility hotels must design processes that restrict access to guest information stored in their PMS by means of user rights, following the example of ARH in one of the best case scenarios reported previously. To go a step further, hotels can seek to join forces to negotiate with TPIs for a safe and respectful handling of guest data, and can, for example, require a guarantee for and an explanation of how guest data is stored securely. When hotels request TPIs for additional privacy guarantees in addition to the guarantees already required by law, then they are complying with the ethical approach of Carroll.

In our opinion, both hotels and TPIs have reached a point where more and more attention will be paid to the way in which they protect guest data. Based on our knowledge, the information shared by the 'best case' hotels and the realisation that sustainability and corporate social responsibility require more than just literally following the letter of the law, we conclude that TPIs and hotels need to explore new ways to securely collect and store guest data, and find ways to handle and share data that clearly benefit the end user. In this respect they can follow the lines set out in this section. In the next section we will look at the second sustainability challenge, namely the challenge that is related to a TPI business model and the dependence of hotels on TPIs as a distribution channel.

TPIs' business model and marketing

In illustrating the sustainability challenges that hotels face when using TPI services, we have already noticed that global TPIs are the most important channels for hotel bookings. Moreover, hotels can benefit from the so-called billboard effect when they use a TPI, i.e., the fact that a hotel brand can appear in the search results even if a guest has not entered that specific brand name. It is therefore not wise to stop working with a TPI. However, as demonstrated in the JAH best case scenario, a possible solution is to seek a better balance between reservations via TPIs and via other channels such as the brand website. To this end, a hotel must purposefully apply insights from distribution channel management (Hayes and Miller, 2011). Distribution channel management starts with identifying the hotel's market segmentation and determining the desired balance between the various segments, including the business and leisure segments. The hotel must then determine which market segment makes the most reservations via which channel. This analysis is important because, as the JAH best case has shown, not all TPIs attract the same market segment. Moreover, hotels want to reap the benefits of the billboard effect and appear in the search results in the alternatives assessment phase of the guest journey. Next, hotels must determine the number of rooms to be sold via each distribution channel. This decision should be taken carefully, looking at the best balance per day and taking into consideration changes in booking patterns due to, for example, high and low seasons or events in the area.

Once all this has been determined and implemented, it is time to consider the evaluation phase in the guest journey and the impact that guest reviews have on potential bookings by the same or other guests. A good reputation management strategy is essential to ensure that proper attention is given to and action taken on reviews. However, this is not the place to discuss online reputation management in detail. Research shows that the way in which hotels respond to guest reviews, be they positive or negative, differs greatly. Research also shows that a timely and effective response is essential in a world where user-generated online reviews have an increasing impact on the choices of guests (Sparks and Bradley, 2014).

Once guests have stayed in a particular hotel and their personal details are known, the hotel can approach them directly in order to encourage them to book their next stay via the brand website. To achieve this goal, hotels need to reconsider their marketing approach and in particular their online marketing efforts such as their use of Search Engine Marketing (SEM), web design, Search Engine Optimization (SEO) and content marketing. SEM and SEO are of specific importance here because they can be used to steer bookings away from a TPI website and towards the website of a hotel brand. To achieve this, hotels can use the savings on commission costs to invest in training their employees in both techniques. To see how SEM and SEO work, let us go back to the example of a guest who is looking for a room in Amsterdam for specific nights. In the Image/Perception creation phase of the guest journey, a search engine on the Internet is used in almost 50% of the cases so it is important that a hotel is displayed in the guest's search results (eMarketer, 2016). The fact that guests enter only 1 to 3 keywords for their search, and around 80% view only the listings on the first page, Search Engine Optimization (SEO) is very important for hotels (Paraskevas *et al.*, 2011). According to Paraskevas *et al.* (2011) "Search Engine Marketing (SEM) is a form of online marketing whereby marketers and webmasters use a range of techniques to ensure that their webpage listing appears in a favourable location in search engines' results pages (e.g., Google, Bing, AlltheWeb, Altavista)" (p.1). Organic Search Engine Optimization (SEO) is important for hotels in the alternatives assessment phase in the guest journey. Implementing both SEM and SEO techniques, indicating that a hotel operates in a sustainable manner, is a solution for hotels for generating more bookings via TPIs who support the sustainability approach.

Conclusion

The two pivotal questions in this chapter were: 1) What happens to the information that you send to Booking.com in the seemingly innocent process of booking a room via the Internet? And 2) What are the consequences for a hotel when you book a room via a so-called Third-party Internet site (TPI) instead of directly via the hotel's website?

As regards the first question, we have established by means of the guest journey and our example of a guest who wants to book a hotel room in Amsterdam, that the main issues lie in collecting, handling and storing guest data. Privacy and security are the main sustainable challenges. In our opinion, hotels and TPIs can generate solutions to these challenges by applying Carroll's understanding of Corporate Social Responsibility and extending compliance to include a more ethical attitude.

With regard to the second question, we have identified the dependence of hotels on TPIs as a distribution channel as the main sustainability challenge in connection with the TPI business model. The solution we propose is to continue to work with TPIs, but to address the balance by re-examining the hotel's market segmentation and selecting distribution channels on that basis. We also propose that hotels apply online marketing techniques to stimulate bookings via the brand website.

Instead of recommending some further reading or articles and books that may well no longer be up to date when you read this, we strongly recommend that you follow developments in the field of privacy data security and online marketing possibilities. These are such rapid developments that by the time you peruse this book, some of the information might already have been overtaken by new facts.

References

Agost, R.A. (2016) *5 examples of predictive analytics in the travel industry*, Amadeus, available at http://www.amadeus.com/blog/07/04/5-examples-predictive-analytics-travel-industry/. Accessed 23 July 2017.

Ali, R. (2015) *Lifestyle Habits of the 24/7 Business Traveler*, report prepared for Skift and American Express.

Canzoniere, F. (2014) *Crack the Booking.com algorithm.* https://www.tnooz.com/article/crack-the-booking-com-algorithm/. Accessed: 23 July 2017.

Carroll, A.B. (1991) The pyramid of corporate social responsibility: toward the moral management of organizational stakeholders, *Business Horizons*, **34** (4), 39-48.

Chibili, M.N. (2016) *Modern Hotel Operations*, 1st edn, Groningen Houten: Noordhoff Uitgevers bv.

Deloitte (2017) *Dealing efficiently with cybercrime – Cyber value at risk in The Netherlands 2017.* https://www.sbs.ox.ac.uk/cybersecurity-capacity/system/files/Deloitte_Cyber%20VaR%20NL%202017.pdf. Accessed 19 March 2018

eMarketer (2016) *Most travelers use search engines when planning a trip.* https://www.emarketer.com/Articles/Print.aspx?R=1013745. Accessed: 20 August 2017.

European Commission (2017) *Commission proposes a comprehensive reform of data protection rules to increase users' control of their data and to cut costs for businesses.* http://europa.eu/rapid/press-release_IP-12-46_en.htm. Accessed: 22 October 2017.

Guo, X., Ling, L., Dong, Y. and Liang, L. (2013) Cooperation contract in tourism supply chains: The optimal pricing strategy of hotels for cooperative third party strategic websites, *Annals of Tourism Research*, **41**, 20-41.

Hayes, D.K. and Miller, A. (2011) *Revenue Management for Hospitality Industry*, 2nd edn, Hoboken New Jersey: John Wiley & Sons Inc.

Lanz, L. (2015) *Digital marketing budgets for independent hotels: continuously shifting to remain competitive in the online world.* https://www.hospitalitynet.org/opinion/4072042.html. Accessed: 23 July 2017.

Larisch, J., Choffnes, D., Levin, D., Bruce, M.M., Alan. M. and Christo, W. (2017) CRLite: A Scalable System for Pushing All TLS Revocations to All Browsers, paper presented at the *ISSS Symposium on Security and Privacy*, 22-24 May, San Fransisco.

Nikiforakis, N., Kapravelos, A. Joosen, W. Kruegel, C., Piessens, F. and Vigna, G. (2013) Cookieless monster: exploring the ecosystem of web-based device fingerprinting, paper presented at the *IEEE Symposium on Security and Privacy*, 19-22 May, San Fransisco.

Paraskevas, A., Ioannis Katsogridakis, I., Law, R. and Buhalis, D. (2011) Search engine marketing: transforming search engines into hotel distribution channels, *Cornell Hospitality Quarterly*, **20** (10), 1-9.

Priceline.com (2017) *Web Site Terms & Conditions*. https://www.priceline.com/static-pages/terms_en.html. Accessed: 25 September 2017.

Rabobank Cijfers & Trends (2016) *Branche Hotels*. https://www.rabobankcijfersentrends.nl/INDEX.CFM?action=branche&branche=Hotels. Accessed 2 October 2016.

Rauch, M., Blutstein, M., Jong, A., Wright, B. and Quinby, D. (2017) *2017 Phocus Forward – The Year Ahead in Digital Travel*, report prepared for Phocuswright. https://www.phocuswright.com/Free-Travel-Research/2017-Phocus-Forward-The-Year-Ahead-in-Digital-Travel. Accessed 24 March 2018.

Sohrabi, B. and Khanlari, A. (2009) Ethics, information technology and organizational citizenship behavior, *Iranian Journal of Ethics in Science and Technology*, **4** (1), 1-13.

Sparks, B. A. and Bradley, G. L. (2014) A 'Triple A' typology of responding to negative consumer-generated online reviews, *Journal of Hospitality & Tourism Research*, **41**(6), 719–745.

Xiang Z., Wang, D., O'Leary, J.T. and Fesenmaier, D.R. (2015) Adapting to the Internet: trends in traveler use of the web for trip planning, *Journal of Travel Research*, **54** (4), 1-52.

Zwitter, A. (2015) Big data and international relations, *Ethics & International Affairs*, **29** (4), 377-389.

5

The Impact of Third-Party Internet Sites on the Hotel Guest Journey

Niels van Felius, Elena Cavagnaro and Marit de Vries

Learning goals

This chapter focuses on the sustainability challenges that arise from the increased influence of Third-Party Internet sites on the guest journey, in particular during the gathering of information and judgement of alternatives phase. After studying this chapter, readers will have the ability to:

1 Define the growth in the use of online information communication technology from a hotel perspective;

2 Describe the guest journey focussing on how a hotel guest uses a Third-Party Internet site (TPI) as a booking tool;

3 Describe the main technology for data gathering behind TPIs, and the resulting bubble effect;

4 Explain the sustainability challenges connected with the bubble effect;

5 Identify tools to address the challenges of the bubble effect considering also best-case examples.

Introduction

Reservations are essential for hotels to plan their operations. When considering reservations for their planning, hotel departments usually refer to the reservation horizon, that is the number of rooms booked on a day in the future, and the predicted pick-ups, that is the number of room reservations a hotel expects to get confirmed over a certain period. These figures are used to decide upon, for example, the number of employees needed in the F&B department for the breakfast shift or in Housekeeping to clean the rooms; the volume of ingredients needed for breakfast; and planning hotel rooms' maintenance during less busy periods.

Nowadays hotel reservations are highly dependent on information technology. Most of the reservations enter the hotel's Property Management System (PMS) via interfaces linked to different booking websites. These are owned and controlled by Online Travel Agencies (OTAs) and are generally referred to as Third-Party Internet sites (TPIs), because OTAs are independent organisations and not directly related to a hotel or a hotel chains, but exist to provide hotels with reservations. These concepts have already been discussed in Chapter 5, to which you are referred if you wish to know more about how TPIs work. In line with this, a TPI is defined as "an Internet Distribution System (IDS) operated by a variety of travel intermediaries not directly controlled by a hotel" (Hayes and Miller, 2011: 289). Chapter 5 also addressed the question of what happens with the information that guests provide while making a booking via an IDS, and have shown that large quantities of data and information are gathered by TPIs. Following up on this discussion, this chapter focuses on the sustainability challenges that arise from the increased influence of TPIs on the process through which travellers gather, select and judge information about their next trip.

It is important to know that this chapter, if not otherwise stated, is written from the guest perspective. We generally agree with the statement that the use and abuse of a tool is in the hand of the user, although the developer or owner of the tool can nudge its users towards a more sustainable practice, and a more sustainable selection, and that is exactly where the sustainable challenges are.

In closing this brief introduction we wish to share a word of caution. Considering that developments in innovation technology are quick and continuous, and that regulations impacting the use of technology are inevitability changing, the authors would like to acknowledge that from a future perspective the issues discussed in this chapter might seem obsolete, and that in a few years and even in a few months more urgent issues might occur.

Main sustainability challenges

During the *Guest on Earth* conference held at Stenden University of Applied Sciences (Leeuwarden, The Netherlands) in 2015 one of the attendees raised the issue whether staying at home would not be the most sustainable form of tourism. An interesting question, and this person might be right that, at least from an environmental perspective, no-tourism may qualify as the best option. On the other side, going on a holiday can potentially change guests' perspectives on the environment and open up their mind regarding different cultures and customs (Falk *et al.*, 2012; Cavagnaro *et al.*, 2018). The transformative power of tourism can help guests to understand that different cultures should be nurtured and natural beauty protected. This understanding, in its turn, may motivate tourists to behave more sustainably even when they are back home. Moreover, as other chapters in this book show (e.g. Chapter 4) tourism has the potential to impact positively on the socio-economic conditions of local people. It would therefore be a pity to forego tourism, and the transformational, positive opportunities it might bring to tourists, local people and service providers. Yet, as all chapters in this book show, to achieve sustainable tourism several daunting challenges have to be addressed. Also sharing data online while booking and experiencing a trip presents challenges to sustainable tourism. The points we will make below are twofold. First, we will argue that TPIs use the information that they possess about their users to make to potential travellers offers that suit their needs so perfectly, that travellers are pushed to travel more often – with all consequent environmental damages. Second, we will argue that by following the hassle-free offer of TPIs, travellers are caught in their own bubble thus missing, for example, the opportunity to truly get in contact with other people and cultures. The transformative power of tourism is therefore impaired while the environment is negatively affected. Under these circumstances staying at home is surely the most sustainable form of tourism.

The section on challenges is divided in four subsections. The first subsection offers a historic overview of the development of the World Wide Web, and the implications of this development for marketing in hospitality and tourism. If you are already well aware of these issues, you may wish to skip this part and go directly to the following subsection, on the impact of TPIs on the guest decision-making process (page 97). The third subsection is dedicated to the impact of pre-set filters on the guest journey, the so-called bubble effect, and the final subsection addresses wearables.

The development of the World Wide Web and its implications for hospitality and tourism marketing

Currently we find ourselves in an era where almost all communication between hotels and their guests is computer mediated, meaning that computers are the main medium through which information is shared. This era has been labelled Web 3.0. Yet, how did we get here? We need to answer this question to better understand not only the link between online marketing and the guest journey, but also the sustainability challenges that arise from this link. This section first gives a short explanation about how the sharing of information between hosts and guests has evolved over time, and then looks more in depth into the implications of this evolution for the guest's journey.

Let us start this brief history of (online) marketing by giving an overview of the different distribution channels used by hotels nowadays (Figure 6.1). As you can see, hotels have a vast number of options to choose from, including old-style but still very useful options such as a phone call.

From the present, depicted in Figure 6.1, let us then step back to the good old days before 1993 when guests gathered information by visiting a travel agency or a booking agent (both brick and mortar style companies), by consulting hotel information distributed through mailings and brochures, or by requesting hotel information via telephone. Information was circulated on paper and only the quantity of brochures or hotel catalogues distributed per area could be measured. This was the only information hotel marketers could use in planning their sales activities. In 1993, when Internet went public, this situation changed dramatically.

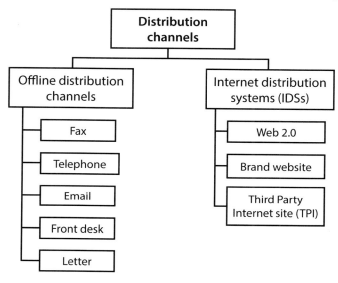

Figure 6.1: Overview of distribution channels (designed by the authors)

The year 1993 marks the start of what is now sometimes called Web 1.0, the first phase in the development of the World Wide Web. During Web 1.0 websites were static, that is they did not provided interactive content, while webpages were only connected via hyperlinks. Taking advantage of the opportunities offered by Web 1.0, hotels and travel agencies started sharing information with potential guests via their company or brand websites. Yet, out of all the channels illustrated in Figure 6.1, offline distribution channels were still the most commonly used. During the Web 1.0 phase, in fact, brand websites were no more and no less than online hotel brochures. Information and reservation requests were still handled via e-mail, and usually answered via fax or by sending a brochure per post. Online information that, for example, could allow guests to compare different offers was scattered over a multitude of websites. Moreover, potential guests generally needed to know the hotel's web address to view its website.

During the next development phase, known as Web 2.0 (2004–2015), the Internet not only became an interactive medium but also upheld the growth of social media websites, where users create content. Interaction in a Web 2.0 environment means that not only hotels could send out information to guests, but guests could also respond to the hotel by e-mail and using chat options. During Web 2.0 interaction was still one-to-one (i.e. from the hotel to the guest and vice-versa), or one-to-many (i.e. from the hotel to potential guests), and not yet many-to-many as in the current development phase, Web 3.0. Interactive communication, though, paved the way for Search Engine Marketing (SEM), a form of Internet marketing that allows the ranking of websites on the results pages of search engines like Goggle (for more on SEM see Chapter 5).

Alongside multichannel and many-to-many communication, the next step in the development of online communication has been ubiquity. Ubiquity is the capacity to access and create content using applications from any place where one is, thanks to the connection of multiple devices with the web. In a Web 3.0 environment, for example, guests can evaluate their experience on review sites and their social media profiles using their laptop or mobile phone. They are thus able to reach not only the hotel, but also many other users wherever they are. Though experts still debate whether we are already experiencing Web 3.0, for the sake of this chapter is it important to consider that the main difference between Web 2.0 and Web 3.0 for us lies in the massive, extensive and all-pervasive use of the Web for communication purposes in Web 3.0.

Since Web 1.0 and Web 3.0 are already embedded in the brand website and the TPI site, they are not separately listed in Figure 6.1. Consequently, also the hotel's presence on social media platforms like Facebook, Twitter or Instagram is not reported in this overview, since our focus is on the use of TPI.

During the first phases of development of the World Wide Web comparing hotels' locations and prices was still not easy for a guest. Search engines were not available yet, nor services like Google maps. Moreover, hotels were hesitant to put their prices online in full view not only of guests but also of their competitors. Yet, thanks to the Web development, hotels started understanding their guests better. Marketers had now more instruments than just counting the number of brochures distributed per area, as in the pre-digital era. They could in fact already collect information on the age, gender, address, and if lucky, marital status, of their guests on the registration forms filled out by the guests during their check-in.

From a marketing perspective the next big jump was made possible by the development of search engines in the 1990s. For example, Archie become available in 1990 and Google in 1998. Search engines made the Web easy to navigate so that entrepreneurs could better help potential guests to find and book their preferred hotel room. Booking a new trip, reserving a hotel room and asking for a brochure all become only a mouse click away.

In the mid-1990s booking search engines started to develop into TPIs open for the general public, linked to hotel PMS technology via interfaces. TPIs work with subscriptions for hotels on mostly a 'no cure no pay' basis, meaning that hotels pay a fee per room sold via the TPI website. Usually these fees are based upon a percentage of the room price. Consequently, one of the business models of a TPI is to sell as many hotel rooms as possible. To be able to successfully and efficiently market hotel rooms TPIs need specific information from the hotel such as tangibles and services. When booking a hotel room via a TPI, a guest shares information with the TPI and that information ends up in the in the hands of (the

TPI's) marketers who can then convince the guest to book a specific hotel.

A last (at least for now) step was set when TPIs got access to information shared on social media platforms, a technology that, as we saw above, emerged during Web 2.0. Social media platforms offer to people the opportunity to share stories, videos, comments, blogs, and vlogs with their friends or with the world at large. Most social media platforms started from an idealistic or social activist perspective, and some of them have evolved to become billion dollar companies (Forbes, 2018). The larger platforms, like Facebook and LinkedIn, are masters in the art of acquiring personal user information. They know what music their users listen to; which movies they like; which activities they prefer; at which companies they shop; what kind of friends they have; which school they have attended and so on. Obviously this information is very valuable for marketers.

In a moment we will see how TPIs get access to the information on social media websites. For now let us notice that TPIs' websites are very successful. The main reason of this success is their user friendliness: the websites are easy to navigate and make the comparison of different hotels very convenient. Moreover, when guests book a hotel room via a TPI's website, they do not have the bother of communicating with a real person – such as by sending an e-mail, calling the hotel's reservation department, or searching for the right hotel website. A search results page quickly and neatly present a choice of hotel rooms, which can be compared on price, location, tangibles and service level, and also on reviews of previous guests. This information is already visible for the potential guest before registering with a TPI. In other words, to use basic TPI's features, such as viewing a list of hotels in a certain location, a guest does not need to register with the TPI. To get tailor-made services, for example an overview of hotels suiting specific needs such as sauna facilities, a guest has to register with a TPI. When registering, the potential guest needs to submit information to make the search for hotel rooms "as convenient and tailor-made as possible". This information consists of data such as demographics (age, gender, marital status), travel preferences and way of payment. Another way of registration is via a social login. A social login is a single registration to a TPI using the information from a user's social media platform. The TPI then can see and use the social media information that the user consents to share.

Before we start discussing the sustainable challenges that derive from a guest booking a room or travel experience using a TPI, let us look a bit longer at the consequences of data sharing online. To do so we wish to refer to the 2015 study by Zuboff, and her observation that a new form of capitalism is emerging, thanks to the mechanism used by companies like Google and Facebook, but also TPIs, to gather and analyse data. She identifies data extraction and analysis, new contractual forms due to better monitoring, personalization and customization, and continuous experiments as the main tools through which these firms constantly follow users online (Zuboff, 2015). In the previous chapter data gathering and analysis have already been addressed, and we refer you to that for more specific information. For our analysis it is important to note that the rapid harvesting of data made possible by algorithms has led to a whole new market in data exchange, data mining (a technique to discover patterns in large data sets) and data brokerage (aggregating information from a variety of sources, analysing it and allowing other organisations to use it for a fee). Consequently enormous investments were possible in start-ups that possess users' data like AirBnB, Facebook and Booking.com (Houtman, 2005). Thanks to the money invested in them, these companies could increase the pace of continuous experimentation, and learn how to influence people to show profitable (online) behaviour, like making a booking to the hotel yield the highest revenue. Let us emphasise this point: the constant extraction and analysis of data brings profit opportunities, because over time data gathering companies learn not only what people prefer but also how people react online. With this knowledge it is relatively easy to influence online behaviour, and then companies can use influencing techniques to boost the value of advertising on their websites, and consequently to increase their own income. This point reached, the circle can start again: the increased cash-flow makes new experimentation possible; leading to even more subtle ways to gather and analyse data, and influence people. The other side of the medal, as Zuboff (2015) puts it, is the rise of surveillance capitalism, a form of capitalism where Big Brother is not only watching you but also presenting you with offers that are impossible to resist because they are perfectly tailored to your needs and wants. In surveillance capitalism, human private data has become a commodity, a product to sell and to use to increase business profits.

Though the mechanism behind the surveillance capitalism may not be known to everyone, by now almost everybody knows that when you join a social site for free, you actually pay with your personal data. Why then do we still join these sites and share so much information on them? Users like you and me feel compelled to participate mostly because we fear that, if we do not, we will be excluded from the social buzz. Moreover, these sites play skillfully with our need for status (look at how many friends you have compared to person X!) and instant gratification (look at how many likes you have!).

The impact of TPIs on the guest decision making process

Now that we have at least a basic understanding of how data are shared online and gathered by TPIs, let us get to the heart of this section and assess how TPIs use these data, and the information on the user that they provide to steer the guest journey. To do so we will use Figure 6.2 as guidance. The main steps in the guest journeys have already been explained in Chapter 5. We will therefore not repeat this information here.

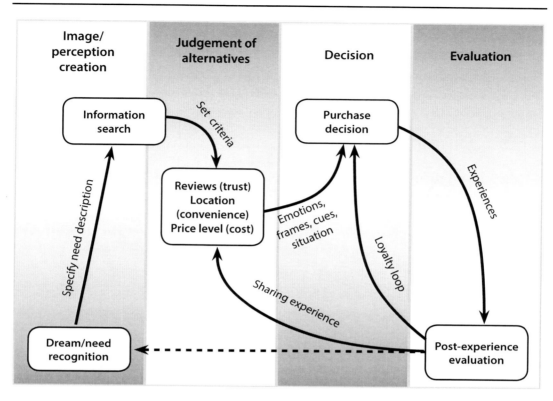

Figure 6.2: The guest journey (designed by the authors)

Already at the start of a search, on the left side of Figure 6.2, a TPI is able to select information tailored on 'you' by using algorithms. Algorithms can predict your travel preferences using the information that the TPI receives from own cookies and third party cookies, that is cookies set by companies other than the company of the visited website. If you log in via a social network, as we have seen above, the information in hands of the TPI increases. It is also important to notice that a TPI can see the location from which you visit the website either via IP addresses or via the use of a GPS chip (such as when you use a hotel room booking app on a smartphone). Finally, if you have already booked a trip or a hotel via a TPI, then specific preferences like price category, service level and location (e.g. city centre or outskirts) are known (see Chapter 5). Till this moment no financial transaction between the guest and the provider has taken place. The search for information seems for free, but, since personal data has become a commodity, the potential guest has in fact already paid with personal data.

Let us go back to the guest journey. When you, or another potential guest who shares with you the same characteristics (the *persona*), start a search, a TPI has already enough information to give you dedicated advice for the type of travel that you are most likely to select. Still more fascinating is that, even if you have not yet started a specific search, a TPI will reach out to you and tempt you to undertake a new travel experience. The ones among you who recently booked a hotel room via a TPI must have noticed that in the weeks prior and after staying in that hotel room, a barrage of e-mails with catchy subjects like "Great deals in Osnabruck, Niels – take a look!"; "Elena! Where does your next trip go? You deserve it!"; or "Marit, Lima has never been this cheap!" appear in your e-mail box.

These messages normally use *push technology*, which is essentially a mailing list, whereby the TPI repetitively sends information on categories selected by the provider and matched to the user's personal information; or *pull technology*, where the website visitor accepts a link that retrieves messages from the service provider, in this case a TPI website. Messages will then either appear in their mailbox, or pop up on the home screen of a portable device or computer. These messages can be very persuasive and tempt the potential guest to click the link and act exactly as the provider desires by, for example, booking a new journey to an exotic destination.

These techniques are not completely new. They were and are also applied in television and radio commercials, but with less success. Different from TPIs, television and radio use a one-to-many form of communication that is targeted to a specific group but not to a specific persona. Moreover if consumers wish to act on the promoted offer they need to make an effort, such as going to a specific shop. In contrast, e-mails and messages pushed by a TPI are not only tailor-made for the receiver but also offer an instant action, like pushing a button to book a room or click a bar to visit the TPI website, the perks of Web 2.0.

The debate whether it is ethical to push a consumer this strongly is fascinating. The provider usually argues that users consented to receiving these messages, even though it is widely known that users mostly agree with the terms and conditions without reading them properly (Steinfeld, 2016). Nevertheless, the intentions of the TPI are clear: impact the guest decision making process from the start, or even before, by motivating the guest to book another travel experience, and preferably as many as possible. The implication for sustainability of the TPI business model is that the more trips are taken, the higher is the impact on the natural environment because travellers generally will make use of transport options that are not yet sustainable (see Chapter 3), and even the more sustainability or environmentally aware guests generally use more resources while away from home, since on holidays we tend to indulge ourselves (Barr *et al.*, 2010).

The unavoidable conclusion is that, if a company constantly pushes guests to book hotel rooms in other cities, it may stimulate behaviour that negatively impacts the use of resources while just minimally benefitting the guest (Gössling, 2017). The challenge for hotels is mainly that they may depend from these bookings for a sound financial position (but see the observations in Chapter 5) while in the meantime increased travel is harmful to the environment.

The remark by the attendee to the *Guests on Earth* Conference quoted above that the most sustainable travel is no travel at all, not only gains more force when one considers these new developments, but appears also as an even more remote and idealistic solution to the challenge of achieving sustainable hospitality and tourism. Before we try to look at solutions for this challenge, let us consider a second major issue arising from the way TPIs handle our data: the impact of pre-set filters on our ability to see the whole picture in the next stage of the guest journey; the selection stage.

The impact of pre-set filters or the bubble

This sub-section explores three related questions: when searching, does a guest see the whole picture? What is the influence of TPIs on the judgement and selection of alternatives? And what is the consequence of this all on the transformative power of tourism? It is clear by now that while searching on the Internet we share, both intentionally and unintentionally, massive amounts of personal data. It is also clear that, thanks to this data, search engines and TPIs can provide tailor made, personalised answers to our online searches. This phenomenon is called web personalisation.

Personalised service is the holy grail of marketers, because the recipient of an offer perfectly tailored to his wishes is supposed to be a perfectly satisfied and thus loyal guest. Therefore personalised services, including web personalisation, are very well perceived by business organisations. Who is indeed not looking for satisfied and loyal guests?

Notwithstanding the promise of web personalisation, an ethical discussion on its merits quickly started to emerge. The issue is that personalisation can go as far as to create a web environment to the liking of the user and to exclude from his notice any facts or events that may be unpleasant to him. Let us clarify a point: web personalisation builds here on an intrinsic need of most people, and that is to reach out to other people who share similar values and beliefs. Yet, web personalisation has opened up possibilities to cope with this need in a way that was unthinkable before, and that has the danger to almost hermetically seal off people from what they do not like to see. A quote by Marc Zuckerberg, the co-founder of Facebook, illustrates this effect in a quite disturbing way: 'A squirrel dying in front of your house may be more relevant to your interests right now than people dying in Africa' (CNN, 2011).

Thanks to the power of their algorithms, search engines and TPIs can come to know users' preferences almost better than themselves. They are then able to filter out all information or (travel) offers that are even remotely in conflict with the user's preferences. In the end users will find themselves in a kind of bubble: a world where everybody seems to think like they do; book the same type of hotel; take the same type of travel experience and so on. While this world may seem paradisical, it is not real. Moreover, it is ethically questionable whether an organisation should have the power to seal off people from reality, and impede them from seeing the whole picture by keeping them in a 'filter bubble'.

The term 'filter bubble' comes from the book *The Filter Bubble: How the new personalized web is changing what we read and how we think* by Eli Pariser (2011). Pariser points to the race by giants such as Facebook, Google and Apple to win our favour and our business by customizing our online experiences. In the process, these companies create for us unique worlds in which we mainly receive news that is pleasant to us, confirms our views, and encourages us in thinking that we are right (and other people are wrong). Unpleasant information is filtered out and does not reach us – so that the unique universe in which each of us ends up is in fact a 'filter bubble'. In other words, search engines and social websites may have started as idealistic platforms but are still organisations focusing on profit. To make money they want to keep you on their platforms, and to do so they are ready to show you what they think you would like to see, rather than what you were really looking for or should see.

Importantly, Pariser (2011) also warns that filters are invisible to the user, and that therefore the user does not know what is left out of the bubble. Since people are not aware of the mechanisms leading them to the bubble, moreover, it is unethical not only to push people into a specific bubble but also to keep them there so that they form an easy target to business offers.

Summing up, and answering the first two questions posed above, there is a high chance that during the guest journey guests do not see the whole picture due to the 'filter bubble' created by TPIs.

To answer the third question and in analogy with the 'filter bubble', we wish to introduce the concept of 'experience bubble'. With this concept we mean that, using the information that they posses, TPIs are able to create a bubble around a traveller or hotel guest by showing them only experiences that are to their liking. Travelling in their own bubbles, travellers will only visit places where they meet people who have the same characteristics, opinions, and life experiences as themselves. They will only experience what similar travellers have experienced. The encounter with another culture will be domesticated to fit with their personal ideas of that culture, so that it does not raise any unpleasant feelings. The question that arises is whether a traveller caught in the experience bubble will ever be able to feel the transformative power of tourism, i.e. to have the opportunity to change one's mind-set and worldview by truly experiencing other cultures and meeting people who do not belong to the 'in-group'. Travelling, in fact, has been valued for its capacity to increase the traveller's social, cultural and self-awareness (Falk *et al.*, 2012). Yet, what is left of this capacity if everyone travels in their own bubble? Will guests still be able to see the beauty that lies beyond the bubble, if they enjoy a highly personalized service? Will they ever experience the unexpected, and feel the beauty and fragility of nature and other cultures beyond the boundaries of the bubble? Very probably the answer to these question is a negative. Guests and travellers have no idea they are in a bubble and have therefore do not realise that there is a world outside it. They do not see the whole picture, because of the personalized service offered by search engines and TPIs, and will not be able to chose for experiences that question their own values and believes.

Looking at the issue from another perspective, one may ask whether local communities, operators and service providers (e.g. tour guides) will ever have access to the bubble where the traveller is kept. It may be too early to give a definitive answer. Yet, by posing this question, a scenario presents itself where tourism's contribution to the local economy is impaired by a new, technologically driven form of inclusive vacations, where TPIs (invisibly) organize the whole experience, leaving only crumbs to the local community that is not connected to them – or cannot afford their fees. This is a bleak picture, opposite to an equitable and sustainable tourism development (see Chapters 4 and 9 on tourism and the local community).

By thus answering the questions posted at the beginning of this subsection, we bring new water to the mill of people who think that the most sustainable form of travel is no travelling at all. In fact, if travelling fails in leading to personal development and growth through the confrontation with 'the other', why should we uphold travelling in face of its massive, negative impact on the natural environment and on local heritage?

Wearables and their influence on the guest journey

In our brief history of data sharing between hosts and guests, and ultimately between users and TPIs, we have seen how marketers got access to an increasing number of channels to gather data about us. The development of the World Wide Web has had, as we have seen, a remarkable impact on the width and depth of personal data that may be gathered and analysed. We have also touched on the role of mobile phones, and indeed, since the introduction of the iPhone on the 27 April 2007, smartphones are increasingly used by guests to search for information and shop online. A smartphone is a piece of equipment that stores massive amount of private information, such agendas, photo albums, notes, e-mail boxes and music libraries. At an even closer look, a smartphone reveals itself as a mini computer combined with sensors such as a GPS, a barometer, a speedometer and a gyroscope. By combining data from these sensors, a smartphone is already able to decide where your home is (the place where it most often rests at nights) and where you work or study (the place to which you commute most often from home), without you telling it. This might seem handy and smart, but may be also seen as a breach of privacy, if this data is visible to the provider (see Chapter 5).

'Wearables', such as the smart watch, represent the next step in a world where very private data is shared. Smart watches, for example, may feature a thermometer and a heart rate sensor. It is widely know that the heartbeat changes under the influence of specific emotions. Thus if a smart watch owner has accidentally or by design decided to share all this data with a provider, the provider may be able to conclude that the user is aroused when he or she is in a certain location at a certain time (say looking at the window of shop X during lunch break; or looking at a sunset), and add this knowledge to the other data about the person. Electronic Customer Relationship Management (eCRM) has already been called the next success factor in customer management and communication (Xiang *et al.*, 2015a).

Indeed, it is expected that buying decisions will be increasingly made via mobile devices and therefore providers also want to be there, to further gather data (Xiang *et al.*, 2015a). It goes without saying that all this information will make further personalisation possible.

To conclude the discussion of challenges linked to the increasing use of digital devices in the guest's decision making process in general (Gustavo, 2013) and in tourism in particular (Xiang *et al.*, 2015b), let us look at Figure 6.3. The dark area in the figure shows the increased influence of TPIs.

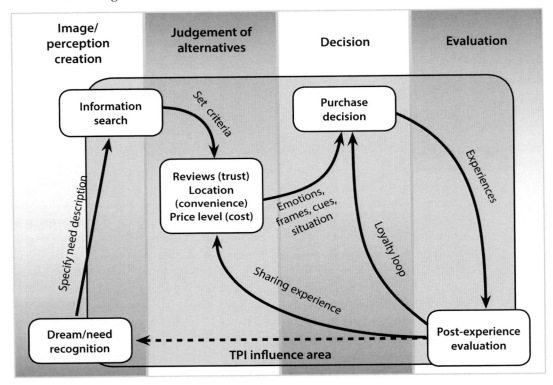

Figure 6.3: The influence area of a TPI in the guest journey (authors)

As the figure shows, the influence of TPIs is remarkable. Our discussion above has demonstrated that TPIs run the risk of using this influence to push users to an ever-increasing number of trips, thus exacerbating the negative environmental impact of tourism. Moreover, by perfectly tailoring their offer to suit the guest's needs, they may form around him a 'bubble' impenetrable to local providers, thus weakening the positive socio-economic impact of tourism on the local community. Finally, by the same means, they may lower the chance that a traveller gets in touch with beliefs different from his own, thus diminishing the transformative power of travelling.

While the profit motive of TPIs, tour operators and hospitality establishments increases the probability that these risks are incurred, they do not represent the destiny of these organisations. In fact, as the best cases below will show, there are organisations that think that with the power of influencing the guest journey comes the responsibility to use this power wisely to promote a more sustainable form of tourism.

Best cases

Case 6.1: Online Travel Agency BookDifferent

Book Different sees itself as the booking site for responsible travellers. Their mission is "to contribute to a better world through a clean, green and fair tourism sector'". They consider themselves as "a social enterprise and stand for maximizing impact rather than profit maximization'".

Using BookDifferent guests can book a green hotel and support a charity once the hotel is booked. When searching, a guest may choose among hotels with an eco-label, a low carbon footprint, or both. In other words, guests can decide how sustainably they want to spend the night. BookDifferent nudges guests in choosing the most sustainable option (a third party eco-certified hotel) by showing these results first. As eco-certification is not yet mainstream, BookDifferent resorted to CO_2 emissions as a second-level indicator of sustainability. This is a smart choice for at least two reasons. First, small hotels may not be able to afford a certification, while they are operating sustainably; second eco-certification is uncommon in certain regions and in several developing countries. By using the carbon footprint alongside eco-certification, BookDifferent is inclusive and is able to offer guests a choice of destinations where a hotel with an eco-label is not available.

In the search result page, BookDifferent shows only hotels available for the chosen period. Each hotel features icons indicating whether it has an eco-label or not, and the carbon footprint per room per night. If a hotel is eco-certified, this is displayed by means of a white leaf in a green icon. The carbon footprint is presented by means of a green (small) or red (large) footprint icon. Alongside it, a figure shows the CO_2 emission in kilos. BookDifferent donates 10% of its gross turnover to charity. They partner with organisations, such as The Travel Foundation, The Global Forest Fund and the WWF, that help destinations and their stakeholders to benefit from the tourists visiting their destinations. Remarkably, on the opening page of their website, BookDifferent prominently features the United Nations Sustainable Development Goals, and by a mouse click offers more information on how, as an organisation, they help to achieve four out of the seventeen goals. These are goal 8 on decent work and economic growth; goal 12 on responsible production and consumption; goal 13 on climate action and goal 14 on protecting life below the water.

BookDifferent is part of Booking.com and therefore part of priceline.com, and won the 2018 Sustainable Travel Award.

Sources: BookDifferent, 2018a, b, & c.

6

Case 6.2: TripAdvisor and the GreenLeaders Program

TripAdvisor presents itself as 'the world's largest travel site' and proudly boasts about its 600 million reviews and the 7.5 million accommodations on offer. TripAdvisor compares hotel prices by checking over 200 websites, but does not perform the booking itself. In April 2013 Tripadvisor launched the GreenLeaders Program in the United States, and in 2014 extended it to other countries, including Canada, the United Kingdom and Italy. "Developed in consultation with the United Nations Environment Programme, the U.S. Green Building Council, ENERGY STAR®, and the International Center for Responsible Tourism Canada, the TripAdvisor GreenLeaders program aims to help travellers around the world plan greener trips by highlighting hotels and B&Bs engaging in environmentally friendly practices" (TripAdavisor 2018b).

Accommodations participating in the GreenLeader Program are rated on the basis of their sustainable status (bronze, silver, gold or platinum). On the search results page GreenLeader Program accommodations are identified by a leaf. By clicking on the leaf, a guest gets to know which green practices are implemented by the property. The greater the impact of these practices, the higher the sustainability status of the property. To become a member of this program, a hotel has to apply by filling out a survey. On a yearly basis, the hotel must reapply for the program. Guests can give their feedback upon the sustainable practices of an accommodation that they visited by leaving a review in a special section of the TripAdvisor website. In addition, audits are conducted by independent organizations.

In October 2016, TripAdvisor took a second step towards offering sustainable products by banning the sale of tickets of attractions where personal contact with wild animals is allowed (The Guardian, 2016).

Sources: TripAdavisor 2018a & c.

Tools to address the challenges

This section presents and discusses possible actions or solutions for the challenges illustrated at the start of this chapter. It follows a similar structure, and dedicates separate sub-sections to online marketing and the impact of TPIs on the guest journey; to the filter-effect and the resulting travel bubble; and concludes with some thoughts on the increasing impact of wearables on the guest journey.

Online marketing and the impact of TPIs on the guest journey

As noted earlier, users often agree with a provider's terms and conditions without fully reading them and rarely use the options to limit a provider's access to personal data (Steinfeld, 2016). The first step in lowering the influence of TPIs on your guest journey lies therefore in your hands: read the terms and conditions so that you are aware of how your data is used, and limit the provider's access to your personal data. There are several possibilities ranging from banning the use of sites that misuse private information, to softer options such as declining cookies and surfing the Internet on incognito mode or with a non-traceable browser like Comodo Dragon Browser. Another action is to stay logged out from a booking-platform till the moment that you make the purchasing decision, or using one browser to search and another to book. In this way you make it more difficult for a TPI to link your search to your profile, to learn about your preferences, and to subsequently nudge you to travel to previously researched locations or hotels. You can also make sure that, if you sign-in on a TPI website through social media, you have logged out from these platforms, and that you have deleted all cookies from the device you are using. Otherwise the cookies will connect the digital dots that you have left behind and link your profile to your device.

Most purchasing decision are made on a TPI website, because these are easy to use and very conveniently compare prices, location and service levels of different options. From a hotel perspective, a solution to this challenge could be to invest or reinvest in loyalty programs. Loyalty programs aim to convert one-time guests to returning guests by offering them privileges such as booking at a discount, a welcome drink or a free upgrade. However, the best 'tool' for retaining guests is providing quality service, which is still considered to be the best predictor of guest satisfaction (Delafrooz *et al.*, 2014). Hotels may also encourage guests that have already stayed at the hotel, to book via the hotel's brand website or to call one of the hotel's employees the next time they need a room. It looks like going back to the old days, but with emerging technologies such as chat bots and eCRM, hotel organisations can get back in the driver's seat and exclude the middleman (the TPI). Of course, when following this route, hotels should make the booking process – from information inquiry till decision making – as easy as possible for potential guests. The benefits of this solution are evident, because a hotel may re-appropriate for itself information on its guests that is now only known by TPIs, and may lower the amount of fees paid to a TPI. There are though several challenges of which the most serious is probably that only 8% of the frequent guests are loyal bookers of a hotel brand (Ballantyne *et al.*, 2017). Moreover, the addiction of guests to booking apps should not be underestimated. One of the authors of this chapter experienced personally how walk-in guests who just arrived at the parking lot of the hotel, made a booking via a TPI app on their smartphones and only then entered the hotel. The consequence of this behaviour was on one side that the hotel had to pay 12% commission costs to a third party and on the other that the guest missed a walk-in discount. A small sign on the hotel's parking lot, on room availability and price, might already nudge guests into walking in, and not use their smart phones to book.

The impact of pre-set filters or the bubble

Legislation has taken on the challenge to protect the web users' privacy and to make the use of filters more transparent For example, the European legislation on cookies and the guidelines by the European Commission dictates that websites cannot gather unnecessary information, and that websites should ask users for their consent when installing cookies on their devices (EU Commission, 2016). As already mentioned, users usually consent, either because they are not aware of the consequences or because they are afraid to harm the streamlined Internet experience when they do not consent.

Before giving some suggestions on how to escape the filter and experience bubble, we would like to note that web personalisation is not by definition a bad development. Thanks to it, results are shown that are the most relevant to the searcher, for example based on their location. This is, of course, very handy if you are in a foreign city and are looking for the nearest ATM or restaurant. On the other hand, web personalisation makes it easier for us to fall prey to *confirmation bias*. "Confirmation bias suggests that we don't perceive circumstances objectively. We pick out those bits of data that make us feel good because they confirm our prejudices. Thus, we may become prisoners of our assumptions" (Heshmat, 2015). As a consequence, a searcher is often unknowingly trapped in his own bubble.

Most guests' journeys start with an enquiry on a search engine, and, as we have seen, this is enough for TPIs to push to us offers that fit our bubble. To get search results that are as unbiased and non-personalised as possible, the searcher needs to escape the bubble. We suggest the following steps:

1 Use a non-pre-set filter search engine like DuckDuckgo.com, Wolframalpha, Yippy or Hulbee. When using these your location, social profiles and interests stay private and cannot be turned into commodities to be traded or used to influence your decisions;

2 Log out from all your Google accounts on your devices;

3 Turn off your personal search history;

4 Use a browser extension that disables tracking or adds like Addblock plus, Privacy Badger, Do Not Track Me; and,

5 Use the private browser setting on your device (though this only helps a little).

Finally, a guest who is already alerted towards sustainability may chose a browser or booking site that shares that goal, such as BookDifferent (see the case and the box below). Paradoxically this may mean entering a new 'bubble', yet at least a more sustainable one.

Box 6.1: Examples of sustainable TPIs

GreenHotelWorld is an OTA that partnered with Expedia. GreenHotelWorld offers the customer a range of hotels based upon their certified green practices. In addition, Green-HotelWorld compensate for the customer's CO_2 emission related to the travel, without any additional costs. (Green Hotel World, 2018)

BookDifferent is also an OTA and is affiliated with Booking.com. Similar to GreenHotel-World it offers to the customer a wide range of hotels and shows whether the hotel has an eco-label and what the carbon footprint will be per night. It also donates a percentage of its gross revenues to affiliated charities, as has been noted in Case 6.1.

GreenLeaders Program is a referral site related to TripAdvisor. GreenLeaders Program shows how sustainable a hotel is by means of a leaf alongside the hotel name. For more information see Case 6.2.

Bennu is a sustainable Web 2.0 site and sees itself as the leader in green social media marketing. Its main goal is to promote a greener new lifestyle. (Bennuworld, 2018)

Wearables and their influence on the guest journey

The solution to this challenge is hard to find. The pace of innovation and development in mobile devices and wearables is unrelenting, and it is therefore hard to predict what the future will bring. Nevertheless, signs are emerging that point towards a change in the use of smartphones. Increasingly young people feel they have become addicted to their phone, and look for opportunities to 'take a holiday from it or use it more responsibly'. In several European cities there are bars and restaurants where guests may chose to leave their phone at the entrance, and pick it up when they leave. In 2016 the owner of Hove bar in Sussex (United Kingdom) was featured on the BBC news for having build a Faraday cage around his property so that guests could not use their mobile phone and would start socializing with each other again (BBC, 2016). Less invasive is the solution proposed by the advertising agency Fischer & Friends: a beer glass that can only stand upright when balanced on the guests' mobile phone. It has been tested in Salve Jorge a bar in Rio de Janeiro (Brazil) whose owners also wished to encourage people to talk to each other and not to their phone (The Telegraph, 2017). One may laugh at these initiatives and neglect them as being marginal. And yet there is a growing consensus that we are witnessing the rise of a less materially-orientated and more meaning-orientated approach to life (Drewell and Larsson, 2017).

Before reaching that point, change will probably occur due to regulations, education and learning by mistakes. Regulations will better protect our privacy while education will help us to become 'tech-savvy' and be careful in sharing data on the Internet. It will also remind us of an old saying that is still true in the Web 3.0 era: only the sun comes up for free.

Old and new generations might also learn from the mistakes that are made by their role models, such as the vlogger Paul Logan. On 31 December 2017, Logan uploaded a disturbing video made at Aokigahara, a forest on the slopes of Mount Fuji (Japan). Aokigahara is known as the "suicide forest" because it is the site of hundreds of suicides. The video hit 6.3 million views within 24 hours of being uploaded and caused massive attacks to Logan for disrespect. People accused him of using emotional images to boost views and thus his monetary value to advertisers (Swearingen, 2018). In the end, Logan's action not only led to his open apologies but also to a public debate on suicide. As a last step in acknowledging his mistake, on 24 January 2018, Logan uploaded a suicide prevention video. With 22 million views in four days, the video had undoubtedly a massive impact on his followers, mostly youngsters (DramaAlert, 2018).

Connecting all these tiny dots, we expect that the quest for meaning and authenticity will encorage travellers to turn off their phones and wearables, and explore their surroundings with a book, a notebook and a pencil. We believe that awareness of the consequences of the filter and experience bubble will lead people to more critically assess what has been put on their plate.

Conclusion

Filling rooms with satisfied guests is one of the hotel's core businesses. In an era where communication is fully computer-mediated, guests can book rooms with a click of a mouse. Availing themselves of web 2.0 technologies, TPIs took the centre stage and by now control most of the bookings. This chapter has discussed the sustainable impact of data gathering, analysis, and usage in personalising the potential traveller's search for a trip. We have argued that web personalisation leads to a 'bubble' that reduces the traveller's power of choice and limits his experience.

We have argued that this process is not irreversible, and that guests have several opportunities to prick the bubble. They may book responsibly using more sustainable options or may search incognito for third parties. In the end, looking beyond the bubble, exploring new cultures and areas, and getting the chance to be changed, is what travel is all about.

References

Ballantyne, R., Kerr, F., Rate, S. and Mouthinho, L. (2017) Exploring tourist transformation: From need to desire to experience, in Dixit, S.K. (ed.) *The Routledge Handbook of Consumer Behaviour in Hospitality and Tourism*, pp. 26-31.

Barr, S., Shaw, G., Coles, T. and Prillwitz, J. (2010) 'A holiday is a holiday': practicing sustainability, home and away, *Journal of Transport Geography*, **18** (3) 474–481.

BBC (2016) www.bbc.com/news/technology-36954687. Accessed on 22 February 2018.

Bennuworld (2018) www.bennuworld.com/our-story/. Accessed on 22 February 2018.

BookDifferent (2018a) *About BookDifferent*. https://www.bookdifferent.com/en/page/about-bookdifferent. Accessed 22 February 2018.

BookDifferent (2018b) *BookDifferent: make the world a better place by booking a hotel*. https://www.bookdifferent.com/en/. Accessed 22 February 2018.

BookDifferent (2018c) *Sustainable Development Goals*. https://www.bookdifferent.com/en/page/sustainable-development-goals-2/. Accessed 22 February 2018.

Cavagnaro, E., Staffieri, S. and Postma, A. (2018) Understanding millennials' tourism experience: values and meaning to travel as a key for identifying target clusters for youth (sustainable) tourism, *Journal of Tourism Futures*, https://doi.org/10.1108/JTF-12-2017-0058.

CNN (2018) *What the Internet is hiding from you*. http://edition.cnn.com/2011/TECH/web/05/19/online.privacy.pariser/index.html. Accessed 19 February 2018.

Delafrooz, N., Taleghani, M. and Nouri, B. (2014) Effect of green marketing on consumer purchase behavior, *QScience Connect*, **5**, 1–9.

DramaAlert (2018) *Paul Logan is back!* 24 January 2018. https://www.youtube.com/watch?v=_NpiOJ_21Zg,Accessed on 23 February 2018.

Drewell, M. and Larsson, B. (2017) *The Rise of the Meaningful Economy: a megatrend where meaning is the new currency*, Kindley Edition, Amazon Digital Services LLC

European Commision (2016) *Information providers guide, the EU internet handbook.* http://ec.europa.eu/ipg/index_en.htm. Accessed 4 February 2018.

Falk, J. H., Ballantyne, R., Packer, J. and Benckendorff, P. (2012) Travel and learning: A neglected tourism research area, *Annals of Tourism Research*, **39** (2) 908–927.

Forbes (2018) *The Priceline Group on the Forbes Growth Champions List.* https://www.forbes.com/companies/priceline/. Accessed 11 February 2018.

Gössling, S. (2017) Tourism information technology and sustainability: an exploratory reiew, *Journal of sustainable tourism*, **25** (7), 1024 – 1041.

Green Hotel World (2018) *Want to make your overnight hotel stay 100% climate friendly?.* https://www.greenhotelworld.com. Accessed 22 February 2018.

Gustavo, N. (2013) Marketing management trends in tourism and hospitality industry: facing the 21st century environment, *International Journal of Marketing Studies*, **5** (3) 13–25.

Hayes, D.K. and Miller, A. (2011) *Revenue Management for Hospitality Industry*, 2nd edn, Hoboken New Jersey: John Wiley & Sons Inc.

Heshmat, S. (2015) *What is confirmation bias?* https://www.psychologytoday.com/blog/science-choice/201504/what-is-confirmation-bias,Accessed 5 February 2018.

Houtman, J. (2005) *Priceline koopt Bookings voor 110 miljoen euro.* https://www.emerce.nl/nieuws/priceline-koopt-bookings-voor-110-miljoen-euro, Accessed 24 June 2017.

Pariser, E. (2011) *The Filter Bubble: What the Internet Is Hiding from You*, London: Penguin.

Steinfeld, N. (2016) 'I agree to the terms and conditions': (How) do users read privacy policies online? An eye-tracking experiment, *Computers in Human Behavior*, **55**, 992–1000.

Swearingen, J. (2018) *Logan Paul posts footage of apparent suicide victim on YouTube*, 1 Jan. http://nymag.com/selectall/2018/01/logan-paul-suicide-forest-video-youtube.html. Accessed on 23 February 2017.

The Telegraph (2017) http://www.telegraph.co.uk/news/worldnews/southamerica/brazil/10113715/The-beer-glass-that-only-stands-upright-when-balanced-on-your-phone.html. Accessed on 23 February 2017.

TripAdvisor (2018) *About Tripadvisor*, https://tripadvisor.mediaroom.com/us-about-us, Accessed 22 February 2018.

TripAdvisor (2018) *TripAdvisor GreenLeaders(TM) launches in Canada and Europe to showcase eco-friendly hotels.* https://tripadvisor.mediaroom.com/2014-03-17-TripAdvisor-GreenLeaders-TM-Launches-In-Canada-And-Europe-To-Showcase-Eco-Friendly-Hotels. Accessed 22 February 2018.

6

TripAdvisor (2018) *What is the TripAdvisor GreenLeaders Program?*, https://www.tripadvisorsupport.com/hc/en-us/articles/200614147-What-is-the-TripAdvisor-GreenLeaders-Program. Accessed 22 February 2018.

Xiang, Z., Wang, D., O'Leary, J. T. and Fesenmaier, D. R. . (2015a) Adapting to the Internet: trends in travelers' use of the web for trip planning, *Journal of Travel Research*, **54** (4), 244-249.

Xiang, Z., Magnini, V. P. and Fesenmaier, D. R. (2015b) Information technology and consumer behavior in travel and tourism: Insights from travel planning using the internet, *Journal of Retailing and Consumer Services. Elsevier*, **22**, 244–249.

Zuboff, S. (2015) Big other: Surveillance capitalism and the prospects of an information civilization, *Journal of Information Technology*, **30** (1), 75–89.

Part II: Buildings

Introduction

Elena Cavagnaro

The quadrant named 'Buildings' in the Sustainable Hospitality Value Chain contains three boxes: technology, equipment and buildings:

While some readers may have doubted by reading that a book dedicated to sustainability in hospitality contains a part on distribution, no one will raise questions about discussing buildings. In fact, it is quite inevitable that while we think of hospitality we also conjure in our minds the image of a building, as Thulani Xhali notes in his chapter on 'Equipping better buildings'.

Buildings, moreover, consume a vast amount of resources. During the construction phase, scarce natural resources such as timber, stone and metals are used, while energy and water consumption are high during both construction and use of the building. Hotels are particularly resource intensive. A study comparing water use by tourists and residents found that tourists use three to eight times more water than locals in countries such as the Philippines, China, India and Sri Lanka (Becken, 2014).

If not repurposed, buildings are knocked down, causing waste, or left to decay, spoiling neighbourhoods. Moreover, buildings may, literally, make people sick. Infamous is the case of asbestos, used as insulation and fire retardant material. As was already discovered at the beginning of the 20th century, asbestos is highly toxic and causes lung cancer, not only in people mining it but also in people exposed to it in buildings. The use of asbestos has been banned in most countries from the 1970s onwards.

As the examples above illustrate, buildings have a major impact on the social and environmental dimension of sustainability. Therefore their discussion is appropriate in a book dedicated to sustainability in hospitality. In his chapter Thulani Xhali connects the discussion of buildings' sustainability to the appropriate choice for equipment. He focuses on challenges faced by building developers in choosing the correct accreditation tools, the most sustainable building materials, the most suitable equipment and in financing sustainable development projects.

The case of asbestos is interesting, also because it shows that technological progress may have unintended effects. Asbestos was prized and used for its remarkable insulation quality, and as a fire retardant. Yet, by and by, its negative effects on people's health got noticed, leading to its ban. Technology is indeed a double-edged sword, as the title of the chapter on technology by Elena Cavagnaro indicates. This chapter is a stand-alone but is also written as an introduction to 'Equipping better buildings' by Thulani Xhali. It discusses the difference between cradle-to-grave and cradle-to-cradle technology and shows that human behaviour should be considered, too, when deploying technological solutions to sustainability problems.

References

Becken, S. (2014) Water equity – Contrasting tourism water use with that of the local community, *Water resources and industry*, **7-8,** 9-22.

7 Technology: A Double Edged Sword

Elena Cavagnaro

Learning goals

After studying this chapter, a reader will have the ability to

1 Define technology in general;
2 Distinguish between cradle-to-grave and cradle-to-cradle technology;
3 Exemplify how cradle-to-cradle technology can be applied in a hospitality settings.

Introduction

This chapter functions as a brief introduction to the section on building and aims at clarifying what technology is and under which conditions it supports a more sustainable development of the hospitality industry.

The term 'technology' is composed by two words from ancient Greek: *techne* and *logos*. *Techne* means art, skills and a cunning hand; while *logos* refers to the capacity to explain something, to science. Thus, literally, technology is the science of crafting, i.e. turning an input, which can be raw martials or energy, into an end product or a service. In other words, technology is a group of (human designed) tools, or knowledge, that transform inputs into outputs.

Humans have used technology since the beginnings. Think at stones thrown to animals to chase them; at the domestication of fire; at pottery – and so on. Animals, such as chimpanzees, use technology too: for example wooden sticks to fish for termites or stones to crack nuts open. To use technology one does not need to exactly know how it works. Think for example of driving a car or sending a message on a mobile phone: some may know exactly how these devices work; most of us know only how to use them.

Technology has been and still is widely used to make our life more comfortable and secure. Yet, technology can also be used to less noble scopes. The automatic gun used by suspected shooter Nikolas Cruz at Majory Stoneman Douglas High

School in Parkland (Florida) on 14 February 2018 to kill seventeen people and wound fourteen is also a fruit of technology. In this chapter we will not discuss this type of technology, but will only consider the (unintended) negative consequences of technology developed to ease people's life. Because technology has unintended consequences we called it in the chapter's title 'a double-edged sword'. In this chapter we will look at technology in general, and then give some examples applied to hospitality. The bottom line of our discussion is that in the context of sustainability, when evaluating technological solutions, managers should not only ask themselves whether the proposed solution improves productivity; increases profit or gives a competitive advantage. They should also ask themselves whether it also add value to people and planet.

Main sustainability challenges

In this section we will consider three main sustainability challenges connected with technology. First we will show how technology that was introduced to solve an issue may cause unintended negative consequences. Then we will discuss in-built obsolescence, and, third, the issue of recycling products made of mixed materials. As a conclusion to this section, we will look at the main paradigm underlying the development of modern technology, i.e. that the world has an unlimited capacity to provide us with raw materials and to cope with our waste.

To start with, let us emphasise that generally speaking technological development is fuelled by a desire to make people's life more easy and comfortable. Think for example of refrigerators. Before they were invented, conserving food was a time intensive, costly and risky activity. Food has to be smoked, for example, or dried to keep it from rotting; or ice had to be collected from mountains and brought into cities to keep food cold. This last was an expensive activity, and only few could afford to cool their food in this way during summer. Conserving food was risky in the sense that, notwithstanding efforts to conserve it properly, food could still get spoiled, and had then to be thrown away. Several languages have proverbs that remind us of this difficulty, such as the saying 'a rotten apple spoils the whole barrel'. In the absence of other technologies to conserve or produce food during winters, the consequence was that families had to endure hunger.

The fridge was therefore saluted as a lifesaving discovery. Yet, the first fridges used ammonia for the cooling. Ammonia is toxic for people and animals, and therefore producers kept looking for other options. One of these options was chlorofluorocarbons, a low toxic and not easily inflammable man-made cooling substance. Since the 1930s ammonia was gradually replaced by chlorofluorocarbons, also known as freon. All's well that end's well, you might say. Yet, in the early 1970s it become evident that chlorofluorocarbons were responsible for the breaking down of the ozone layer in the upper atmosphere, that filters ultraviolet rays. Ultraviolet rays are damaging to humans and other animals living on the Earth's surface. The international community reacted rather quickly, and freon was banned during a meeting in Montreal in 1987 (see Cavagnaro and Curiel, 2012: 35-36). This story illustrates that technologies – even when they are designed to improve a product – may have unintended negative consequences.

Sometimes, thought, technology is used intentionally not to improve but to worsen a product. A typical example is the light bulb. Incandescent light bulbs work because a thin wire filament is heated to such a high temperature that it glows with visible light. Their usual life span is few years, as anybody who still uses them knows. It may therefore sound quite extraordinary that at the Livermore's Fire station in California (US) there is an incandescent light bulb that has been burning since 1901. The bulb was made by Adoplhe Chaillet in his own factory, Shelby Electric Company; is a hand-blown bulb with carbon filament; is left burning continuously as a nightlight over the fire trucks; and in 2015 reached 1 million light hours (Centennial Light, n.d.). Some people think that the bulb in Livermore is a fake. Others think that it is still burning thanks to a special procedure, not well explained in the documentation left by Chaillet. Still others see the bulb as an example of planned obsolescence (Krajewski, 2014). Planned obsolescence refers to in-built weaknesses in a product so that it does not last long and should be replaced. While at the time that Chaillet build his bulbs quality and durability of a product were central to marketing campaigns, later on the focus shifted and longevity was seen as bad to business. The reasoning goes that if things last too long, people will buy less, and thus profits will be affected. In the case of bulbs, there is evidence suggesting that all big producers, including the American General Electrics and the Dutch Philips, agreed in the 1920s to reduce the maximum burning hours of a bulb to 1,000 hours, an amount significantly lower than the 1,500 to 2,000 hours that had previously been common. The new, short-lived bulbs were of higher quality and brighter than previous ones, but also more expensive. It seems therefore that the major bulb-producing companies were motivated by the desire to increase sales and thus profit at the expense (literally) of consumers (Krajewski, 2014).

In-built weaknesses come in different kinds. Think for example of materials, such as a thinner wire in the case of bulbs, and at the power of marketing, such as new colours and shapes dictated by the new fashion. In our digital era a weakness might be hidden in the software or be the consequence of (the absence of) updates – as everyone who possesses an 'out-dated' phone or computer model will know. We put 'out-dated' in quotation marks because 'out-dated' nowadays may mean two to three years old. Out-dated products may be reused or recycled, but often they are discarded and become waste. Waste is, as we have seen in several places of this book, environmentally and socially unsound (see, for example, Chapter 1). Moreover, it should be rememberd that, to produce goods, raw materials have to be sourced; transported, often across long distances; assembled using energy and labour; and transported again to the outlets where they are sold. The question arises therefore whether the environmental impact of an economy based on consumption of goods and services that are replaced faster and faster is environmentally and socially sustainable. We will come back to this point later on, in the conclusion to this section. Le us now briefly consider why goods are not easily recyclable, and why therefore our economy is still so much in need of new raw materials.

Most goods are composed of mixed materials. Consider for example a water bottle, an item that is often considered as an essential amenity in up-scale hotels. The bottle itself and its cap are made of plastic. Yet, usually, these are two different types of plastic that cannot be simultaneously recycled. The bottle label is generally of paper, a material that is easy recyclable. Yet the label is usually attached to the bottle with glue and the glue makes not only difficult to detach the label but impacts also the process of recycling the whole bottle. More often than not, therefore, recycled plastic from bottles is of an inferior quality and cannot be used for making new bottles, or other high-end products (Hopewell *et al.*, 2009). Consider now that most items in a hotel are composed of mixed materials: beds, chairs and tables may be made of wood but their pieces are kept together by glue or metal screws. Wood may be plywood, which is thin layers of wood glued together. Carpet tiles are usually made of plastic fibres glued to a backing. Mattresses might feature metal springs, latex, wood and cloths of, for example, cotton or wool – usually in a combination. These examples may suffice, we think, to conclude that most if not all items in a hotel room are made of mixed materials, and thus difficult to recycle. It is a well-known and accepted fact in the industry that at least once in the seven years a hotel room should be totally refurbished. In other words all rooms are emptied and tables, chairs, carpet tiles, mattresses and so on are wasted because they cannot be easily recycled. One may object: some hotels donate these goods to charities, so that they are reused. Indeed some hotels do, and they should be praised for their good intentions. Consider, though, that even in this case the life of the donated products is only prolonged by some years. Eventually they will be discarded. Someone else may object that products nowadays are not discarded in landfill, but burned thus creating energy. Yet, even without setting the energy needed to manufacture new goods against the energy produced by burning old ones, burned materials are gone forever while the process of burning generates pollution. All in all, the conclusion is unavoidable that the way we transform inputs to outputs, and that is (as we have seen) technology, produces waste and it does so at an increasing pace, due to planned obsolescence. In other words, technology as we know it is cradle-to-grave: it takes raw materials; transforms them efficiently into products; and then quickly discard them.

Cradle-to-grave technology would not be a problem if our world could provide us with raw materials indefinitely and could process the waste generated during the manufacturing, use and disposal of products notwithstanding how much it is. Waste here includes not only trashed materials but also water and air contamination, such as the emission of greenhouse gases that occurs when using fossil fuels. As Ray Anderson, former CEO of Interface, noticed, contemporary technological development rests on the assumption that our world is unlimited in its capacity to provide materials and cope with waste. Yet, the Earth is not unlimited, as everyone who has seen a photograph of the Earth from space should know (Anderson, 2009). Scientists, moreover, have chartered Earth's limits quite accurately (Rockström *et al.*, 2009). We know for sure that Earth is not unlimited, and that we have not only reached but even passed some of the boundaries that define a safe space in which humanity could live and thrive (Rockström *et al.*, 2009).

Because Earth's capacity to cope with waste is limited, cradle-to-grave technology exacerbates environmental problems and the more so the more people make use of it, and the more quickly products are discarded. This insight has been caught in a formula, called $I=P{\times}A{\times}T$ (Ehrlich and Holdren, 1971): Impact on the natural Environment (I) equals number of people using a certain good (P) multiplied by level of consumption or affluence (A) multiplied by technology (T).

Cradle-to-grave technology is not only environmentally unsound but also socially unsustainable, because it is not able to fulfil the needs of poorer people without increasing pollution and environmental damage. Moreover by exhausting natural resources it jeopardizes the ability of present and future generations to meet their own needs. Luckily, an entirely different approach to technology is possible, as these best cases show.

Best cases

Case 7.1: Philips and light as a service

In the section above we have cited Dutch Philips as having allegedly been one of the companies that applied planned obsolescence to shorten the lifespan of light bulbs. It is fair to say that times have changed also for Philips, who are now pioneering a revolutionary business model: 'product as service'. The basic idea behind this model is that people generally are not looking for a product, but for the service that it provides. For example, a hotel owner does not need lamps and lamp frames but light. In a 'product as service' concept the hotel's owner pays not for the lamp but for the light. The lamp itself and its frame stay in the ownership of the producer, in this case Philips. Philips does not only take care for them during use, for example by changing a frame if it is broken; but also takes them back after use. By keeping ownership of its products, a manufacturer is encouraged to design products so that they can be easily recycled, or, even better, so that the raw materials composing them can be recovered without loss of quality. Consequently, waste is minimized, the customer gets what he really wants, and the two businesses (in our case a hotel and Philips) stay in contact thus maximizing the possibility of recurred business for the producer. See e.g. Philips (2015)

Case 7.2: Bakeys' edible cutlery

Though there is some food that traditionally is eaten with the hands, such as pizza in Italy, most people use cutlery. In homes and restaurants cutlery is often made of metal and sometimes of wood, and is thus (at least in principle) recyclable. Yet more and more people eat convenience food, using plastic cutlery. Plastic is, as we have seen, not easy to recycle and is, moreover, often thrown on the ground. If not disposed of properly, plastic easily reaches rivers and seas, thus adding to the so-called 'plastic soup'. It has been reckoned that if this issue is not addressed quickly by 2050 there will be more plastic than fish in the ocean (Plastic Soup Foundation, n.d.). Moreover, plastic contains chemical compounds, several of which are toxic and carcinogenic. These compounds may leak into food. Though leaked quantities are limited, some people doubt whether there is a safe limit for substances that may attack our nervous system or cause cancer. Moved by the desire to address plastic waste in India, his home country, Narayana Peesapaty invented edible cutlery. The cutlery is made of sorghum; rice and wheat flours with hot water added to it. Then it is baked. After much experimentation, Narayana Peesapaty established Bakeys Foods Private Limited in 2010 in Hyderabad, Andhra Pradesh (India). Spoons, the only model available in February 2018, come in three flavours: plain, sweet and savoury. Bakeys supplies only India, but has already attracted the attention of the world thanks to a video that went viral; invitations for TEDxTalks (for example in Amsterdam, The Netherlands, in 2016: YouTube 2016) and press articles such as in The Wall Street Journal (See Bakeys, n.d. ; Zhong, 2016)

Case 7.3: Dancing and walking generate energy

One may think that dancing and walking cost energy. Yet they can also generate it.

For a club in Rotterdam (The Netherlands) the Dutch architect bureau Studio Roosegaarde created an interactive dance floor that generates electricity through the act of dancing. It produces up to 25 watts per module. By covering the whole floor, enough energy is generated for the lighting and DJ booth (Studio Roosegaarde, n.d.).

The UK based company Pavegen offers tiles that produce energy when people walk on them. As the company explains on its website, "as people step on the tiles, their weight causes electromagnetic induction generators to vertically displace, which results in a rotatory motion that generates off-grid electricity" (Pavegen, n.d.).

Both technologies engage the user into the process of generating energy. When connected to a display featuring the amount of energy thus created against the energy need of, e.g., the building where they are used, they may also contribute to create awareness about energy consumption.

Tools to address the challenges

The best cases presented above illustrate how technology can be used to ease people's lives while staying within Earth limits. In particular, Case 7.1 shows that it is possible to create conditions under which products' components are designed to be reused. This is an example of *cradle-to-cradle* technology. Cradle-to-cradle is a concept introduced by William McDonough and Michael Braungart in 2002. The idea is simple: products should be designed so that at the end of their life they can either be disposed of in nature without damaging it or disassembled so that all components can be used again in the production cycle without loss of quality. In the production process, ideally, only renewable energy (for example solar) should be used and labour should be paid fairly. McDonough and Braungart insist that cradle-to-cradle products are guilt free, because they do not have any negative impact on people and the planet. From an environmental perspective, no waste is generated because each component of a cradle-to-cradle product is actually food for a new cycle. Cradle-to-cradle products may therefore be 'discarded' if a new, cradle-to-cradle product with better specifications enters the market. In-built obsolescence is not inevitable.

7

Even though the idea is simple, its application has several difficulties. To start with, in the cradle-to-cradle approach all materials should fall into one of two categories: technological nutrients or biological nutrients. Materials qualify as technological nutrients only if they are not toxic for people and not harmful for nature. Moreover, they should re-enter the production process (also referred to as technical cycle) indefinitely without any loss of quality. As we have seen, most products are made of mixed materials that are not easily detached the one from the other. All these products by definition do not qualify as cradle-to-cradle. Moreover, even if products may be easily reduced to their initial components, these qualify as cradle-to-cradle if and only if they are non-toxic and non-harmful. Consider a coloured cotton tablecloth. Cotton, if not organically grown, contains residues of pesticides, while chemicals are used in the dying process. Of the used chemicals, some may not be harmful, some may be. Therefore, to qualify a material as 'technical nutrient' a very complex in-depth analysis is needed all along its life span, from production via processing to use and disposal. In other words, a life cycle assessment of each of its components is needed before a product can be certified as cradle-to-cradle.

Biological nutrients are organic materials that can be disposed of in nature safely and become food for new natural processes. Think for example of food waste, that may be composted and used to fertilize gardens. Here, too, however, one should consider the specific ecological conditions of each region. In fact a 'biological nutrient' that is not harmful in one geographic area may be harmful in another, for example the seeds of exotic plants. In a region different from their original one, these seeds may have no enemies. By growing and reproducing undisturbed, they may destroy the local flora. Therefore, to define a biological nutrient as cradle-to-cradle research is needed.

Notwithstanding these difficulties cradle-to-cradle has become a central concept in the transition towards a more sustainable economy. More interestingly, the number of cradle-to-cradle certified products is increasing, and comprises items that are commonly used in hotels such as paper, cleaners, beds and chairs (c2ccertified.org, n.d.).

Cradle-to-cradle is central to the so-called circular economy. In a circular economy the loop of energy and materials is narrowed or closed so that waste is minimized. It opposes the (still mainstream) linear economy where products are made, used and disposed of, and aims at keeping materials 'in the loop' as long as possible. This can be achieved by cradle-to-cradle design, but also by better maintenance, repair and reuse. The circular economy focuses mainly on environmental sustainability. Indirectly, it touches upon social sustainability too because by not wasting scarce resources it enables future generations to meet their own needs. However, social issues such as fair pay and distribution of wealth are usually not considered in the circular economy, while these too should be addressed to achieve a more sustainable form of development. It falls beyond the scope of this book to explain this point further. If you wish to know more you are referred to Cavagnaro and Curiel (2012) or Raworth (2017).

Cradle-to-cradle technology is complex. There are, though, less complex forms of technology that can be applied to reach sustainability. Some of these are proven, traditional technologies such as the building taking the location into consideration, so that (for example) in hot countries windows are turned from the sun (See also Chapter 8). Some are a mix of old and new, such as organic farming. Some are new ones, such as the use of solar energy to cook (One Earth Design, n.d.). The bottom line is that all these technologies respect the Earth's limits to cope with our waste and provide us with resources. Looking back at the $I=P\times A\times T$ formula introduced by Ehrich and Holdern, these technology do not intensify the negative impact on the environment of people's consumption, but lessen it. The formula for sustainable technologies therefore reads $I=P\times A/T$.

As a final note we wish to add a reflection on human behaviour. First we wish to note that technology may help people, including hotel guests, to behave sustainably without effort. Think for example of low-water flush toilets or sensors switching off the lights when a guest leaves a room. As in general people shrink from efforts, and the more so when they are in a relaxing environment such as a hotel, technologies that reduce water and energy consumption without involving guests are welcomed and widely used in a hotel environment. However, exactly because they work unnoticed, if a hotel does not tell guests, they will be less likely to appreciate the hotel's choice of these sustainability measures. Guests appreciate communication and storytelling about sustainability (Cavagnaro *et al.*, 2018), and therefore we encourage hospitality managers to communicate with their guests about the technological solutions that they implement on their premises.

Second, we wish to spend some words on the so-called 'rebound effect'. The rebound effect occurs when consumption of a service increases after the costs for using it have decreased thanks to efficiency (Guerra Santin, 2013). A typical everyday example is car use. Fuel efficiency in cars has dramatically improved in the last few years. The positive environmental effects of this improvement, however, are counteracted because people tend to use their cars more often. It is as if car users have in their mind a certain budget that can be spend on fuel. Therefore they drive till that budget is exhausted, instead of continuing to drive the same distance they did before and thus save on costs and help to protect the environment. A similar effect has been observed in houses: although energy consumption is lower in energy efficient homes, research indicates that their occupants tend to prefer higher indoor temperatures and to ventilate less than people living in less well insulated houses. The energy saving and consequent positive impact on the environment is therefore reduced (Guerra Santin, 2013). People's behaviour cannot be easily changed by external means, such as laws and regulations. It may, though, be changed by careful communication. A well-known example is the experiment conducted by a company called OPower in San Diego, California. People were shown their energy consumption compared to the consumption of their neighbours. To the surprise of the researchers, occupants with a lower than average consumption started consuming more after receiving the information. Yet, the simple addition of a smiley was sufficient to eliminate this effect (Soto, 2011). Showing appreciation for reduced consumption may be enough to help people keeping to their 'sustainable' habit even in the face of reduced costs thanks to more efficient technology. Well-crafted communication can also help guests in showing sustainable behaviour in hotels, such as switching off lights in absence of a sensor or reusing their towels (Goldstein *et al.*, 2008).

Conclusion

This chapter has discussed technology and shown that to achieve sustainability we need to switch from a cradle-to-grave to a cradle-to-cradle approach. Cradle-to-grave is not sustainable because by destroying scarce resources it threatens the ability of present and future generations to fulfil their needs. This is the exact contrary than the aim of sustainable development as avowed in its classic definition by the World Commission on Environment and Development (WCED, 1987). The WCED defines sustainable development as a form of development that meets the needs of the present generation without making its impossible for future generations to meet their own need, wherever and whenever they will live (WCED, 1987). To achieve sustainable development, therefore, we all, including the hospitality industry, will have to embrace cradle-to-cradle technology. If a cradle-to-cradle solution is not yet available, then the choice should be of products and services that resemble it the most, because, for example, they are eco-efficient or enable reuse and recycling.

In our view a cradle-to-cradle approach means that the energy used in all processes is sustainably harvested and that people's right to a decent and secure life are upheld not only for consumers but also for producers. Finally, we have argued that human behaviour should be considered, so that increased consumption does not nullify the environmental benefits achieved with new technologies. Technology remains indeed a double-edged sword and should be applied prudently to harness its benefits for sustainability.

References

Anderson, R.C. (2009) *Confessions of a Radical Industrialist, Profits, People, Purpose: Doing Business by Respecting the Earth*, New York: St Martin's Press.

Bakeys (n.d) http://www.bakeys.com. Accessed 26 February 2018.

Cavagnaro, E. and Curiel, G.H. (2012) *The Three Levels of Sustainability*, Sheffield: Greenleaf.

Cavagnaro, E. Melissen, F.W. and Düweke, A. (2018) The host-guest relationship is the key to sustainable hospitality: Lessons learned from a Dutch case study, *Hospitality & Society*, **8** (1) 23-44.

Centennial Light (n.d.) http://www.centennialbulb.org, accessed on 26 February 2018

c2ccertified.org (n.d.) http://www.c2ccertified.org/products/registry. Accessed 27 February 2018.

Ehrlich, P.R. and Holdren, J.P. (1971) Impact of population growth, *Science*, **171** (3977) 1212-17.

Goldstein, N.J., Cialdini, R.B. and Griskevicius, V. (2008) A room with a viewpoint: using social norms to motivate environmental conservation in hotels, *Journal of Consumer Research*, **35** (3) 472-482.

Guerra Santin, O. J. (2013) Occupant behaviour in energy efficient dwellings: evidence of a rebound effect, *Housing and the Built Environment*, **28** (2) 311-327, https://doi.org/10.1007/s10901-012-9297-2. Accessed 27 February 2018.

Hopewell, J., Dvorak R. and Kosior, E. (2009) Plastics recycling: challenges and opportunities, *Philosophical Transactions of the Royal Society B: Biological Sciences*, **364** (1526), 2115–2126.

Krajewski, M. (2014) *The Great Lightbulb Conspiracy, The Phoebus cartel engineered a shorter-lived lightbulb and gave birth to planned obsolescence.* https://spectrum.ieee.org/geek-life/history/the-great-lightbulb-conspiracy/. Accessed 26 February 2018.

McDonough, W. and M. Braungart (2002) *Cradle to Cradle: Remaking the Way We Make Things*, New York: North Point Press.

One Earth Design (n.d.) https://www.oneearthdesigns.com/blog/compare-solar-cookers/. Accessed 27 February 2018.

Pavegen (n.d.) http://www.pavegen.com/about/. Accessed on 26 February 2018)

Philips (2015) www.philips.com/a-w/about/news/archive/standard/news/press/2015/20150416-Philips-provides-Light-as-a-Service-to-Schiphol-Airport.html. Accessed on February 2018.

Plastic Soup Foundation (n.d.) https://www.plasticsoupfoundation.org/en/. Accessed 27 February 2018.

Raworth, K. (2017) *Doughnut Economics: Seven ways to think like a 21st century economist*, White River Junction: Chelsea Green Publishing

Rockström, J., W. Steffen, K. Noone, Å. Persson, F. S. Chapin, III, E. Lambin, T. M. Lenton, M. Scheffer, C. Folke, H. Schellnhuber, B. Nykvist, C. A. De Wit, T. Hughes, S. van der Leeuw, H. Rodhe, S. Sörlin, P. K. Snyder, R. Costanza, U. Svedin, M. Falkenmark, L. Karlberg, R. W. Corell, V. J. Fabry, J. Hansen, B. Walker, D. Liverman, K. Richardson, P. Crutzen, and J. Foley (2009) Planetary boundaries: exploring the safe operating space for humanity, *Ecology and Society*, **14** (2) 32. http://www.ecologyandsociety.org/vol14/iss2/art32/. Accessed 26 February 2018.

Soto, O.R. (2011) *Energy savings through peer pressure*, www.sandiegouniontribune.com/sdut-efficiency-with-a-smile-2011feb11-htmlstory.html. Accessed 27 February 2018.

Studio Roosegaarde (n.d.) https://www.studioroosegaarde.net/project/sustainable-dance-floor/. Accessed 26 February 2018.

WCED (World Commission on Environment and Development) (1987) *Our Common Future*, Oxford: Oxford University Press.

YouTube (2016), https://www.youtube.com/watch?v=73jPh0eRP-Y. Accessed 27 February 2018.

Zhong, R. (2016) Can an edible spoon save the world?, *The Wall Street Journal*, 25 October.

7

8 Equipping Better Buildings

Thulani Xhali and Philipp Kanthack

Learning goals

This chapter is dedicated to buildings and how to equip them better from a sustainability perspective. After studying this chapter, readers will have the ability to:

1 Discuss buildings and their impact on profit, people and planet;

2 Describe the main sustainability challenges faced by building developers considering the correct accreditation tools, the use of building materials, the use of equipment and financing of development projects;

3 Provide examples of ways to address some of these challenges;

4 Identify good practices in sustainable building.

Introduction

When discussing hotels, it is very difficult to do so without conjuring an image of a beautiful tower in a city centre or perhaps a majestic chateau in the countryside. Regardless of the initial image, chances are that the first thought was of a building of some kind. These types of buildings have existed for as long as the profession of hospitality has existed and have often demonstrated little regard for energy efficiency or the larger economic, environmental or social impacts of the built environment.

Sustainable building attempts to break with these practices by reducing negative impact and, when possible, restore the balance between the social, environmental and economic dimension of sustainability. By understanding the main challenges in this topic, one can begin to address them by considering the past and present in order to build for the future. Early efforts to bring change to the building sector in the 1960s through the 1980s generally focused on single issues such as energy efficiency and conservation of natural resources, but a movement to formalize led to the rise of committees and institutes in the late 1980s to the mid 2000s.

This included the American Institute of Architects (AIA) forming the Committee of Environment in 1989 and the United States Green Building Council (USGBC) forming in 1993 and them piloting their Leadership in Energy and Environmental Design (LEED) programme in 1998. Today green building features can include high-tech, modern practices such as geothermal heating as well as simple and often time-tested practices like attention to building orientation and design.

In this chapter, challenges and solutions of sustainable accreditation of buildings, selection of the best materials and equipment and financing options will be explored alongside some best-case practices of the same.

In reading this, please keep in mind that technological and organizational advancements in the areas covered here are developing at an increasingly fast pace. Though we have chosen examples carefully, it may be that at the moment that you are reading this, options are available that are better from a sustainability point of view than the ones presented here. Therefore, to enable you to evaluate existing and new options we would like to remind you of the general sustainability principles presented in Chapters 1 and 2: avoiding harm and doing good. When applying these principles to buildings one should consider the design, construction, usage and end-of life phases. In the design and construction phase, avoiding harm means designing the building so that it may take the most advantage from its position, for example, by letting sunlight in so that less artificial light is needed; respect as much as possible the local flora and fauna on the location, during construction and in landscaping; choose materials and building methods that consume as little natural resources as possible and minimize any health and safety risk for the people involved. Doing good in this phase would mean choosing a regenerative or restorative building, i.e. one that is purposefully designed to improve the surrounding environment by, for example, restoring a site's natural hydrology; providing for lost wildlife and plant habitat or producing more energy than the building itself consumes. A restorative building, moreover, chooses materials that, following the cradle-to-cradle philosophy, can be reused without loss of quality or can be safely disposed of in the natural environment. It is in the design phase, too, that one can choose options that permit repurposing of the building if it is no longer needed as a hotel. During usage, similar considerations are at play: reduce the use of natural resource and services, and care for the health and safety of staff and guests. In the end-of-life phase, if the building cannot be repurposed, demolition should be managed so that materials are recovered for new uses.

We have chosen the examples in this chapter by keeping the general sustainability principles in mind, and by considering the same principles we hope that you will be able to evaluate any new options available for hotel building in the future.

As any other chapter in this book, this one starts with a discussion of sustainability challenges; proceeds to best cases and closes with highlighting tools to address the challenges.

Main sustainability challenges

Below we will discuss what we consider to be the most pressing sustainability challenges in hotel building: accreditation of 'green' buildings; materials and energy; equipment and financing sustainable buildings.

Accreditation systems

There are several views and definitions on what makes a building sustainable and with that, there are several ways in which a building's impact may be measured. Some may focus on either environmental, economic or social impacts and others on a combination of those.

From an environmental perspective, it is estimated that buildings use about 30-40% of all primary energy, which is the energy contained in raw fuels before they are converted for human use. It should be moreover considered that "most of this energy is derived from fossil sources, and the hotel sector's contribution to global warming and climate change is estimated to include annual releases between 160 and 200 kg of CO_2 per m² of room floor area, depending on the fuel mix used to provide energy. Global hotel-based CO_2 emissions were assumed to be at the level of 55.7 Mt in 2001, while the estimated annual energy consumption for a European hotel of 39 TWh, would result in emissions of more than 10 Mt of CO_2 each year" (Hotel Energy Solutions, 2011: 2).

Buildings are energy intensive in all phases of their life. It is therefore logical that, from an investor's perspective, the best known economic argument for building with sustainability intent is the decrease in operating costs. These refer to the costs of the energy used by a building in its life-cycle for heating, cooling, lighting and ventilation. They also incorporate various maintenance activities and factors including insurance and property taxes.

In a social perspective, it is estimated that people spend 90% of their time indoors and poor health issues, allergies, asthma, acute respiratory illness have been associated with poor building design (Lackman and Bourdeau, 2008). Alongside the individual suffering associated with building-related illness, there are also major social costs. In the United States alone, the annual amount of these costs has been estimated at 58 billion dollars (CEC, 2008).

Consider that a developer intends of being sustainable with their construction choices; how can they be sure that they have made the right ones? This discussion may be the reason for confusion and is why there are institutions that allow clear definitions and set procedures to indicate the sustainability of a building. For the past few decades, building professionals have been refining their expertise and consolidating their efforts in the area of sustainable building design. To ensure coherence as well as consistency, and to respond to the need for a documented approach, tools and methodologies have been developed and are now recognized as a key element of achieving green building practices. Since the early 1990s, a number of organizations have developed green building rating systems that provide specific performance objectives and frameworks for assessing overall build-ing design and performance. Each of these rating systems allocate points in areas such as energy use, water use, pollution, material and product inputs, indoor air quality and occupant comfort, transport, site ecology, and other sustainable design features. Their differences stem from the standard development process, philosophy on particular issues, and stringency (CEC, 2008). The challenge is in choosing which of the multitude of available systems is best. Whether the inves-tors reasoning is principle based, financially based or a combination of the two, there are considerations to be made.

Materials and energy

Form a 'no harm' perspective, in the process of design to delivery of a (hotel) building, the aim is for an optimum use of resources such as energy, water and materials while reducing building impacts on human and environmental health. However, there are direct environmental impacts that result from the construction and operation of buildings including greenhouse gases and other air emissions related to energy use, water use and discharge, storm water runoff and impacts related to building materials (for some figures see Chapters 14 and 15). All these impacts represent sustainability challenges and will be briefly addressed in this sub-section.

According to a report from the University of Michigan, there are three life-cycle phases related to the flow of materials through the life of a building. Phase 1, the pre-building phase, describes the production and delivery process of a mate-rial up to, but not including, the point of installation. This includes extraction, processing, packaging and shipping of materials. Phase 2, the building phase, refers to a building material's useful life and in that factors such as construction, installation, operation and maintenance are considered. Phase 3, the post-building phase refers to the building materials when their usefulness in a building has expired, with considerations of recycling and reuse (Jong-Jin and Rigdon, 1998). The figure below shows these phases; the main areas in which impact may occur and options for reusing and recycling of materials.

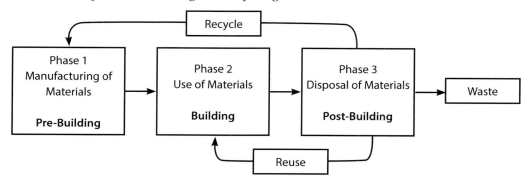

Figure 8.1: Lifecycle of materials (Designed by the author on the basis of an illustration by Jong-Jin and Rigdon, 1998).

A report prepared by the Secretariat of the Commission for Environmental Cooperation (CEC) states that data collected from Canada, Mexico and the United States show the negative environmental impacts of buildings. In Canada, buildings are responsible for 33% of all energy used, 50% of natural resources consumed, 12% of non-industrial water used, 25% of landfill waste generated, 10% of airborne particulates produced, and 35% of greenhouse gases emitted. In Mexico, buildings are responsible for 17% of all energy used, 25% of all electricity used, 20% of all carbon dioxide emissions, 5% of potable water consumption and 20% of the waste generated. While in the United States, buildings account for 40% of total energy use, 12% of the total water consumption, 68% of total electricity consumption, 38% of total carbon dioxide emissions, and 60% of total non-industrial waste generation (CEC, 2008). In the construction of buildings, it is therefore important to consider the materials used in an effort to reduce or eradicate these impacts.

Individual and social costs connected to building-related illnesses have already been mentioned. To these we should add social issues that may arise all along the chain, such as forced labour or unsafe working conditions. In Chapter 15 on Food and Beverage, for example, the unsafe working conditions for stone workers in China have been pointed out (Bjurling *et al.*, 2008). Similar issues are known for other building materials such as wood: forestry is in fact at high risk of forced and child labour, especially in Latin America (ILO, 2001) and Indonesia (ILO, 2010).

Looking at the post-building phase, from an environmental perspective waste and non-proper disposal of materials is a major issue. Socially, if buildings are not repurposed or dismantled, they may become ruined and unsafe. Ruined buildings may affect the whole surrounding community because by giving the impression that nobody cares they may encourage vandalism and other forms of asocial behaviour (Wilson and Kelling, 1982).

Equipment

When building a property, the developer has choices of the equipment to use in day-to-day operations. This equipment choice ranges from small to large units that are complimentary to the ideals of the developer, and in this case, responsible practices in looking after people, the planet and profit.

When looking at equipment sustainability challenges, there are three main areas of concern in the procurement, use and maintenance of operational equipment; and these are waste, energy and water. Waste includes hazardous material and operators should aim to reduce, reuse and recycle it. The issue of energy has already been raised earlier and will be discussed further on, as will water, which includes domestic and facilities use.

Waste is estimated to cost the United Kingdom approximately €48 per ton in landfill costs. A typical hotel guest generates one kilogram of waste per night with more than half of it in paper and plastic (Green Hotelier, 2009). From an environmental perspective, waste is problematic due to the carbon emissions generated, the amount of resources lost and landfill take-up.

Water scarcity is a well-known problem the world over and as global institutions, hotels have the moral responsibility to address this issue. Only 1% of global water is available in rivers, lakes and groundwater and it is this 1% that may be used while the remaining 99% is in oceans, the Poles and in glaciers. In many hotels water is known to account for 10% of the utility bill (Tuppen, 2013). This cost implication does not account for the double usage, in that water must first be purchased fresh, hence the utility expense, and then also disposed of as waste, which also has cost considerations.

From a socio-cultural perspective, it is important to note that the choice in equipment needs to be as thought out as the intention. For example, a property I am familiar with, located in South Africa, made a well-intended and expensive investment in a geothermal system. This system worked, until it didn't. By that I mean that whenever there were maintenance problems, the local support needed to fly experts in from the United States, and one could argue that the footprint of placing and maintaining the system was counter-efficient to the system itself. Never mind the feelings of frustration from all parties that had to work with it!

Financing

It is well known in the hospitality industry that a tremendous amount of energy, water and other resources are required to run a property and serve its guests. Research done by Hotel Energy Solution in 2011 states that hotels rank in the top five of energy consumers in the tertiary building sector with an estimated annual usage of 305-330 kilowatts per square meter versus a typical urban apartment building which uses 260 kilowatts per square meter (HES, 2011). Older hotel facilities can be especially costly to operate from an energy use and efficiency perspective, as they generally lack newer technology designed with sustainability in mind. Despite the potential benefits the hospitality industry may enjoy with the implementation of sustainability improvements, there have been significant obstacles to the development of energy efficiency and water conservation measures.

The most obvious obstacle is simply the significant additional capital investment required from a hotel developer. Many are concerned that adopting green features into their buildings will involve high upfront costs. Compared to conventional buildings, green building projects are often perceived as having higher initial design and construction costs (Mahendriyani, 2016).

Additionally, the developer may have concerns regarding their ability to recoup their investment within an acceptable time frame, as well as have challenges in accessing the financing necessary for these initial costs. With regards to framing an acceptable payback period, it is difficult because the nature of hotel valuation is difficult. Payback is one of the simplest methods in measuring a return on investment, as the calculation is simply the number of years the cash flows would take to payback the initial investment. Hotels may be valued purely as real estate or just the business or both, and this can be either 3-5 years for the business or as much as 15 years for the total package (Sviatlana, 2011).

Later in this chapter, we suggest tools and possible solutions to each of the three main considerations in the challenges of equipment use and selection, and explore financing options and opportunities.

Best cases

Case 8.1: Accreditation systems: Van der Valk and BREEAM – Deliberate sustainability

Femke Vrenegoor, NHL Stenden University of Applied Sciences

Van der Valk is a Dutch hotel chain for which sustainability in their buildings and in their operations is important. For a recent development, the Van der Valk hotel in Leeuwarden (the Netherlands) that opened in January 2018 with 115 rooms, they received the BREEAM Excellent certificate based on the building plans drawn in 2015. BREEAM is the leading organization for assessing the sustainability of buildings, and awards an internationally renowned certificate based on a buildings' technical specifications and its ability to minimize impacts on the environment. The Van der Valk chain does not require new hotels to be built according to this standard, nor does Leeuwarden municipality have any demands with regard to sustainable building. Regardless, the owners of the Van der Valk Leeuwarden hotel opted for this BREEAM certificate, because they believed it is the right thing to do. The BREEAM Excellent certificate is the second most sustainable level within this certificate, and this level on average saves 32% CO_2 emission compared to non-BREEAM certified buildings.

The BREEAM certificate follows very stringent guidelines, and to obtain it, Van der Valk Leeuwarden had to implement several measures in their hotel construction. Some actions that Van der Valk had to take are by now considered quite standard such as using only FSC certified wood, installing heat pump systems for heating, and LED lighting. However, the owners also implemented less standard measures such as using triple pane glazing. As a consequence, the new hotel has no need for gas, and is self-sufficient in its energy needs. Cooking for example is done with induction, thus using electricity rather than gas. However, Van der Valk Leeuwarden does have two small kettles as a backup.

In some instances Van der Valk had to look for a workable balance between the BREEAM requirements and the usability of the building. For example, the hotel could have earned extra points by using gypsum and iron profiles for their walls. However, the choice was made for bricks as they absorb sound better. To demonstrate how serious Van der Valk Leeuwarden is in their implementation of the BREEAM Excellent certificate, one can consider that the hotel deliberately chose not to use solar panels (yet). According to the hotel, it is an easy way to score extra points and they would rather use this only if other more stringent options do not work out as planned.

Part of assessment that leads to a BREEAM certificate in the Excellent category is the reduction of maintenance. For example, hotels' walls, and especially corners, are damaged by vacuum cleaners, suitcases and housekeeping trolleys. This is common knowledge in hotels, and therefore the corners are reinforced. At Van der Valk Leeuwarden, they sought an even more robust solution: implementing an integrated RVS slat. They measured the height of the damages at other hotels (25-30 cm) and implemented the RVS slat up until the height of the damages, and no more. This measure avoids damage to the wallpaper and corners and thus reduces future maintenance, and also avoids using more natural resources than needed.

In the grounds of the hotel there was an old barn they had to tear down. Hotel Van der Valk Leeuwarden realized that rather than having this debris removed, and order new debris to put under their parking lot, they could use the debris from the barn. This insight allowed for a closed resource loop, as well as preventing unnecessary transport.

Interesting to note is that during the building phase, Van der Valk Leeuwarden consulted with the local neighbours about the progress of the construction, the sustainability of the building, and their concerns and wishes with regard to the hotel. For example, the possibility to build a bike path behind the hotel was discussed, as well as possible future uses for the archaeological protected farm which is on the building's premises and social activities with and/or in the hotel.

Overall, hotel Van der Valk Leeuwarden has not only demonstrated true commitment to building their hotel in a sustainable manner but has also shown that building sustainably is a suitable and viable option for hotels.

If you are interested, more information about their BREAAM certificate can be found on their website (http://www.breeam.com).

Case 8.2: Materials and energy: The Madaster Foundation and 'Material Passports'

Thomas Rau is a silver-haired architect based in the Netherlands but originally of German descent. To simply call him an architect would be a disservice to his accomplishments, as many have called him an innovator, a visionary and an inspiration. His decision to settle in the Netherlands was inspired by his love for architecture as he found that it had some of the most charming architecture that he had ever seen. Thomas Rau is also co-founder of Madaster, a foundation that aims to eliminate waste, starting in the building and construction sector.

In February 2017, the Madaster foundation was launched in Amsterdam with the aim of preventing building materials from ending up as waste, by giving that material an identity whereby one may know exactly how much of each material was used and where the remainder is. This effort of giving waste an identity is done through a Material Passport for buildings, thus ensuring a closed system of accountability where resources should not be wasted. Rau has stated that waste is a raw material that has ended up in anonymity.

The Material Passport gives waste anew an identity. The Material Passport service offered by Madaster is an automated process that is monitored and supervised by the foundation, where they promote and oversee the development and usage of the Passport while ensuring security, privacy and availability of data. The foundation is of the belief that a building is a deposit of materials that hold an intrinsic value at a product, component and material level. By listing and valuating all materials used, it creates opportunities to save costs, and increase re-usage of materials, to reduce and ultimately eliminate waste.

Liander is a Dutch network company whose head office in Duiven was designed by Thomas's firm, RAU Architects. It is a sustainable building that generates more energy than it consumes and has a Material Passport. Triodos Bank in Driebergen (The Netherlands) is another of the architectural firm's projects and is being realized at the time of writing (January 2018). It goes a few steps further by not only registering the materials but also recording how the value of the materials develops over time, with the principal belief that if financial value is placed on the materials, then destroying them would be akin to destroying capital. Another major project under this principal is the delivery of a Material Passport for the renovation of the Schiphol Tunnel in Amsterdam.

It is clear that Rau is a radical who believes that waste is not a necessary evil but rather a commercial construct developed through the practice of deliberate product obsolescence. In an interview with fd.nl, Thomas Rau gives an example of the light bulb, noting that one of the first ever light bulbs still burns today and that this technology is not only available but inexpensive. He states that the collusion of light bulb manufacturers led to a decision that bulbs should be deisgned to burn for more than 1,000 hours, therefore creating a need for repurchases from consumers. And ultimately, waste. (See also p. 17.)

The Materials Passport of a building can be downloaded via the online platform (https://www.madaster.com/en). The aim is to have 10,000 buildings registered in the Netherlands with the promise that other countries will promptly follow suit.

Case 8.3: Financing: The Hilton Universal City and PACE – Partner in responsible financing

Hilton Universal City (Hollywood, USA) is located within walking distance of several major film studios, the Universal CityWalk Hollywood shopping and entertainment centre, and Universal Studios Hollywood theme park, which attracts more than six million visitors a year. This 23-story building has nearly 500 guest rooms, a top floor presidential suite, and 32,000 square feet of flexible meeting space. There are several public courts and gardens surrounding the property and banquet facilities located above a three-story hillside parking garage. Additional amenities include a lobby bar and restaurants, an outdoor pool, business centre, and a fitness facility.

The hotel was built 30 years ago and improvements were necessary for the property to remain competitive in the current hospitality market. Initially, the goal was to focus on 'low hanging fruit' upgrades that offered a quick payoff. Before long though, the Hilton Universal City executive board saw an opportunity to expand the scope to encompass upgrades with a much longer payoff, including improvements such as elevators and control systems. Additionally, the hotel aspired to reach LEED certification and PACE was the solution that helped in reaching that goal. PACE (Property Assessed Clean Energy) financing is an innovative way for commercial property owners to pay for energy efficiency upgrades, on-site renewable energy projects, and water conservation measures. PACE funding can cover 100% of a project's costs, and is repaid over a term of up to 20 years. This financing is broadly applicable to commercial, industrial, agricultural, multi-family housing and non-profit properties. Since 2009, in the United States the size of commercial PACE projects has ranged from $2,000 to $7 million. Several real estate market leaders have used PACE to fund energy efficiency upgrades to their buildings. In the Hilton case, long-term PACE financing made a deeper retrofit possible and the final project price tag includes construction costs, fees, and other expenses. The major goals for a new expanded project included:

- Increase guests' comfort and overall experience;
- Improve overall building performance;
- Replace old equipment – heating, ventilation and air conditioning (HAVC), lights, water pumps, etc.;
- Reduce energy costs;
- Reduce operating and maintenance costs;
- Improve the environment;
- Adhere to the 'Hilton global' standard of sustainability and design.

The idea for the project was born at a US Green Building Council workshop in Los Angeles attended by the building owner's sustainability manager. A conversation then began between the building owner and PACE program on ways to fund fairly modest upgrades to address maintenance that had been deferred for the past 10 years without incurring additional debt.

Hilton's comprehensive retrofit included energy efficiency glass installations and new LED lighting, which is expected to reduce energy consumption by 50%. Additionally, 500 low-flow showerheads were installed and 250 bathtubs with showers were replaced as part of the conservation upgrade to save the equivalent to one month of the property's current water usage. Older HVAC systems were replaced with new energy efficient ones.

The hotel management was very involved with planning and project design. The contractors were selected through a competitive bidding process and ReNewAll, a Los Angeles County PACE project developer, assisted Hilton in the selection process by pre-screening and interviewing the candidates. Hilton's general manager, Mark Davis notes, "The interest and commitment to sustainable energy and saving earth resources are largely due to being informed. It was a great opportunity to share how easily PACE empowered our decision to commit to this responsible effort on our journey to improve the property's saving of valuable resources. We are indeed grateful for the professionals who supported and collaborated in making this project a reality." (PACE, n.d.).

This project serves as a great example of proactive use of rebates. The initial energy audit identified a number of possible rebate opportunities on the state and federal level. The local utility, Los Angeles Department of Water and Power, offered $80,000 in incentives for replacing an old chiller. The hotel applied the $80,000 towards a new 125-ton chiller. On the federal level, the Section 179D of the Internal Revenue Code for Commercial Building Tax Deductions allows for the deduction of 40 cents per square foot for the replacement of old lights with LED fixtures. Overall, the Hilton took advantage of nearly $1.1 million in federal rebates. The value of the improvements along with the additional value of added net operating income was in excess of $13 million and the value of the property increased by more than $30 million.

The PACE assessment equalled $7 million with a term up to 20 years. The net operating income for year one was a $335,000 increase (afar PACE Assessment payment) and a return on investment of 78%. The total project return was $12.5 million and the building value increase was approximately $30 million while the list of improvements included:

- Four elevators - full system upgrade;
- 520 HVAC fan motors in guestrooms;
- HVAC controls system;
- Eleven refrigerators & freezer motors;
- Two 450-ton chillers;
- LED lighting upgrade;
- Lighting controls;
- Glass replacement in select areas;
- 250 bathtubs and showers;
- 500 shower heads;
- Dynamic tinting glass units;
- High capacity washers and dryers;
- EV charging station.

Overall, this project addressed a number of concerns, including deferred equipment maintenance, compliance with the Hilton global design standards, and adherence to sustainable practices while solving the financial conundrum.

Adapted by Thulani Xhali from PACE/Hilton case study (PACE, n.d.)

Tools to address challenges

In this section tools to address the challenges in accreditation system, use of materials and financing sustainable buildings will be presented.

Accreditation systems

As it has been highlighted in the section on challenges, in the construction and use phases, buildings consume a vast quantity of energy. Moreover, they may negatively impact people's health and safety. Sustainable buildings address both challenges, through energy and water management, waste management, materials recycling, resource conservation and protection of biodiversity. They also do this by being highly sensitive to the well-being of the occupants and incorporating features that promote their comfort and health. To assist financers, owners, and managers in choosing the best available option, various countries have developed 'Green' building standards in accordance with their environment. As not all regions are equal from a social and environmental perspective, some of the green building standards in the world are discussed below with a focus on Europe (BREEAM), Asia (CASBEE) and the United States (LEED).

BREEAM

8

The first standard that we will present here is BREEAM (Building Research Establishment's Environmental Assessment Method), the standard referred to in Case 8.1. BREEAM was launched in 1990 in the United Kingdom and has become a widely used means of reviewing and improving the environmental performance of a range of different building types, for not only hotels but also offices, homes, industrial units, retail units and schools. The organization determines the BREEAM rating based on quantifiable sustainable design achievements. When a building is assessed, points are awarded for each criterion and the points are tallied for a total score. The overall building performance is awarded a 'Pass', 'Good', 'Very Good' or 'Excellent' rating.

BREEAM major categories of criteria for Design and Procurement include (Fowler and Rauch 2006):

- **Management**: commissioning, monitoring, waste recycling, pollution minimization, materials minimization;
- **Health & Wellbeing**: adequate ventilation, humidification, lighting, thermal comfort;
- **Energy**: sub-metering, efficiency and CO2 impact of systems;
- **Transport**: emissions, alternate transport facilities;
- **Water**: consumption reduction, metering, leak detection;
- **Materials**: asbestos mitigation, recycling facilities, reuse of structures, facade or materials, use of crushed aggregate and sustainable timber;
- **Land use**: previously used land, use of remediated contaminated land;

■ **Ecology**: land with low ecological value or minimal change in value, maintaining major ecological systems on the land, minimization of biodiversity impacts;

■ **Pollution**: leak detection systems, on-site treatment, local or renewable energy sources, light pollution design, avoid use of ozone depleting and global warming substances.

CASBEE

CASBEE (Comprehensive Assessment System for Building Environmental Efficiency) is the second standard we present. It was developed in Japan and introduced in 2004. The system requires documentation of quantifiable sustainable design achievements, which are assessed by trained architects who have passed the CASBEE assessor examination.

The community of assessment tools is based on the building's life cycle: pre-design, new construction, existing buildings, and renovation. Results are plotted on a graph, with environmental load on one axis and quality on the other and the best buildings will fall in the section representing lowest environmental load and highest quality. Each criterion is scored from level one to level five, with level one defined as meeting minimum requirements, level three defined as meeting typical technical and social levels at the time of the assessment, and level five representing a high level of achievement. An example of such a graph is given below.

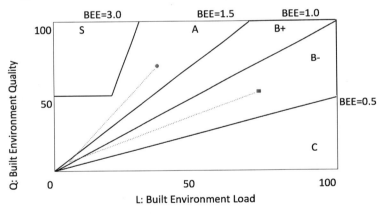

Graph 8.1: Example of a CASBEE Graph (Adapted by author, based on Fowler and Rauch, 2006)

CASBEE major categories of criteria include the following: Building Environmental Quality and Performance (Fowler and Rauch 2006);

■ **Indoor environment**: noise and acoustics, thermal comfort, lighting and illumination, and air quality;

■ **Quality of services**: functionality and usability, amenities, durability and reliability, flexibility and adaptability:

- **Outdoor environment on site**: preservation and creation of biotope, townscape and landscape, and outdoor amenities;

- **Energy**: thermal load, use of natural energy, efficiency of systems, and efficient operations;

- **Resources and materials**: water conservation, recycled materials, sustainably harvested timber, materials with low health risks, reuse and reusability, and avoidance of CFCs and halons:

- **Off-site environment:** air pollution, noise and vibration, odour, sunlight obstruction, light pollution, heat island effect, and local on local infrastructure

LEED

The last standard presented here is LEED (Leadership in Energy and Environment Design). LEED is owned by the US Green Building Council and promotes a whole-building approach by recognizing performance in sustainable site development, water savings, energy efficiency, materials selection, and indoor environment quality. Documentation of the quantifiable sustainable design measures are provided to the US Green Building Council, the developer of the LEED rating system, for third-party verification. The assessors have been trained and must pass an assessor examination.

The LEED Reference Guide presents detailed information on how to achieve the credits within the following major categories (Fowler and Rauch 2006):

- **Sustainable sites**: construction-related pollution prevention, site development impacts, transportation alternatives, storm water management, heat island effect, and light pollution;

- **Water efficiency**: landscaping water use reduction, indoor water use reduction, and wastewater strategies;

- **Energy and atmosphere**: commissioning, whole building energy performance optimization, refrigerant management, renewable energy use, and measurement and verification:

- **Materials and resources**: recycling collection locations, building reuse, construction waste management, and the purchase of regionally manufactured materials, materials with recycled content, rapidly renewable materials, salvaged materials, and sustainably forested wood products;

- **Indoor environmental quality**: environmental tobacco smoke control, outdoor air delivery monitoring, increased ventilation, construction indoor air quality, use low emitting materials, source control, and controllability of thermal and lighting systems;

- **Innovation and design process**: LEED accredited professional, and innovative strategies for sustainable design.

Although there are differences in how the world sees the priority of sustainability in buildings, the fact that throughout the planet, accreditation boards exist is a clear indicator that this topic is a priority. These accreditations provide consistencies in conversations whether they are being had in the east or the west. Consistencies such as similar views on the use of energy resources, the use of water, the management of materials, recycling and the importance of design in construction. One could argue the legitimacy of points versus levels versus credits and how they are weighted, but what matters is that they all encourage more sustainable building.

Materials and energy

In an effort to address the energy and material concern of sustainable buildings, there are some key options when considering what to use in these buildings. These are discussed below looking at materials first, then at energy and then at sustainable options in landscaping and repurposing buildings.

When considering materials, the first step in addressing energy and water consumption is reducing it, for example by insulation and the use of water- and energy-saving mechanisms. Before construction begins, the developer should consider the differences in building materials and new developments such as the so-called *bio-based* materials. Generally speaking 'bio-based' means that materials are derived or made from renewable resources, with the understanding that these resources are harvested taking into account the time they need to recover. In this sense, sustainably harvested wood and wool also count as bio-based. Yet, more specifically, bio-based refers to innovative materials of mineral or vegetable origin and to materials enhancing industrial by-products coming from recycling, such as concrete made of elephant grass (Nakanishi *et al.*, 2016). Bio-based materials are durable, recyclable without loss of quality or safe to dispose of in the environment, and answer high performances requirements, such as thermal, hydric, physical or mechanical ones. Compared with traditional materials such as concrete and aluminium, generally speaking, bio-based materials embed less energy (Jones and Brischke, 2017). Although bio-based are the ideal, there is the reality of availability and affordability, and for that one must consider alternatives. For this, concrete, wood, insulation and glass are discussed as the main material components of a building.

Concrete is a building material which is made entirely from water, cement, gravel and sand. Concrete is used either as a binding material to fix bricks or can be poured into modular elements which can be connected and put into form. In order to create cement, clay and limestone are heated 1045°C and are then ground into powder. Due to the intense energy usage while creating cement, concrete it is one of the most energy intense building materials on the market. Building with concrete provides a very durable and long-lasting structure, though, that can be used over and over again. Concrete can be produced today with different characteristics depending on the individual need. Lightweight or high-performance concretes do not only have different production steps but entirely different utilization. For a residential property, different characteristics are needed than for bridges for example. Although there is intense energy usage of concrete in its production, the materials allow for recycling. In this regards the material, when produced can be reused in further construction projects (Baunetz Wissen, 2016).

When considering using wood it is important to note its origins. While local types of wood are generally accepted to be sustainable when forested correctly, using tropical wood can have a contrary effect. It is not only important to choose a sustainable type of wood but also to ensure that the forestation companies are fair employers and transparent in their market approach. Sustainability includes, in fact, a three-dimensional approach where care is required not only for planet and profit but also for the human component. Especially types of woods originating from jungles cannot be considered sustainable, due to deforestation, the destruction of living space of varied species, the negative impact this may have on the lifehood of the local inhabitants and the risk of forced and child labour (ILO, 2001 and 2010). Certification, such as that from the Forest Stewardship Council, should therefore be sought when using wood. Wood has the advantage that it has an high strength to weight ratio, and that depending on the type and treatment it can have great insulation characteristics. Bamboo, for example, can be used to insulate, as walls, floors or even as construction side scaffolding (Baunetz Wissen, 2016).

When it comes to choosing which insulation to use, three main types are applicable. Options are organic, mineral or cellular insulation materials. When choosing organic, choices include lamb's wool, wood, cotton, coconut leaves, flax or other natural materials with similar attributes. Even though these options are organic at their core, they need to be treated with different chemicals like flame retardants for fire protection or biocide in order to prevent the natural fabrics from vermin infestation. Moreover, some of these materials, require a vast amount of water and pesticide to be grown, and even more so for non-organic varieties (see the example of cotton in Chapter 15). Attention to certification, both environmental and social, is therefore essential when looking for a sustainable insulation option. (Baunetz Wissen, 2016).

The right type of glass can significantly improve the energy usage of a property. When considering window glass, it is important to adjust the need to the individual destination. When making use of insulating glass the windows are made out of two or more panes which have an air barrier built between them. They possess insulation properties, which can significantly help to decrease the energy usage needed to heat or cool down rooms. In very sunny and heated areas it can make sense to use shaded windows, which reflect the sunlight and allow for a lower energy intput for air conditioning (Baunetz Wissen, 2016).

Through proper insulation, energy needs are reduced. Reduction makes it easier to cover the remaining energy needs with renewable sources, such as wind and solar energy. In fact, consensus has it that the first step to be taken is to design so that the energy consumption during the usage phase of a building is reduced. Electricity consumptions entails, basically, everything from lighting, appliances, IT, air conditioning, and so on. The sustainable solution entails two separate approaches in order to identify potential savings, either to create the demanded energy on the property or to look for energy efficient technology. First, we want to look at the option of creating energy on the property itself.

Depending on the location of a property the number of sun days differs greatly. Thus, the energy concept for any property must meet the demands of its usable energy sources that it can tap into locally. When there is an abundance of sun, solar panels should be considered, where strong winds are common wind use collectors, when there is a stream or river nearby the use of a water generator should be taken into consideration. In areas like northern Europe, where each of these sources can be found and are unevenly distributed, a mix of those energy collecting technologies should be considered. Independent consulting companies can help determine the optimal mix and they can help find subsidiaries and public funding.

The residual energy needs should then be as far as possible covered by renewable energy, i.e. energy that is not derived from fossil fuels.

Designing to reduce energy consumption mainly means taking advantage of the building location so that, for example, sunlight may enter the building for illumination and the roof is properly orientated for the maximum yield of solar panels and heating systems. Here we will briefly touch upon these considerations.

The most commonly used technology to generate clean energy is the installation of solar panels on the property. In order to be able to generate the best yield, these solar panels are commonly installed on the roof top. They can generate up to 1,000 kWh per year per individual module (Mertens, 2015). A property in a sunny area can easily produce more energy than needed. The extra generated energy which is not repurposed for heating or warm water can be directed back into the local electricity network and thus generate extra revenue. Solar panels have come a long way and are now producing energy in some areas of the world at lower cost than fossil fuels. A study undertaken by the Fraunhofer Institute predicts an average cost level of 4-6 cents per kWH by 2025 generated by solar energy alone. A kilowatt-hour electricity in Germany, for example, costs at the moment on average 29.17 cents (Podewils, 2015).

There are multiple examples of hotels that have already made changes towards their energy production with the use of solar panels.

Even though wind turbines are mainly used in offshore parks and in long rows on land, small turbines can be installed on properties as well. The investment is feasible when a certain amount of wind can be estimated. Due to their size and design these turbines need to be viewed as a small addendum to the energy mix.

LED lightning is considered to be the best choice in low-energy lighting. LED stands for light-emitting diodes and are at their core the most sustainable light source based on technology. LED lights can last up to 50,000 hours (>5 years). Depending on the wanted illumination factors (measured in Kelvin) the cost reduction compared to equivalent conventional light bulbs can be up to 90%. Not only does the reduction of energy save costs but the decrease of waste creates an additional positive effect for the environment. The average household electricity bill can be lowered by up to 8% when making use of LED lamps.

When considering heating systems different options are feasible. Currently the majority of properties still use oil or gas heating systems, which not only make the operations dependant on the fluctuations on the energy markets and thus offers a variable in the costs calculations, but also negatively affect the environment with greenhouse gas emissions. Therefore both for financial and environmental reasons, when considering replacing an old heating system or planning a new property, developers should consider more sustainable systems. The most feasible option depends again mostly on the individual circumstances of the property. The developer first needs to establish the demand of heating for the property. This varies, based on the climate surrounding the property, the degree of insulation, the type of windows, the availability of radiant barriers and type of outlets. Options for sustainable heating systems include wood based and solar powered systems, heat pumps, district heating, and heat recovery or cogeneration systems. In the following we will take a closer look on these available systems and their benefits.

Wood pellet heating systems are considered sustainable for different reasons. First, when burned the wood pellets are CO_2 emission neutral. Due to the use of fast growing trees such as poplars or willows, which are grown in short rotation forestry, these trees can be harvested after three to six years. Wood pellets are not only CO_2 friendly but cost less than oil. The wood pellets price per kilo in January 2018 was €24.17 cents per kilo, while oil cost €55.23 cents per litre (Holzpellets, n.d). A study of 13 business style hotels in Germany found the estimated average heating consumption was 72 kWh per square meter (Voss, Bernard, 2015). Oil generates an average of 9.8 kWh per litre with a litre price of 0.5523 €/l; wood pellets are estimated to produce around 4.8 kWh per kg, with a cost price of 0.2417 €/kg. On this basis, heating with oil would cost €4.05 per square metre while the wooden pellets cost €3.63 per square metre. Considering the cost and CO_2-foot print of distribution, a wooden pellet heating system is the most sustainable, when its production source is as close by as possible and wood is properly harvested.

The principle of a heat pump is basically the same as the idea of a fridge – just the other way around. Small heat differences in the depth of the ground, for example, are harvested and transported into storage. The differences in heat can be stored and then used in order to either heat up the building or do the opposite and cool it down. With intelligent construction such as pipelines in the floor and the façade, heated or cooled water can be pumped through the entire building in order to generate the desired temperatures. When establishing an energy mix in the property, the needed electricity to run the heat pump comes out the solar panel electricity production. The advantages of this system are not only the sustainability but even more important in regards to a hospitable operation that the perceived temperature is not transported through air flow, as for example in classic air conditioners, but distributed through the entire building structure. In order to generate the best possible outcome, this system is best installed when a hotel is constructed.

A district heating system is one in which energy is generated in a central power plant and then distributed via an underground network directly to residential or commercial properties. When in place, this system allows the end user to obtain heating without having to install and run their own heating system. Due to the increased burning of bio mass and wooden pellets in those central facilities, the generated heat can often be considered sustainable. When offered in the region, this system not only provides a green solution for the heating demand but also is very cost effective since no extra maintenance needs to be considered.

Designing a building sustainably means also, as observed above, considering its end-phase. Two main options may be considered here: design for repurposing and design for demolition. In time the purpose of buildings may change. Consider, for example, the consequences of the on-going stream of people in developing countries leaving rural areas and occupying the ever-larger growing international metropolises in the pursuit of a better life. Urbanization poses significant essential challenges, which must be met by the local authorities in order to provide the infrastructure of growing cities and houses to the new city dwellers. Repurposing buildings in the inner city or its direct outskirts may then be an option. In developed countries, the ageing population is looking for properties suitable for their needs, such as having no thresholds between rooms and lift. Hotel properties, if properly designed, may be easily repurposed to meet these challenges.

From a sustainability perspective, designing for demolition means choosing for a cradle-to-cradle (or circular) approach instead of a cradle-to-grave. This means, as in Case 8.3 above, to consider materials as intrinsically valuable and wasting them as a destruction of capital. Materials and methods of construction should therefore be chosen that allow for easy dismantling of a property structure so that (almost) all materials can be reused without loss of quality. Unfortunately, most buildings have not yet been built considering repurposing or circularity. Even then, demolition may be carried out so as to recover materials as far as possible, recycle and re-purpose them. This strategy is financially and environmentally sound. Financially, because saved materials may be either reused to build a new or sold. Environmentally because energy may be regained from existing building materials in order to reduce the embodied energy in the next new built building. Recycling has been found to have the highest energy saving potential (53%), followed by reusing (6.2%) while incineration gave only a minimum energy saving of 0.4% (Ng and Chau, 2015).

Finally, when planning or revitalizing, a hotel property developer should consider the environmental impact on the local flora and fauna. Water reduction in the hotel industry has a long history and is generally seen in the activity of recycling and composting. Recycled water can decrease the water costs significantly and composted organic waste can be used as a fertilizer for the landscaping needs on the properties. Planting local and water non-intensive plants, which also support the local variety of insects and animals, can have significant impact on the positive environmental effects of any property. Not only do guests value biodiversity but also municipalities and local government are often very much in favour of a rich variety of plants and animals. These efforts are not only seen very positively on a community level but can greatly enhance the acceptance of comprehensive building applications and support from local authorities.

Besides the obviously positive impact on local biodiversity, the right choice of trees, plants and bushes can greatly reduce landscaping costs and contributes to the long-term development and growth of the landscape itself. When typical local trees, for example, are planted as young plants, the gradual growth over time will improve the architecture, design and the overall impression of the property. Resort properties in the countryside as much as inner city hotels can, for example, get involved with bee-keeping. Not only can the necessary demand for honey be self-produced, marketed and maintained but more importantly the property performs active duty to the community.

When properties are located in the countryside, it is of great benefit to consider starting their own small-scale fields for home grown herbs, vegetables and fruit. Providing these infrastructural opportunities allows and offers the kitchen operations, for example, to get more involved with local greens, experiment with products and greatly reduce costs for ingredients. Besides the obvious opportunity to distinguish the F&B offers from its competitors, the social environmental impact on employees and guests cannot be overstated (see also Chapter 15).

Concluding, though some options such as bio-materials and design for repurposing may be at the moment still a bridge too far for the hospitality industry, there are several ways to lower the economic, social and environmental impact of building by wisely choosing materials and energy solutions that follow the circular economy of cradle to cradle.

Equipment

As the challenges section included discussions about equipment and how to choose it, this section aims to address these challenges through identifying equipment options for the various areas of a hotel's rooms division and food and beverage departments by focusing on waste, energy and water examples.

When it comes to implementing sustainable strategies at the front office, the topic of the key card may be considered for the waste perspective. A report from the company Sustainable Cards, states that a typical 200-bedroom hotel in the United States goes through approximately 12,000 plastic key cards per year and these are added to the 1,300 ton plastic landfills (Nastu, 2009). A replacement option for plastic key cards are green key cards which exists in a variety of sustainable options but are ultimately made up of recycled PVC, paperboard, corn and/or wood. Another option for consideration is a mobile key card instead of handing over environmentally unfriendly plastic cards. A hotel may offer to transfer a digital code to a guest's smartphone with which he or she can enter the room. Mobile key is a relatively new form of accessing rooms and will be found mostly in recently constructed properties but new technology has also made it a viable option as an inexpensive retrofit.

In the restaurant, one may consider the use of linen as a sustainable action point in reference to the energy perspective. To meet the global demand of linen from cotton every year, 256 cubic kilometres of water is needed. This vast amount of water would be enough to provide every human on the planet with 120 litres of water per day. Even though only 1/40th of the world's agricultural area is used to farm cotton, a quarter of the pesticide consumption is allocated at cotton production (see also Chapters 14 and 15). Programs like the *Sustainable Cotton Project* are not only about reducing the amount of toxins that are used in production, but are able to increase the yield from an average of 210 kilograms per hectare of conventional production, to up to 285 kilograms with the initiative *Cleaner Cotton* (Virtuelles Wasser, 2017). Therefore, the first step should be to identify in which capacity linen is actually needed, within an F&B outlet. When a restaurant concept dictates linen, there are certified green linen alternatives on the market, which should be considered. In this regard, it depends on the structure, size of woven threads and the level of difficulty in cleaning. If linen is not to be given up on the table, reducing its use to napkins and sparing table cloths can be a cost saving and first approach for existing outlets.

In the kitchen, a heavily used appliance is the dishwasher and this is useful for the water perspective. When it comes to washing dishes, innovation has produced machines which can reuse water by making use of built-in water treatment unit where dishwashers can not only reuse water and use less chemicals but can also clean glasses and crockery in the same appliance. By reusing water on the same basis as car wash companies do, water waste can be dramatically reduced. Innovative companies are driving so-called energy recovery concepts. Exhaust air heat exchangers in combination with waste water heat exchangers build into dish-washing machines are now able to harvest the energy of the already heated (and paid for) waste water to quickly heat fresh water up to 42 degrees Celsius. With this technology, not only can the air quality in the stewarding department be greatly increased (with direct benefits for people's health and comfort) but furthermore operating costs can be reduced up to 24% per year (Ehrhardt, 2012).

There are many considerations to be made for equipment and the above are some examples of things to be taken into account. This broad scope of considerations is made more easily digestible through product specific standards and certification programs. A 2012 report from HVS sustainability solutions (Goldstein and Primlani, 2012) highlights some of these. They are summarised in Table 8.1.

Table 8.1: Taken in part from Goldstein and Primlani, 2012

Product-Specific Standards and Certification Programs		
Energy Star www.energystar.gov	U.S. Environmental Protection Agency	Voluntary governmental program that provides free benchmarking services to a variety of building types. Also rates appliances and provides resources for owners/operators.
Green Seal www.greenseal.org	Green Seal	Develops life-cycle based certification of products and services. Provides green building guidance for public housing facilities and environmental certification for hotels and lodging properties.
Green Tag www.ecospecifer.com.au	Ecospecifier	Database of vetted products in infrastructure, residential, commercial, industrial, and other construction. Subscription based service.
Greenguard www.greenguard.org	Greenguard Environmental Institute	Evaluates emissions from interior products and building materials.

The persistent theme in managing sustainability in equipment is the wish to reduce the amount used, to reuse what is possible and then recycle what is left. The combination of considerations leads to a decision that all people involved know has been thoughtfully reached so that the products can be used with good conscience.

Financing

As the challenges section included discussions about the higher than conventional initial costs as well as difficulties in accessing financing, this section aims identify options to address these challenges.

One such option is loans. According to Etrecia Van Dyk, Provincial Sales Manager at Ooba, South Africa's largest bond originator, a building loan is used to financially support the construction of a building on a piece of vacant land or to finance additions and renovations to an already existing property. When it comes to building loans, it's important to bear in mind that a portion of the approved loan amount is retained by the bank and the funds are advanced to the borrower in stages as progress payments during the construction period (Ooba, 2017). In recent years, loans specifically geared towards sustainable (building) initiatives have been developed. For example, Bridgeway Capital, an American firm that provides capital and business education to markets that will result in positive economic and social impact, has a Green Loans initiative. This initiative assists local building owners and developers with the implementation of sustainable building practices in order to create green buildings and achieve LEED (Leadership in Energy and Environmental Design) certification. These loans are flexible, long-term, and offer low rates (Bridgeway Capital, 2017).

One of the most effective and more popular strategies to encourage sustainable building is to stimulate the market through financial or structural incentives. *Structural incentives* work by encouraging developers to practice sustainable building through rewards such as additional density bonuses or expedited permitting processes. At low or no cost to the municipality, building green can be made a more attractive option to developers. *Financial incentives* are in the form of tax credits, fee reduction and waivers, low interest loans, revolving loan funds and grants to developers who propose and build sustainable buildings.

Technical assistance may be offered by many municipalities through allowing access to free planning or certification training and assistance, and this assistance may allow a developer who is unfamiliar with green building practices to build green. In some municipalities, developers who are LEED certified may be offered marketing assistance via signage, awards, websites, press releases, and other means as an incentive for developers to build according to sustainable standards (USGBC, 2017). For instance, Sustainable development bonuses in the City of Pittsburgh provide benefits for LEED certified buildings and include floor areas and maximum building heights exceeding base standards by up to 20% (Library Municode, 2017).

A third option is formed by sustainable, responsible and impact investing (SRI). SRI is an investment discipline that considers environmental, social and corporate governance criteria to generate long-term competitive financial returns and positive societal impact. Leading up to and including 2015, $8.72 trillion was invested according to SRI strategies in the United States alone. There are several motivations for SRI, including personal values, institutional missions, and the demands of clients. Sustainable investors aim for strong financial performance, but also believe that these investments should be used to contribute to advancements in social, environmental and governance practices. They may actively seek out investments such as community development loan funds or clean tech portfolios, that are likely to provide important societal and environmental benefits (USSIF, 2017).

Conclusion

In this chapter, we have discussed sustainability challenges concerning a hotel building with a focus on certification, materials and energy use, equipment and financing. In the introduction and in discussing sustainable solutions we have shown the new frontier of restorative building and bio-based materials. The best cases have shown that several ground-breaking measures are already implemented in hotels. Yet, some of the most innovative options may still be a bridge too far for the hotel industry, so here as a conclusion we wish to tie the discussion together by presenting an ideal image of a hotel that is not only trying to reduce its negative impact on the environment, but also aims at nullifying it by choosing for zero-emission. A zero-emission hotel is a property that generates as much energy on its own as it consumes. The way to go is to actively increase the generation of renewable energy through technology and decrease at the same time consumption by intelligently replacing, updating or eliminating out-dated energy consuming appliances or structures. The advantages of such a property are not only the sustainable overall balance with its positive effects on its surroundings and for the environment, but also, that it allows for a very stable energy cost prediction. When done correctly the heat and cooling be air-based, and the hotel will be powered by a hybrid solar system which generates electricity through sunlight and generates warm water, equipped with a short-term energy storage facility and a long-term phase change material, has double glazed windows and has a sun blocking curtain façade.

So, what would a zero-emission hotel look like? We assume that the property is planned as a medium sized inner-city business hotel in the 4-star category in an urbanized area with 70 rooms. The investors have laid out their projections through financing options and the positive exploitation of grants and benefits. It is paramount for the funding that the building itself could potentially be repurposed for other commercial use in case the hotel operation would default. The building will be built in order to facilitate a BREEAM-certificate and will be built with a bearing façade, centralized riser slots, a flat roof and the rooms will be formed by non-bearing but insulated walls. The insulation will be composed of mineral materials. Hardwood floors will be in used all the rooms. The developers have outlined that a wood pellet central heating system will be used in the basement to produce energy. The basement will also hold space for a water treatment plant in order to provide clean drinking water, as well as reduce the harmful waste by-products. The windows will be treated and double sided, in order to provide a lower vulnerability to UV-beams and temperature changes caused by weather outside the rooms. The bearing walls will be constructed out of a steel and concrete structure. The façade will not only be bearing but also equipped with a cooling system. Through this system hot and cold air will be pumped in order to regulate temperature changes. Via solar panels on the roof the electricity will be generated and the overproduction will be sent into the electricity supply system. The rooms will be equipped with green key card wall slots which activate lights and lamps in the room, motion sensors will automatically provide light, when needed. All lamps and lights will be LED-based with warm light characteristics of around 2,700 Kelvin. Finally, the equipment and fittings will be chosen based on their water saving qualities, energy saving qualities and waste reduction qualities.

The above is an attempt to tie the discussed concepts together. There may be many alternatives to creating such a property but the aim is to opt for the most sustainable solution.

References

Baunetz Wissen (2016) *Sustainable Building*. https://www.baunetzwissen.de/nachhaltig-bauen/fachwissen/baustoffe--teile/beton-1291381. Accessed 15 10 2017.

Bjurling, K., Weyzig, F. and Wong, S. (2008) *Improving the working conditions at Chinese natural stone companies, SL: SwedWatch and SOMO.* http://www.somo.nl/publications-en/Publication_2459. Accessed 28 June 2016.

Bridgeway Capital (2017) *Loans.* www.bridgewaycapital.org/loans/overview/. Accessed 15 October 2017.

CEC (2008) *Green Building in America: Opportunities and Challenges, Quebec.* /www3.cec.org/islandora/en/item/2335-green-building-in-north-america-opportunities-and-challenges-en.pdf. Accessed 15 October 2017.

Ehrhardt, W. (2012) *Perfekte Hygiene Trifft Nachhaltigkeit.* https://www.ahgz.de/archiv/perfekte-hygiene-trifft-nachhaltigkeit,200012197199.html. Accessed 23 November 2017.

Fowler, K. and Rauch, E. (2006) *Pacific Northwest National Laboratory: Sustainable Building Rating Systems Summary, USA.*www.pnl.gov/main/publications/external/technical_reports/PNNL-15858.pdf. Accessed 15 October 2017.

Goldstein, K and Primlani, R. (2012) *HVS Sustainability Services: Current Trends and Opportunities in Hotel Sustainability, Mineola.* https://www.hvs.com/content/3218.pdf. Accessed 23 November 2017.

Green hotelier (2009) *Waste Management.* www.greenhotelier.org/our-themes/waste-management/. Accessed 10 November 2017.

Holzpellets (n.d) *Energiekosten- und CO 2-Vergleich Pellets-Heizol-Erdgas,* https://www.holzpellets.net/service/energie-vergleichsrechner.php. Accessed 15 October 2017.

Hotel Energy Solutions (2011) *Analysis on Energy Use by European Hotels: Online Survey and Desk Research,* Madrid: Hotel Energy Solutions project publications.

ILO (2001) *Stopping forced labour – Global Report under the follow-up to the ILO Declaration on Fundamental Principles and Rights at Work,* Geneva: ILO.

ILO (2010) *Labour Conditions in Forestry in Indonesia,* Jakarta: ILO (International Labour Organization).

Jones, D. and Brischke, C. (eds.) (2017) *Performance of Bio-based Building Materials,* Duxfors: Woodhead Publishing.

Jong-Jin, K. and Rigdon, B. (1998) *Sustainable Architecture Module: Qualities, Use, and Examples of Sustainable Building Materials, Michigan.* http://www.umich.edu/~nppcpub/resources/compendia/ARCHpdfs/ARCHsbmIntro.pdf. Accessed 15 October 2017.

Lackman, T. and Bourdeau, M. (2008) *Fasken Martineau DuMoulin LLP: The Advantages of Building Green, Montreal.* http://www.fasken.com/files/Publication/564bddae-8a66-4203-ac10-72f069bd05aa/Presentation/PublicationAttachment/e673d22d-1ccc-4b8e-b90b-3155890acba7/Real_Estate_Bulletin_Sept2008.pdf. Accessed on 15 October 2017.

Library Municode (2017) *Pittsburg.* https://library.municode.com/pa/pittsburgh/codes/code_of_ordinances?nodeId=PIZOCO_TITNINEZOCO_ARTVIDEST_CH915ENPEST_915.04SUDEBO. Accessed 15 October 2017.

Mahendriyani, D. (2016) *What's the main challenge for Green Building development in Asia?* https://www.linkedin.com/pulse/whats-main-challenge-green-building-development-asia-mahendriyani. Accessed 15 10 2017.

Nakanishi, E. Y., Frías, M., Santos, S. F., Rodrigues, M. S., Vigil de la Villa, R., Rodriguez, O. and Junior, H. S. (2016) Investigating the possible usage of elephant grass ash to manufacture the eco-friendly binary cement', *Journal of Cleaner Production*, **116**(Supplement C), 236–243. http://doi.org/https://doi.org/10.1016/j.jclepro.2015.12.113.

Nastu, P. (2009) *Green Hotel Key Card Offerings*. https://www.environmentalleader.com/2009/02/green-hotel-key-card-offerings/. Accessed 23 November 2017.

Ng, W. Y., and Chau, C. K. (2015) New Life of the building materials - recycle, reuse and recovery, *Energy Procedia*, **75**(Supplement C), 2884–2891. http://doi.org/https://doi.org/10.1016/j.egypro.2015.07.581.

Ooba (2017) *Ins and Outs of Building Loans*. https://www.ooba.co.za/news-archive/ins-and-outs-building-loans. Accessed 15 October 2017.

PACE (n.d.) *The Hilton Los Angeles/Universal City completes $7 million upgrade*. http://pace.lacounty.gov/pdf/Hilton_Case_Study.pdf. Accessed on 15 October 2017.

Podewils, C. (2015) *Sonnenergie wird in vielen Teilen der Welt gunstigste stromquelle*. https://www.agora-energiewende.de/de/presse/agoranews/news-detail/news/sonnenergie-wird-in-vielen-teilen-der-welt-guenstigste-stromquelle/). Accessed 15 October 2017.

Sviatlana, A. (2011) *Valuation and Management of Hotel Property: Swedish Experience*. http://www.diva-portal.org/smash/get/diva2:500982/fulltext01.pdf. Accessed 23 November 2017.

Tuppen, H. (2013) *Water Manageent and Responsibilty in Hotels*. www.greenhotelier.org/know-how-guides/water-management-and-responsibility-in-hotels/. Accessed 5 Jnauary 2018.

USGBC (2017) *Good to Know Green Incentive Strategies*. https://www.usgbc.org/articles/good-know-green-building-incentive-strategies-0. Accessed 15 October 2017.

USSIF (2017) *SRI Basics*. http://www.ussif.org/sribasics. Accessed 15 October 2017.

Virtuelles Wasser (2017) *Baumwolle*. http://virtuelles-wasser.de/baumwolle.html. Accessed 23 November 2017.

Voss, K. and Bernard, S. (2015) *Energieverbrauch und Energieeffizienz in der Hotellerie, hotel+ energie*. https://www.hotelbau.de/download/downloadarchiv/hotel+energie2015.pdf. Accessed 20 March 2018.

Wilson, J.Q. and Kelling, G.L. (1982) Broken Windows: The police and neighborhood safety, *The Atlantic*. https://www.theatlantic.com/magazine/archive/1982/03/broken-windows/304465/. Accessed 21 October 2017.

8

Part III: Purchasing

Introduction

Elena Cavagnaro

The third quadrant of the Sustainable Hospitality Value Chain is dedicated to purchasing. In the broadest sense purchasing does not only refer to buying those goods and services that are needed to provide guests with a hospitable experience. It also encompasses all those activities for which an organisation receives an invoice, thus including advertising contracts and hiring temporary staff. While traditionally purchasing aims at getting external resources at the most favourable economic conditions, sustainable purchasing aims at generating social and environmental value while contributing to the financial profitability of the organisation.

The power of purchasing in the transition of the hospitality and tourism industry toward sustainability cannot be underestimated. In fact, sustainable value creation depends not only on how an organisation is internally organised (a subject that will be addressed in the next part of this book), but as also on how a business relates to other businesses all along its supply chain, as Ko Koens and Harry Reinders show in their chapter. Moreover, purchasing departments handle a considerable amount of money. The impact that they can generate by sourcing sustainably is therefore also huge. To better understand what we are trying to say, think about the amount of money that you spend each month on groceries. Then add the costs for using your mobile phone, your travelling expenses, costs for energy and water – in short all the expenses for which you get a bill. Now compare this amount to what you donate to charities. Even if you are a very generous individual, your donations are probably vastly inferior to the amount of money that you spend on buying goods and services. Imagine now that when buying you chose organic food, fair trade goods, sustainable energy and the like. The positive impact that you then cause all along the chain is much higher than if you buy traditionally sourced goods and services, considering only their price. A similar reasoning can be made for all organisations, including hotels and restaurants, and this why it is important to consider purchasing in hospitality and tourism.

Purchasing may occur locally or (inter)nationally. In the chapter by Sarah Seidel and Elena Cavagnaro, the opportunities and challenges of purchasing locally are discussed. They argue that, even though the term 'local' is still contested, there is enough evidence to suggest that, if properly managed, buying locally contributes to creating value on all three dimensions of sustainability. Seidel and Cavagnaro also show that the hospitality industry is in the best possible position to create value by buying locally, because of the wide range of products and services that they need.

In their chapter on international purchasing, Ko Koens and Harry Reinders stress that sustainable purchasing not only goes beyond the economic paradigm from which traditionally managers operate, but goes further than environmentally sustainable (or 'green') purchasing. Sustainable purchasing should also include social and ethical considerations, while responsibility should be extended to suppliers all along the supply chain. This is a daunting task, and even more so in international purchasing where chains are usually complex and blurred. To address these challenges Koens and Reinders propose a relational approach to international purchasing in which trustworthy business relations are created with all parties involved.

Even when bought locally, goods have to be transported. Therefore the third chapter of this part is dedicated to the sustainable transport of goods. In this chapter Jörn Fricke discusses economic, social and environmental challenges and shows how transport can help achieving efficiency, equity and environmentally sound development. In line with Koens and Reinders' conclusion, Fricke states that coordination between all the private and public stakeholders involved is necessary to achieve sustainability in transport and purchasing.

9 Purchasing Local for Sustainable Development

— and improved hospitality experiences

Sarah Seidel and Elena Cavagnaro

Learning goals

This chapter will help readers to understand and critically reflect on the benefits and challenges of purchasing locally on the three dimensions of sustainability. After reading this chapter, readers will have the ability to:

1 Understand the term local, its ambiguity and its connection to sustainability;

2 Understand the social, economic and environmental benefits of local purchase;

3 Be aware of the importance of local purchasing to enhance sustainability, yet, be able to reflect that buying local does not automatically mean being sustainable;

4 Know different movements and trends supporting a more sustainable hospitality industry by purchasing local goods.

Introduction

You might have heard the famous slogan "think global, act local" already. The thought behind this slogan is simple: the idea is that you should nurture a 'care for all' mentality and think of all humans and of the Earth itself (Cavagnaro and Curiel, 2012), while the actions that you take need to be local because these local steps can be of benefit to all of us. If you research that matter or the issue of sustainability further, you will find more slogans that are related to and inspired by the original slogan, such as "think global, buy local" or "think global, eat local" (Flint, 2004). So, apparently people believe that by eating and buying local they can not only generate significant benefits for their local surrounding and the direct stakeholders, but also contribute to a more sustainable society or world. This chapter is going to analyse these ideas further and show that – while the general idea is true – the matter is a bit more complicated than these statements seem to imply. In general, buying and consuming local can indeed be a significant contributor on all three sustainability dimensions. However, these benefits are seldom immediate and should therefore be sought after by design.

Sustainable purchasing is defined as creating sustainable value. Creating sustainable value is defined as assessing sustainability on the "return that is created with a resource" (Manzhynski *et al.*, 2015: 638) or with several resources. As a way to assess the sustainability impact of human activities, the concept of value creation breaks with traditional assessments practices that largely focus on the burden created, such as measuring environmental damage. In general, in recent years it has been argued that resources should be considered as rare and that not using a resource or using less of it should be considered as the most sustainable strategy (Cavagnaro and Curiel, 2012). In other words, and combining both perspectives, resources should be used so that burdens are minimized and value creation is maximized on the economic, social and environmental dimension of sustainability. Considering this point, local purchasing is linked to four of the most significant burdens that the hospitality industry often brings with it: CO_2 emissions either due to transport or other energy use, waste, economic leakage and social impacts at a destination of guests and tourists from outside the community. The relationship between these four potential burdens is discussed in the following section on sustainability challenges. But first, let us have a look at the general idea of why local purchasing is considered to be more sustainable.

To elaborate on the benefits of local purchasing on the economic, environmental and social dimension of sustainability in more detail, this chapter uses the example of local food. Local food is chosen as an example because of two main reasons. First, food is an essential component of hospitality, and therefore sustainable food procurement may play a significant role in the transition of the hospitality industry to a more sustainable stance. Second, as most hospitality settings offer food to their guests, the triple bottom line benefits of offering local food may be reaped by a high number of hospitality businesses. Yet which exactly are these benefits?

Let us consider first the impact of local food purchasing on the economic dimension of sustainability. The amount of money spent by tourists on food, and thus potentially on local food, is quite considerable. It has, for example, been found that tourists spend up to one third of their budget on food and food-related products (Hall and Sharples, 2003; Skuras and Dimara, 2005; Telfer and Wall, 2000). This means that tourists bring money from outside to a region; that this money is spent in the region and that it can therewith support the local economy. Moreover, tourists' spending gives a particular boost to the local economy due to the so-called tourism multiplier effect. The multiplier effect is defined as the rise in final income emerging from any new injection of expenditure (Page and Connell, 2014). It relies on the assumption that the money spent by the tourists can be spent again. To exemplify: if a tourist pays for their stay at the hotel, the hotel then uses the money to pay their staff (who then have an income that they can potentially spend on something else) and their suppliers. Considering that hospitality is labour intensive and supposing that jobs are sourced locally, it is easy to see how hospitality may support a broad section of the community economically (Minta, 2015; Shuman, 1998, Hjalager and Johansen, 2013). On a similar line, if the food supplier is local, another member of the community (in this case even one who is usually not involved in the tourism sector) will receive financial benefits from the hotel operations. Hence, a particular advantage of the tourism multiplier effect is that it benefits parties that may otherwise have no relationship with the hospitality industry. These parties may be local food suppliers, as in the example, but also suppliers of services, such as cleaning, and people employed in primary industries such as farmers and fisheries (Hjalager and Johansen, 2013).

An additional economic benefit of local food is the (perceived) added value of a food product if it is local. Local food is often considered to be fresher and healthier than other food products. Tourists are also often quite keen on experiencing the authentic destination (Yeoman, 2006). Hence, by offering local food the perceived value of the whole tourism experience increases and therefore a guest might be willing to spend more on it and may appreciate it more.

Alongside economic benefits, the integration of local food products in the hospitality and tourism offer also brings several social benefits to the community (Hall and Gössling, 2013; Long, 2004). An important benefit is that locals become more visible to the guests of the hospitality providers and therefore it may become easier for tourists to relate to locals. Local food offered in hospitality businesses can foster the dialogue and the connection between locals and tourists. Local dishes, recipes, beverages and eating habits represent the local culture. Therefore, while local people might derive pride and feel recognised when tourists are interested in the local culture, tourists are attracted by the authenticity of the offer and come to appreciate the hospitableness of the locals who are willing to share their culture with them (Hall and Gössling, 2013; Minta, 2015).

For the hospitality industry, integrating local food and recipes into their products means also taking advantage of a unique opportunity to provide special experiences to their guests. Upholding the local cuisine may become a means for hospitality providers to differentiate themselves from competitors located in other regions. Simultaneously, they support and benefit the local community by preserving local food traditions or preparation methods (Everett and Aitchison, 2008; Long, 2004). While this might seem like a small step, it might be of real importance and value to locals, particularly when recipes and traditional ways of food preparation are part of a family heritage and have personal significance. Just imagine if your favourite apple pie, prepared according to the recipe of your grandmother is suddenly sold at local cafes (Abate, 2008).

On the environmental dimension, choosing local food will in many cases have significant advantages. Let us start with the landscape. Many food products such as fruits and vegetables termed 'local' grow naturally in the landscape and are able to grow under the given climate and geological conditions. This means that no or less interventions in the landscape are needed to grow these crops, and that, in certain cases, local crop varieties are preserved. Moreover, produce that traditionally grows in a specific region often needs less energy, fewer pesticides or chemicals to grow than non-indigenous crops. Here, however, it is important to consider each crop separately as this claim is often, but not always, true. Some fruits or vegetables, such as tomatoes in Northern Europe, are grown in regions where they do not fit originally and therefore need extra pesticides or energy such as heated green-houses. A point that is often not considered when mentioning the environmental benefits of local food is the preservation of farmland in the middle of the current increase of urban development and therewith the preservation of more open natural spaces, which need fewer artificial agricultural adaptions than non-local plants might need (Abate, 2008). Local food can indirectly protect rural development, help preserve the existing biodiversity and natural habitats, and also the original wildlife (including bees), which in turn again might contribute to the success of the local harvest.

Though the benefits of a local food offer are manifold, they usually can only be reaped by design. There are challenges that have to be considered and addressed so that purchasing local can deliver on its promise to create value on the economic, social and environmental dimensions of sustainability. The next section is dedicated to these challenges, and is followed by best cases. Then tools to address the challenges will be presented and a short conclusion will close this chapter.

Main sustainability challenges

Following the general structure of the book, in this section sustainability challenges related to purchasing are discussed in the context of local purchasing. Chapter 10 on international purchasing by Ko Koens and Harry Reinders also discusses some of these impacts; therefore, if you wish to know more, please have a look at this chapter as well. The section starts with the challenge of the paradigm shift from traditional purchasing to sustainable purchasing. Then negative impacts, such as CO_2 and waste, are discussed, followed by a discussion of the challenges related to defining the term 'local' in local purchasing. Last but not least, the improper promotion as 'local' of products that are not 'local' is considered.

Traditional purchasing and sustainable purchasing in hospitality

Sustainable purchasing represents a paradigm shift from traditional purchasing. To understand this claim, we need first to briefly define purchasing and its functions. According to Weele (2010), the purchasing process consists of several activities. First of all, purchasing does not only refer to buying materials, goods or services, but it also covers all those activities for which the company receives an invoice. Therefore, advertising contracts, counter trade agreements or hiring of temporary staff can also be considered as purchasing. Consequently, purchasing is not confined to the purchasing department but involves several other departments such as marketing (Weele, 2010). In general, management books and also Porters' Value Chain will insist that purchasing should be as efficient as possible, where efficiency is defined as reducing the costs and obtaining the highest (economic) value for the money spent (Oehler and Buer, 2017).

To achieve efficiency and high economic returns, procurement in hospitality businesses is often focussed and structured. For example, quite often hotels, and in particularly hotel chains, enlarge their power as buyer by concentrated buying (e.g. ordering the same goods in a high quantity for several hotels) which usually lowers the prices of the goods acquired. In addition, to save time and keep the number of suppliers for different products low, hotels often buy their goods from contractors instead of from smaller suppliers (Oehler and Buer, 2017). Hence, the traditional view on purchasing is focussed on keeping the financial costs of the products and the procurement process low.

However, only considering the economic return is not sufficient when talking about sustainable purchasing, because social and environmental return should also be considered. Let us go through some concrete examples by looking at the different steps of purchasing. First of all, during the process of determining specifications, the hospitality business that wishes to purchase sustainably should not only look what kind of products are needed but also if there are alternatives with a higher sustainable value. Concerning the choice of the supplier, Stead and Stead (2004) state that companies that follow the goal of sustainable purchase practices require sustainability-based supplier relationships. Therefore, the hospitality business would need to include the integration of sustainability criteria in their purchase decisions and determine which suppliers meet these criteria or even require suppliers to fulfil these criteria in the first place before contracting takes place (Stead and Stead, 2004). Hence, if you consider the purchasing process as a sustainable purchasing process, the hospitality business has more responsibility than just considering its own financial return. It should not only consider social and environmental return, but it should also take responsibility all along the supply chain, starting with the actions towards sustainable value created by their suppliers. It is enough to look at most hotel management books and consider the operations of most hotels, to see that this is not a common thought in the hospitality industry. Sustainable purchasing represents therefore a paradigm shift compared to business as usual.

Transport and waste management in the purchasing process

Transportation of tourists, day-trippers and in general the guests of the hospitality providers is discussed in Chapter 3 by Matthias Olthaar. However, transportation is also an issue in purchasing. Jauhari (2014) stated that transportation is required to provide hotels with the products that they need to operate successfully. The transport needs differ from hotel to hotel depending, among other things, on the offered products and services (such as drinks, food and laundry services) and on whether services are catered for in-house or outsourced to an external company. Transportation services for guests from the hotel to another place, such as transfer services to the airport or the city centre, might also be included in the offer (see Chapter 3 for a discussion).

To operate successfully hotels need to purchase quite a lot of different products and services. These ranges from interior decoration to food; from room amenities to hardware; from services for the hotel (e.g. craftsmen) to services for the guest (e.g. a tour guide for an excursion or the musician in a bar). Transportation is required for most if not all the needed products and services. Therefore, as a general rule it could be stated that the closer the purchased good or service is to the premises of the hospitality buyer, the shorter is the transportation chain and the less CO_2 is emitted. In other words, buying 'local' is considered to minimize negative environmental impacts of transportation. Yet, there is no consensus in the literature on how 'local' should be understood. The definition that is most used refers to the range from which a certain product or service should be sourced. Yet, even in this case authors disagree. For instance, Nabhan (2002) defined a range of 200 miles (around 320 kms) of the organisation's surrounding as local purchasing. Pretty and Lang (2005) and Flint (2004), however, defined local purchasing with a purchasing/delivery distance of 12 to 30 miles, that is around 20 to 50 kms. Of course the environmental impact of transporting goods to a hotel from 300 or from 30 kms may be significantly different. To avoid such discussions, other authors, such as Devine (2004), proposed a different definition by referring to the number of daily round-trip drives.

To dig deeper in the impact of transportation, let us go back to the example of local foods. One of the most important concepts concerning local food and its contribution particularly to the environmental dimension of sustainability is the concept of food miles. You might have heard the term in relation to CO_2 miles, the miles that you travel when you go on holiday. However, your food travels too, and in some cases significantly. Just check in any supermarket and you will find fruits from all over the world. Food miles specifically refer to the distance food is transported from the point of production until it reaches the customer (Pretty and Lang, 2005). Transport usually equals negative impact on the natural environment (see for further explanation Chapters 3 and 10). So, as stated above, it is not only the tourist that is travelling but, in many instances, also the food. Sometimes the food miles take bizarre forms, such as in the famous example of crabs from the European North Sea. Many of the shrimps from the German North Sea that you can buy a couple of hundred kilometres away in mid-Germany are not just caught in the Northern part of Germany and then transported a few hundred kilometres to areas not along the coast – they are first shipped to Algeria for shelling, then shipped back and then sold to the areas not along the coast. Hence, before they reach the plate these shrimps have travelled a couple of thousands of kilometres.

If you carefully check the transport chains of a lot of food products that you can buy in your supermarket, you will notice that your daily food has travelled enormous distances. In general, it is accepted that the distance travelled by food travel has increased dramatically due to globalisation. Globalisation shifted the focus of food supply to fewer and larger districts where costs are lower, taking advantage of the possibility to transport goods on longer distances quickly, and of changes in customer habits such as buying more packaged food and buying at supermarkets instead of local markets (Hall and Gössling, 2013). These patterns seemingly work against local purchasing.

The second point that we wish to address in the context of sustainable purchasing and specifically local purchasing is waste management (Sloan *et al.*, 2015). It might sound a bit odd to call waste management an important factor in purchasing. However, products that are ordered and delivered to a hotel will be packaged, and packaging often depends on the way they are transported and/or the distance they travel. When the products are used, the packaging is usually wasted. Packaging, of course, is not the only form of waste a hotel produces. Along with packaging, Lin-Heng *et al.* (2010) identify hotels 'solid waste as bottles, cans, food scraps, oils and fat, garden waste, paper, old furniture and equipment. Looking specifically at hotels' on-site restaurants, the main waste accrues due to food, packaging and consumed energy, as is also discussed in Chapter 15.

To highlight the relationship between sustainable purchasing and waste management (and, consequently, transport and energy use), we would like to take as an example something that you will find on every menu of a restaurant: fish. Fish is usually flown in from all over the world. The European Union has a self-sufficiency – that is the rate to which internal supply can cover local demand – of 55%, so almost every second fish needs to be imported from outside the EU to cover demand (Kleinjans and Vardakoulias, 2017). This means the fish needs to be transported. As fish tends to deteriorate rather quickly, it is usually flown in by plane, which causes a lot of CO_2 emissions. In addition to that, it needs to be cooled, which uses a lot of energy. Last but not least, it will need to be packaged carefully. Packaging may be needed several times, such as when fish is divided into smaller quantities after being imported into the country but before delivery to the hotel. Most packaging involves the use of plastic to keep the fish unspoiled. The first point that we wish to make here is that, while packaging may prevent food spoilage and thus waste, it becomes waste when the packaged food is used.

Fish is here only considered as an example of a product that needs special (plastic) packaging to keep it unspoiled and that is often repackaged during the delivery chain. The second point to make is that food bought locally will at least need less repackaging than non-local food. Therefore buying local may contribute to lowering waste in the production cycle and to reducing the amount of resources used. Consequently, more value is created per resource. Moreover, some food-stuffs, such as fruits, tend not to be packaged in plastic but in reusable boxes when they only travel short distances. By choosing local food in reusable packaging,

9

hotels do not only contribute to reducing waste in the chain but may also save costs for waste disposal (Sloan *et al.*, 2015). The use of local food is therefore seen as a possible way to redress some major negative environmental impacts of hotel operation, while simultaneously reducing costs. However, understanding what is, and how to manage, local food so that these issues are addressed without creating new ones, is again another challenge, as is shown below.

Finding the 'local' in local purchasing and related issues

In discussing food transportation above it has already be noticed that there is no consensus on what qualifies as 'local'. Indeed, while the word 'local' is quite commonly used – and in fact you have already read quite a few pages on *local* purchasing – its exact meaning is less well understood, in general and in the context of purchasing in particular. The terms 'national' and 'international' purchasing are rather clear, as they refer respectively to buying within and outside of the country. However, how can we exactly determine what is 'local'? Should it be determined using the number of kilometres as in the definitions reported in the sub-section above? Should it be bound to a region with similar geographical and/ or cultural characteristics, in which case the size of regions and therefore the term local would vary significantly? Can a product be bought from a neighbouring country and still be considered local? What if a local grown product is not locally processed? Several products are the results of different basic ingredients or the combination of several raw materials – think of a food dish or a washing machine. Would they qualify as 'local' only if all components are locally sourced and processed (Touzard *et al.*, 2016)? Finally, an essential part of the hospitality business are the guests, but if the guests are not able to recognise a local product as local, can you still call it local?

To make the definition issue even more complicated, one might argue that buying local is a concept that is not up to date anymore, because in a globalised society the whole world is our 'region'. On the other side, other people (and even some political parties) claim that, in a globalised world, regions are more important than nations, and that therefore buying in the region and producing in the region should be enhanced even at the expense of the nation's socio-economic development.

Finally, one could argue that buying local may negatively affects regions, whose economies rely on export to other countries. This argument wins strength if one considers that several of these regions were former colonies and that their economies were designed by the colonial power to serve the needs of its own economy. Typical examples are cocoa and coffee: both are grown in specific areas in Africa and South America but are mainly processed, traded and consumed in northern countries. Cocoa and coffee farmers are dependent on this trade for their survival. What if western consumers decided to 'go local' and forego the pleasure of cocoa and coffee? This example may be farfetched, but it is important to consider that several of the products used in hotels, including not only food but also for example cotton and chinaware, are in the rule not 'local' (Vermeulen and Ras, 2006; see also Chapter 10).

As discussed above, people tend to identify products as local if they see that these are farmed or produced in the surrounding area. Particularly local fruit and vegetables can often be easily spotted in the landscape around a hospitality business (Long, 2004). As explained before, these products might even be the main reason for some kinds of guests, namely food tourists, to come to the region. However, whether you think of vineyards, the blossom time of fruit trees or the fisherman selling fresh fish at the harbour: all of these have in common that they are seasonal. Indeed, particularly if you think of fruit and vegetables, most of them can only be purchased regionally during a limited seasonal period. To take an example: in northern Europe, strawberries have an extremely limited season that usually starts in May and ends in July. Yet, the success and length of the harvesting season is unpredictable because it is heavily dependent on the weather conditions and a sudden change in weather could quickly end or extend it. If now a restaurant or hotel chooses to offer strawberries on its menu, it can neither calculate properly the available quantities (and therefore also the purchasing costs), nor the timeframe in which the strawberries are locally available. Last but not least, such a restaurant would need to change the menu quite often. While nowadays restaurants generally do have an additional card to take advantage of seasonal products, usually hotels will not ban strawberries and other seasonal produce from the menu during the off-season. The consequences of going fully local and thus seasonal, are such that restaurants are often not willing to go the full way, and adapt their menus largely or even completely to correspond to seasonality. The guests play a significant role here as well, as often they are not able to distinguish between seasonal and non-seasonal products, and even more often do not consider this issue at all. Think about yourself, how often have you considered, when ordering a meal, whether the ingredients were seasonal? Hence, while seasonal regional food products in total might have the biggest added value on all three sustainability dimensions, their seasonality represents a challenge for hospitality providers.

Apart from the consequences of seasonality, there is another issue related to the guests' perspective that seems to be often forgotten when considering local food: the eating habits and preferences of people. The point that we wish to make here is not only that guests might not consider seasonality when ordering food at a restaurant, but also that their choices will be steered by their preferences. To sum it up simply: not every (possible) local food product has the potential to be a favourite among guests and, more strongly, guests might prefer food that is not from the region at all.

Starting with the first possibility, let us consider as an example chicken consumption in Western Europe. If there is chicken on the menu card of a restaurant, in Western Europe you will most likely find chicken breast or chicken leg. In many restaurants there will even be only chicken breast as this is supposed to be the best part of the chicken. Now, a chicken consists of more parts then just the breast, hence, quite often the whole chicken is not used and part of the chicken might be wasted (thus contributing to the waste problem addressed in the sub-section above). Moreover, these restaurants need a consistent all year around provision of large quantities of chicken, which in turn means that either one supplier has the capacity to deliver the needed quantities or several suppliers in the region should be contracted. Both options have drawbacks, in terms of local and sustainable purchasing. Finding a regional supplier for large quantities of goods may in fact not be possible, while contracting to a larger number of local suppliers implies more transport; more time spent in communication, negotiations and aligning delivery; and facing the risk of scarcity if several small suppliers cannot provide in moments of higher demand. Similar difficulties arise for other products and also for the supply of services, such as contracting local craftsmen, who tend to be organised in independent, small-sized businesses and might be overwhelmed by the amount of work, and be also more expensive than larger businesses.

Looking at the second possibility, guests might have preferences for products that cannot be produced locally at all. This is particularly tricky for guests that come from a different culture. In the Netherlands and Northwest Germany, green cabbage, prepared in different regions according to the regional traditions but usually served with potatoes and pork, is clearly a favoured dish among locals. However, tourists from China (one of the fastest growing tourist segments in the region) or guests with a Muslim background will not eat it. At the same time, restaurants like the Avocaderia in New York, proudly claiming to be the world's first avocado bar, attract masses of tourists and locals, while it is widely known that avocado trees are not found in the United States – or, in fact, basically in any of the places where you can now find avocado restaurants or bars. When people go out to eat, they will often select according to the food they prefer and not necessarily consider if the products served are local. Lastly, even if guests consider a product to be local or better for the environment, on a holiday trip or a nice evening out they might rather focus on having a good time instead of considering what is best for them or for everybody else. There might be exceptions, such as day-trippers visiting a farm café to eat homemade apple pie and to support the farmers, or guest selecting a local dish they believe to be fresh and healthy. However, generally speaking, and though times are changing (Cavagnaro *et al.*, 2018), guests are driven by hedonic more than normative values when travelling, and may need a bit of nudging before choosing for local, as we will see below.

Promoting and selling products as local that are not

Often goods, craft and food are promoted as local in order to attract those customers that are looking for an authentic experience. Unfortunately, as with many trends, the word 'local' is easily abused, to promote as 'local' products that are not locally grown or produced. As it has been explained above, the term local is rather unspecific and there is no agreed upon definition of it. Therefore, in good faith, vendors may consider what they sell as 'local', while people in less good faith may easily refer to the confusion around the term to cover their intentions. To complicate the issue even more, 'local' is not a protected term and, therefore, it is very difficult to reveal fraud. It is no surprise that several studies, particularly from the United States, have shown that in many restaurants promoting local food, the proportion of ingredients that are grown, processed and then consumed locally (and are thus truly local) are far lower than stated. There are quite a few studies which support this claim. The article by food critic and investigative reporter Laura Reiley of *Tampa Bay Times* gained quite a bit of attention, because she listed the restaurants by name and elaborated each false claim in detail (Reilly, 2016). While one could point to the restaurateurs as being the culprit, Laura Reiley offers a differentiated view. She notes that, while sometimes indeed hospitality providers do claim incorrectly that they use local food, purely for profit, many do so because they have an incorrect understanding of such terms as 'farm to table' (which is elaborated further below); are not aware of who their actual provider is, because they deal with contractors and intermediaries; or are simply not able to deal with small scale farms and therefore change back to a larger distributor for efficiency's sake. Offering 'local' food therefore is less straightforward that it may seem, and needs careful consideration of all these challenges before being implemented. As the best cases show, though, this is not an impossible task.

Best cases

9

Case 9.1: Fogo Island Inn

The Fogo Island Inn situated in Canada is a multiple award-winning hotel – not only for its stance on sustainability but mainly for its uniqueness and guest services. The hotel is situated on Fogo, an island measuring 35 kms East-West and 24 kms North-South with fewer than 2500 inhabitants. The Fogo Island Inn decided to have a clear focus on purchasing local with the general purpose of leaving 'a gentle footprint'. *Local* in their definition is quite simple: everything that the island itself has to offer and, if a product is not available on the island, it will be bought from the nearest province on the mainland, Newfoundland and Labrador. In addition, local acquisition for them means also using commodities available for free such as collecting rain water for toilets and laundry, or solar panels to collect energy for hot water supply. Last but not least, the personnel are locals and each stay at the hotel includes a half-a-day guided orientation tour with a so-called community host, 'a livelong Fogo islander'.

There are several ideas behind this. First and foremost, the owners state that this is just what Fogo Island and the Fogo Island Inn are and stand for. They then add two rather simply motives from a business point of view: on the one hand the Fogo Island Inn, situated as it is in a small community limited by the size of the island, recognises the need to restrict its use of resources to protect the unspoiled nature which attracts the guests; and on the other hand the Inn wants to use the local products as a special gift to their guests.

Part of this gift is the food at the Fogo Island Inn. The food served to the guests in the restaurant, including seasonal grown vegetables and fresh seafood, is locally sourced with the complete production-process taking place on the island. The production and transportation chain are thus very short. The Fogo Island Inn also recognises the social-cultural importance of food and, therefore, the dishes are prepared according to local recipes, which is also communicated to the guests.

Last but not least, all the purchasing processes (purchasing as defined as everything which is paid for and not just goods directly used in production) are recorded for the Shorefast label. You might not have heard of this label, but the idea behind it is incredibly simple. On every food package you find a nutrition label, which tells you exactly how many calories and what ingredients you find in the food. The Shorefast is an 'Economic Nutrition Label', which tells the customer where the money spent goes and how much stays in the community. By using this label, the Fogo Island Inn recognises the importance of enhancing the socio-economic development of the community and the role that the multiplier effect can play in the process. The Shorefast label of the Fogo Island Inn, as published on their website, shows that two thirds of the economic benefits stay on the island while a total of over 90% stays in Canada.

Source: Fogo Island Inn (n.d.)

Case 9.2: Healthy Kansas Hospitals

With the idea of 'Keeping it Fresh and Local', Healthy Kansas Hospitals is one of the many 'Farm to Institution' programs. The aim of this program is to increase the cooperation and supply from small to medium-sized local food providers to an organisation. In this case, the organisation involved is not a hotel but a hospital. Hospitals need food for their patients, their employees and guests, and usually feature a canteen or cafeteria. From the perspective of a health care institution, an additional benefit of offering local food is that, as Healthy Kansas Hospitals also point out, local food is supposed to be more flavourful and more nutritious than food imported over longer distances. Therefore, offering local food may help the patients to recover sooner and, on the long run, may nudge patients, employees and guests into changing their eating habits and consuming more local food.

Healthy Kansas Hospitals offer support and share specific actions that can be implemented to support the integration of local food. One of these actions is developing community gardens on the grounds of the hospitals. Hence, in the green zones around the hospitals' buildings local food can be produced and patients who are able to, and employees who are willing to, may get directly involved in tending the gardens. By exposing people to the challenge and satisfaction of growing food, their awareness and knowledge may be educated increased in the process. At the same time, the gardens add beauty and green spaces to the often rather sterile atmosphere of the hospitals. The closeness of the hospital and the farming grounds might also stimulate more dialogue and create a sense of ownership and community, which might blossom into further business relationships.

Last but not least, sharing with people knowledge about vegetable gardens may be a way to address malnutrition, a serious issue not only in developing countries but also in developed ones, particularly among lower income or less educated groups. In fact malnutrition has been recognised as a serious threat to the health of United States citizens. Former first lady Michelle Obama has been a spokesperson for programmes to ensure a healthier eating culture in the United States particularly for youngsters. In this context, it is not surprising that one of the foci of Healthy Kansas Hospitals is to educate on the benefits of fresh local food and to make it accessible. Therefore, while Healthy Kansas Hospitals mentions the benefits of locally grown food on all three sustainability dimensions, it highlights its aim to educate on healthy nutrition and the importance of accessible healthy food for the wellbeing of the community. On the same line, another initiative suggested by Healthy Kansas Hospitals is the establishment of hospital-based food shelves to provide particularly low-income groups or people with specific nutritional needs with fresh local food (KHA, n.d.).

Although this best case regards hospitals, some of the initiatives there deployed – such as tending own gardens – may be easily transferred to a hospitality environment.

Tools to address the challenges

In this section we first consider the economic, environmental and social benefits of local food. Then we share some ways to address the challenges identified above.

Trends in local (food) purchasing in hospitality

One of the challenges that impede reaping the full sustainability benefits of local food is, as it has been shown above, the complexity of handling the chain and the need for guidance on how to implement local purchasing. As a first answer to this challenge, the social movement of farm-to-table (sometimes also called farm-to-fork, farm-to-plate or, in relation to schools, farm-to-school) should be mentioned. This movement promotes serving local food at restaurants, cafes, school cafeterias and all other organisations serving food. It focuses on benefitting locals and on closing the circle of consumption. Therefore, they recommend that direct acquisitions so that, as the name implies, the food may end up fresh from the field on the plate without time-consuming further distribution stages. The movement may be understood as community support for local agriculture, which often suffers as prices for agricultural products decline to an extent that only large farming operations can sustain themselves. While benefitting local producers, the end consumers also profit from the farm-to-table approach because they enjoy fresher and healthier (see the case on Healthy Kansas Hospitals) food and know exactly where their food is coming from.

While the term farm-to-plate is quite catchy, it does not necessarily only refer to businesses of the primary industry such as farms, fisheries or ranches. It may also refer to secondary businesses like breweries, wineries, cheese dairies and bakeries. Therefore, the term 'local' might not be appropriate according to the most strict definition, yet the general concept of supporting local farms/firms, serving fresh and healthy food, knowing where the food is coming from and economically benefitting other businesses of the region is still upheld.

A key aim of the farm-to-table movement is increasing awareness of local food and of the importance of knowing where the food is coming from. Therefore, farm-to-table is often framed as the opposite to fast food, where food needs to be cheap, ready to eat while the ingredients' origins and their production process are often unknown. In this context it is unsurprising that the farm-to-plate movement also encourages the growth of own food, so that for example a school, a restaurant or a café may grown food in its garden that is then offered to pupils or guests. The catch phrase "knowing where your food is coming from" is an important motto of the movement.

The farm-to-table movement has become a trend, and this is mostly due to changing social attitudes. More and more people want to support their own community, want to know where their food is coming from and are concerned with environmental sustainability and their own well-being. Increased social attention to climate change and to the link with long transport chains, encourage people not only to buy local, but also to choose seasonal food. Indeed, in most European countries you will be able to recognise this trend in many supermarkets and wet markets where the term 'local' and 'seasonal' food is used as a promotion tool. Increasingly, guests expect that also hospitality businesses catch on this trend (Cavagnaro *et al.*, 2018). Therefore by offering local and seasonal produce hotels and restaurants may enhance their customer satisfaction.

Alongside meeting guests' expectations, hotels that apply the concept farm-to-table may reap other advantages. Hotel guests are usually tourists that come to visit and experience the place. The hotel is not the main attraction of the stay, but a place where to sleep safely while exploring the surroundings. Therefore, by using local foods, hospitality providers can offer extra experiences to their customers. First, as the food is grown in the local area, it is usually visible (during the growing season) to the guests and they will often recognise it while exploring the surroundings. The tourists might thus feel their meals to be connected to the region. Second, if hospitality providers prepare the food accordingly to regional dishes, guests experience an interaction with local customs and to some extent even local heritage, which many tourists strive for. Think here of the popularity of food festivals and markets selling local food. Consumption food may also be designed as an experience of the regional culture. Think for example of eating with chopsticks in China or eating with your hands in some Arabic countries. Consuming food is also an important social experience. In many families the meals are a moment to sit together and talk with each other while eating together. Something similar happens during holidays where often travel parties sit together and talk, sometimes also with people other than their travel companions. Eating dinner is often more than just a means to cope with your primary needs of hunger and thirst, and fulfils a social function as well.

Eating with locals is a trend that builds further on the social importance of eating, the meaning that tourists attach to authenticity and their desire to experience the local culture. One of the first international companies offering this experience was 'Eat With' that started in 2014 and now offers travellers the opportunity to eat at someone else's home in more than 130 countries, including Israel and Italy. The concept is simple: instead of promoting local restaurants or offering local menus in their own restaurants, the tourists are invited to eat with locals, so actually visiting a local family and eat with them. Hence, tourists experience hospitality in the houses of local families, who cook for them traditional food in their own kitchen and then sit together with them and have the meal. So, suddenly the hospitality provider here is a local family that offers traditional meals to visitors. By now this concept has spread also to residents of a city. Hence, if you do not wish to eat on your own or you really would like to cook your favourite dishes for other people, platforms as Eat With can be used to get into contact with people who either would like to be offered hospitality or wish to offer hospitality in a private home with literally home-made food.

Taking the guest and the deep experience of the guest into account the trend of 'slow food' cannot stay unmentioned. To start with, we wish to stress that, even though farm-to-table and slow food overlap and follow similar principles, they are not the same. Slow food is defined as food prepared in accordance with local traditions and recipes and consciously consumed, often according to local habits, using, if possible, locally grown, high quality ingredients. You might have recognised that the name slow food is the direct opposite to one of the most prominent movements in the food industry: the fast food movement. In this it indeed resembles the farm-to-table approach. Alongside slow food, you might have also heard of another concept important for hospitality providers: the trend of slow tourism. Slow food and slow tourism may be seen as examples of a broader social movement, the so-called 'slow movement' which aims at slowing down life's perceived pace. The end goal of slow food, slow tourism and everything else related to the slow movement is enhancing the quality of life of the participant. You should be aware of where your food comes from, and the consumption process should be deliberate, slow and free of any other influences. In other words, the core of the slow food movement is to be aware of where your food comes from and consume it with a 'care for all' mentality (Cavagnaro and Curiel, 2012; see also Chapter 1). Important steps in the slow food movement are therefore to buy local, organic produce or ideally grow it yourself; then to prepare the food according to traditional recipes or local customs; and finally to consciously enjoy the food without any disturbances in an atmosphere supporting your well-being. The slow food movement is very much focused on the person participating in it and on enhancing the quality of life of oneself and others (such as the producer). It is sometimes also accompanied by a political program aiming at protecting local eco-systems and supporting local communities. Summing this discussion up, the philosophies behind farm-to-table and slow food (at least when it started) are different because the first focuses on the regional welfare while the second sets the quality of life of the consumer in the spotlight. However, in their application both approaches are quite similar. As a consequence, by now the philosophy and the application of the two concepts are mixed, so it might be difficult to distinguish between the two. Given that both focus on the conscious consumption of local produce, it might not be necessary to distinguish between them.

When one considers the advantages of local purchasing together with the above-mentioned trends in local (food) consumption, a picture arises that seems to be almost too good to be true. Directly in the core of the hospitality industry, the hospitality business (a hotel, a restaurant, a café, a caterer) benefits by strengthening its ties with the surrounding communities and by offering special experiences to its guests, who value the local products as being a part of the region they visit. In its turn, the surrounding community, including other local businesses, benefits directly and indirectly thanks to the multiplier effect as the money that the guest spends in the hospitality business is spent on local products of other local businesses. As we have seen, usually this includes businesses such as farms, wineries or craftsmen that have no direct link to the hospitality industry and would often be cut out of the benefits trickling down from the success of other industries in the region. Lastly, some of the biggest negative impacts on the environment of the hospitality industry are avoided as local purchasing usually means less CO_2 and less energy use due to short production and transportation chain, as well as less waste due to a reduced packaging. However, there are also significant challenges that hospitality providers need to deal with. Particularly the way that larger hotel or restaurant chains procure their products needs to be questioned, as the development of a local purchasing strategy would require changes and more effort at some of the stages of the purchasing process. The purchasing system needs therefore to be rethought, from a sustainability paradigm. How to address this challenge is the focus of the next subsection.

Rethinking purchasing systems

The increase in complexity of the purchase chain might be one of the biggest challenges that hinder hospitality businesses from providing more local products on their premises. As elaborated in the purchasing-related activities section, the existing philosophies are based on a financially efficient buying process, and not on selecting suppliers on the basis of other sustainability-related indicators such as choosing local providers to enhance the multiplier effect for the community, or purchasing fair trade products to benefit the producers' employees. Also the idea that an organisation is not only responsible for its internal processes but somehow also considered liable for its suppliers' deeds is rather new and still uncommon. In regions with a fragmented supplier structure purchasing locally may become even more daunting. Think of regions with small-scale farms or specialised businesses, such as vineyards, cheese dairies and so on. If the hotel wants to procure products locally, contracts will be negotiated with a lot of suppliers and the logistics for all these products need to be arranged. This extra effort does not only require time but may also cause higher costs. Last but not least, small-scale suppliers might not be able to offer the same prices as large contractors. So, to sum up, the acquisition of local goods makes the procurement process more complex and possibly more expensive. Regardless of the fact that costs might be reduced elsewhere and value might be added to the guest experience, the thinking process behind it can also be an issue. After all, most managers will be trained in regular management courses where keeping purchasing costs low and the purchasing process as efficient as possible are the major success factors in the procurement of good for their business. Hence, a step towards a more sustainable, local purchasing process also requires a paradigm shift of the hotel management, and in particular the managers in charge of purchasing.

Hence, the important first step is to help managers to see the benefits of local purchasing in terms of, for example, guest satisfaction, linkages with the community, and image (Shuman, 1998). These benefits may then be weighted against the costs of redesigning the purchasing system. The second step is to start rethinking the system by considering it as a value adding process on all three dimensions of sustainability, instead of keeping it as tight and short with its only focus to be cheap and efficient. The third step is then to consider specific goods and services: what is bought and where is it bought? can it be bought locally, as well? Of course, the answer will depend on what kind of hospitality business we are referring to – a café has different suppliers than a hotel. Yet the process is the same: to check which products and services are bought or regularly needed and to research if these can be bought local. Depending on where the business is and what kind of business it is, this will be possible with some goods and not with others, because some goods might not be available in the needed quality or quantity. However, even starting with small quantities is an important first step. In regions where the economy is not much developed yet, it is very important to create demand for small local businesses. As stated, this is a particular important step for hospitality businesses, as many of them will have different providers in different industries and local purchasing may greatly stimulate the economic activity in a region. To come back to a food related example: a hotel that buys food from the market benefits farms, who are a part of the primary industry. Yet, if the hotel also buys goods like table and bed cloths, pillows, chairs and tables locally, its purchases will benefit the secondary industry. Finally, if local tour guides and mechanics are hired, the tertiary industry benefits as well and in the end the positive economic impact of the tourism multiplier effect can benefit a lot of different people in a lot of different industries in a region. The capacity to benefit so many different organizations in all types of industries is typical of hospitality: a steel manufacturer, for example, will not have these many links to other types of businesses.

The complexity of handling many suppliers is still an issue in sourcing locally. This has to be recognised, and yet some solutions are appearing. Of these we will wish to mention here two that we consider may develop strongly in the future. One is the use of new media, such as WhatsApp, to easily communicate between producer and hotel or restaurant. For example, the executive chef of Wannee restaurant in the Netherlands has daily and quick contacts with his supplier via WhatsApp (personal communication, January 2018). The second is forming a cooperative among producers. For example, a group of farms may supply one or more restaurants. This solution brings interaction between supply and demand that will very likely lead to a better alignment between producer's capacity and restaurant's demands (Nijboer *et al.*, 2015). Cooperatives, moreover, may be designed to guarantee not only a more stable supply in terms of quality and quantity, but also to supply from a central point thus avoiding the need for each producer to drive to the supplied organisation separately.

Defining 'local' and applying it to a business

As discussed, there are many definitions of what 'local' is and this is an issue because as long as the definition is vague, the term may be knowingly or unknowingly abused.

In absence of an overall definition, attempts have been made to specifically define for some goods what '(buy) local' means. Certification schemes have also been developed such as the Shorefast label used by the Fogo Island Inn (Case 9.1). Yet, certification costs may be high and thus a barrier for small, local consumers, while certification may not even been the best way to communicate with guests (Baddeley and Font, 2011).

Considering the drawbacks of certification, we wish to present here a tool that has been proposed by Dr. Peter Klosse, professor of Gastronomy, in collaboration with Jaap Peter Nijboer and Jan A. Schulp (Nijboer *et al.*, 2015). It has been developed to help the restaurant of the Hotel Management School Maastricht (the Netherlands) making more sustainable buying decisions, but may be easily applied to other purchased good and services than food. It is called the Foodzone Model, and it gives an indication on where food should come from to achieve a more sustainable stance as a restaurant. The figure shows the model applied from the perspective of the city of Maastricht, in the Netherlands.

The zones in the model represent areas of increasing distance from the location where the food is offered to guests. Zone 1 is in the immediate surrounding of the food provider. Zone 2 is the wider area where the business is located, for example the province. In the Dutch situation this will generally stay inside a limit of 50 km. The Zone 3 comprises the Netherlands as a whole, a country where the maximum distance between North and South is 300 kms and between East and West 200 kms. The Zone 4 is Europe, and Zone 5 the tropic and sub-tropic regionWitih the zones product groups are identified, so that it is clear to both hosts and guests from where they come. Each restaurant applying the model should make its own analysis and choices. Yet, the higher the percentage of food sourced form the first two zones, the clearer it is that the restaurant intends to support local farmers and the region (Nijboer *et al.*, 2015).

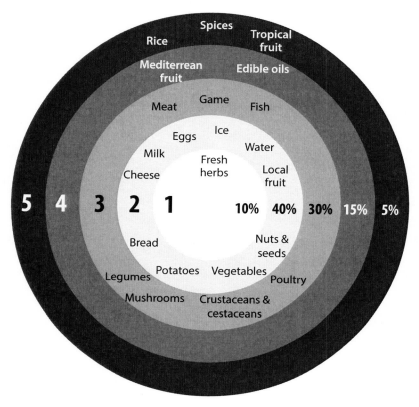

Figure 9.1: Food zone model (by kind permission of Dr. P. Klosse)

As the model suggests, 80% of the offered food should come from a radius of max 300 kms from the business. This division between locally and non-locally sourced food corresponds to the advice of executive chef and proponent of the 'Dutch Cuisine' Albert Kooy (2011; see also Chapter 15). Neither Albert Kooy nor the authors of the Zone Model wish to ban food from elsewhere; they rather wish to set the focus on local food. For example, tropical fruit, rice and coffee are not available in the Netherlands, and Mediterranean fruit and vegetable is and can be a nice addition to the kitchen of a Dutch restaurant. However, still a main focus should be on the products than can be easily bought directly in the neighbourhood or even grown on their own grounds, such as fresh salad or herbs. A lot of other fruit and vegetables or items such as milk and cheese should be derived from close by, a distance of less than 50 kilometres, while meat and fish can be sourced from a distance up with 300 kilometres, which will ensure also animal welfare but still avoid long transportation, a problem highlighted above. Even though some may argue that some of the goods might be easier to source from even closer, we do think that this model is a sensible starting point. Following this example, moreover, hospitality providers might not only more easily define what is local food to them but also apply the same process to other goods and services as well.

Conclusion

To sum up, 'local product' remains a difficult term, as there is no agreement on one single definition. However, it is generally agreed that 'local food product' refers to a product whose production process took place in the same region where it is consumed, and which has had a short transport chain. This results in income for hospitality and non-hospitality providers in the region, less CO_2 and packaging as well as social benefits for both locals and guests. It should be also stressed that the hospitality industry is in the best possible position to create value for a large group of people simply because it draws from a large range of suppliers and supplies a wide range of guests. When choosing local products, therefore, its positive impact can be considerable.

It needs to be stated that hospitality-related businesses can contribute to a more sustainable hospitality sector by purchasing local products. Generally speaking, local products tend to contribute to all three dimensions of sustainability to a varying degree. At the same time, being more sustainable by local purchasing also requires some efforts in the purchasing process which hospitality businesses are not necessarily used to, at least not to the extent that is required for local purchasing. Hence, the first step in the process of reaping and sharing the fruits of buying local is to become aware of the unique position of hospitality. Hopefully this awareness will generate a sense of responsibility, and will make the benefits that derive from purchasing local more salient to management than the efforts and time involved in, for example, setting up a network of local suppliers instead of buying from contractors and taking responsibility to choose their suppliers using sustainability criteria and not only cost-efficiency considerations.

References

Abate, G. (2008) Local food economies: driving forces, challenges, and future prospects, *Journal of Hunger & Environmental Nutrition*, **3** (4) 384-399.

Baddeley, J. and Font, X. (2011) Barriers to tour operator sustainable supply chain management, *Tourism and Recreation Research*, **36** (3) 205–14.

Cavagnaro, E. and Curiel, G.H. (2012) *The Three Levels of Sustainability*, Sheffield: Greenleaf Publishing.

Cavagnaro, E. Melissen, F.W. and Düweke, A. (2018) The host-guest relationship is the key to sustainable hospitality: Lessons learned from a Dutch case study, *Hospitality & Society*, **8** (1) 23-44.

Devine, D. (2004) Local food makes a global impact: the case for shopping locally, *North Country Times*. 4 December, San Diego, CA.

Everett, S. and Aitchison, C. (2008) Role of food tourism in sustaining regional identity: A case study of Cornwall, South West England, *Journal of Sustainable Tourism*, **16** (2) 150–167.

Flint, A. (2004) Think Globally, Eat Locally: A new socially conscious food movement wants to reset the American table, 15 August, *Boston Globe*.

Fogo Island Inn (n. d.) www.fogoislandinn.ca/in-between#!fogo-island-foodways and www.fogoislandinn.ca/in-between#!economic-nutrition. Accessed 15 February 2018.

Hall, C. M. and Gössling, S. (2013) *Sustainable Culinary Systems: Local foods, innovation, tourism and hospitality*, New York: Routledge.

Hall, C. M. and Sharples, E. (2003), The consumption of experiences or the experience of consumption? An introduction to the tourism taste, in Hall, C. M. (ed.), *Food Tourism Around the World: Development, management and markets*, Amsterdam: Butterworth-Heinemann, pp.1-24.

Hjalager, A.-M. and Johansen, P.H. (2013) Food tourism in protected areas – sustainability for producers, the environment and tourism?, *Journal of Sustainable Tourism*, **21** (3) 417–433.

Jauhari, V. (2014) *Managing Sustainability in the Hospitality and Tourism Industry: Paradigms and Directions for the Future*. Oakville, Canada: Apple Academic Press.

KHA (n.d.) www.kha-net.org/criticalissues/healthykansashospitals/. Accessed 21 February 2018.

Kleinjans, R. and Vardakoulias, O. (2017) *Fish Dependence – 2017 Update – the reliance of the EU on fish from elsewhere*, report for the New Economies Foundation. http://neweconomics.org/wp-content/uploads/2017/03/NEF_Fish_Dependence_2017_2.pdf. Accessed 24 March 2018.

Kooy, A. (2011) *The New Dutch Cuisine*, Zutphen: KunstMag.

Long, L. (2004) Culinary tourism: A folkloristic perspective on eating and otherness in Long, L. (ed.), *Culinary Tourism*, Kentucky: The University Press of Kentucky, pp.20-50.

Lin-Heng; L., Ofori, G, Lee Lei Choo, M, Savage, V.R. and Yen-Peng, T. (2010) *Sustainability Matters - Environmental Management in Asia*, Singapore: World Scientific Publishing Co.

Manzhynski, S., Figge, F. and Hassel, L. (2015) Sustainable value creation of nine countries of the Baltic region: Value, changes and drivers, *Journal of Cleaner Production*, **108** 637-646.

Minta, S. (2015) Regional food products: only for tourists or also for residents, *Agriculture and Forestry*, **61**(1), 51-58.

Nabhan, G. P. (2002). *Coming Home to Eat: The Pleasures and Politics of Local Foods*, New York: W.W. Norton.

Nijboer, J.P., Klosse, P.R. and Schulp, J.A. (2015) How self-sufficient can a restaurant be? Introducing the Foodzone model, a managerial tool, in Sloan, P. and Legrand, W. (eds.), *Handbook of Sustainable Food, Beverages and Gastronomy*, Ch. 25, London: Routledge.

Oehler, J. and Buer, C. (2017) *Macht Einkauf- Power-Methoden für erfolgreiches Einkaufsmanagement in der Hotellerie [The power of purchase – power-methods for a successful purchasing management]*, Frankfurt am Main: Matthaes Verlag.

Page, S. and Connell, J. (2014) *Tourism: A Modern Synthesis*, 4th edn, Andover UK: Cengage Learning EMEA.

Pretty, J. and Lang, T. (2005) Farm costs and food miles: an assessment of the full cost of the UK weekly food basket, *Food Policy*, **30** (1) 1-19.

9

Reilly (2016) www.tampabay.com/projects/2016/food/farm-to-fable/restaurants/. Accessed 20 February 2018.

Shuman, M. H. (1998) *Going Local: Creating Self-reliant Communities in a Global Age*, New York: Free Press.

Skuras, D and Dimara, E. (2005) Consumer demand for informative labelling of quality food and drink products: a European Union case study, *Journal of consumer marketing*, **22** (2) 90-100.

Sloan, P., Legrand, W. and Hindley, C. (2015) *The Routledge Handbook of Sustainable Food and Gastronomy*, Bungay, Suffolk: Routledge.

Stead, E.W. and Stead, J.G. (2004) *Sustainable Strategic Management*, New York: M.E. Shape.

Telfer, D. J. and Wall, G. (2000) Strengthening backward economic linkages: Local food purchasing by three Indonesian hotels, *Tourism Geographies*, **2** (4) 421-447.

Touzard, J.-M., Chiffoleau, Y. and Maffezzoli, C. (2016). What is local or global about wine? an attempt to objectivize a social construction, *Sustainability*, **8** (5) 417.

Vermeulen, W.J.V. and Ras, P.J. (2006). The challenge of greening global product chains: meeting both ends, *Sustainable Development*, **14** (4), 245–256.

Weele, A.J.V. (2010) *Purchasing and Supply Chain Management: Analysis, Strategy, Planning and Practice*, 5th edn, Hampshire, England: Nelson Education.

Yeoman, I., Brass, D. and McMahon-Beattie, U. (2006) Current issues in tourism: The authentic tourist, *Tourism Management*, **28** (4) 1128–1138.

10 Sustainable Purchasing in an International Context: A relational perspective

Ko Koens and Harry Reinders

Learning goals

After studying this chapter, readers will have the ability to:

1 Appreciate the difference between standard purchasing and *sustainable* purchasing;

2 Understand the complexity of ensuring sustainable development in international purchasing;

3 Know that sustainable purchasing goes further than environmental sustainable purchasing;

4 Appreciate solutions to ensure more sustainable international purchasing practices.

Introduction

Sustainable value creation depends not only on the internal organisation of businesses, but also on their relations with others in the wider international supply chain. Particularly with increasing levels of outsourcing, it can be argued that businesses nowadays are no more sustainable than their suppliers (Krause *et al.*, 2009). Although this is increasingly acknowledged within manufacturing industry, it is as much the case in service-oriented industries, such as hospitality and tourism. However, awareness, willingness and ability to act and integrate measures of sustainability into purchasing and supply management has only received limited attention from hospitality and tourism stakeholders (Schwartz *et al.*, 2008). In the academic literature too, ways of achieving sustainable development within purchasing and supply chain management in the hospitality industry have received little attention – to the extent that some have argued "there is a clear dearth in existing research" (Al-Aomar and Hussain, 2017: 42). This suggests that there is a lack of knowledge and understanding about this topic, which can lead to purchasing not being done in the most sustainable way possible, even when there is a willingness to do so. This chapter deals with this issue by focusing on the international aspects of purchasing in the value chain.

Purchasing is closely related to supply management and to appreciate the relationships a concise version of a hotel supply chain is provided in Figure 10.1.

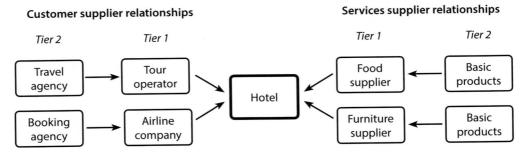

Figure 10.1: Simplified depiction of hotel supply chain (based on Lambert and Cooper, 2000: 68)

It is important to highlight the distinction between different tiers of suppliers, before detailing the different chains that can be identified in the hotel industry. First tier suppliers directly supply to the hotel, second tier suppliers supply the service providers of the first tier, third tier suppliers supply the second tier service providers, and so on (Zhang *et al.*, 2009). Within the current chapter the focus lies on purchasing activities with first tier suppliers, although there may be some discussion of second tier activities too.

When looking at the supply chains, it is important to recognise that there are two distinct channels within the hospitality industry supply chain, both with different purchasing characteristics. Hotels (and other hospitality providers) commonly purchase goods and services in order to be able to offer a good-quality product. These suppliers of goods and services form the first supply channel. The first tier here tends to be product and service providers (e.g. food, facilities, furniture) who in their turn purchase their products from second tier producers. Whereas there is an increasing tendency of hospitality providers to purchase from local suppliers, at least for the first tier, second or third tier providers can still be based abroad. The second channel concerns the way in which hotels are 'supplied' with customers. Here first tier suppliers are tour operators, taxis and/or airline companies, whereas second tier agents are inbound travel agents or travel agencies in the country of origin of the visitor. At the same time hotels provide tour operators and others also with customers, thus inverting the supply chain relationship. As will be argued below, this characteristic may offer possibilities to make the purchasing process within the hospitality sector more sustainable.

Given that the subject of this chapter is *sustainable* purchasing in the hotel sector, it is useful to provide greater clarity on this concept, as it may be interpreted in different ways. Whereas *purchasing* commonly entails the management of external resources with the aim of managing a company's activities at the most favourable economic conditions (Van Weele, 2014), *sustainable purchasing* goes beyond this economic paradigm. It can be defined as "the consideration of environmental, social, ethical and economic issues in the management of the organization's external resources in such a way that the supply of all goods, services, capabilities and knowledge that are necessary for running, maintaining and managing the organization's primary and support activities provide value not only to the organization but also to society and the economy" (Miemczyk *et al.*, 2012: 489).

Three main types of buyer-supplier relationships can be discerned, largely depending on the interdependency of buyers and sellers. *Transactional* relationships are the most common. The focus in these relationships is mostly on price, with neither party is particularly involved in the well-being of the other and there is little sharing of information. Within *collaborative* relationships there is an awareness of interdependence and the benefits of long-term cooperation. This will require trust, planning and communication, but makes it less likely that supplies will be disrupted and allows for easier implementation of improvements. *Supply alliances* differ from collaborative relationships in that they include institutional trust, where trust is placed in the rules, roles and norms or even the 'values' of the organisation rather than the people who occupy these roles. Such alliances are difficult to achieve, but allow for greater openness and shared responsibilities. In this way supply alliances allow for more sustainable purchasing (Burt *et al.*, 2002).

The scope of sustainable purchasing may be wider than with normal purchasing, but the purchasing concept itself remains largely the same. Commonly purchasing is said to cover six core activities (Van Weele, 2014):

1 Determining the purchasing specifications of products and services;
2 Selecting the best possible suppliers;
3 Conducting negations to come to a legal contractual agreement;
4 Placing the order with the chosen suppliers;
5 Monitoring and controlling the order;
6 Follow up and evaluation.

In describing the scope of purchasing, it is important to acknowledge that these activities are closely interrelated and intermingled, so actions do not necessarily happen in this order and in this structured a fashion. Instead, the purchasing process can be seen as one of continuous negotiation, where decisions are based not simply on rational decision making, but also on the basis of the quality of networks and relations between old and new potential stakeholders (Van der Duim and Caalders, 2008). These characteristics complicate international purchasing practices, as will be discussed in the following section where sustainability challenges regarding international purchasing in the hospitality sector are discussed.

When looking at the international context in business, it is tempting to focus on geographical distance as a potential hindrance. However, while geographical distance undoubtedly provides limitations, distance can also be determined by other characteristics (Van der Duim, 2005). Equally important in an international context are cultural differences, the quality of the communication channels, the technological divides between the stakeholders and the number of stakeholders involved. All of these have a significant impact on the international purchasing process. While this can be observed both for the 'services and goods' supply chain as well as the 'customer' supply chain there are certain specific purchasing challenges of each channel that merit a closer look. This chapter first looks at the sustainability challenges involved when purchasing services and goods, following which challenges in the customer supply chain are discussed. Finally, a set of best-practice examples are provided and tools to address the sustainability challenge are introduced.

Main sustainability challenges

As stated at the end of the introduction, we discuss sustainability challenges in the focusing firstly on the supplier's and secondly on the customer's supply chain.

Sustainability challenges in the service supplier supply chain

A clear challenge when purchasing services and goods, is the limited knowledge regarding sustainable development in the hospitality industry (Melissen *et al.*, 2016; Yeh, 2012) and the limited importance given to the subject (Beck *et al.*, 2007). Possibly as a result, the emphasis in purchasing remains largely on cost-efficiency, while many purchasing practices remain largely based on habit (Mosgaard, 2015). Although this is slowly changing and businesses increasingly have started to use local products, sustainability still comes into view mostly through its association with food quality, freshness and localness, not as a concept as such. Unfortunately, current handbooks dealing with purchasing are outdated on this subject. They do not just fail to highlight the importance of and ways to ensure an ethical purchasing process, but the subject of ethics or sustainability is often simply not mentioned at all (e.g. Feinstein and Stefanelli, 2011; Hayes and Ninemeier, 2009). Such a lack of knowledge leaves purchasers underprepared should they want to pursue a more ethical path. For example, they may be too extreme when determining the environmental or social specifications of products and services, and end up with an impossible specifications list that makes the ethical purchasing process hugely frustrating or very expensive, creating negative sentiments.

A number of cases specific to the hospitality industry illustrate this point. To start with, we may remember some examples that are already mentioned in other chapters in this book, such as the lower environmental norms when producing plates and glass in China, as well as wage issues (see Chapter 15). However, the same issue can be observed within the purchasing of other goods too. For example, when buying furniture or kitchen equipment, it is not evident under what environmental and social circumstances they have been produced. This can even come down to very simple questions, such as, among others: to what extent are materials sustainably sourced (i.e. is primary rainforest cut down); how many pollutants come into the environment (air, water, solid waste) as a result of the production process; are workers paid a living wage; is child or slave labour used in the production process; to what extent do companies stimulate a diverse, local, workforce and/or women empowerment? While it is difficult enough to gain insights on these issues in themselves, these considerations are but part of the larger discussion when purchasing goods, and may compete with economic considerations or with quality, health and safety assurances that may be easier to determine (Lawlor and Jayawardena, 2003). This means that in practice managers may have to choose between what they believe are more ethically produced goods versus goods that are either cheaper, or have better assured quality control.

The lack of knowledge also limits the ability of hospitality businesses to stimulate ethical standards among second and third tier providers by encouraging sustainability initiatives among suppliers. In practice this is not always easy, as control and regulation among these providers may be lacking in an international context (Kirezieva et al., 2015). In addition corruption and financial kickbacks for preferential treatment are not uncommon, particularly in situations where there is limited transparency in the supply chain and one party has more or better information than the other party. It is important to realise here that such practices are not limited to developing countries where there may be less transparency regarding business, but also happen in developed countries. Moreover, the potential for corruption is enhanced in global purchasing arrangements, due to the "multitude of entities involved, varying ethical standards, and the numerous pass-off points in the acquisition and transportation of goods and services" (Arnold et al., 2012: 136). In other words, the more complicated the supply chains become, the greater the potential for corruption and kickbacks. Whilst certification (e.g. ISO 14001; ISO 20400) may be able to deal with some of these issues, it can be a costly affair for suppliers, and exclude smaller suppliers who are unfamiliar with certification schemes or cannot afford them (Wilhelm et al., 2016).

The recent focus on purchasing locally products can be considered a positive thing from an environmental and sustainability perspective (see Chapter 9). Not only does it lead to reputational gains, but it also supports building stronger partnerships with greater mutual understanding and increased efficiency (Camilleri, 2012). However, more localised purchasing may have the consequence of making it more difficult for international suppliers to participate. For suppliers from developing countries in particular this can have a negative impact on economic livelihoods. One example of this is serving local wines, which can harm economic development in developing countries (Vermeulen and Ras, 2006). At the same time, it is important to realise that in the purchasing process it is increasingly difficult to distinguish between local and global chains. For example, several local products include food products from abroad. This means that, even when the actual purchasing is done locally, the value chain behind the product is commonly a mix of local and international (Touzard et al., 2016).

A completely different issue arises when international hotel companies, aimed at customers from the Global North, operate in developing countries. In their hotels the use of local suppliers often remains limited. As argued by Mgonja *et al*. (2017) this can be attributed to a lack of communication. Given that local food patterns can be different from what guests are used to, guests are less likely to try local food if this is not promoted by the hotel. Local producers can lack the knowledge to produce the food that hotel customers prefer and be unable to deliver a high enough quality of this kind of food. Experiences from Latin America and the Caribbean also point to language barriers between local farmers and hospitality providers, as well as difficulties with inconsistent supply, quality issues and a lack of trust (Pattullo, 2005; Torres and Momsen, 2004).

Sustainability challenges in the customer supply chain

Increased internationalisation has meant that the centres of power in the customer purchasing chain tend to move away from the location where the hospitality business is based. Whereas previously, local intermediaries were used to ensure the quality (and sustainability) of a business, improved ICT communication has made it easier to guage this information from afar. As such the centres of power have switched further towards tour operators, travel agents and, increasingly, online travel agencies that are not based in the destination country, and offer many alternatives to choose from (Van der Duim and Caalders, 2008; see also Chapter 5). Unless a hospitality operation can make itself an obligatory part of itineraries (e.g. through location or attractiveness), it can be easily replaced. This makes it difficult to establish long-lasting relationships. At the same time, it makes it easier for innovative and unique providers to gain a larger share of the market, even when commission percentages are not necessarily lower.

A key issue is the fact that it is difficult for guests and buyers to see beforehand the extent to which businesses take sustainable development seriously. There is a discrepancy between the way ethical considerations are communicated and the practices on the ground. Communication tends to paint too positive a picture of the way actors deal with their business, including their relations with suppliers (Font *et al*., 2012; Font *et al*., 2016). The extent to which businesses do ethical purchasing becomes visible only when guests are at their destination and have already purchased the product (e.g. through communication regarding food origins or detailed information regarding the sourcing of furniture). In addition, the question remains to what extent sustainability influences customers' decisions. There is a lack of tangible evidence that ethical business practices throughout the supply chain leads to greater willingness by customers to purchase or to pay more for a product, which may limit the willingness of businesses to take ethical aspects into consideration (Schwartz *et al*., 2008).

Also difficult is the fact that sustainable purchasing can be mistaken for 'green' purchasing. In recent years the opportunities for environmentally sustainable purchasing have increased strongly, due to increased availability of green suppliers and greater clarity due to eco-labelling. Unfortunately, social sustainability is not always taken into account as much (Pullman *et al.*, 2009). Particularly when purchasing from developing countries, it is important to ensure that social elements such as ensuring local employment, decent working conditiond, stimulating a good quality of life among nearby residents, etc. are also taken into account. Doing so helps provide local legitimacy and may have a positive impact on local economies, as well as the long-term economic performance for the businesses involved (Reimann *et al.*, 2012; Riikkinen *et al.*, 2017).

An interesting aspect in the customer supply chain is that hospitality businesses act both as suppliers and purchasers of services. They largely depend on tour operators and travel agents for their customers. This means they have to 'purchase' guests by offering good service, commission or a lower general price. At the same time, hospitality businesses can act as suppliers to tour operators and travel agents with independent travellers. This puts them in a unique position and may provide them with some essential tools to address the sustainability challenge when it comes to sustainable purchasing in an international context.

Best cases

Case 10.1: Fairmont Hotels – sustainable development as a core value

Fairmont Hotels and Resorts is a global group of hotels and resorts, part of the ACCOR group. It views sustainable development as one of its core values and cooperates with agencies like the World Wide Furnd for Nature (WWF) to enhance its sustainable credentials. As part of their sustainability strategy, Fairmont has switched its global supplier of cleaning products to an environmentally friendly one, has removed threatened fish from their menu and only procures FSC-certified stationary. They have developed a green procurement policy and supplier code of conduct for their hotels. This code of conduct focuses on guaranteeing that all the suppliers of a hotel are aware of and participate in the environmental mandate of the company.

Rather than simply implementing this procurement policy, Fairmont has taken the initiative to support its main suppliers and educate them to ensure that they can provide products that are in accordance with this new policy. In addition they work with suppliers to improve energy efficiency of their operations and product design, as well as limiting shipping frequencies and packaging waste.

(Green Hotelier, 2017; Jia *et al.*, 2015).

10

Case 10.2: How a horse became a cow

Although it is physically impossible to turn a horse into a cow, long supply chains and insufficient transparency mean that, within international purchasing at least, this can be achieved. Around 2013, a meat trading scandal was unveiled in Europe. A Dutch-owned, Cypriot-registered company, run from the Antwerp area of Belgium, called "Draap Trading Ltd" was accused of selling horsemeat as beef. It bought the meat from an abattoir in Romania. The people at this abattoir and the local residents were very aware and open about the fact that the meat produced there was horse. Draap Trading stored the frozen meat in Breda, the Netherlands. They subsequently delivered the meat to a French company for processing, which then supplied it to another French company that made consumer products of it (e.g. lasagne) in Luxemburg. These products were then sold by a Swedish company to supermarkets in Belgium, France, Great Britain and the Netherlands. Allegedly, the owner of Draap Trading falsified papers somewhere along the way. Four years later the same owner was arrested again, for similar charges.

This story highlights how international purchasing processes can quickly become very complex with several tiers of suppliers. A lack of transparency and clarity somewhere in the supply chain, makes it possible for strange things to occur, including the miraculous change from horse to cow. Ironically, the company's name "Draap" is the Dutch word for horse (*paard*) spelled backwards, which makes it all the more intriguing, why this issue was not found out about earlier.

The lack of transparency in international supply chains is a well-known phenomenon and not just restricted to beef. For example, Dutch restaurants have been found to serve a relatively cheap tropical fish *Cynoglossus senegalensis* as common sole (*solea solea*), which looks and tastes similar, yet is far more expensive. Another example comes from the notoriously opaque cocoa supply chain, which makes it impossible to ascertain whether or not chocolate has been produced with slave labour. The worrying thing is that this may be the case even for organic or fair-trade chocolate (see www.slavefreechocolate.org for more).

To prevent problems such as these when purchasing food products in the hospitality industry, several steps can be taken. The most obvious solution is to create smaller supply chains and focus on local sourcing. Indeed, this solution is advocated and implemented by 'Conscious Hotels', a small Dutch hotel chain that actively seeks to work with local food suppliers and designers to limit the negative environmental and social impact of their hotel (for more information, see www.conscioushotels.com).

For large international chains, such an approach is more difficult and sometimes impossible to implement. A solution here can be to stimulate diversity and transparency within food supply chains by creating long-term relationships, trusted networks of suppliers and only using sustainably certified products. An example of this is the Hilton sustainable seafood project, which aims to ban the procurement of endangered species from all properties by 2022, have at least 25% of all seafood supplied from Marine Stewardship Council or Aquaculture Stewardship Council certified sources and the rest from sources working towards certification (based on the 'green list' of the World Wildlife Fund). This is done by training staff and involving guests, deepening partnerships with suppliers as well as NGOs, whilst transparently measuring and reporting on the progress (MSC, 2015). Although, it remains to be seen how the project will work out exactly in practice, it contains a number of actions and strategies that hotel chains can take to prevent, for instance, a *Cynoglossus* becoming a sole.

Case 10.3: Eurostar – creating long-term supplier relationships

Eurostar is a high speed railway company that links London with various other European destinations (e.g. Brussels, Paris, Amsterdam). Over the years it has gained a reputation as being forward-thinking with regards to implementing sustainable development into its business practices. This also stretches to its (international) purchasing practices. The company has taken measures to ensure it takes a holistic approach to sustainability on this matter. For example, the paints used for the outside and inside of the train are water-based and eco-friendly, food and drinks on board nearly all come from fair-trade or organic, preferably local suppliers (using seasonal vegetables) and seat covers and staff uniforms are upcycled into bags for train managers after their initial use.

Eurostar has a clear focus on transparency in their procurement practices, including a zero-tolerance approach to bribery and corruption, which it actively communicates to its suppliers. With their Supplier Engagement Strategy, the company actively works together with its suppliers to join up data to get an integrated perspective of the supply chain. Whilst this helps in detecting issues with non-compliance, the focus of the strategy is on building long-term relationships with suppliers that have a similar perspective on sustainable development. Their digital procurement portal, for example, records suppliers' emissions management, but at the same time acts as a learning platform as it contains tools and information to improve sustainable practices. In this way it not only acts as a means to control the sustainability and quality of suppliers, but also actively helps them to improve their practices.

(Eurostar, 2017; Responsibletravel, 2011)

Tools to address the challenges

The literature on sustainable purchasing is relatively consistent when it comes to potential ways to address the challenges in achieving sustainable purchasing. Solutions that are offered mostly are related to interdependence and the benefits coming from longer-term strategic cooperation between partners (Dabhilkar *et al.*, 2015; Walker *et al.*, 2012). These can be applied to both supply channels that were discussed earlier. For a clearer understanding of the proposed solutions, it is useful to frame the challenges mentioned previously with Cox's (2001) matrix of buyer-supplier power relationships (Figure 10.2).

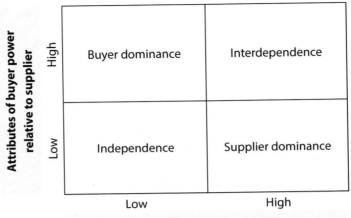

Figure 10.2: Types of buyer-supplier power relationships (Cox, 2001)

Cox largely follows Bensaou (1999) who argues that the relationship between buyer and supplier is largely related to the mutual exchange of investments that may lose their value when they are diverted to other suppliers or customers. This can be tangible products or financial investments, but it can also be intangible investments (time, effort). In addition, it relates to the options that stakeholders have to switch buyers or suppliers. If buyer and supplier make limited investments to improve their relationship, they will have several other options and will view purchasing as a simple market exchange. Both can easily exit the relationship and the emphasis here tends to move to cost reduction. It may be possible that suppliers or buyers hold other parties with limited other options 'captive' – they are the main supplying or buying party and thus critical for the survival of the other. In this case, the ability to enforce change lies largely with the most powerful actor, who can relatively easily switch supplier or buyer. In the case of a strategic partnership both supplier and buyer invest much in the relationship and are likely to want to continue their collaboration. While sustainable purchasing can be achieved in all types of relationships, for international purchasing, interdependent relationships are said to hold particular potential (albeit with certain caveats, as described below).

Solutions focused on strategic interdependent relationships commonly fit within what can be considered an advanced professionalized approach to the purchasing process (Van Weele *et al.*, 1998). They contain three main elements to ensure more efficient and sustainable purchasing practices (Van Weele, 2014):

1 An integration of thinking on purchasing practices within the core business process and product development;

2 A shared vision carried by all stakeholders in the value supply chain;

3 Integrated information systems with partners both upstream and downstream.

Commonly, the emphasis within these three elements is on maximizing economic benefits and increased revenues by ensuring a better quality of products, clearer specifications and more price- and time-efficient purchasing. However, the same elements can also provide social and environmental returns and help address at least some of the challenges described above.

With regards to the first element, the integration of thinking on purchasing practices within the core processes of an organisation, it should be noted that international purchasing practices are complex and as such may also include other actors within the business (e.g. marketing department). Increasingly companies have a Corporate Social Responsibility (CSR) strategy that includes purchasing practices. In most large hotel chains there are regulations to ensure that the purchasing process complies with the overarching CSR strategy. This can lead to corporate responsibility performance measurement platforms or specific goals for sustainable sourcing of food, for example, to only use certified food products or cooperate with businesses that also adhere to certain ethical standards (e.g. fair trade businesses). These can be useful points of reference and help purchasing managers. To go further, it is possible to work with specialised agencies that can support hospitality businesses. For example, the ACCOR group works with ECO VADIS, a renowned supplier sustainability ratings, to provide a more 'objective' perspective on the sustainability of their suppliers.

To ensure sustainable purchasing is understood and supported within the business, it is not enough for only purchasers to take note of the CSR strategy of the company. Instead, they need to communicate and cooperate with others within the business, with the aim of a joint understanding *and* application of the CSR strategy and procedures in practice. Developing strategies and procedures to stimulate ethical, integrated purchasing practices alone is not enough. These strategies need to be combined with training and education to ensure that the CSR strategy of the company is applied throughout, to result in sustainable purchasing practices (Mosgaard, 2015). Doing so allows for far greater integration of sustainable practices in the company, for example by using refurbished furnishings, instead of new furnishings, in the re-design of a hotel, creating a marketing strategy that highlights sustainability of products and services to guests, or by implementing sustainable product indicators in customer satisfaction surveys (Bohdanowicz, 2006). Trent and Monczka (2005: 24) refer to this more integrated way as 'global sourcing' rather than 'international purchasing'. Even though global sourcing is generally more complicated and can be difficult to achieve, it also leads to greater economic and environmental efficiency. To learn more about the specific ways in which to create greater integration, it can be highly useful to become involved in networks aimed at stimulating sustainable development. This allows for learning from others who may struggle with similar issues. Provided that there is a level of trust, which may take time to develop, these networks can be effective vehicles for sharing stories of success and failure. Alternatively, there is information that can be freely gathered from the Internet – see, for example, www.greenhotelier.org.

Turning towards the second element, a shared vision among all stakeholders, recent work on stakeholder theory emphasises the importance of relationship management as well as taking a networked approach that goes further than looking only at direct dyadic ties, that is ties between two actors (Johnsen *et al.*, 2017). This means that purchasers have to maintain a certain level of awareness of additional stakeholders besides the suppliers and purchasers. This includes, for example, the environment or the interests of local communities, both of which are affected (both positively and negatively) by the decision to purchase from a certain supplier or not. The difficulty in the international context is that it is not easy to learn about the social and environmental impact of suppliers. However, hospitality businesses can still exert significant influence, both when purchasing services and goods, as well as when dealing with the customer's supply chain. To start with the former, hospitality businesses can choose suppliers and partners that value sustainable development. This can, for example, be done by persuading suppliers to certify their products or services (Bohdanowicz, 2006). Such an approach may lead to additional costs for them and can be difficult when dealing with smaller international suppliers and may lead to them feeling abused (Koens and Thomas, 2016). An alternative way to achieve the same goal, can be to base partnerships on a shared vision on sustainable development with purchasing partners. In such cases, suppliers still work on the basis of sustainable development, without seeking labelling from a potentially costly certification scheme (Margaryan and Stensland, 2017).

In addition to this, hospitality providers can support their suppliers with capacity building to improve sustainable practices. Even if this incurs costs, it will be beneficial for the hospitality provider, given that such sustainability education leads to a higher level of commitment of suppliers (Wilhelm *et al.*, 2016). An example of a tool that can help with capacity building is the Travelife Sustainability Auditing (www.travelife.org), albeit that additional training and professional development may be required, particularly as the focus of this auditing tends to be on environmental aspects of sustainable development (Baddeley and Font, 2011). As a relationship deepens, purchaser and supplier can focus on better integration and joint problem solving based on joint responsibilities and shared values. This can be through long-term commitments, but also through better logistics integration, information sharing and even involvement in the product development of suppliers (Paulraj *et al.*, 2006). Provided both parties have a shared understanding of sustainable development, such integration between international partners can lead to the development of long-term supply alliances where sustainable development is accepted as a given, rather than an additional cost.

With regards to the customer supply chain, the unique characteristics of the hospitality and tourism industry – where hotels and tour operators operate more in a network, than through one-sided customer-supplier relationships – give hospitality businesses specific opportunities to achieve sustainable development through interdependent relationships. Sustainable hospitality providers can actively seek out specialist sustainable tour operators and travel agents to create 'networks of sustainable supply'. These networks will help businesses to collaborate and 'share' customers through preferred supplier agreements or joint operations. Whilst such networks are quite common within destinations, the advent of ICT solutions has made it possible to create virtual networks. There even are online travel agencies (e.g. bookdifferent.com and responsibletravel.com) that are aimed specifically at working with sustainable providers. In addition, platforms like TripAdvisor provide useful networking and promotion possibilities to create linkages with other sustainable operators (for more information on the role of online distribution channels see Chapter 5).

The third element, integrated information systems, attempts to deal with a potential issue by a more networked approach to purchasing, which entails interdependent relationships that require a certain level of trust. As mentioned previously, better connections between stakeholders require a level of institutional trust, and trust can easily be damaged by the careless actions of individuals (Shi and Liao, 2013). To ensure trust in the international purchasing process, a level of openness and transparency is key. This includes good administration and communication with potential suppliers and partners. Openness and transparency may be difficult to achieve, but are particularly important in an international context where it is impossible to easily verify claims of suppliers in person. One way of creating a sense of trust is to develop a policy to require suppliers or their products to have a certain level of certifications (e.g. that of the Marine Stewardship Council for fish or the Green Key certification). While not without their issues, this gives at least some clarity regarding what suppliers can or cannot do. Recently, online tools have become available that, at a cost, will allow for some form of verified transparency as they provide insights into the practices of potential suppliers (Bonanni *et al.,* 2010). Alternatively, NGOs are actively monitoring suppliers of a wide variety of products and share this via websites and other outlets (see e.g. www.ethicalconsumer.org and www.sourcemap.com). Whilst aimed largely at consumers, this information can be useful for industry too and is already seen as a source of trusted information by several organisations. This may be an effective way to start building trust in new relations and help create successful long-term sustainable partnerships.

Conclusion

Companies increasingly focus on sustainable purchasing in striving to operate in a more sustainable way. As the discussion in this chapter has highlighted, this is not easy. It is always difficult to find the balance between environmental and social sustainable impact of purchasing practices, and in the case of international purchasing the purchasing process is further complicated by the myriad of actors and stakeholders involved, not all of which are easy to identify, nor is the sustainability of their practices. A number of solutions have been put forward in this chapter to ensure a more sustainable international purchasing process, be it by providing more objective insights into the sustainability of goods and services, or by creating trustworthy business relations in which all parties involved work together to achieve sustainable purchasing.

Further reading

Green Hotelier (2017) *Responsible Procurement.* http://www.greenhotelier.org/our-themes/responsible-procurement/ Accessed: 31 January 2018.

Johnsen, T. E., Miemczyk, J. and Howard, M. (2017) A systematic literature review of sustainable purchasing and supply research: Theoretical perspectives and opportunities for IMP-based research, *Industrial Marketing Management*, **61**, 130–143.

Pattullo, P. (2005) *Last Resorts: The cost of tourism in the Caribbean.* New York: NYU Press.

References

Al-Aomar, R. and Hussain, M. (2017) An assessment of green practices in a hotel supply chain: A study of UAE hotels, *Journal of Hospitality and Tourism Management*, **32**, 71–81.

Arnold, U., Neubauer, J. and Schoenherr, T. (2012) Explicating factors for companies' inclination towards corruption in operations and supply chain management: An exploratory study in Germany, *International Journal of Production Economics*, **138** (1), 136–147.

Baddeley, J. and Font, X. (2011) Barriers to tour operator sustainable supply chain management, *Tourism Recreation Research*, **36** (3), 205–214

Beck, J. A., Lazer, W. and Schmidgall, R. (2007) Hotel marketing managers' responses to ethical dilemmas, *International Journal of Hospitality and Tourism Administration*, **8** (3), 35–48.

Bensaou, M. (1999) Portfolios of buyer-supplier relationships, *MIT Sloan Management Review*, **40** (4), 35.

Bohdanowicz, P. (2006) Environmental awareness and initiatives in the Swedish and Polish hotel industries—survey results, *International Journal of Hospitality Management*, **25** (4), 662–682.

Bonanni, L., Hockenberry, M., Zwarg, D., Csikszentmihalyi, C. and Ishii, H. (2010) Small business applications of Sourcemap: a web tool for sustainable design and supply chain transparency, in *Proceedings of the 28ᵗʰ SIGCHI Conference on Human Factors in Computing Systems*, Atlanta (Georgia): ACM, pp. 937–946.

Burt, D., Dobler, D. and Starling, S. (2002) *World Class Supply Management: The Key to Supply Chain Management* (7 edition), Boston: McGraw-Hill/Irwin.

Camilleri, M. A. (2012) *Creating shared value through strategic CSR in tourism* (PhD thesis), University of Edinburgh: Edinburgh. https://www.era.lib.ed.ac.uk/handle/1842/6564. Accessed on 31 January 2018.

Cox, A. (2001) Understanding Buyer and supplier power: a framework for procurement and supply competence, *Journal of Supply Chain Management*, **37** (1), 8–15.

Dabhilkar, M., Bengtsson, L. and Lakemond, N. (2015) Sustainable supply management as a purchasing capability: A power and dependence perspective, *International Journal of Operations and Production Management*, **36** (1), 2–22.

Eurostar (2017) *Sustainable Procurement Policy*, London: Eurostar.

Feinstein, A. H. and Stefanelli, J. M. (2011) *Purchasing: Selection and Procurement for the Hospitality Industry* (8th edition), Hoboken, N.J.: Wiley.

Font, X., Guix, M. and Bonilla-Priego, M. J. (2016) Corporate social responsibility in cruising: Using materiality analysis to create shared value, *Tourism Management*, **53**, 175–186.

Font, X., Walmsley, A., Cogotti, S., McCombes, L. and Häusler, N. (2012) Corporate social responsibility: The disclosure–performance gap, *Tourism Management*, **33** (6), 1544–1553.

Green Hotelier (2017) *Responsible Procurement*. http://www.greenhotelier.org/our-themes/responsible-procurement/. Accessed: 31 January 2018.

Hayes, D. K. and Ninemeier, J. D. (2009) *Purchasing: A Guide for Hospitality Professionals*, Upper Saddle River: Pearson.

Jia, F., Gosling, J. and Witzel, M. (2015) *Sustainable Champions: How International Companies are Changing the Face of Business in China*, Sheffield: Greenleaf Publishing.

Johnsen, T. E., Miemczyk, J. and Howard, M. (2017) A systematic literature review of sustainable purchasing and supply research: Theoretical perspectives and opportunities for IMP-based research, *Industrial Marketing Management*, **61**, 130–143.

Kirezieva, K., Luning, P. A., Jacxsens, L., Allende, A., Johannessen, G. S., Tondo, E. C. and van Boekel, M. A. J. S. (2015) Factors affecting the status of food safety management systems in the global fresh produce chain, *Food Control*, **52**, 85–97.

Koens, K. and Thomas, R. (2016) "You know that's a rip-off": policies and practices surrounding micro-enterprises and poverty alleviation in South African township tourism, *Journal of Sustainable Tourism*, **24** (12), 1641–1654.

Krause, D. R., Vachon, S. and Klassen, R. D. (2009) Special topic forum on sustainable supply chain management: introduction and reflections on the role of purchasing management, *Journal of Supply Chain Management*, **45** (4), 18–25.

Lambert, D. M. and Cooper, M. C. (2000) Issues in supply chain management, *Industrial Marketing Management*, **29** (1), 65–83.

Lawlor, F. and Jayawardena, C. (2003) Purchasing for 4,000 hotels: the case of Avendra, *International Journal of Contemporary Hospitality Management*, **15** (6), 346–348.

Margaryan, L. and Stensland, S. (2017) Sustainable by nature? The case of (non)adoption of eco-certification among the nature-based tourism companies in Scandinavia, *Journal of Cleaner Production*, **162**, 559-567.

Melissen, F., Cavagnaro, E., Damen, M. and Düweke, A. (2016) Is the hotel industry prepared to face the challenge of sustainable development?, *Journal of Vacation Marketing*, **22** (3), 227–238.

Mgonja, J. T., Backman, K. F., Backman, S. J., Moore, D. D. and Hallo, J. C. (2017) A structural model to assess international visitors' perceptions about local foods in Tanzania, *Journal of Sustainable Tourism*, **25** (6), 796–816.

10

Miemczyk, J., Johnsen, T.E. and Macquet, M. (2012) Sustainable purchasing and supply management: a structured literature review of definitions and measures at the dyad, chain and network levels, *Supply Chain Management: An International Journal*, **17** (5), 478–496.

Mosgaard, M. A. (2015) Improving the practices of green procurement of minor items, *Journal of Cleaner Production*, **90**, 264–274.

MSC (2015) *Hilton Worldwide Becomes First Global Hotel Company to Serve MSC Certified Sustainable Cod across Europe*, Marine Stewardship Council. https://www.msc.org/newsroom/news/hilton-worldwide-becomes-first-global-hotel-company-to-serve-msc-certified-sustainable-cod-across-europe. Accessed on 31 January 2018.

Pattullo, P. (2005) *Last Resorts: The cost of tourism in the Caribbean*, New York: NYU Press.

Paulraj, A., Chen, I. J. and Flynn, J. (2006) Levels of strategic purchasing: Impact on supply integration and performance, *Journal of Purchasing and Supply Management*, **12** (3), 107–122.

Pullman, M. E., Maloni, M. J. and Carter, C. R. (2009) Food for thought: social versus environmental sustainability practices and performance outcomes, *Journal of Supply Chain Management*, **45** (4), 38–54.

Reimann, F., Ehrgott, M., Kaufmann, L. and Carter, C. R. (2012) Local stakeholders and local legitimacy: MNEs' social strategies in emerging economies, *Journal of International Management*, **18** (1), 1–17.

Responsibletravel (2011). *2011 Responsible Tourism Awards*. https://www.responsibletravel.com/holidays/responsible-tourism/travel-guide/2011-awards-winners. Accessed on 31 January 2018.

Riikkinen, R., Kauppi, K. and Salmi, A. (2017) Learning sustainability? Absorptive capacities as drivers of sustainability in MNCs' purchasing, *International Business Review*, **26** (6), 1075-1087.

Schwartz, K., Tapper, R. and Font, X. (2008) A sustainable supply chain management framework for tour operators, *Journal of Sustainable Tourism*, **16** (3), 298–314.

Shi, X. and Liao, Z. (2013) Managing supply chain relationships in the hospitality services: An empirical study of hotels and restaurants, *International Journal of Hospitality Management*, **35**, 112–121.

Torres, R. and Momsen, J. H. (2004) Challenges and potential for linking tourism and agriculture to achieve pro-poor tourism objectives, *Progress in Development Studies*, **4**, 294–318.

Touzard, J.-M., Chiffoleau, Y. and Maffezzoli, C. (2016) What is local or global about wine? An attempt to objectivize a social construction, *Sustainability*, **8** (5), 417. https://doi.org/10.3390/su8050417

Trent, R. J. and Monczka, R. M. (2005) Achieving excellence in global sourcing, *MIT Sloan Management Review*, **47** (1), 24.

Van der Duim, V. R. (2005) *Tourismscapes* (PhD thesis), Wageningen: Wageningen University.

Van der Duim, V. R. and Caalders, J. (2008) Tourism chains and pro-poor tourism development: an actor-network analysis of a pilot project in Costa Rica', *Current Issues in Tourism*, **11**, 1–17.

Van Weele, A. J. (2014) *Purchasing and Supply Chain Management: Analysis, Strategy, Planning and Practice* (6th Revised edition). Andover: Cengage Learning EMEA.

Van Weele, A. J., Rozemeijer, F. A. and Rietveld, G. (1998) Professionalizing purchasing organization: toward a purchasing development model, in *Proceedings of the 7th IPSERA Conference, London, Great Britain*, ISPERA: London, pp. 515–523.

Vermeulen, W. J. V. and Ras, P. J. (2006) The challenge of greening global product chains: meeting both ends, *Sustainable Development*, **14** (4), 245–256.

Walker, H., Miemczyk, J., Johnsen, T. and Spencer, R. (2012) Sustainable procurement: Past, present and future, *Journal of Purchasing and Supply Management*, **18** (4), 201–206.

Wilhelm, M. M., Blome, C., Bhakoo, V. and Paulraj, A. (2016) Sustainability in multi-tier supply chains: Understanding the double agency role of the first-tier supplier, *Journal of Operations Management*, **41**, 42–60.

Yeh, R. (2012) Hotel general managers' perceptions of business ethics education: implications for hospitality educators, professionals, and students, *Journal of Human Resources in Hospitality and Tourism*, **11** (1), 72–86.

Zhang, X., Song, H. and Huang, G. Q. (2009) Tourism supply chain management: A new research agenda, *Tourism Management*, **30** (3), 345–358.

10

11 Sustainable Transport of Goods:
Tackling backstage challenges of the hospitality industry

Jörn Fricke

Learning goals

After studying this chapter, readers will have the ability to:

1 Define sustainable procurement and its link to profit, people and planet;
2 Describe the main sustainability challenges faced by transport and purchases;
3 Provide examples of how to tackle challenges faced by sustainable transport and purchases;
4 Identify good practices in sustainable transport and purchases.

Introduction

The tourism supply chain can be defined as "a network of tourism organizations engaged in different activities ranging from the supply side to the distribution and marketing of the final tourism product; it involves a wide range of participants in both the private and public sectors" (Zhang *et al.*, 2009: 345). Hotels, restaurants, cafes and other hospitality-related companies are at the heart of this network of tourism organizations. Vujoševic (2004) and Quah and Zulkifli (2011) show that taking small steps in any area of the supply chain can have large effects within the company and can have a positive impact on the competitive advantage of the company. Management of this supply chain and, within it, transport and logistics management are therefore also named as the areas where efficacy and effectiveness of economic systems can be achieved. The logistic supply chain can be seen as a system of links between partners who are all part of the distribution channel that supplies buyers and consumers with products and materials. Only when the product of choice is delivered to the right place in the right time, with optimized amounts under adequate conditions, with the participation of carriers that move through air or over road and rails, can it fulfil its task successfully. Wilson (2009) states that, while companies have become increasingly aware of the fact that transport and logistics management are linked to competitive advantage, they still struggle as they are seen as a separate entity within the company's operation.

Within the field of purchases, there are three elements that need to be looked at in detail in order to understand the whole supply chain and its management: purchasing, vendors and transport or logistics. Tourists' transportation is covered in Chapter 3 by Matthias Olthaar; while purchasing locally is discussed by Sarah Seidel and Elena Cavagnaro (Chapter 9) and purchasing internationally by Ko Koens and Harry Reinders (Chapter 10). In this chapter we cover transport dealing with the movement of goods and materials by air, rail, road or sea. Some argue that logistics should also cover non-tangible products such as information and data – that a business must source in order to function properly.

Value creation is a term widely used in academia and in practical contexts. It deals with achieving competitive advantage through efficiency and effectiveness. Yet value itself is defined by the customer and created through product and service improvement. Rather than simply increasing profit for shareholders, the aim of value creation is to add value to customers and suppliers (Shamah, 2013). Included in this concept is the idea of sustainable development through the reduction of waste and the preservation of resources, as Chapter 2 on the Sustainable Hospitality Value Chain has already shown. Companies differ with regards to the level of awareness and especially implementation of sustainable practices along their supply chain. With higher awareness comes the ability to overcome obstacles regarding the implementation of sustainable supply chain management.

Sustainable transport in the hospitality industry, especially in tourism which often involves air transport to get tourists to their destination, is a somewhat difficult topic just because this part of the industry is where most of the CO_2 emissions and greenhouse gasses are produced (see Chapter 3). The focus here, however, shall be on transport within procurement, i.e. the products and materials that are transported to and from businesses in the hospitality sector along the supply chain and where higher levels of sustainability can be achieved.

Numerous businesses in the hospitality sector are now looking at options to reduce the environmental impact, while at the same time cutting costs. The shift to a more sustainable procurement involves moving away from a traditional cost-benefit analysis to the inclusion of environmental criteria. Asking suppliers to follow these criteria before signing a contract can enhance cooperation between partners, with the opportunity of win-win situations. Worldwide, between 6,000 and 7,000 procurement professionals (Palmer, 2013) are in charge of institutional purchasing. It is this purchasing power that offers the opportunity to effectively change supply chains to a more sustainable future. Instead of changing the mindset of millions of people, it is these professionals who could help the industry to

11

take a large step forward towards a more sustainable future. Sustainable transport planning recognizes that transport decisions affect people in many ways, so a variety of objectives and impacts should be considered in the planning process.

This chapter will start with a description of the major sustainability challenges that transport and logistics face in the area of purchasing in the hospitality industry, followed by three best cases, of which each is set in one of the three dimensions of sustainability (economic, social and environmental issues). Finally, it will conclude with a series of tools that could help address these challenges.

Main sustainability challenges

In 2015, the United Nations Conference on Trade and Development (UNCTAD) secretariat devised a concept of sustainable freight transport with criteria for each of the three dimensions of sustainability – economic, environmental and social (UNCTAD, 2015). Within the economic dimension, (energy) efficiency and productivity, employment and revenue generation, access, connectivity and competitiveness as well as infrastructural development are mentioned, while in the social pillar, equity and fairness, social inclusiveness and value, community involvement, health and safety as well as the quality of the labour conditions were included. Finally, with regards to the environmental pillar, water, air and soil pollution, air emissions and greenhouse gases, climate change impact and resilience, resource depletion and land use should be taken into consideration. In this section we focus on these challenges in the economic, the social and the environmental dimension of sustainability.

Economic challenges

Within a company's overall expenditure, transportation can be a significant part, sometimes amounting to more than half the logistics spend (Rodrigue, 2017). Once these expenses have been established, they are passed on to the customer, increaseing the price of the offering. Due to the fact that transportation costs can be such a considerable share of the overall expenses, companies are interested in trimming these costs, and there are a variety of ways to achieve this: using fewer carriers, consolidating shipments and single sourcing (Murray, 2017).

In the same way that the purchasing department attempts to streamline vendors in order to minimize costs and gain higher volumes, a comparable strategy could be adopted with respect to the number of carriers (Murray, 2017). Simply looking for the best carrier for the best price can have the effect that you end up with too many carriers. To avoid this situation, an overall view is required of the transportation system around the company, and by reducing the number of carriers, each one will carry more load and the transport companies will be able to offer better rates. Fewer kilometres with the same amount of goods is linked directly to the environmental dimension through the reduction of emissions (see also Figure 11.1).

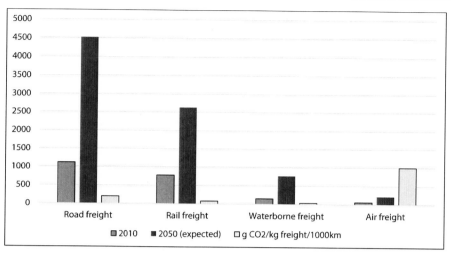

Figure 11.1: CO_2 emissions worldwide of different freight carriers in 2010 (in million tonnes and g CO_2 per kg per 1000km).
Source: adapted by the authors from CO2-emissionen-vergleichen (2010); Statista (2010)

One major challenge with this approach is that the company runs the risk of developing a high dependency on too few carriers. Should one of them drop out, this could lead to delivery failures, unsatisfied customers and in the end, lower revenues. With a larger number of carriers, losing one of them has less of an impact on the overall transport service, and the company can be more resilient to such events.

Another way of reducing costs and increasing efficiency is by consolidating shipments (Farris, 1998), with the aim of reducing the number of shipments and receiving lower rates. However, even though this is not always possible, transportation managers will always have a look at whether they can combine shipments in larger units to reduce costs.

Finally, using a single source for a large variety, if not all, shipments and transports can be an option, and is often used by purchasing managers and transport managers (Murray, 2017). It does mean that the company needs to thoroughly evaluate the transport company's ability to provide quality service, and whether it is financially stable. You are entering a very delicate dependency relationship and should not underestimate the risks. Once the transport company has been checked and appears to fulfil the needs, a company can attain considerable savings on costs. This should allow companies to provide their customers the same quality of service at a better price.

One of the main arenas where hospitality businesses have to make decisions is between a global and a local supply chain (Piboonrungroj and Disney, 2015). Both have advantages and disadvantages that need to be considered. Global supply chains offer economies of scale that reduce cost per kilometre, while adding a global market makes it possible to improve sales and increase efficiency of the

11

supply chain, with full loads rather than fractional loads. Opening up to a global market also allows a company to choose from a wider variety of supply chain partners, among which are transport businesses. This in turn can reduce costs, which will then allow for a more competitive product and/or service to sell on the market. In other words, there will be more value for the customer.

However, a global supply chain also presents challenges, such as language and differing quality expectations, which can result in varying levels of quality and dissatisfied customers. Especially for transport, global supply chain means longer distances to travel. Should there be backorders, these can be more difficult to fill compared to a local supply chain. With local supply chains, the overall environmental cost – especially when taking into consideration waste – can be less than in a global supply chain (Solér *et al.*, 2010). Transporting all kinds of goods from all over the world to their destinations can also increase the complexity to such a level that the system becomes prone to disturbances (Woxenius *et al.*, 2001).

Another challenge is the hidden transport costs if the vendor takes care of the transport (Rogers *et al.*, 2012).

Environmental challenges

Khairat and Maher (2012) indicate that some hospitality businesses – in their case tour operators – still consider sustainability in the supply chain management to be motivated primarily by the aim of 'building a positive public image', while the main benefits that are reported are 'increased operational efficiency & business opportunities', 'competitive advantage' and 'improved image of company in general' (p.136). There appears to be a major gap between strategy and actual implementation, due to a lack of stakeholder support, high levels of actual or perceived complexity with numerous partners, and difficulties of having to invest extra funds into environmental and social activities. In a similar fashion, most hotels continue to see sustainable transport as an environmental or a cost-cutting issue, whereby products with less packaging and clean transport as a part of the input are considered paramount to performing 'green' (Al-Aomar and Hussain, 2017). As part of a bigger picture, where suppliers, input, processes, output and the customer are combined in the supply chain, transport is therefore only a 'small' part of the whole chain.

Next to increasing efficiency and effectiveness of transport in the supply chain, companies who want to work sustainably, however, cannot ignore the impact it has on the environment and society as a whole. Increasing awareness of corporate social responsibility commands that companies become aware of the social and environmental impact of their supply chain and look into how they can reduce the negative impact of their businesses activities. Transport issues, being so tightly linked to the use of fossil fuels and therefore greenhouse gases and emissions into the air, present a major environmental dilemma. And while financial data that can be used to analyse the costs and benefits are quite straightforward, environmental and social data are highly complex and require a very different approach and a certain level of simplification. What is needed is quantified data of a product or system not only during its production, but throughout its lifetime – a whole-life cycle analysis.

As transport in logistics is still based on the use of fossil fuels, its environmental impact and the related challenges become immediately apparent. The overall transport sector accounts for a quarter of greenhouse gas emissions in the EU, with road transport taking the largest share (European Commission, 2016). Numbers from New Zealand reveal that the transport sector accounts for 17.4% of total CO_2 emissions (New Zealand Ministry for the Environment, 2016), and assuming that 20% of light duty road transport emissions arise from business activities, the business sectors accounts for roughly a third of the total transport emissions in that country.

The direct environmental effects of transport are, of course, the use of energy and the emissions that are caused by moving materials and goods with vehicles from one place to another. Any vehicle that uses gasoline will break hydrocarbon molecules, and the combustion process produces emissions which contain chemicals such as carbon dioxide – known to cause global warming – but also carbon monoxide, sulphur oxides, nitrogen oxides, particulate matter and others. In transport lingo, these are called *direct emissions* as they are linked to the primary aim of making the transport of goods and materials possible.

Even though road vehicles have become more efficient with their use of fuel, overall transport volumes have continuously increased. Air pollution is therefore a problem that we are facing more and more, as we can tell by the measures taken by some countries, especially in urban areas, to reduce traffic. Companies can either opt for an energy-efficient transport system and enhance transport efficiency of energy use, or they can opt to attempt reducing transport vehicle mileage (Chiu and Hsieh, 2016). There are options such as electric and alternative-fuelled cars, but until now, with regards to sustainability none of them have managed to tackle the environmental issues of transports and logistics successfully, either because the mining of raw materials and the recycling of lithium-ion batteries is considered unsustainable, because the energy that charges the batteries is generated in an unsustainable way (Majeau-Bettez *et al.*, 2011) or because biofuels compete with other crops for land use (Rathore *et al.*, 2016).

There are also ancillary processes, which enable the primary process to exist and whose impacts on the environment have to be taken into account: vehicle, infrastructure and energy production services. Any truck, ship or plane that will move goods first needs to be built. You also need a road network, ports and airports, all of which need to be constructed, operated and maintained. In order for the energy to be available, there needs to be a system that extracts and produces (mostly fossil) fuels that can then be used as a source of energy. Each of these ancillary processes has its own system of life-cycle processes that are needed for the overall system to work.

Some companies choose to set up a system with a central distribution depot whereby a large number of relatively short transport distances are covered by the carriers. This leads to longer journeys made by trucks, and two trips for each item: from the supplier to the depot, and from the depot to the company. This common practice cannot be considered environmentally sound.

Another challenge for a sustainable transport infrastructure in the hospitality sector is the seasonality of demand for mobility and transport services (also a social issue because of temporary/seasonal employment), with peak periods producing a large traffic volume with extremely high emission levels compared to low seasons where sometimes there can be no transport specifically for hospitality businesses and tourists (European Commission, 2017). In this case, a multi-stakeholder approach is required to address these issues, involving the transport sector, environmental organizations and the hospitality sector.

If a business chooses to go 'all the way', some products, goods and materials – especially food – can even be produced 'on-site' in order to reduce the environmental impact of transport by eliminating it altogether. Figure 11.1 displays the total emissions of CO_2 worldwide of various freight carriers as well as the emission per kg per 1000km of transport. With the figures on total emission through road transport and the high level of CO_2 emissions per transported kg through the air in mind, even though on-site production might look radical to some, it is definitely paramount to prevent any unnecessary or avoidable transport of goods to and from the business.

Social challenges

While increasing attention has been paid to the environmental and economic dimensions of sustainable procurement and more specifically the transport of goods and materials in the hospitality sector, so far limited information has been made available regarding the social impact of a more sustainable supply chain management and more specifically in transport. While the aims of equity and fairness, inclusiveness, community involvement, health and safety in the production part of the supply chains are relatively straightforward, albeit challenging to achieve, the concept of sustainability of the entire supply chain should ensure that the same elements be considered in the transport sector. What about the social risks, bribery and corruption, poor working conditions, discrimination and the overall ethical standards in the transport of goods and products in the hospitality industry? Investment in these areas often does not provide immediate financial gains but is aimed at long-term revenues and 'soft' benefits. However, with increasing public awareness of the impact of business activities, hospitality businesses have started to become increasingly aware of the need to address social issues in their supply chain (CERES, n.d.). Especially when companies are active in regions with strong levels of inequality, and discrimination of certain members of society, businesses can make a change for the better by considering the needs of people within their sustainable supply chain management. Nonetheless, the overall social sustainability of transport – which is a highly competitive market – appears to be more an issue of (legal) regulation, and often more at home with public services than with the private sector (see also UN, 2012).

Many hospitality businesses source their materials, their food and services from where it is most cost-efficient, most easily accessible, most reliable and of an assured quality. As mentioned under global supply chains above, these criteria often lead to businesses selecting large international suppliers rather than local small and medium-sized enterprises or from disadvantaged entrepreneurs. However, in the context of transport management, local sourcing of food and drinks has a variety of benefits such as reducing costs, helping local service providers and therefore the local economy while at the same time having the potential to enhance community relationships and a higher predictability of delivery (Green Hotelier, 2012; see also Chapter 9).

With regards to transport services, one main issue is the responsibility along the supply chain: at what point does this responsibility for the supplier end and where does the responsibility of the hospitality business start. This has a strong impact as to what extent the company can put into practice its internal sustainability policy, or at what point the tendering process will have to include sustainability criteria when choosing a certain supplier and transport service.

Best cases

Case 11.1: Economic challenge

With an increasing number of Muslim travellers and of increasing expenditure (US$ 155 billion in 2016) especially in Asia and the Middle East (Elliott, 2017), halal-certified food transport will play an greater role in customer choices in the hotel industry (Malaysia Institute of Transport, 2012). The Malaysian government has acknowledged the market potential for halal food logistics, with a value of the halal industry of around US$ 2.3 trillion (excluding finance) in 2013 and moving beyond the traditional sector into pharmaceuticals, health products and medical devices, and into the service sector with logistics, marketing, branding, packaging and more (Edbiz Consulting, 2013). A key issue for transport in the hotel industry is the fact that with an increasing market segment of Muslim customers, service providers in the food and beverage industry – and therefore the hotel industry – will need more halal certified services, which ensure that food and beverages follow Islamic rules and principles. Service providers need to ensure that the products are not haram (i.e. 'contaminated') for instance through contact with pork along the logistics chain. In 2015, Yusen Logistics, a major Japanese shipping company, received halal certification in Indonesia (Nikkei, 2017) with its growing Muslim middle class, and has recently opened a warehouse in other Southeast Asian countries, such as Thailand (Yusen Logistics, 2017) where the first halal hotel opened in 2016 (South China Morning Post, 2016).

11

Case 11.2: Environmental challenge

In the Austrian resort of Bad Hofgastein, which is located in the touristically well-developed but ecologically very sensitive Alpine region, car and freight traffic has resulted in high levels of pollution (Sammer, 2013). Within the framework of the EU-funded LIFE project, various measures were planned, of which an emission-free freight distribution system was implemented. Other projects such as CO_2 free public transport were not realized, due to technical difficulties of electric vehicles in such a mountainous region. However, as a result, shops and hotels managed to jointly organize deliveries with the help of electric powered vans. CO_2 emissions were thereby reduced by 13% and noise exposure was reduced. The intention in Bad Hofgastein was not only to reduce the environmental impact of freight, but to serve as an example for other tourist destinations in the region, such as Werfenweng. While individual hospitality businesses often appear to be lagging behind with regards to environmentally friendly logistics, results of this project suggest that regions in environmentally fragile areas can benefit from the economies of scale when clusters of businesses join forces to improve the footprint of their logistics (European Union, 2001).

Case 11.3: Social challenge

This case study will help you understand how the challenge of using a social approach in developing transport services can be addressed – here with the help of a hotel in South Africa. Spier is a family-run wine farm accommodation in Stellenbosch (South Africa) that has been running since 1692 (Spier, 2017). It offers farm-to-table services with products that are sourced from local producers. Next to serving food and drinks in their restaurant, Spier also acts as a hotel with more than 150 rooms and conference venue. The company has been awarded conservation awards, is organically certified and follows sustainable production methods of wine, with numerous certificates that have been recognized by external organizations. The company was a pioneer in fair trade production methods in the country (Demhardt, 2008). In post-Apartheid South Africa, empowerment of black-owned companies is at the heart of developing the economy and drives business activities to a more equitable distribution of wealth in the country (Hiam *et al.*, 2017).

Before 2003, Spier had already realized sustainable development as part of their business activities, but rather than integrating it into the base philosophy of the company, it was project-based and ad hoc. The company culture needed to reflect their dedication to achieve higher levels of sustainability, and move beyond purely financial success into actual care for the environment and society. The idea was to create a number of businesses that would help contribute successfully to environmental conservation and social justice, by making business operations sustainable, not only on the basis of individual projects but for every single business activity. One of the major challenges in this respect was the diversity of a large company, where each part of the company required a customized approach rather than a common approach for all (Spier, 2017).

After some thorough research, a director of sustainability was appointed, with the remit to drive the whole move towards sustainability. With a large number of suppliers of goods and services, there was a need to identify major issues and with the help of a questionnaire, the company attempted to find small, local, black-owned businesses to work with. At the same time, it was necessary to find out which of the products and services could be provided by local, black-owned small and medium-sized enterprises (Demhardt, 2008).

One black driver, who had worked for Spier for a long time, and had always wished to run a self-owned transport company, got in touch with Spier in 2008. The idea was to become self-employed and continue working as a service provider. Convinced by his work performance and spirit, Spier looked for a way to help him on his way to having his own company, and at the same time continue transforming the supply chain. After getting in touch with an existing transport partner who was responsible for the entire transport of wine across South Africa, the company suggested the establishment of a joint venture to subcontract services in order to cope with excess transport that the company could not take care of. The joint venture was established, a black entrepreneur was successful in borrowing money for his own truck and the black-empowered joint venture – called *Debinisa*, which is Xhosa for joy – is assured of a regular income in order for the loan to be paid off. Spier can continue being successful with its procurement, a black entrepreneur has managed to start up his own business, and the transport company can look for more jobs now with the help of the joint venture which is guaranteed a share of the transport so as to finance the first stages of the company (Spier, 2017).

Compared to other wine and leisure businesses in South Africa, transforming the supply chain, and making use of procurement to push change forward, has turned into a competitive advantage and increased the overall level of innovative practices at Spier.

Tools to address the challenges

In order to address these challenges of sustainable transport in the supply chain, three broad steps need to be taken. First, there must be a sustainable supply chain policy and management system that integrates and structures the company's sustainability policies. Second, suppliers must be supported in reaching sustainability goals, as the procurement system as a whole needs to be sustainable to function properly. Third, sustainability criteria must be integrated into suppliers' contracts to assure the partners of accountability in regard to sustainability. Some common solutions with respect to efficiency and economic benefits have been addressed in the challenges section above, so here the intention is to focus on the economic benefits for the company and the community where it is located.

Economic tools

Making use of locally available logistics increases regional differential multiplier effects – these effects indicate the monetary value that is retained within the network of first and second-line individuals and businesses that work with a company in a certain region – while preventing leakages – the monetary value that drains outside the region through imports – to the outside. Businesses can reduce the amount of fossil fuels that lead to greenhouse gas emissions and air pollution. Moreover, making use of local transport services not only promotes the local economy and reduces pollution levels, but it can have social benefits that extend beyond the immediate and create a strong relationship with the community. However, in some cases (Pratt *et al.*, 2017) sustainability is affected negatively when local sourcing results in the supply of products and goods that fail to meet standard health regulations. Failure to perform in one area of the value chain can then have serious ripple effects through the supply chain, and shows how intertwined the various areas of sustainability are. Designing a service that simplifies the coordination of product system with shorter transport distances and with fewer carriers can be the solution to purchasing issues in global supply chains.

The challenge of hidden transport costs that were mentioned in the economic challenge section can be tackled by outsourcing transport to a third party that is transparent in handling the shipment and billing for the service of transport. The hospitality business can then monitor service choices and leverage its purchasing power. One example would, for instance, be the replacement of rooms, adding upgrades, or the improvement of facilities, all of which require base materials and labour.

In any case, wherever and whenever possible, a business aiming for economic efficiency while considering environmental and especially social sustainability should always try to find the shortest possible distance for transport.

Environmental tools

Life-cycle assessment (LCA), sometimes also called life-cycle analysis, is a method that helps you measure and evaluate the impact on the environment, by describing and assessing energy and materials that are extracted from and released into the environment over a life cycle of a product or good, from cradle to grave. It has been around since the 1970s, and any quantifiable flow, such as labour, costs, materials, water, energy and pollutants, can be measured and evaluated. LCA is a method that is relevant to sustainable development as it offers the opportunity to identify in which part of the life cycle a company can improve its performance. In this section we will elaborate on LCAs by first looking at how to reduce CO_2 emissions and then the use of environmental certification standards.

Reducing CO_2 emissions

In order to minimize the ecological impact of business activities, the aim should be to make transport as resource-efficient and hazard-free as possible. Ways of achieving this include local sourcing, and if it is not possible to make use of energy-efficient means of transport, at least prioritizing bulk orders. Requesting local suppliers to ship their goods via ground rather than air can help reduce the CO_2 footprint of the company. When goods cannot be sourced locally, choosing the environmentally friendly option for transporting goods should always have priority. Airfreight therefore should always be the last option (see Figure 11.1). Bulk shipment with sea freight – despite the fact that it has environmental consequences – can be a good option, especially considering the move to slower shipment speeds, which in turn reduces CO_2 emissions. Another option is to choose companies that consolidate shipments and schedule deliveries in order to reduce the environmental impact of individualized shipping. Rail transport offers the chance to use renewable energy resources and at the same time transport large volumes of goods. Rail shipments are high-speed, and as a high-density transport can provide plenty of opportunities for future improvement. Last but not least, there is road transport where a company can choose to transport goods with a supplier that tries to use fuel-efficient and low-emission vehicles.

Moreover, packing material that is required during the transport should come from certified sources and be recyclable. When choosing transport services, one criteria should be to check whether the packaging will be re-used or recycled. Choose packaging that can be recycled locally rather than be transported to a recycling facility far away. Recycling in general will eliminate a part of transport costs, which in itself can be a step forward to more sustainable business practices.

Finally, when emissions cannot be reduced, or there is a lack of alternatives for transporting goods, there is still the opportunity to practice carbon-offsetting (Zotz, 2008), whereby there is a compensation through the support of carbon emission reduction elsewhere. This can either be done by the company itself, or by utilizing retail carbon off-sets. The issue with carbon-offsetting is that there is no single methodology with which it is calculated. Offsetting can therefore be seen as a positive yet quite subjective practice.

Certifying environmental standards

The aim of environmental certification is for companies to meet the requirements of processes as defined by a certification service. Once certified, the company can use the logo as a proof to relevant stakeholders that the company adheres to principles of corporate social responsibility beyond the limits set through legal requirements. One of the most important organizations which provide such certification services is the International Organization for Standardization (ISO). First launched in 1996, ISO 14001 was revised in 2015 as the issues surrounding climate change needed to be included (ISO, 2015). As a risk-based environmental management system, ISO 14001 intends to meet expectations of policy makers regarding water utilization or energy usage. During a three-year transition period, certified organizations will be allowed to adapt and integrate the requirements of the most recent transition, or they will lose their ISO certification. These challenges need to be addressed in order for stakeholders to be assured that companies are ready to tackle the multitude of problems surrounding sustainable business practices. ISO certifications are a tool that helps with the process of continuously improving environmental performances. They have gained increasing recognition as

11

a self-improvement tool for third-party recognition. In 2017 more than 300,000 certified companies made use of ISO as a tool on the way to achieving sustainable development globally (Deutsche Gesellschaft für Nachhaltigkeit, 2017). Internally, employees can be taken on board to work on a shared commitment, and it makes companies 'stand out' compared to their competitors while helping to increase efficiency levels. The 2015 revision of the ISO certificate was devised by 70 ISO certified companies with the intention of making the transport of goods more sustainable.

Integrating *whole life-cycle costing* and *life-cycle analysis* is an important way of addressing the challenge of making transport of goods for the hospitality industry more sustainable. These terms are often used interchangeably, which makes it difficult to distinguish one from the other. Whole life-cycle cost (WLC) is a tool that is defined by ISO standard 15686 to "assist in assessing all significant and relevant initial and future costs and benefits of an asset, throughout its life cycle, while fulfilling the performance requirements" (ISO, 2017). This includes the operational costs that follow after initial purchasing costs. With respect to transport and purchases, it is worth noting that WLC is a systematic way of considering all costs and revenues that are related to the acquisition, use and maintenance as well as the disposal of an asset. Other terms such as *life-cycle cost* and *through life cost* also exist, but are less common nowadays.

There are two kinds of LCAs: retrospective and prospective ones. The former were the most common but the latter is gaining in importance to help decision-making. Retrospective LCAs such as one for a train ride would include direct effects such as the movement of the train, ancillary effects, as for instance the evaluation of the greenhouse gas emission because of the construction of a rail network divided by the number of train rides, and supply chain effects, which are, for instance, greenhouse gas emissions from extracting raw materials that are used to build a train, and then divided by the number of rides a train will make throughout its lifetime. Prospective LCAs look at what would happen if a new transportation system made use of existing infrastructure in a more efficient way. In that case there would not be increasing greenhouse gas emissions, as no new infrastructure would need to be built. This can help decision-makers in companies opt for alternatives in line with environmental considerations.

Social tools

Economic and social aspects and impacts are, typically, outside the scope of the LCA. Other tools may be combined with LCA for more extensive assessments. At least in the public arena, and in the context of sustainable procurement, awareness of the fact that organizations have to move beyond the purchase price of a good to include financial and non-financial gains by looking also at social costs and benefits are considered. However, depending on the socio-political context, private companies often tend to neglect social costs. While public authorities are held accountable by the electorate, traditionally, companies often would not move further than the legal obligations with regards to their impact analysis. However, more recently, managers have realized that merely complying with regulatory or contractual frameworks is often not sufficient, as environmental and social awareness can improve public perception and add to the competitive advantage (Theyel, 2001). Moreover, the public eye often does not discern between the environmental and social performance of a company and its suppliers, but holds the company itself accountable for the overall performance within a supply chain (Rao and Holt, 2005; Kovacs, 2008).

Noteworthy exceptions exist in countries where business activities are embedded in a highly politicized society and where the government has a strong pro-poor policy, with legal requirements for companies to abide. South Africa is such as country, where in the post-Apartheid era, the national government made sure that the black population would get access to beneficial treatment in order to overcome the division between races. The example of Spier illustrated this, showing how the company helped established black-empowered businesses successfully.

In order to address the issues of global supply chains, companies can design the transport within their supply based on a certain sustainability goals and look for partners that are compatible with the firm's goal. However, especially in a global context, cultural, language and political factors can render this difficult and the company will need to find a way to assess the compatibility of its service providers.

Regarding deeper social issues such as disadvantaged communities or individuals, companies can select transport services based on pro-poor criteria, helping long-term unemployed or maybe integrating smaller, emerging companies into the supply chain. Due to the fact that they are often limited by capacity, they would need to be mentored or receive other additional support in the beginning. While this might be a small difference for the businesses, it can potentially have a large impact on those transport companies, triggering a ripple effect throughout the supply chain with second and third tier suppliers of services in the long-term. This can sometimes be achieved simply by asking for social responsibility from service providers, thereby raising awareness which can lead to changes in the future.

Conclusion

Regulation and the quest for competitive advantage appear to be the driving forces behind the improvement of environmental, social and economic performances of the transport sector. Greater use of (fuel) technologies and improved energy efficiency give industries a competitive advantage, with an especially high potential for industries in emerging economies to improve their performance. Another driver for change is consumer demands for sustainability and corporate social responsibility in supply chains worldwide, with a more a transparent and reliable performance and as a result, a reduced ecological footprint.

Transport stands at the core of achieving sustainable development in procurement procedures. Not only does it trigger economic growth, promote trade, and enhance access, but it also creates links between communities and societies. Transport systems can play an important role in achieving efficiency, equity and environmentally sound development. Crucial to an improvement of the sector's performance is ongoing coordination between all the private and public stakeholders involved.

Supply chain management is traditionally based on price and quality with the aim of maximizing benefits/profits. Externalities such as the impact on the environment or social costs are often not part of the equation, and it was only recently that policymakers started to create a legal framework that pushed companies towards sustainability reporting and that companies began to include non-economic figures in their sustainable procurement, where consequences for third parties are taken into account. Some progress has been made with regards to the environmental impact, yet, until today, social factors are often neglected, and environmental factors included often only if they lead to price advantages.

Choosing transport services that meet the desired sustainability criteria can be a challenge, but it is here that hospitality businesses can show their dedication to the task by not resorting to the obvious choice of the most cost-efficient transport service in the short-term, but by including those businesses that show readiness to improve on their sustainability performance across the board in environmental, social or economic areas. The task of the hospitality businesses would then be to educate those service providers and thereby increase sustainability performances in every step of the supply chain. This would be a strategic, in-depth approach to reforming procurement, initiated by the management with the aim of not only improving the overall sustainability performance, but also gaining knowledge of the individual performances of all the actors, providing information for assessment of transport services, improving knowledge levels about sustainability inside the company, and increasing accountability of managers with respect to working on improved sustainability performance throughout the supply chain. For more on these points, see Chapter 10 on International Purchasing.

The transport sector itself needs to move towards a culture of collaboration and partnership through raising awareness while at the same time influencing owners' and consumers' expectations and decisions. To move forward in sustainability also requires services to move beyond cost alone, through the inclusion of health and safety, benefits for the environment, innovation, standardization and a higher level of transparency. All in all, it is crucial for a variety of private and public stakeholders to collaborate on achieving efficiency in this area.

One specific challenge remains: how credible is an industry that depends to a great extent on transporting guests by long- and short-haul air travel to their destination, with regards to their efforts to tackle sustainability by transporting goods and materials to their facilities in a more sustainable way? This is a question that has been repeatedly asked in this book, for example in Chapters 1 (the

Introduction) and 3 on Tourist mobility. Here, I wish to stress that climate protection (among others) needs to be the guiding principle in existing business strategies, and top-level management needs to develop measurable targets, as it must be committed to these goals (and held accountable) and devise key performance indicators. Not only vendors, but also transport services should be selected on their mitigation performance and, if need be, the carbon footprint can be offset through credible offset schemes. Offset schemes are likely to be the initial step for many of the larger organizations on their way to more sustainable business activities, as it allows them to work on their performance without having to make immediate structural changes.

Urban areas might provide the opportunity to implement highly-advanced sustainable transport and mobility solutions. Increasing purchaser and end-user awareness about technologies and processes in applying these urban solutions can boost market demand in general. As such, sustainable transport and procurement in the hospitality industry is obviously not limited to that sector alone, but part of a 'bigger picture' that needs to be addressed by all stakeholders involved.

The transport sector is one of the main contributor to greenhouse gases and air pollution, and with the effects that carbon emissions and fossil fuels have on the environment, it is of utmost importance to make its performance more efficient in terms of people and goods transported per kilometre. Most importantly for the image in the eye of the customer to improve, businesses need to cooperate with NGOs and public authorities and communicate their progress through adequate and trustworthy channels.

Further readings

Hyard, A. (2014) *Non-technological Innovations for Sustainable Transport – Four Transport Case Studies*, London: Springer.

Kersten, W., Blecker, T. and Ringle, C.M. (eds.) (2015) *Sustainability in Logistics and Supply Chain Management – New Designs and Strategies, Proceedings at the Hamburg International Conference of Logistics* (HICL) – 21, Berlin: epubli GmbH, accessed on 11 January 2018 from https://tubdok.tub.tuhh.de/bitstream/11420/1266/1/HICL%202015%20-%20 Vol%2021%20-%20Sustainability%20in%20Logistics%20and%20Supply%20Chain%20 Management.pdf

Kramberger, T., Potocan, V. and Ipavec, V.M. (2016) *Sustainable Logistics and Strategic Transportation Planning*, Hershey, USA: Business Science Reference.

11

References

Al-Aomar, R. and Hussain, M. (2017) An assessment of green practices in a hotel supply chain: A study of UAE hotels', *Journal of Hospitality and Tourism Management*, **32**, 71-81.

CERES (n.d.) *Performance: Supply Chain*. https://www.ceres.org/roadmap/performance/supply-chain. Accessed 23 September 2017.

CO2-Emissionen-Vergleichen (2010) *CO_2-Vergleich beim Lebensmitteltransport*. http://www.co2-emissionen-vergleichen.de/Lebensmittel/Transport/CO2-Transport-Lebensmittel.html. Accessed 10 October 2017.

Chiu, J-Z. and Hsieh, C-C. (2016) The impact of restaurants' green supply chain practices on firm performance, *Sustainability* **8** (1), 42. www.mdpi.com/2071-1050/8/1/42/htm. Accessed 11 January 2018.

Demhardt, I. J. (2003) Wine and Tourism at the "Fairest Cape", *Journal of Travel & Tourism Marketing*, **14** (3-4), 113-130.

Deutsche Gesellschaft für Nachhaltigkeit (2017) *ISO 14001:2015 Die wichtigsten Änderungen*. http://dqs-cfs.com/de/2014/10/iso-140012015-die-wichtigsten-neuerungen/. Accessed 17 October 2017.

Edbiz Consulting (2013) *Global Islamic Finance Report 2013*. www.gifr.net/gifr2013/ch_13. PDF. Accessed 17 September 2017.

Elliott, M. (2017) *Southeast Asia drives growth of Muslim travel market, in: TravelDailyMedia*, posted on 3rd May. www.traveldailymedia.com/250063/southeast-asia-drives-growth-of-muslim-travel-market/. Accessed 16 October 2017.

European Commission (2016) *Buying Green! A handbook on green public procurement*. http://ec.europa.eu/environment/gpp/pdf/Buying-Green-Handbook-3rd-Edition.pdf. Accessed 16 October 2017.

European Commission (2017) *Sustainable Transport for Areas with Tourism through Energy Reduction (STARTER)*. https://ec.europa.eu/energy/intelligent/projects/en/projects/starter. Accessed 1 January 2018.

European Union (2001) *Sustainable transport logistic - Environmental sustainable vehicles and transport logistic for public transport and freight distribution in tourist resorts*. http://ec.europa.eu/environment/life/project/Projects/index.cfm?fuseaction=search.dspPage&n_proj_id=840. Accessed 10 June 2017.

Farris, M. T. (1998) Reduce total purchased cost by 5% through inbound freight management, *Institute for Supply Management 83rd Annual International Conference Proceedings*.https://www.instituteforsupplymanagement.org/pubs/Proceedings/confproceedingsdetail.cfm?ItemNumber=10778&SSO=1. Accessed 11 January 2018.

Green Hotelier (2012) *Responsible Procurement*. www.greenhotelier.org/our-themes/responsible-procurement/. Accessed 10 June 2017.

Hiam, C. M., Eshghi, G. and Eshghi A. (2017) Business impact of the black economic empowerment in South Africa: A critical review of four case studies, *Journal of Research in Business, Economics and Management*, **8** (2), 1370-1380.

International Organization for Standardization (2015) *ISO 14001:2015 - Environmental management systems - Requirements with guidance for use*. https://www.iso.org/standard/60857.html. Accessed 17 October 2017

International Organization for Standardization (2017) *ISO 15686-5:2017 - Buildings and constructed assets - Service life planning - Part 5: Life-cycle costing.* https://www.iso.org/obp/ui/#iso:std:iso:15686:-5:ed-2:v1:en. Accessed 13 December 2017.

Khairat, G. and Maher, A. (2012) Integrating sustainability into tour operator business: an innovative approach to sustainable tourism, *Tourismos: An International Multidisciplinary Journal of Tourism*, **7** (1), 213-233.

Kovacs, G. (2008) Corporate environmental responsibility in the supply chain, *Journal of Cleaner Production*, **16** (15), 1571–1578.

Majeau Bettez, G., Hawkins, T.R. and Stromman, A.H. (2011) Life cycle environmental assessment of lithium-ion and nickel metal hydride batteries for plug-in hybrid and battery electric vehicles, *Environmental Science & Technology*, **45** (10), 4548 - 4554

Malaysia Institute of Transport (2012) *The Value and Advantage of Halal Logistics*, Presentation at Halal Logistics Conference, Penang (Malaysia), 28th June, http://www.hdcglobal.com/upload-web/cms-editor-files/21bc5b40-5eff-40e8-b4ff-5b6a20931fed/file/The%20Value%20and%20Advantage%20of%20Halal%20Logistics_AZLINA.pdf. Accessed 5 October 2017.

Murray, M. (2017) *Reducing Supply Chain Transportation Logistics Costs.* https://www.thebalance.com/reducing-transportation-costs-2221049, Accessed 10 August 2017.

New Zealand Ministry for the Environment (2016) *New Zealand's Greenhouse Gas Inventory 1990–2014.* www.mfe.govt.nz/publications/climate-change/new-zealand-greenhouse-gas-inventory-1990-2014. Accessed 24 October 2017.

Nikkei (2017) Japanese shipper expands halal logistics to Indonesia, *Nikkei Asian Review*, **14** (October). https://asia.nikkei.com/Business/Companies/Japanese-shipper-expands-halal-logistics-to-Indonesia. Accessed 17 October 2017.

Palmer, L. (2013) The power of procurement: can sustainable purchasing save the world?, *The Guardian*, 24 October. https://www.theguardian.com/sustainable-business/blog/procurement-professionals-sustainable-supply-chain. Accessed 11 January 2018.

Piboonrungroj P. and Disney, S.M. (2015) Supply chain collaboration in tourism: a transaction cost economics analysis, *International Supply Chain Management*, **4** (3), 25-31.

Pratt, S., Mackenzie, M. and Sutton, J.L. (2017) Food miles and food choices: the case of an upscale urban hotel in Hong Kong, *Journal of Sustainable Tourism*, **25** (6), 779-795.

Quah, H.S. and Zulkifli, M.U. (2011) Supply chain management from perspective of value chain flexibility: an exploratory study, *Journal of Manufacturing Technology Management*, **22** (4), 506-526.

Rao, P. and Holt, D. (2005) Do green supply chains lead to competitiveness and economic performance?, *International Journal of Operations and Production Management*, **25** (9), 898–916.

Rathore, D., Nizami, A., Singh, A. and Pant, D. (2016) Key issues in estimating energy and greenhouse gas savings of biofuels: challenges and perspectives, *Biofuel Research Journal*, **3** (2), 380-393.

Rodrigue, J.-P. (2017) *The Geography of Transport Systems.* https://people.hofstra.edu/geotrans/eng/ch5en/conc5en/logistic_costs_breakdown.html. Accessed 17 July 2017.

Rogers H., Pawar K. and Braziotis C. (2012) Supply chain disturbances: contextualising the cost of risk and uncertainty in outsourcing, in: Chan H., Lettice F. and Durowoju O.

11

(eds.) *Decision-Making for Supply Chain Integration. Decision Engineering, vol. 1*, London: Springer, pp. 145-164.

Sammer, G. (2013) *Nachhaltige Mobilität für touristische Gebiete. Handbuch der kommunalen Verkehrsplanung*, Berlin: Wichmann Verlag.

Shamah, R. A. (2013) Measuring and building lean thinking for value creation in supply chains, *International Journal of Lean Six Sigma*, **4** (1), 17-35.

Solér, C., Bergström, K. and Shanahan, H. (2010) Green supply chains and the missing link between environmental information and practice, *Business Strategy and the Environment*, **19** (1), 14-25.

South China Morning Post (2016) Thailand's first halal hotel hopes to help entice Muslim tourists, In: *South China Morning Post*, 30th August. www.scmp.com/news/asia/southeast-asia/article/2011232/thailands-first-halal-hotel-hopes-help-entice-muslim. Accessed 16 October 2017.

Spier (2017) *Transforming our Supply Chain*. www.spier.co.za/spier_sustainability/flash_assets/data/content.xml. Accessed 5 October 2017.

Statista (2010) *Weltweit ausgestoßene CO_2 -Emissionen im Frachtverkehr im Vergleich der Jahre 2010 und 2050 nach Verkehrsträgern (in Millionen Tonnen)*. https://de.statista.com/statistik/daten/studie/483039/umfrage/co2-emissionen-des-frachtverkehrs-weltweit-nach-verkehrstraegern/. Accessed 10 October 2017.

Theyel, G. (2001) Customer and supplier relations for environmental performance, *Greener Management International*, **35** (3), 61–69.

UNCTAD (2015) *Sustainable Freight Transport Systems: Opportunities for Developing Countries*. http://unctad.org/meetings/en/SessionalDocuments/cimem7d11_en.pdf. Accessed 10 October 2017.

United Nations (2012) *UN Procurement Practitioners Handbook*. https://www.ungm.org/Areas/Public/pph/ch04s05.html. Accessed 10 October 2017.

Vujoševic, M. (2004) Koordinacija i kooperacija kao uslov uspešnosti lanca snabdevanja, in *Zbornik radova XI. naucnog skupa, Tehnologija, kultura i razvoj*, Beograd, pp. 110-120

Wilson, D. (2009) Today's logistics management challenges, *Dairy Foods*, **110** (12), 66.

Woxenius, J., Arnas, P.O. and Ohnell, S. (2001) Approach for handling the increased complexity of European Intermodal freight flows, Article presented at the *World Conference on Transport Research*, WCTR 2001, Seoul, 23-27 July 2001.

Yusen Logistics (2017) *Yusen Logistics launches Halal warehouse operation in Laem Chabang*, Retrieved from: https://www.yusen-logistics.com/en/resources/press-and-media/16790. Accessed 17 October 2017.

Zhang, X., Song, H. and Huang, G. Q. (2009) Tourism supply chain management: A new research agenda, *Tourism Management*, **30** (3), 345-358.

Zotz, A. (2008) *Efficiency is not enough. Tourism Watch – Informationsdienst Tourismus und Entwicklung*. https://www.tourism-watch.de/en/content/efficiency-not-enough-0. Accessed 10 October 2017.

Part IV: Operations

Introduction

Elena Cavagnaro

The fourth and last quadrant of the Sustainable Hospitality Value Chain is dedicated to operations. These are the activities under the most direct influence of a hospitality manager. In this quadrant human resource management (HRM) issues are discussed, alongside operations in the Rooms Divisions and Food and Beverage department.

Sustainability cannot become part of any business if employees do not support it and make it alive in their daily work. Moreover, we believe that the social responsibility of organisations starts with responsible behaviour toward employees. Finally, a special responsibility rests on the shoulder of the hospitality industry because it is one of the largest employers in the world.

To stress the importance of the social dimension of sustainability, in this book two chapters are dedicated to human resource management: one focussing on the business's own employees and one on outsourced staff. The first chapter is authored by Frans Melissen and Nadia Teunissen. After a general introduction on HRM in hospitality, Melissen and Teunissen exemplify the challenges of social responsible HRM by focussing on diversity. Then they explain how and why good HRM not only addresses diversity but is also able to engage and involve employees in sustainability practices. They conclude that investing in human capital is not only crucial to achieve sustainability in hospitality, but is also in the best interest of hospitality firms.

The second chapter, authored by Bill Rowson and Elena Cavagnaro, is dedicated to the challenges and opportunities of outsourcing. It considers organisational arrangements for the effective utilization of human capital, such as flexible employment contracts, and then digs into the specific challenges arising from globalisation and the so-called 'gig-economy'. They show that collaboration between hospitality organisation, unions and policy makers is needed to fully address the darkest side of employment practices in the globalized labour market.

In her chapter, Femke Vrenegoor shows that Rooms Division (RD) offers numerous opportunities to implement sustainability in the core of hotels. She discusses challenges and opportunities linked to water and energy use; waste and the well-being of guests and employees. Vrenegoor also highlight that a common effort of all these stakeholders is needed because, in their own ways, they all contribute to (environmental) value creation or destruction in RD.

The next and last chapter in the quadrant Operations is dedicated to Food and Beverage (F&B). Alongside Rooms Division, F&B is one of the core operational departments within a hotel. The offer of food, moreover, is seen by all cultures as a token of hospitality. Therefore F&B is central to the hospitality proposition of most hotels. F&B is a complex department, where several activities take place such as selecting, purchasing, storing, preparing and serving food. Consequently, like the RD department, it offers several challenges and opportunities in the context of sustainability. To structure the chapter its author, Elena Cavagnaro, discusses challenges and opportunities in separate sections dedicated to the physical environment in which the provision of food and services takes place; the selection of food and beverage ingredients; the vessels used to offer food and drinks; and, finally, the role of hosts and guests. Storage and preparation are also briefly addressed in these sections. Cavagnaro concludes that a proper approach to F&B not only offers several opportunities for sustainable value creation, but also enables the hotel to further engage its employees and to cater for the emerging wishes of its guests.

12 Social Responsibility – Your Employees

Frans Melissen and Nadia Teunissen

Learning goals

After studying this chapter, readers will have the ability to:

1 Understand the relevance of the social dimension of sustainability from both a sustainable development and a business economic perspective;

2 Understand the relevance of working conditions, salary, empowerment and development of employees;

3 Understand the relevance of embracing diversity;

4 Understand the fact that proper working conditions and salary, empowerment and development of employees, and embracing diversity do not represent a technical challenge but a choice;

5 Understand the benefits of good working conditions and salary, empowerment, development, engagement of employees, and embracing diversity for sustainability initiatives in general, and for the planet and profit dimensions in particular; and

6 Understand the relevance and benefits of creating a sustainability-oriented organizational culture.

Introduction

Sustainable development is increasingly important to and applied within the hospitality sector. Interestingly, efforts in this field often prioritize environmental issues above social ones (Cavagnaro, 2017: 377). This is remarkable, given that hospitality is an industry with a people-oriented nature, which is dependent on the quality of its relationships with others on all levels of the socio-economic system (Melissen, 2017: 2). Therefore, one would expect this sector to invest significantly in this dimension of sustainability. Unfortunately, short-term cost reduction strategies, such as eco-efficient practices, are instead prioritized (see Chapter 1 and Cavagnaro, 2017: 377).

However, if one intends to take sustainable development seriously, the social dimension simply needs to be addressed as well. For the hospitality sector, being one of the largest employers in the world, the focus of addressing this dimension could for instance be on well-being and engagement of employees. In fact, creating a more humane and inclusive work environment is in itself a goal of sustainability (Glavas, 2012; Cavagnaro, 2017). Moreover, if one wants to operate sustainably, engaged employees are a necessity. Employees will only engage in sustainability initiatives if they feel engaged with and taken care of by the company or organization they work for. To date though, the hospitality sector is not exactly known for its employee friendly reputation (Baum, 2007; Melissen, 2013). Significant steps still need to be taken within this field in order to live up to a holistic perspective on sustainable development. As this chapter will show, employee engagement and well-being is not only an important *aspect* of sustainability, it is also essential in *achieving* sustainability goals. Sustainability initiatives can enhance employee engagement and satisfaction and by doing so function as a mechanism to foster further sustainable development (Glavas, 2012). In this way, the hospitality industry can make a start in fulfilling its potential to create value not only for its own economic sake, but also for society as a whole (Cavagnaro, 2017; Melissen, 2017).

The remainder of this chapter discusses these issues in more detail by first focusing on the generic challenge of social sustainability, illustrated by the specific challenges of HRM and diversity management. Subsequently, the way to address these challenges and the benefits of doing so, both from a business economic and sustainable development perspective, are presented.

Social sustainability challenges

Worldwide, the hospitality sector offers a diversity of work opportunities, for people in various areas and levels of society. In turn, employees are a critical element within the qualitative execution of tourism and hospitality services, and are seen as the most important element of hospitality firms' organizational performance (Baum, 2007; Kusluvan *et al.*, 2010). Without employees, there would be no business. Not only do they run and support operational management, but most importantly they interact and build relations with guests and other stakeholders which are indispensable for the existence of a hospitality firm. The sector is thus heavily reliant upon human capital and therefore one would expect this sector to invest significantly in the well-being of its employees and their skills necessary to deliver these services. Unfortunately, existing literature draws a rather different picture. Over 20 years ago, Wood (1997) portrayed the sector as follows:

> Hospitality work is largely exploitative, degrading, poorly paid, unpleasant, insecure and taken as a last resort or because it can be tolerated in the light of wider social and economic commitments and constraints (p. 198).

Although the sector has made some progress since Wood's pessimistic assessment, there remains little evidence that the sector has improved to levels that can be referred to as sustainable from a social perspective (Baum, 2007; Melissen, 2013; Williamson, 2017).

HRM in hospitality

Employees nowadays still face "perceptions of low social status and prestige, along with poor employment conditions and unsocial and irregular working hours [...] together with a [high] physical and emotional workload" (Kusluvan *et al.*, 2010: 196). Also, jobs within hospitality have become fragmented, as people no longer work at one place for their entire career but (have to) change jobs often due to 'flexible capitalism' (Sennett, 1998: 9; see also Chapter 13), causing uncertainty and ambiguity for both employees and employers (Baum, 2007). This, in turn, may result in burnout or turnover of employees with all its financial consequences. It is therefore not surprising that human resource management in the hospitality industry is described as "unprofessional, underdeveloped, and inferior" (Kusluvan *et al.*, 2010: 177). Research suggests that those who are in charge of people management or human resources management not always fully understand "what this strategic role means in practice" (Baum, 2007: 1388). Clearly this points to an imbalance or even contradiction within the sector, considering the earlier stated fact concerning the importance of employees for its existence. Change in this area is thus required precisely because, as Melissen (2017: 450) states, sustainable development could be best achieved by using a "collaborative learning" approach for which all relevant stakeholders need to equally engage. For this, the easiest and most pressing step is to involve and invest in employees, both on a professional as on a personal level.

However, investments in human capital are not only crucial from a sustainability perspective, they are also crucial for creating a "sustained competitive advantage" (Kusluvan *et al.*, 2010: 172). Thus, development and management of employees and their competencies should be a priority in the agendas of managers within the hospitality industry, as can be illustrated by the following statement of the National Tourism Development Authority of Ireland:

> The story of successful tourism enterprises is one that is largely about people – how they are recruited, how they are managed, how they are trained and educated, how they are valued and rewarded, and how they are supported through a process of continuous learning and career development (Fáilte Ireland, 2005: 8, in Baum, 2007).

Embracing diversity

Within the social dimension of sustainability, diversity, with its related concepts of inclusiveness and accessibility, is also an important theme. The United Nations even framed it as a "necessary prerequisite for sustainable development" (UN, 2013, in Cavagnaro, 2017: 379). Although the concept is not new to the hospitality

12

sector, managerial implications for working with these concepts are still explored and tested (Baum, 2007). Diversity management concerns "the utilization of a variety of human characteristics, orientations and dispositions in satisfaction of ethical precepts and the pursuit of business goals" (Wood, 2003: 93, in Baum, 2007: 1393). Diversity policies in organizational management usually stress respect for human beings regardless of any ethnical backgrounds, gender, age or (physical) disabilities. Working with sustainability therefore not only requires direct investment in present employees, as discussed before, but also providing and creating opportunities and equal chances for future personnel regardless of their background or abilities. As hospitality is intertwined with all levels of society both nationally and internationally (Melissen, 2013), it is exactly this sector that needs a workforce that equally reflects those differing backgrounds and abilities to strengthen both its relationship with and contribution to the sustainable development of our society.

An important issue in embracing diversity is to tackle discrimination and prejudice. Baum (2007) points to the fact that migrant labour is still commonly used to fulfil the lowest-valued jobs, at low cost with minimal investment in training. Gender roles still influence career opportunities, rewards and status within the hospitality sector. For example, some areas are primarily male-dominated (e.g. chefs) whilst others largely consist of female workers (e.g. housekeeping). Furthermore, the sector is often perceived as "an industry for the young, beautiful and super-fit" (Baum, 2007: 1395). This has implications for older workers, as well as those facing a disability. Cavagnaro (2017) stresses that the inclusion of less advantaged groups, such as disabled people, is a pressing social issue in our current economy. These social and ethical issues are in need of change in most existing business and labour models. This is important because, as Washington states: "We need social inclusion, social justice and greater equity […] precisely because without it we will not solve the environmental problems"(2015: 107).

Obviously, Washington's statement relates to the interconnectedness of the environmental, social and economic dimensions of sustainable development. Truly putting our societies on a sustainable course cannot focus on just one of these dimensions; this requires simultaneously addressing all three, and their interdependencies.

Embedding diversity within an organization can provide other positive outcomes, as innovation is more likely to arise when people of various backgrounds work together (Herring, 2009). It challenges organizations, and its employees, to "think outside the box" which requires and simultaneously stimulates creativity and open-minded attitudes. Embracing diversity and respecting differences is therefore a "necessity not a nicety" (Groggins and Ryan, 2013: 269) for organizations and society as a whole.

Best cases

Case 12.1: The inclusive project 'Hotel with 6 stars' of the Meliá Roma Aurelia Antica

At the Meliá Roma Aurelia Antica, part of Meliá Hotels International (MHI), something extraordinary is taking place. Together with the Italian Association of People with Down Syndrome, the project 'Hotel with 6 stars' was set up, aimed at closing the gap between youngster with Down Syndrome and the labour market. Six youngsters were selected and offered professional experience in a real work environment. They became the 'six stars' of the hotel. At MHI, sustainability has been part of the company from the start. Among other things, they are committed to protecting the environment, sharing the local culture and contributing to cultural integration, which all reflect their fundamental values and are embedded in the company´s strategy, processes and procedures. Within these, the social and environmental dimensions of sustainability are equally present. MHI explicitly states that they value the social dimension, as "MHI's activity will only be sustainable in the long term if it is able to contribute to the reduction of social differences and poverty" (Cavagnaro, 2017:380), and look for opportunities for inclusion of less advantaged groups. With this background, the project 'Hotel with 6 stars' was developed and implemented at Meliá Roma Aurelia Antica. The project shows that it is possible and beneficial to include the social dimension of sustainability, and that by doing so value is created inside and outside the company. During the project, the six youngsters were professionally trained as hotel employees with a focus on their ability rather than their disability. They joined all departments of the hotel and actively contributed to the various daily activities within six different roles: receptionist, chambermaid, waitress during breakfast, waitress at the bar and restaurant, cook and maintenance. Each t rainee was tutored by a selected staff member. The traineeship took around three months and was organized as a part-time job. The design of the working hours and job activities were adjusted to the abilities of the trainees, but at the same time they would be challenged to reach the next level. The following quote of one of the trainees illustrates the personal growth they experienced during the traineeship:

"I wasn't able to do anything at first … I could not match the required timings, the bathroom was not perfect … Yet in the end I managed it!" (Martina in Cavagnaro, 2016: 382). In turn, the presence of the trainees had a positive impact on the hotel's staff because of their genuine enthusiasm: "My trainee's passion, proactive attitude and uncomplicated approach to life are a constant inspiration for me and the Front Office Team today. His presence here represented an undisputed enrichment for us, from both a professional and a human point of view" (Tutor in Cavagnaro, 2017: 382).

These quotes show how projects like 'Hotel with 6 stars' can be an enriching experience for both employees and employers and how it informs the corporate culture. For applying such a project successfully, three key conditions are needed: "first, careful preparation with the support of a specialized organization; second, a thorough choice both of trainees and tutors; and, last but not least, an unrelenting commitment to make a difference by creating value for all" (Cavagnaro, 2017: 382).

12

Case 12.2: Design your employees' customer journey

Hotels are experts on designing customer journeys. The ultimate product they offer and sell to their guests is not just a hotel room or breakfast or a meeting room; rather, the customer journey created by all these elements and the way staff interacts with guests will determine how guests will perceive the quality of the overall experience staged for them. Interestingly, this also means that if any type of companies should be able to accommodate for the needs and wishes of employees, it should be those operating in the hospitality industry. All theories, models, tools and techniques that can be used to design and realize an optimal customer journey for guests could also be used to design and realize an optimal customer journey for employees. Ensuring proper working conditions for and improving the overall well-being of employees could very well be addressed in the same way. A working day of an employee is also a customer journey made up of a range of touch points that together determine how an employee will experience his or her working day. An extended period of working in a hotel is not different from an extended period of staying in a hotel; both represent extended experiences that can purposely be designed and need to be managed properly. What's more, one could even argue that designing the working days or careers of employees is actually less challenging than designing the customer journeys of guests because you know the people for whom you are designing this experience personally. You can talk to them, you can involve them in the design process, you could even have them test/try out specific designs of or alternatives for touch points in their overall customer journey. Therefore, if any type of company should be able to address the needs and wishes of employees, it should be those that have made staging hospitality experiences their core business!

Based on Smit and Melissen, 2018.

Case 12.3: Travellers café Viavia Jogja

Out of a concern of the growing impact of mass-tourism on the environment and local communities, the Belgium travel agency Joker developed the concept of 'Viavia' cafes. These cafes, spread over different locations all over the world, can serve as intermediaries between tourists and locals. The cafes are set up in synch with the unique local environment and are co-owned and managed by locals. They support local people and initiatives while at the same time providing an experience in which tourists are able to really connect with local people and in this way enhance mutual understanding. Their focus is not on profit, but on making a positive impact in the community and on tourists. In Jogjakarta, Indonesia, they have a few key issues as their focus. One of them is the focus on the inclusion of women. In Indonesia, women working in tourism are most often related to sex workers. By hiring women in tour guide and management positions, Viavia Jogja tries to change this perception. The same attention is given to the LGBT community, which is in a very vulnerable position. Next to these kinds of social initiatives, they work on several environmental issues as well. Most importantly, they educate their staff about sustainable development via focus groups and personnel excursions. By informing their employees and asking their guides to actively inform tourists about it as well, their awareness increases and they start to inform their neighbours, families and even the local market sales man. An employee stated: "[at Viavia] I learned a lot; from how I treat people to how I treat my surroundings. [..] I learned to have more respect for nature" [Tourguide].

Sources: http://viavia.world/ and http://www.viaviajogja.com/

Tools to address the challenges

This section addresses some specific reference points and guidelines for addressing sustainability from the perspective of how (current and potential future) staff are treated but also how to ensure that this contributes to the other two dimensions of sustainable development: planet and profit.

Diversity

Let us first address the issue of embracing diversity. One could argue that the hospitality sector is perfectly poised to contribute in this area; it has the capacity and possibilities to host a variety of employees irrespective of their cultural background, gender, age and/or physical and mental abilities due to the variety of tasks and jobs available within its business model. Doing so would allow hospitality firms to move beyond only addressing eco-efficiency and to engage in sustainability by "tackling a social challenge" (Cavagnaro, 2017: 378). The case of Meliá Roma Aurelia Antica is an illustration of how hospitality firms can take on this responsibility and by doing so fulfil their potential on the social dimension of sustainability. It clearly illustrates that embracing diversity is not complicated. It does not require specific complicated tools or techniques; it requires making a choice and committing to that choice. In other words, there is really no excuse for the hospitality sector not to contribute to tackling this social challenge.

Proper HRM, involvement and engagement: why and how

As indicated in the previous section, proper HRM – in terms of working conditions, salary, empowerment and development of employees – is an important dimension of sustainability. Similar to embracing diversity, it is also something that does not require complicated tools, techniques and management philosophies. Rather, it represents a choice. A choice that is not only the right choice from a social sustainability or ethical perspective, but also from a profit perspective. Some business leaders might argue that investing in employees is costly, however, it turns out that "companies with highly engaged workforces are 18% more effective, 15% more innovative, and 10% better at serving their customers than other companies" (McElligott, 2013: 5). Employees should thus be perceived as "valuable assets to be invested in and developed, rather than costs to be controlled" (Kusluvan *et al.*, 2010: 176). In other words, investment in empowerment and development of employees results in better employee performance and productivity, improved

12

organizational commitment, job satisfaction, improved interaction with guests and thus guest satisfaction (Kusluvan *et al.*, 2010) – and it is the logical and right thing to do from a sustainable development perspective. It is a no brainer, really. The tools to do so are widely available, and are discussed and described in an almost endless range of scientific and popular (general) management books and papers. To be very blunt: there is really no excuse for the hospitality industry not to improve on the current situation through proper job design, recruitment, training, job rotation, leadership, motivational techniques, reward policies, and so on.

Simultaneously, working on environmental sustainability initiatives and social sustainability initiatives beyond the borders of the company can only succeed with support of employees, which in turn requires involved and engaged employees. This section therefore specifically focuses on why and how one can involve employees in sustainability initiatives, and what the benefits of engaged employees are for both the enterprise and sustainable development. This is done based on the reference point that social sustainability is also about creating a workable social structure, in enterprises *and* society, through which sustainability can be achieved (Washington, 2015).

In other words, regardless of the specific dimension you focus on, working with and succeeding in sustainability requires engaged and supportive employees. In general, however, employees will only engage in sustainability initiatives if they feel engaged with the company, organization or enterprise in the first place. This engagement can be achieved in several ways, depending on why one wants to involve employees and how 'engaged employees' are interpreted.

As Sinek (2009) states, the success of every company, project, initiative or policy starts with *why*. Most companies know *what* they do, but very few articulate *why* they do what they do. Why does one want to work with sustainability, and why do employees need to be involved? By asking 'why', the core purpose, cause or belief of one's actions can be clarified, which is needed to inspire, initiate innovation and maintain the sustainable success and growth that makes a company thrive (Sinek, 2009). In other words: you need to have a story; a story that inspires and motivates employees to get involved; a story they can be proud of and share with others. Next to the *why*, it is just as important to consider *who* is involved and in *what* way. Does one make a distinction between management and support staff? Does one inform employees about decisions after they have been made, consult them for input or co-create from the beginning? Decisions made in these areas determine whether the participation of employees will turn out to be *passive* or *active* involvement (Pretty and Hine, 1999). When an employee is *passively* involved, he or she is the recipient of the decisions made by external actors and will only be involved in the *execution* of those decisions, e.g. because they 'have to'. Concerning sustainability, this usually results in an external motivation to work with sustainability. Employees execute the required tasks because it is expected, but not because they acknowledge the value or importance of the underlying ideology. *Active* participation, on the other hand, alludes to an approach in which employees have had the opportunity to *engage* in brainstorm sessions, provide their own ideas and input or contribute in any other way to the initiation of sustainability initiatives. This mode of participation supports the development of internal motivation, as employees (learn to) understand and acknowledge the importance of sustainability and are willing to commit.

Research suggests that engaged employees are beneficial for both the organization and for sustainability, and the other way around, that working with sustainability can enhance employee engagement (Glavas, 2012; PwC, 2014; Melissen, 2013, 2017). First, having genuine interest in employees' ideas, and in turn, providing insight into the decision-making processes, creates work environments in which employees feel taken seriously and valued (PwC, 2014). Involved employees express a feeling of being part of something, which increases connectivity and motivation for their work, and loyalty towards the company grows. Additionally, when employees have been taking part in the decision making process, they will feel more responsible for the efficient and accurate execution of the specific tasks related to those decisions. This is also a crucial element while working on sustainability. By informing and involving employees in decisions concerning sustainability, their understanding and knowledge of the topic will increase. And with a better understanding of what sustainability entails, support for sustainability initiatives will grow. What's more, working with sustainability provides purposeful work or work activities. Nowadays, employees are increasingly searching for work with meaning, work through which they can make a difference:

> Employees are living lives that are becoming faster and more efficient, doing work that does not fulfill them and with little time left to find fulfillment outside work. [...] Employees are therefore looking to find increased meaning in their work. As such, the impact of companies engaging in sustainability practices might have a positive influence on the engagement, productivity and well-being of employees (Glavas, 2012: 14).

McElligott *et al.* (2013) show that employees who find fulfilment within their work by directly contributing to social or environmental issues, report higher job satisfaction compared to their colleagues who do not, which in turn results in higher productivity. Additionally, the majority of graduates indicate that "making a difference through their next job [is] a priority" and that they are willing to accept a lower salary for meaningful work (McElligott *et al.* 2013: 5). Glavas (2012) points to the fact that companies which focus solely on profit might find themselves with a disengaged workforce as employees cannot bring their 'whole selves' to work (2012: 18): "Profit alone does not move some employees as much as if work was found to provide greater alignment with one's own concept of self, values, virtues and morals" (2012: 19).

Working with sustainability issues thus brings meaningfulness to the work floor. A division exists between meaningfulness *at* work and *in* work (Glavas, 2012: 20). Meaningfulness *at* work refers to the company's efforts towards

12

sustainability, meaningfulness *in* work to what an employee does personally, how a job directly contributes to sustainability. If there is meaningfulness *at* work, this can stimulate feelings of pride and reciprocity amongst employees. When a company acts fair towards employees and others in society, employees will be motivated to "return the favour". Meaningfulness *in* work can increase job satisfaction by giving work activities a "higher purpose". When meaningfulness at work and in work are combined, this is known as the "embedded sustainability" approach (Laszlo and Zhexembayeva, 2011) which is proposed to be "the most powerful pathway for engaging employees" (Glavas, 2012: 20) and achieving the company's sustainability goals. For achieving embedded sustainability, it is not only necessary to "see the big picture, but also understand the linkages within the system" (Laszlo and Zhexembayeva, 2011: 41). This requires a critical reflection on the relations, motivations, shared assumptions and beliefs, and the business model of the enterprise. Therefore, embedding sustainability in the company's DNA is about transforming its organizational culture.

Culture

Employees are, especially within hospitality, the engine of every enterprise. They bridge the gap between goals and realization, between theory and practice. It is therefore not surprising that companies need to reach out to their most important resource – the employees – for pursuing sustainability goals (McElligott *et al.*, 2013). But how does one get employees on board, how can they be stimulated to act more sustainable? Employee engagement for sustainability initiatives is especially crucial when one does not want sustainability to represent an 'add-on' to business as usual or an ad hoc measure, but rather something that has become part of the corporate DNA.

It is argued that organizational culture impacts employee behaviour and attitudes (Kusluvan *et al.*, 2010). Integrating sustainability in the minds and behaviour of employees, and thus the company, is therefore largely about a cultural change; from business-as-usual to a work ethic in which people and the environment take a (more) central position. Luckily, businesses increasingly recognize that organizational culture plays a crucial role in the transition towards sustainability (Bertels *et al.*, 2010).

Culture is about learned behaviour and is deeply rooted in the minds and behaviour of people. It arises in an unconscious process in which habits, values, assumptions, behaviour and perspectives on the world are learned and shared through daily interactions and conversations (Braun and Kramer, 2015; Bertels *et al.*, 2010). It is something hard to grasp and yet it is always there, steering the way we act and think about the world. Organizational culture can be described as something that "guides the decisions of its members by establishing and reinforcing expectations about what is valued and how things should be done" (Bertels *et al.*, 2010: 10). When sustainability is embedded in the corporate culture it will thus become an everyday, long-lasting part of the organization, creating a "culture of sustainability".

A sustainable organizational culture "strives to support a healthy environment and improves the lives of others whilst continuing to operate successfully over the long term" (2010: 10).

So how does one shift towards such a sustainable organizational culture? For this, a closer look is needed at its producers: the employees. As is shown, culture is something that arises in daily interactions and conversations. As Braun and Kramer (2015) state: "Culture is produced and changed via human (inter)actions and daily dialogues, step by step" (2015: 271).

It is exactly this process of daily interactions and dialogues that forms an entry point if one wants to change or reshape the organizational culture. Culture is not static, but dynamic, and therefore changes and renews itself constantly over time via these kinds of dialogues and practices (Braun and Kramer, 2015). As employees and their interests are diverse, it is important to gain insight in their perspectives on sustainability. What do they think is important, and why? What are their values, beliefs, assumptions and how do these relate to sustainability? These kinds of dialogues can also be included in evaluation and performance appraisals or taken into account from the very start during job interviews with new employees. By doing so, sustainability will no longer be an add-on but a core topic. Once again, the tools to do so are already widely available – such as proper job design, recruitment, training, job rotation, leadership, motivational techniques, reward policies, and so on – and therefore fine-tuning them to create an organizational culture that supports and stimulates furthering sustainability is anything but rocket science!

Another way of informing organizational culture is via the use of life-altering experiences. For example, Kellert (2002) suggests that the way we perceive nature depends on memorable moments during our middle childhood in nature, which he refers to as 'imprints'. These imprints affect the development of values one holds about nature. As Sobel states: "one transient experience in nature is worth a thousand nature facts" (2008: 13). Based on these kinds of personal experiences, people make decisions, distinctions, and develop values and moral standpoints concerning the environment and other ethical issues. Therefore, in changing organizational culture, one could imitate such an experience by creating one. Glavas (2012) describes a case in which a coffee company sends its employees to the very start of the supply chain to experience life at that part of the chain. When they returned, their perspectives on the supply chain were significantly altered:

> [...] Their experience completely reshaped how they think about the supply chain. It goes beyond fair trade to a point where employees think holistically about the entire value chain and how shared value can be truly created. It also results in deeper and high-quality connections with one's stakeholders. The experience then informs the entire business model but more importantly the culture of the organization to be one that truly looks at the holistic contribution it makes to the community [...] as well as to the planet as a whole (Glavas 2012: 24).

12

This example shows that such an experience not only increases knowledge, but also awareness of the *importance* of that knowledge. In this way, sustainability will not only serve people by engaging them, but employees themselves might become change agents in the quest for sustainable development. Furthermore, in most theories about behaviour change, the underlying structures – such as institutions or commodity chains – that might influence environmentally conscious behaviour are not questioned. However, Hall (2013) states that our patterns of behaviour are determined by our socio-technical systems and organized structures that, via the provision of knowledge and opportunities, enable or constrain us to act in a certain way. Therefore, changing behaviour requires a "system of provision" approach, in which the focus lies on understanding the "contextual collective societal institutions, norms, rules, structures and infrastructures that constrain individual decision-making, consumption and lifestyle and social practices" (2013: 1099). It requires not only reflecting on the internal organizational culture, but also on external structures of provision that might affect the development of that culture. Consider a very practical example. If a hotel would like its guests to use less energy by not using the air conditioning in a room, they could ask them to do so through leaflets. But why not switch it off completely, or at the very least not switch it on before a (new) guest enters his/her room. Change the rules and norms. This applies to employees, but also to guests, as well as suppliers.

Sustainable development thus not only concerns technical and eco-efficient measures, but is also about patterns of human behaviour and attitudes, values and beliefs (Dessein *et al.*, 2015). Hospitality and tourism organizations, as people-oriented businesses, can therefore function as incubators for sustainable development both internally, by establishing a supportive sustainable organization culture, as externally, when employees become change agents by taking sustainability home or via sharing their experiences and knowledge with guests or stakeholders. Tourism and hospitality organizations have the unique possibility to bring people of different (cultural) backgrounds together. They can be described as 'transmission belts' between different lifestyles (Cohen and Kennedy, 2007: 292). As the most important output of tourism and hospitality organizations is services, it is exactly this interaction through which (sustainability) values can be exchanged. This process is nicely explained by Kusluvan *et al.* (2010):

> [...] services are made tangible in the personality, appearance, attitudes, and behavior of the service provider; thus the employees become part of the product, represent the organization, and help form the image of the organization (2010: 172).

This illustrates the importance of employees for sustainable development of the organization and it also underlines their powerful position in becoming change agents towards external actors. Therefore, it would be unwise for tourism and hospitality entrepreneurs to not invest in their employees and a sustainable organization culture, not only for their own sake, but also for the long-term quality of the social, environmental and economic systems of which they are a part.

Conclusion

This chapter has explained that sustainable development is about more than just managing the triple bottom line; it is about actively creating added value for both the company and the socio-economic system of which it is a part. It has also shown that, within this context, it is crucial for hospitality firms to address the social dimension more explicitly than is done so far. It is not only their responsibility but also in the best interest of hospitality firms to invest in human capital – their current employees, and also potential, and different types of, new employees and people in the communities in which they operate. Simultaneously, doing so further supports sustainability initiatives, because sustainability cannot truly become part of business as usual if it is not supported and lived by employees. This chapter has presented a number of reference points and examples that could prove useful in doing so.

References

Baum, T. (2007) Human resources in tourism: still waiting for change, *Tourism Management,* **28** (6), 1383-1399.

Braun, D. and Kramer, J. (2015) *De Corporate Tribe,* Deventer: Vakmedianet.

Bertels, S., Papania, L. and Papania, D. (2010) *Embedding Sustainability in Organizational Culture: A systematic review of the body of knowledge,* Ontario: Network for Business Sustainability.

Cavagnaro, E. (2017) Creating value for all: Sustainability in hospitality, in C. Lashley (Ed.) *The Routledge Handbook of Hospitality Studies: Perspective and cases,* Oxford: Routledge, pp. 377-388.

Cohen, R. and Kennedy, P. (2007) *Global Sociology,* New York: Palgrave.

Dessein, J., Soini, K. Fairclough, G. and Horlings, L. (eds.) (2015) Culture in, for and as sustainable development. Conclusions from the COST Action IS1007, Finland: University of Jyväskylä.

Glavas, A. (2012) Employee engagement and sustainability: a model for implementing meaningfulness at and in work, *Journal of Corporate Citizenship,* **2012** (46), *13-29.*

Groggins, A. and Ryan, A. (2013). Embracing uniqueness: The underpinnings of a positive climate for diversity, *Journal of Occupational and Organizational Psychology,* **86** (2), 264-282.

Hall, M.C. (2013) Framing behavioural approaches to understanding and governing sustainable tourism consumption: beyond neoliberalism, "nudging" and "green growth"?' *Journal of Sustainable Tourism,* **21** (7), 1091-1109.

Herring, C. (2009) Does diversity pay?: Race, gender, and the business case for diversity, *American Sociological Review,* **74** (2), 208-224.

Kellert, S. R. (2002) Experiencing nature: affective, cognitive, and evaluative development in children, in Kahn, P.H. and Kellert, S.R. (Eds.) *Children and Nature: Psychological, Sociocultural, and Evolutionary Investigations,* Cambridge: MIT Press, pp. 117-152.

12

Kusluvan, S., Kusluvan, Z., Ilhan, I., and Buyruk, L. (2010) The human dimension. A review of human resources management issues in the tourism and hospitality industry, *Cornell Hospitality Quarterly*, **51** (2), 171–214.

Laszlo, C. and Zhexembayeva, N. (2011) *Embedded Sustainability: The Next Big Competitive Advantage*, Stanford: Stanford University Press.

McElligott, M, Donnelly, M., Layke, J. and Nesler, C. (2013) *Driving Behavior Change: Engaging Employees in Environmental Sustainability*, Washington: Johnson Controls.

Melissen, F. (2017) Socially responsible and sustainable practices: how to involve tourists and guests?, in S. Kumar Dixit (Ed.) *The Routledge Handbook of Consumer Behaviour in Hospitality and Tourism*, Abingdon /New York: Routledge, pp. 450-458.

Melissen, F. (2013) Sustainable Hospitality: A Meaningful Notion?, *Journal of Sustainable Tourism*, **21** (6), 810-824.

Pretty, J. and Hine, R. (1999) *Participatory Appraisal for Community Assessment: Principles and Methods*, Colchester: University of Essex.

PwC (2014) *The keys to corporate responsibility employee engagement*, US Pricewaterhouse Coopers LLP. http://engageforsuccess.org/wp-content/uploads/2015/10/pwc-employee-engagement.pdf.

Sennett, R. (1998) *The Corrosion of Character. The personal consequences of work in the new capitalism*, New York: W.W. Norton and Company.

Sinek, S. (2009) *Start with Why: How Great Leaders Inspire Everyone to Take Action*, New York: Penguin Group.

Smit, B. and Melissen, F. (2018). *Sustainable Customer Experience Design: Co-creating experiences in Events, Tourism and Hospitality*, Abingdon/New York: Routledge.

Sobel, D. (2008) *Childhood and Nature: Design Principles for Educators*, Portland: Stenhouse Publishers.

Washington, H. (2015) *Demystifying Sustainability: Towards Real Solutions*, London: Routledge.

Williamson, D. (2017) Too close to servility? Why is hospitality in New Zealand still a 'Cinderella' industry?, *Hospitality and Society*, **7** (2) 203-209.

Wood, R. (1997) *Working in Hotels and Catering*, London: International Thomson.

13 The Changing Role of Work:
Staff outsourcing in the 'gig economy'

Bill Rowson and Elena Cavagnaro

When bad men combine, the good must associate; else they will fall, one by one, an unpitied sacrifice in a contemptible struggle.

Edmund Burke (1729-1797) Irish-born politician and man of letters

Learning goals

After studying this chapter, readers will have the ability to:

1 Define the changing role of work in tourism and hospitality;

2 Consider the impact of globalisation and the 'gig economy' on working practices;

3 Evaluate the impact of the changing role of work on sustainability, and specifically on its profit and people dimension;

4 Understand examples of current employment practice and recruitment in the tourism and hospitality sectors;

5 Identify sustainable employment practices for the future.

Introduction

The scale of the tourism, hospitality and leisure industry is enormous. It has become the world's largest employer and, despite the global financial crisis, it is predicted that the decline in international tourism arrivals may have bottomed out (United Nations World Tourism Organisation, 2016). It encompasses virtually every country and culture and has its foundations, according to Baum (2007), in the semi-feudal European society. Today the industry has multiple facets and the terminology can become confusing. For the purposes of this chapter the authors' will use the terms tourism, hospitality, lodging and hotel industry, which will be deemed to include the leisure industry, interchangeably. These industries include multinational companies such as McDonald's, Marriott, Hilton, IHG and Accor, as well as smaller national companies, and the hospitality industry in particular as an array of independent businesses (Rowson *et al.*, 2016; Rowson and Lashley, 2012; Davidson *et al.*, 2011).

Fundamentally, this chapter explores how human resources in the tourism and hospitality sectors are utilized by individual organisations and how recruitment practices are changing under the pressure of socio-economic developments such as globalization. In doing so the authors bring together key issues that individually and collectively have substantial implications for the various parties to the employment relationship. First, the chapter considers organisational arrangements and policies for the effective utilization of human resources within companies, including areas such as flexible employment contracts, outsourcing, zero hour contracts, and quasi-self-employment roles (the so called 'gig economy'). Second, it discusses how globalization and the rise of the 'gig economy' have impacted on employment policies in tourism and hospitality organisations throughout the world. Although at first these may seem discrete areas, it can be shown how they connect with each other. The focus of this chapter is on outsourcing. For a discussion of challenges and opportunities connected to staff directly employed by a hospitality organisation, you may wish to consult Chapter 12.

Following the general lay out of the book, the chapter starts by highlighting sustainability challenges related to these developments, then it presents two best cases and finally looks at possible ways to address these challenges.

Main sustainability challenges

Intransigent human resource issues remain at the forefront of global tourism's challenges (Baum, 2015). In 2007 *Tourism Management*, a leading international journal, published a detailed assessment of the state of play with respect to human resources in tourism, with the somewhat pessimistic sub title of '*Still waiting for change*' (Baum, 2007). The assessment's conclusion was that, in a world of increasing social, economic, political and technological churn, not least within tourism, some dimensions of people management and the role of human resources appeared to be frozen in time (Baum, 2007). Furthermore, and perhaps unfortunately, the reputation of the tourism and hospitality sector as an employer remained very mixed: there was some evidence of very good employment practice, but there was also a widespread perception by many potential employees in hospitality and tourism of poor pay, challenging working conditions and limited opportunities for growth and development particularly for women and minorities (Baum, 2007). More than ten years later the picture has not changed dramatically. Authors keep pointing at the poor perception that potential employees have of the industry, and at the consequences for the labour market of the financial crash of 2008, when most of the major banks in the world effectively went bankrupt, and in most cases were bailed out by the governments of various countries. This led to increased financial pressure on companies, and the tourism and hospitality sector, like many others, started to look seriously at policies for the effective utilization of human resources. While financial resources kept tightening, demand for the so-called flexible and outsourced workforce increased. This increased demand met with a seemingly ever-increasing offer of labour, because many employees lost their jobs in the aftermaths of the 2008 financial crisis. This *perfect storm* led to a race to the bottom that in terms of employment conditions pushed the hospitality and tourism industry back to the challenging situation already described in 2007 (Baum, 2015). The recovery of the world economy to date has shown the unsustainability of a human resource model based on outsourcing. Indeed, sustainability challenges are intrinsic to a staff strategy build upon an external workforce. In this section we will illustrates these challenges focussing first on workforce flexibility, then observing the impact of globalisation and the gig economy on the changing role of work and finally considering the role of algorithmic management in making the gig economy possible.

Workforce flexibility: outsourcing and offshoring

Traditionally many tourism and hospitality organisations have failed to develop strong internal labour markets, where skills are developed via internal promotion and upgrading. Managers have relied instead on the external labour market and on a transient flow of unskilled employees. This led to the use of various forms of employment flexibility. In the UK, for example, during the 1980s and 1990s much of the legislation of the Conservative Government was focused on increasing the flexibility of the labour market. Other European countries, such as the Netherlands, followed. A flexible labour market suits the tourism and hospitality industry employers particularly well, because several job roles had been deskilled so that they could easily be done by anyone in the labour market. In the 1990s there was evidence of a 'churn' of unskilled labour at the lower end of the labour market and often employees in this group circled between tourism organisations, hotels, restaurants and high street retailers or food retailers (Lashley and Rowson, 2000). A similar situation presented itself again after the 2008 financial crisis. Yet, when the world economy recovers and jobs are plentiful, then the hospitality and tourism industry feels the sting of this policy: recruitment and retention of employees becomes difficult as both skilled and unskilled employees may find jobs in industries with a better image and better working conditions. For example, immediately before the 2008 crisis the Dutch hospitality industry hit a record of 16,800 open vacancies. As could be expected, during the crisis vacancies dropped, but midway 2017 the 2008 record was broken and the industry faced 29,000 open vacancies, representing almost 8 per cent of the total workforce (CBS, 2017).

In an effort to curb the negative consequences of relying on an external, flexible workforce while maintaining the benefits of not having to hire and invest directly

13

in employees, the hospitality and tourism industry usually turns on outsourcing and offshoring. Rather than bringing in people to do the company's jobs, outsourcing and offshoring send the jobs out. Outsourcing refers to the transfer of internal organisational provisions to an outside, independent provider. Offshoring is a narrower term. It means having outside vendors or employees *abroad* supply services that the companies' own employees previously did in-house. The nature of transfers and the complexity of provisions is, in practice, varied capturing approaches from simple sub-contracting to the creation of joint-venture partnerships (Taylor, 2010).

In the hospitality industry outsourcing is more common than offshoring. Studies have demonstrated that the most common areas of outsourced activity comprise routine, non-core services such as cleaning, security, buildings, transport, maintenance and catering; alongside certain professional services such as IT, and legal services (Taylor, 2010). Moreover, outsourcing is a particularly important trend in human resource management (HRM). Although in some organisations the human resource departments are entirely outsourced to independent contractors, companies usually outsource one or more of the three main HRM functions: acquiring, administering and developing talent (Bagga, 2015). As already noted above, many hospitality and tourism companies outsource their staff recruitment in an effort to be assured of a stream of employees to comprise the desired flexible workforce even when the economy is strong and job offers in and outside the hospitality industry are plentiful. Outsourcing recruitment may also be chosen because modern recruiting firms apply innovative sourcing strategies, such as the use of social media, that are less known in the industry. Considering administration, companies commonly outsource their payroll processes, employee benefits and the like. Outsourcing firms, finally, can take care of talent development by administering training, assessment and surveys as well as supporting performance management.

Among the benefits of outsourcing, the most important issues are considered to be low costs and more efficient working on one side and time saving on the other. Outsourcing companies tend to be well versed in new technology and the latest trends in their field. For these reasons, they can often perform a function more cheaply than doing it in-house. Outsourcing companies, moreover, frequently employ consultants with specialist skills and so can sometimes offer a better career path for their employees. This can ultimately help the outsourcing firm to retain their employees for a longer period and so provide a better service. Outsourcing companies, finally, can focus on their core strategic functions and so provide them more effectively and through staff who are more specialized and, hence, generally more proficient (Bagga, 2015; Hiamey and Amenumey, 2013).

There are however several disadvantages to outsourcing. Outsourcing firms often employ people on temporary contracts or with very poor working conditions, compared to the permanent employees in the business (see Box 13.1). This can lead to higher staff turnover and lower employee morale. It can also give rise to service quality problems. Outsourcing HRM functions to an off-site location, moreover, often creates a sense of distance between the employees and the company. This can lead to delayed communication or miscommunication. When employees do not have easy access to the HRM department, they can begin to feel frustrated and unimportant. Another challenge of HRM outsourcing is that it reduces the power and control of the principal employer over employees, their work, performance and pay.

Box 13.1: Corporate outsourcing

Check-in your bags on the El Al flight from Madrid to Tel Aviv, and the operation is handled by staff of the Spanish national airline, Iberia. Report a security concern to staff at an Asda supermarket in the UK, and you may well be speaking to an employee of security specialist G4, not an Asda staff member. Receive treatment at the newly opened dialysis centre in Oldham, Greater Manchester, and the nurses caring for you will be employed by global health-care company Fresenius and not the National Health Service. All three are examples of outsourcing, a growing trend as jobs become more complex, and big organizations increasingly seek to achieve greater efficiency by sticking to the core functions that they do best.

Offshoring is also contentious. Particularly in challenging economic times, employees, unions, legislators and even many business owners feel that shipping jobs out (particularly overseas) is ill advised. This notwithstanding, employers are sending more jobs out (Dessler, 2013) and this trend is compounded by one of the most important challenges facing business today: globalisation.

Globalisation and the labour market

Briefly, the concept of globalisation captures the greater interconnectedness of events around the globe (Gilmore and Williams, 2013). In the area of economics and business the process of globalisation is evident in four main respects: levels of international trade; greater financial flows around the world; the growth of foreign investment; and linked to this, the growing activity of multinational companies, which often depend on complex supply chains to source, manufacture, and deliver goods and services across national borders (Gilmore and Williams, 2013; Torrington *et al.*, 2011).

Globalisation brings both benefits and threats, for employers, employees and consumers alike. For employers, globalisation opens up possibilities for international market expansion, and for attracting an international workforce. There has been much discussion of how globalisation might impact on the management of human resources. Just how extensively, and just how easily, trends, policies and practices in human resources can migrate across national borders, thus affecting how workers in other countries are treated, has become a particular concern for many academic authors (Gilmore and Williams, 2013; Dessler, 2013). The point here is whether a global labour market leads to improved human resource management practices in countries where employees have still few or no rights, or whether it leads to a race to the bottom with employers choosing to locate their business or hire in countries with weak labour practices to save on salary and employees' benefits costs.

With the globalisation of the world economy, moreover, even small firms are discovering that success depends on marketing and managing abroad. However, expanding abroad requires putting in place management systems to control overseas activities that require competences not (yet) developed at or available to small companies. These systems include managerial controls, planning systems, and, of course, human resource management systems for recruiting, selecting, training, appraising, and compensating workers at home and abroad (Dessler, 2013). Managing human resources internationally creates challenges. For one thing, differences in cultures and economic and legal systems influence employers' HR practices from country to country. For example, how should we appraise and pay our local employees? How should we deal with the unions in our offices abroad? How do we identify and get the right talent and skills to where we need them? And how do we spread state-of-the-art knowledge to our operations abroad? Challenges like these don't just come from the vast distances involved (though this is important). The bigger issue is coping with the cultural, institutional and economic differences among countries. In China, for instance, government-backed unions are relatively powerful, and in Europe, firing an employee could take a year or more. The bottom line is that it's impossible to effectively manage human resource activities abroad without understanding how countries differ culturally, economically, and legally (Dressler, 2013).

While for consumers globalisation often means better quality products and services at lower prices, the blessings of globalisation for employees are blurred. Although, certainly for highly skilled employees, a global labour market means an increase in job opportunities, for less skilled or less mobile employees it may mean the prospect of working harder in less secure jobs. The increasing use of offshoring jobs, illustrates this threat in real terms. Consider, for example, that there is high youth unemployment in many European cities and parts of America, where once large employers operated, that have moved their operations overseas to achieve cost-benefits not available in the home countries often due to high labour costs. The threat to job security in a globalised world is compounded by another development driven by globalisation, the rise of 'crowd working platforms' often referred to as 'the gig economy'. This area of change is considered to have the biggest impact on employment practice in modern times (Taylor *et al.*, 2017). The remainder of this chapter will consider the impact on employment practices of the 'crowd working platforms' and the 'the gig economy'. From this point forward, the terms will be used interchangeably and in most cases referred to as the gig economy.

The rise of the gig economy

The world of work is changing dramatically and in our increasingly flexible labour market, the notion of a 'job for life' and the concept of a 9 to 5 workday is diminishing fast. In its place, the idea of 'gig working' is rapidly gaining ground. To briefly define this, gig working is when people take temporary, often 'ad hoc', work contracts (or 'gigs') sourced online through digital, cloud-based marketplaces. The recent growth of online platforms such as Uber and Airbnb has given rise to a global sharing economy in which it is becoming ever more commonplace to buy and sell jobs and services online across the world. Digital work platforms such as Upwork and Freelancer.com are symptomatic of the 'Uberisation' of work, as they allow businesses (employers) to contract workers for short-term engagements, or specific projects, for a defined period of time. As the number of crowd working platforms has increased so has the numbers of people working in the area. All these developments have resulted in the rise of the gig economy.

The gig economy is usually understood to include chiefly two forms of work: 'crowd work' and 'work on-demand via apps' (Kessler, 2015; Said, 2015; Smith and Leberstein, 2015). The first term is usually referred to working activities that imply completing a series of tasks through online platforms (Eurofound, 2015; Bergvall-Kåreborn and Howcroft, 2014; Eurofound, 2013; Felstiner, 2011; Cherry, 2009; Howe, 2006). Typically, these platforms put potential workers (employees) in contact with an indefinite number of organisations and individual employers through the Internet, therefore allowing clients and workers to connect on a global basis. 'Work on-demand via apps', in contrast, is a form of work in which the execution of traditional working activities such as transport, cleaning and running errands, but also forms of clerical work, is directed via apps managed by firms that also intervene in setting minimum quality standards of service and in the selection and management of the workforce (Aloisi, 2015; Greenhouse, 2015; Rogers, 2015).

It is difficult to estimate the number of workers in the gig economy. Businesses are sometimes reluctant to disclose these data and, even when figures are available, it is hard to draw a reliable estimate, since workers may be registered and work with several companies in the same month, week or even day (Singer, 2014). Data collected and elaborated by Smith and Leberstein (2015) for the principal platforms and apps, however, show that this is clearly a non-negligible phenomenon (see Table 13.1).

There are many associated difficulties with assessing the number of employees and contractors (those in the gig economy) employed by many of the platforms, because of a high turnover of contractors. However, recent data from Uber.com suggests Uber claims 16,000 employees as of end of 2017 (https://www.uber.com/newsroom/company-info/). Uber also cites 2 million drivers worldwide. A very high turnover rate of drivers complicates this measure of gig workers contracting to Uber (https://www.uber.com/newsroom/company-info/).

13

Table 13.1: Organisations, platforms and apps serving the gig economy (Adapted by the authors from an earlier model by Smith and Leberstein, 2015)

Name	Field	Size of workforce	Operating areas
Uber	Transportation	2,000,000	International
Lyft	Transportation	50,000	US
Sidecar	Transportation	6,000	Major US cities
Handy	Home services	10,000	International
Task Rabbit	Home services	30,000	International
Care.com	Home services	6,600, 000	International
Postmates	Delivery	10,000	US
Hermes	Delivery	50,000	International
Amazon Mechanical Turk	Crowdwork	500,000	International
Crowdflower	Crowdwork	5,000,000	International
Crowdsource	Crowdwork	8,000,000	International
Clickworker	Crowdwork	700,000	International

Hermes has contracts with 10,500 people paid on a piece-work basis to deliver parcels using their own cars. Dubbed 'lifestyle couriers', they are self-employed and so do not receive any paid holiday, sick pay, parental leave or pension contributions. They pay for their own fuel and car insurance but are free to take other jobs and have some flexibility over their working day. They are part of the fast growing gig economy in which big companies, including Hermes, rely on increasing numbers of self-employed contractors, who are not subject to the national living wage, to deliver their core services.

A report by SPERA (2016) indicates that internationally, the gig economy has been having a much bigger impact than was first thought, and currently more than a quarter of the US workforce is officially part of it (SPERA, 2016). To further clarify, nearly 54 million Americans participated in some form of independent work in 2015 (SPERA, 2016) and more than 10 million people – that is about 1 in 12 US households – rely on independent work for more than half of their income (SPERA, 2017). Researchers project that half of the working US and UK population will move into the gig economy within the next five years (SPERA, 2016 and 2017). The European Union also saw a 45 per cent increase in the number of independent workers from 2012 to 2013 and currently independent workers comprise the fastest growing group in the European Union labour market (Goudin, 2016). Other world areas are also affected by these developments. For example, India's independent workforce, at 15 million the second largest in the world, fills about 40 per cent of the world's freelance jobs (SPERA, 2016).

As the gig economy has grown over recent years, so too have debates about its place and value to employment sustainability in the global labour market. Confusion has arisen around what exactly it constitutes and how it impacts employers, recruiters and workers alike. Some see online talent platforms as 'clearing houses' with the potential to inject new momentum into the labour market. The McKinsey Global Institute, for examples, calculates that by 2025 digital work platforms could add $2.7 trillion, or 2.0 per cent, to global GDP, increasing employment by 72 million full-time equivalent positions. For the UK, that equates to £45 billion and extra work for 766,000 people. The study estimates that up to 200 million people around the world could personally benefit from using digital work platforms, specifically by allowing the unemployed to find work as freelancers or by allowing part-time workers to work additional hours on a supplementary basis (Manyika *et al.*, 2015). From the individual perspective of the worker, the argument goes that that the gig economy gives people the opportunity to work when they want to and be more in control of their lives (O'Conner, 2016). There are, though, downsides to the gig economy. To start with, and linked to the reluctance of companies to disclose information and the flexible work patterns of gig workers, there is ambiguity about the employment status of the gig worker: are they self-employed or employees? This is not a rhetorical question, because the status of an employee determines their rights, such maternity leave, overtime pay and health care insurance. Box 13.2 below illustrates a typical ambiguous situation in the gig economy.

Box 13.2: Ambiguity in employment relationships: an illustrative example

Consider a hypothetical work arrangement for a delivery truck driver. He drives for a delivery service whose primary client is a large commerce company. The driver is paid based on the number of deliveries he completes, and he does not receive traditional employment protections such as overtime pay. The driver must purchase his own vehicle, but is not allowed to work for other delivery services. The driver must wear a uniform with the delivery service's logo. He can be removed as a contractor at will for not meeting the service's standards or expectations. What are the sources of classification ambiguity?

For the purposes of IRS classification, the driver may meet some criteria for classification as an independent contractor: he is paid based on the job rather than by the hour, week, or month; he invests in his own facilities (the truck); and he does not perform his work on the business's premises. However, the driver may meet other factors that suggest he is an employee: he must perform services in the order set by the business and he may not work for more than one firm at a time. In addition, the delivery service has the right to terminate the relationship without incurring liability (Joint Committee on Taxation, 2007).

13

As Box 13.2 illustrates, the so-caled 'self-employed' workers in the gig economy are employees in the real sense of the word, in that they often only work for one organisation while the organisation gains value from not having the on-costs of employees by, for example, saving on employee benefits such as pensions, sick pay, paid holidays (Taylor *et al.*, 2017). Second, employees in a gig economy may be free to choose when to work but not how to work or perhaps more crucially, how much they are paid (O'Conner, 2016). Even more crucially, as we will further explain in the next section, many gig workers are not in the position to choose when and how long to work because if they refuse a 'gig' too often they may be offered none in the future and be, in effect, dismissed (Lee *et al.*, 2015). Finally, many of the organisations offering gig work, are often deploying algorithmic management based on the argument that algorithms are better at managing new employment opportunities, and that this offers better and cheaper consumer services. This may be the case, however, the reality is often a tightened control on the gig worker performance, as we will explain more extensively in the next section.

Box 13.3: Taylorism

Frederick Taylor pioneered the 'scientific management' theory, which swept through US factories in the early 20th century. Taylor tested many of his ideas on the 600 or so labourers who worked in the yard of the Bethlehem Steel Company. After a series of experiments, he decided that a "first class" shoveller would be most productive if he lifted 21 pounds of weight with every shovel load. He ordered different-sized shovels for each type of material in the yard: a small shovel to hold 21 pounds of ore; a large one to hold 21 pounds of ash. The men went to a pigeonhole each morning where a piece of paper would tell them which tools to select and where to start work. Another piece of paper would tell them how well they had performed the previous day (O' Conner, 2016). As Taylor said: "Many of these men were foreigners and unable to read and write but they all knew at a glance the essence of his report, because yellow paper showed the man that he had failed to do his full task the day before, and informed him that he had not earned as much as $1.85 a day, and that none but high-priced men would be allowed to stay permanently with this gang" (Taylor, 1911: 68).

Algorithmic management

Algorithmic management might sound like the future but it has uncanny echoes from the past. A hundred years ago, a new theory called 'scientific management' swept through the factories of America. It was the brainchild of Frederick W. Taylor, the son of a well-to-do Philadelphia family who dropped his preparations for Harvard to become an apprentice in a hydraulics factory. At the factory he saw a haphazard workplace where men worked as slowly as they could get away with while their bosses paid them as little as possible. Taylor wanted to replace this rule of thumb approach with "the establishment of many rules, laws and formulae which replace the judgment of the individual workman" (Taylor, 1911: 37). To that end, he sent managers with stopwatches and notebooks to the shop floor.

They observed, timed and recorded every stage of every job, and determined the most efficient way that each one should be done. As Taylor wrote in his 1911 book *The Principles of Scientific Management*: "Perhaps the most prominent single element in modern scientific management is the task idea. This task specifies not only what is to be done but how it is to be done and the exact time allowed for doing it" (Taylor, 1911: 39). For more explanation on Taylorism, see Box 13.3.

Taylor's ideas had almost immediate success, and there was an increase in the use of scientific management, improving productivity in the vast factories of early 20th-century America. Taylorism was the logical precursor to Henry Ford's production lines and its legacy can still be seen in today's factories, call centres and warehouses, although new technology has taken the place of Taylor's instruction cards and stopwatches (O'Conner, 2016). Among these new technologies are algorithms, with their capacity to sweep through an enormous amount of data, discover patterns and formulate in real time the most efficient working process for each given task. Algorithmic management is a system where algorithms rather than humans decide how business operations should be performed, including who should be hired, promoted, dismissed and who should perform which job in which time frame and with which results. Many warehouse workers for companies such as Amazon, for example, use handheld devices that give them step-by-step instructions based on GPS on where to walk and what to pick from the shelves when they get there, all the while measuring their 'pick rate' in real time (Petersen, 2016; see also Chapter 5).

Taylor's scientific management approach has been applied very widely in manufacturing, but the services industry has always been seen as a specialist sector providing customer service at different levels. Hence it has been considered difficult to measure service time without highly standardizing service operations such as it has been the case in companies like McDonald's and Wok to Walk, a Dutch fast food take away that after its start in Amsterdam in 2004 is now represented in four continents (Woktowalk, 2017). More complex operations, such as the ones in most hotel chains, have long been considered safe from the long hand of Taylorism. However, thanks to algorithms, nowadays a vast amount of data can be collected and analysed in real time making possible the measurement of and improvement on processes such as the check-in at hotels. In fact, if a process can be analysed and reduced to its constituent parts, human employees may be (at least partly) substituted by machines thus setting a new step in the de-skilling of hospitality labour. For example, recently on-line check-in and check-out facilities have become available with many hotel groups speeding up the process and reducing staff numbers on front desk in the hotel.

Alongside pushing people to work faster and helping in the de-skilling of labour, the use of algorithms is providing a degree of control and oversight that even the most hardened adept of Taylor could never have dreamt would happen. This 'Taylorism on steroids', as it has been called, generates several moral issues while it often fails to achieve its aim of increased productivity (see Box 13.4).

13

Consider for example Uber, the well-known pioneer company in the sharing economy offering a location-based app that connects drivers to riders. It started in few US cities and by end 2017 is operating in more than 600 cities worldwide. Uber's app controls the fares that drivers charge and raises rates when demand surges. Surge pricing is meant to give both the driver and Uber the opportunity to boost revenues. Yet, research shows that surge pricing failed to reach its aim because rates changed too quickly and suddenly for drivers to utilize the information strategically to improve their income. The interaction between algorithm and people here therefore failed (Lee *et al.*, 2015).

To better understand the degree of control possible with algorithmic management, let us consider again Uber's operations. Uber's app is not only designed to adjust the ride price to the demand; it is also devised to monitor the driver position in order to assign a new client to the driver who is the nearest to the client's location. This process increases efficiency but it also raises issues about the driver's privacy. Moreover, the driver's rate of acceptance of the passengers assigned to him by the algorithm is one of the indicators on which drivers' performance is evaluated. As the process of passengers' assignment is often not transparent to the driver, his motivation and sense of control are negatively affected. Algorithms are also used to analyse passengers' rating of the drivers' service quality, another objective on which a driver's performance is evaluated. If the rating drops below a pre-determined level, drivers are warned or dismissed. Passengers' rating of a driver's quality, however, may not accurately reflect a driver's performance and service level. Consider for example a passenger under stress of missing a flight. He may rate a driver's service based on events beyond the driver's control, such as a traffic jam on the road towards the airport. As an Uber's driver may never meet with a HRM manager during his whole employment period, and may therefore not be able to discuss special circumstances, algorithmic performance management may be perceived as unfair and become a source of stress, disappointment and frustration (Lee *et al.*, 2015).

Box 13.4: The return of Taylorism on steroids

Documents submitted as part of an employment tribunal case brought by the GMB union against Uber in London include an email sent to driver James Farrar in May congratulating him on an average rating above 4.6. "We will continue to monitor your rating every 50 trips and will email you if we see your rating for your past 50 trips falls below 4.4." Uber will 'deactivate' drivers whose ratings drop too low, though it says this is "extremely rare". The court case documents include one instance, in which Uber sent an email on December 23, 2013 to a driver called Ashley Da Gama: "Hi there, we would like to wish you a Merry Xmas and a Happy New Year. We are currently planning for 2014 and would like you to be part of it. However, we do need to see an improvement on your current track record to ensure you are." Two weeks later, Uber emailed again to say his ratings had not improved enough. His account had been "deactivated…as of today" (O'Conner, 2016).

Considering the above discussed drawbacks and the enormous number of people affected by gig work and algorithmic management, it is not surprising that often the word gig economy is code for little more than exploitation of the workforce and that algorithmic management is seen as a tool merely exacerbating the exploitation. As a proportion of the total employees in the population, those who are slaves are relatively small in number, but there are millions of people who are in effect slaves, forced to undertake work at inadequate pay rates that are imposed upon them globally (Lashley, 2016). The use of the word *'wage slaves'* may sound extreme, but there are many arguments to support this as a fact of the modern world.

Concluding this section on challenges connected with outsourcing in a gig economy, we may state that, rather than being driven by workers' preferences to work flexibly, the gig economy is the result of employers' attempts to drive down costs and avoid 'unnecessary' permanent employees, particularly but not exclusively during periods of economic uncertainty (Taylor *et al.*, 2017). The legislative divisions between 'employees' and the 'self-employed' on one side and the mixed blessings of algorithmic management are making it artificially cheaper for businesses to move away from the traditional *'employer employee'* model of working and towards an insecure *'firm–contractor'* relationship instead (Brinkley, 2015). Short-term profit is gained at the expense of people, an unsustainable situation that needs to be addressed.

Best cases

In this section three best cases are presented, one based on information openly shared by NH Hotel Group, on their company website, one based on a conversation with the HRM manager of the Dutch hotel chain Bilderberg and one with the director of HR at Costa Navarino.

Case 13.1: NH Hotel Group's commitment to labour rights

13

Human rights are the basic rights and freedoms that all people are entitled to (UNUDHR, 1948). They include labour rights such as a decent hours, contract and pay. The hotel industry is a people industry where employees are essential to the provision of service to guests. It is therefore striking that, as we have seen above, hotels often fail to respect their employees' basic rights.

There are, though, examples that show that the some in the hotel industry take labour and human rights seriously, and take steps to uphold these rights or at least avoid exploitation of (vulnerable) people. One of these examples is offered by NH Hotel Group. NH is a Spanish chain with worldwide operations that pledged to sustainability in 2010. Five years later, in 2015, NH updated their Code of Conduct to reinforce their commitment to sustainability in-house and all along the supply chain. New in the Code is a clearly articulated commitment to human rights, following the principles laid down in the Global

Compact, the Universal Declaration of Human Rights and in the declarations of the the International Labour Organization. In the Code's section titled 'Workers' and Human Rights' NH states that that:

> In no way, shall safety or working conditions be imposed on the employees that affect, suppress or restrict their rights recognized by legal provisions, collective agreements or individual contracts. No form of illegal labour trafficking or fraudulent immigration shall be allowed, and legislation on foreigners and their entrance and transit shall always be respected. The exercise of rights to demonstration, association, unionization and collective bargaining in the framework of regulatory standards for each and every one of these fundamental rights shall not be inappropriately limited (NH, 2015: 15).

NH, moreover, recognises the threat of modern slavery and not only explicitly requests its suppliers to eliminate any form of child, forced or compulsory labour, but also requires that they respect labour rights such as "the established maximum working hours and minimum working wages," and guarantee safe working conditions (NH, 2015: 19).

Codes of Conduct are stepping stones towards ethical labour practices. However, without proper training of employees and without transparent processes to handle complains they are ineffectual. It is therefore encouraging that NH clearly spells out responsibilities for compliance with the Code, assures opportunity for training and explains procedures for handling norm-breaching behaviour. Finally, it should be noted that NH assures that the implementation of and compliance with the Code will be monitored.

Case 13.2: Bilderberg, a careful approach to outsourcing

Bilderberg is a chain of hotels and restaurants that operates 17 upper scale properties in the Netherlands. At the time of writing (January 2018) Bilderberg is a well-known and esteemed brand in the Netherlands thanks to its centenary history and to events that take place annually on its premises, such as the 'Bilderberg Conference', a private gathering of around 150 people of the European and North American political, industrial, financial and academic elite established in 1954 by Prince Bernhard of the Netherlands. Bilderberg is also committed to environmental and social sustainability. Part and parcel of their sustainability efforts is their policy towards HRM and outsourcing.

The cornerstone of Bilderberg HRM policy is to develop and maintain a sense of ownership in their employees and empower them to deliver the high standard of service to guests for which they are renown. Indeed, as a series of interviews that took place in 2017 in the context of the PhD research by Chris Beuker (personal communication, 5 January 2018), employees identify with Bilderberg, are proud to work for this organisation and voice their loyalty to it. Consequently, Bilderberg develop a very cautious approach to outsourcing.

First of all Bilderberg carefully considered the areas in which outsourcing may be indispensable. In this process, Bilderberg pondered about costs and benefits and concluded that the financial savings of outsourcing were less than expected and that they did not compensated for disadvantages such as a lower bonding of employees with the organisation. As an example, the outsourcing of linen cleaning was shared with us. Outsourcing the cleaning of linen such as towels and bathrobes is a costly operation that, if the right equipment is present at a hotel's premise, may easily be carried out by the hotel's employees outside rush hours. In the end, only three hotels found outsourcing to an external contractor necessary.

To cater for the identified needs, Bilderberg build a first 'circle' of outsourcing possibility inside the group itself. In fact, not all hotels have the same peak moments of demand and, by looking at the whole group, it becomes easier to cover for employees who are, for example, on maternity leave or on vacation. This 'circle' of outsourcing possibilities is supported by another 'circle' formed by managers of a specific department (say RD) of all Bilderberg's hotels. These meet on a regular basis to discuss personnel needs in the short and long term, and can therefore help each other when needed. External contractors with whom Bilderberg has a long-term relationship form the third and final 'circle'.

When outsourcing to an external contractor, Bilderberg makes sure not only that the outsourcing company follows all Dutch law and regulation, but also that it signed the national Code of Conduct for organisation in the cleaning industry. This Code aims at redressing a marked failure that become apparent in the Netherlands around 2015 and that was the result of the quite exclusive focus of the involved parties on price at the expenses of quality and employees' working conditions. The Code is a moral appeal to the industry to take responsibility beyond the minimum set in the law by improving transparency; truly caring for employees' health and safety; and striving for long-term relationships (http://www.codeverantwoordelijkmarktgedrag.nl/home/, accessed 5 January 2018). Moreover, Bilderberg also check that outsourced personnel, when on the chain's premises, are treated as the own personnel and have access to Bilderberg's officers in case they have an issue or a complaint. (Personal communication by Mrs Els van Batum, HRM Bilderberg Group, on 5 January 2018, Bilderberg Headquarters, Remkum, The Netherlands).

Case 13.3: Creating value for employees and the local community at Costa Navarino (Greece)

Costa Navarino is located in Messenia in the southwest Peloponnese, in one of the most unspoiled and breathtaking landscapes in the Mediterranean. Costa Navarino is a luxury resort and home to two 5-star deluxe hotels, Navarino residences (a collection of luxury villas), Anazoe Spa (a 4,000 square meters spa and thalassotherapy centre), two signature golf courses, a conference centre and over 20 fine dining venues.

Its philosophy is driven by a genuine desire to promote Messenia, while protecting and preserving not only its natural beauty but also a remarkable cultural heritage spanning

4,500 years. As the company website states, Costa Navarino's "business philosophy lies a strong commitment to economic, environmental and social responsibility, aiming at sustainable tourism development in harmony with the natural environment and local communities of Messinia"(Costa Navarino, 2018a). This commitment has been not only shown by allocating 10% of the total costs of the resort development to building the infrastructure needed for environmentally sustainable operations, but also by introducing "a new model for tourism development, which bases its success on the success of the destination as a whole" (Costa Navarino, 2018b), where "the success of a tourism business is directly linked with its ability to share the benefits of its operation with local society" (Costa Navarino, 2018c).

Part and parcel of this new, sustainable model of operation is a commitment to hiring people from the area. Before the opening of Costa Navarino in 2010 Messenia was not a tourism destination, and job opportunities were rather scarce. In fact, when before its opening Costa Navarino announced on the local newspapers that it was looking for employees, the HR department received 8000 applications, of which more than 6000 from the area. It should be considered that the nearest town, Pylos, counts only 2,767 inhabitants and the whole region of Messenia less that 160,000 (by the 2011 census population).

Even though Costa Navarino needed around 900 people, the HR department keep their promise to react to all applications and met with all 8000 candidates. Notwithstanding the high number of applicants, most of them were totally unprepared for the hospitality and tourism industry, and several aspirant employees left during the pre-opening training while during the first year of operation the turnover reached 55%.

In seeking to strike the right balance between the lack of skilled people in the region and the promise of giving positions to locals while offering to guests a quality experience, Costa Navarino moved to outsourcing. Yet it quickly relinquished this strategy due to several negative experiences. Two critical incidents were particularly significant. The first was accidentally discovering a blog, by an anonymous writer, claiming that Costa Navarino was employing people without offering social security and a decent wage. As HR knew that all the labour rights of their own employees were fully resected, they quickly concluded that the blog was written by an outsourced employee who – probably unknowingly – revealed that the outsourcing company was neither following the law and not complying with the agreement made with Costa Navarino.

The second incident happened with outsourced security employees, 30 to 35 people. In this case the issue was their reluctance to follow the needed training and security drills. Training is a very important component of Costa Navarino HR philosophy, and is not only intended to help people without or with limited hospitality background to manage the needed skills but also to keep up the high quality service that guests expect. In fact, HR sensed that – even though all outsourced employees enjoyed the same benefits as Costa Navarino employees such as meals and free transportation – employees were falling apart in two groups: one loyal and committed formed by their own people, and one rather uncommitted formed by outsourced personnel.

After some reflection, HR decided to phase out all outsourcing contracts except for highly specialist work such as the position of chef at their Japanese restaurant where an external contractor would offer more value for Costa Navarino's guests than a self-employed and trained chef. In fact, as Elena Gkeka states:

> "The decision of phasing out outsourcing has been taken considering the value that could be created for our employees, the local community and our guests, and not considering only financial costs. In fact, if our brand is damaged by for example a negative review on Tripadvisor due to low quality service, it may cost us much more than what we though to save by outsourcing" (personal communication, 10 January 2018).

Interestingly, Costa Navarino also worked out a solution for peak moments. This solution involves seasonal personnel who work full time during the high, summer season. HR reached out to these employees proposing to them a part time contract during off-season. For the people concerned this meant more income security while Costa Navarino could count on personnel who were already properly trained and embraced the company's culture. The result of this and all HR efforts by Costa Navarino has been an increase in personnel loyalty. From the 55% of the opening year, personnel turnover is down to 10%, a staggeringly low figure in the industry.

As Elena Gkika concludes:

> By believing in our community and investing in our employees we have been able to create a highly committed and loyal workforce. We have delivered on our promise to show respect for our guests, our employees and the local community. And, moreover, we have contributed to the sustainable development of Messenia. (personal communication, 10 January 2018)

(This case has been developed on the basis of public material published on the website of Costa Navarino and of a Skype interview on 10 January 2018 with Elena Gkika, director of Human Resources at Costa Navarino).

Tools to address the challenges:

Towards sustainable employment in tourism and hospitality

When John Elkinton introduced the concept of the triple bottom line of people, planet and profit as a new measure of business success, he noted that social justice is the least well known of the three (Elkington, 1997). More than twenty years after the publication of Elkington's seminal work, we have to recognize that, although the social dimension of sustainability receives increasing attention, there are still several areas that are not well explored. One of these areas is sustainable human resource management in general, and outsourcing of personnel in particular. In discussing sustainable outsourcing, in fact, the attention of scholars and practitioners alike has been directed first of all to issues concerning the environmental impact of the production, processing and transportation of goods.

This environmental focus has resulted in a limited understanding of sustainable outsourcing as greening the supply chain (Bharma, 2012). More recently, when the social dimension of sustainability has been considered, the focus has been kept on the supply chain, and consequently on the labour rights of employees working for suppliers in the chain. Little reflection has been given to how to address sustainability challenges arising from flexibility and gig work for employees who are outsourced but are working in-house. When attention has been given to this topic, moreover, the discussion has focussed on specialized services such as IT services, and has not touched manufacturing (Bhamra, 2012) nor, we add, the hospitality industry.

In our wish to discuss possible solutions to the sustainability challenges presented by outsourcing and the gig economy we are therefore entering uncharted territory. What we offer is a first exploration of this almost unknown territory guided by several sources, including our best cases and discussions on outsourcing in the supply chain. The discussion is divided in two main parts, the first considering workforce flexibility and the second one the gig economy. Considering the novelty of the task, what we offer should be considered as a first view. In other words, we invite you to follow the track that we draw to further explore how human resources may be sustainably manage in the gig economy.

Workforce flexibility: outsourcing and offshoring

Outsourcing is here to stay. A recent report on recruitment approaches (CIPD, 2017) shows that over half of the survey respondents conduct all recruitment activity in-house, but there is an increasing trend to combine in-house and outsourced approaches (2017: 44%; 2015: 40%; 2013: 28%). Although the level in which companies in the hospitality industry rely on outsourced service varies, it is therefore unrealistic to think that all firms in the industry will in the future operate without outsourced or flexible personnel. To approach outsourcing in a more sustainable way, then, we need to address the challenges it poses.

To start with, following the Bilderberg and Costa Navarino examples, a hotel may ask itself if it really needs flexible workforce. If the answer is positive, the second question to be asked is whether to achieve flexibility by using an outsourcing provider. Flexibility may also be achieved by cooperating with other businesses in the area, hiring personnel collectively, or sharing personnel with each other. This 'collegial' form of recruiting may work best among companies that are active in different industries, as these may not have the same peak demand moments. In the Netherlands, for example, three entrepreneurs from three different industries – ICT, installation techniques and interim management – created a platform for businesses that wish to lend personnel to each other, bypassing outsourcing providers and guaranteeing their personnel not only their job during down times but also the same working conditions (Bedrijven Voor Elkaar, 2018).

If a company decides to make use of externally outsourced flexible labour, then, in our view, it should start by investing in increasing awareness about the risks connected with this strategy. Most firms are not aware of the social issues connected with outsourcing and offshoring; they may therefore unknowingly outsource to companies that violate employees' labour rights (Bhama, 2012). Sensitizing personnel in the human resources and purchasing departments about the risks that they may incur in outsourcing is therefore paramount. Sensitizing alone, though, is insufficient without a strong outsourcing policy at the hotel itself where cooperation with companies without their own sustainable HRM policy is excluded, even if they represent the best option from a financial perspective. In other words, when negotiating with outsourcing providers, hotels should ask for evidence of sustainable practices and then take a decision considering the performance of the outsourcing provider on the triple bottom line of people, planet and profit. The point that we are trying to make here is not that a hotel should ignore financial considerations in its outsourcing policy, but that financial considerations should not overshadow respect for the outsourced employees' labour and human rights.

One of the problems of outsourcing noted above is the sense of distance that can be created between the outsourced employees and the company, with a consequence of reduced morale. Moreover, if the working conditions of outsourced employees are poorer compared to the permanent employees in the hotel, this may create resentment. To avoid these risks, the principal employer should find ways of engaging with employees of the contactor by creating an interactive environment within the organisation and should keep a 'close eye on' all the actions of its contractor to reduce the risk of things going wrong. The main employer should supervise, for example, the contractor's working hours, working conditions and performance appraisals. It should also listen to any employee grievances and work with the contractor to rectify them. Supervising and monitoring are essential not only to keep outsourced employees morale up, but also to assess whether outsourcing provider is living up (or not) to the letter of its sustainability policy. If it is not, and if the situation does not improve after warning, the hotel should terminate the outsourcing contract. If the collaboration between a hotel and its outsourcing provider runs well, then, the two firms could take a further step in their cooperation, and focus on standardizing and simplifying HRM processes, and ensuring that they evolve in line with strategic changes in the HRM world generally.

Finally, monitoring is essential also to assess whether outsourcing has brought the expected benefits both in terms of costs reduction and in term of quality of work. Unfortunately many companies are not used to measuring the return on investment (ROI) of their HRM policy, not even of their internal recruitment policy. However, when this measurement is carried out, typically the most used method is cost per hire (81%), followed by the turnover rate of new hires (75%). Half also assess the performance of their new hires as part of their ROI activities. Far fewer assess the quality of the source, candidate satisfaction and interviews per hire (CIPD, 2017). Our recommendation is therefore that monitoring and evaluation should become an integral component of hotels HRM policy,

13

both for the companies own and for outsourced employees. To contribute to the social dimension of sustainability, monitoring should not only consider financial aspects, but also respect of human labour rights.

Globalisation and the gig economy

Having explained the downside of the gig economy and the potential exploitation of workers it is important to recognize that there is also an upside to the gig economy. Gig working through online talent marketplaces can liberate the workforce: it affords people the chance to experiment before maybe changing careers, or simply to have the freedom and flexibility to be their own boss. This can be particularly true for older workers who may want some work on a flexible basis to supplement their pensions or to fit around other activities giving them the freedom that full-time traditional employment does not allow (Goudin, 2016).

As far as businesses are concerned, the gig economy provides particular opportunities for SMEs to access the global talent pool. Sourcing workers from online talent marketplaces allows companies the flexibility to scale their workforce up or down as needed, ultimately helping businesses to keep wage costs low and company morale high (Petersen, 2016). Furthermore, entrepreneurs, in recognising that they cannot do everything themselves, see gig workers as a way of getting talent on board for only as far as needed. The fact that gig workers are also 'management-light' allows clients, moreover, to get on with the day-to-day running of their businesses instead of wasting precious time with administration, recruitment in the true sense of the word, or inductions (Hoque, 2015). Considering that one of the main reasons why SMEs do not fully engage with sustainability is a lack of time and knowledge (Chan, 2011), gig workers may provide the needed knowledge while freeing managers' time for sustainable initiatives.

Finally, it has been noted that there is much more to the application of algorithms to workflows than the pursuit of a further deskilling and even 'dehumanization' of hotel services so that robots can take over people work. Modern technology can also support a healthy working environment while lowering environmental impacts and increasing efficiency, thus truly impacting on the triple bottom line of people, planet and profit. For example, algorithms may help optimizing room cleaning by monitoring the fill levels of towel, soap and toilet paper dispensers through a system of sensors interconnected to each other and to a central server that analyse the data. The cleaning staff are then automatically notified when fill levels drop under a certain norm, making their work more efficient and freeing them from the dull task of fill-level check (Vinke *et al.*, 2017).

Although these positive effects of the gig economy should be recognized and embraced by the hospitality industry to guarantee its success under changing market conditions, the risk of exploitation connected to it should not be forgotten. In order to address this risk, companies can take several measures.

First, they should ensure that the freelancers, interims and contractors who find their next gig this way are protected. One way companies might achieve this is to implement some of the solutions suggested earlier in the chapter when discussing flexible work and outsourcing, such as collegial recruiting. The labour rights of the gig workers should, moreover, be respected, including social benefits and decent pay. We envisage that trade unions may also have a role to play in ensuring protection to gig workers, even though 'gigs' are one-to-one relationships between the contractor and the contractee; these agreements are easy to abuse and hard to monitor; and therefore constitute a tricky environment to control using conventional means, available to trade unions. These difficulties notwithstanding, trade unions could enter the market for collective recruiting and develop into fully-fledged worker co-operatives; hiring out workers to gig employers and providing benefits as members of the co-operative. Alternatively, apps may be created in which gig workers band together, share information and even act together to press for legislation protecting their rights. Indeed the responsibility of governments should not be overlooked. To take the sharpest sting out of the gig economy, a stronger ownership and governance system is needed that part frames, part persuades, part obliges and part incentivises all firms to be fairer and more innovative employers, and to assure everyone they are all acting under the same rules. However, as this book is dedicated to the hospitality industry we will not pursue this argument further, but will come back to tools that may be used by hotels and other companies in the tourism industry to address the sustainability challenges posed by the gig economy.

Second, they should carefully manage the introduction of algorithmic management. In discussing Uber we have seen that some of the features of the app fall short on their promises, because the interaction between the underlying algorithm and the people is not carefully designed and managed. If the user, in Uber's case the taxi driver, does not understand the underlying reason why he and not another taxi driver is asked to pick up a certain client for a specific fee, the readiness to cooperate with the assignment declines. Transparency in the assignment processes is therefore essential, including providing explanation and allowing employees to ask questions about the task (Lee *et al.*, 2015). Following the same line of reasoning we would encourage hotel management to involve employees in analysing tasks and designing norms that will then feed the algorithm. Involving staff in the design process enhances its transparency and easies the implementation of a new technology. New staff should be trained, and involved when possible, in the recalibration processes of the automatic system. Transparency has proven to increase people's trust in the system and help them create better strategies to use the system to their advantage (Lee *et al.*, 2015).

Third, Uber's case demonstrates that when algorithmic management is applied to motivate and control people's behaviour, issues concerning privacy, pace of work and fairness in performance assessment arise. Privacy should be always upheld, and devices such as applications should therefore not be used to over-control people, or monitor them beyond what is required for the proper operation of the system. Moreover, algorithms may be designed to accommodate for the speed of human work and emotions that they may feel on the way their performance is rated (Lee *et al.*, 2015). However, we wish to recommend, that people should be able to meet an HRM employee or a superior to explain situations beyond their control that may affect their pace of work and performance. The averaged evaluation of several guests and even colleagues may reveal itself less accurate than the more holistic evaluation of a well-experienced human resource manager. The human touch should therefore, in our view, not be lost even when algorithmic management will be able to accommodate for differences among employees' work pace, allowing for legitimate reasons or special circumstances to be explained.

Fourth, we should be aware that, like outsourcing, gig work brings with it a sense of distance from the company. Gig workers usually are not socialized in the culture of the company they are working for, and are unable to understand those unwritten expectations between employee and employers that often recognised under the psychological contract. Gig workers may therefore feel disengaged, be less productive, use loops in the system to resist tasks and even engage in unethical behaviour. Recent studies therefore recommend supporting gig workers social interaction via online forums. This may provide an opportunity to share knowledge on the employers' culture, and to at least meet each other online and form a community (Lee *et al.*, 2015).

Last but not least, companies should take care that the time freed by technology and automation is properly used. Consider the example given above of automatic monitoring of dispenser fill levels. One of its benefits is that cleaning personnel do not need to check on the dispensers, because they are automatically notified when they need to be refilled. The increased work efficiency may lead managers to cut o personnel hours, or redirect the freed-up personnel capacity to focus more sharply on quality. In the first case, automation crowds out jobs. In the second case, human talents are freed from tedious tasks and may focus on what makes a hotel experience truly special: the human contact between hosts and guests.

Conclusion

Today's digital capitalism is creating a world of consumers delighting in apps for a cheap taxi or delivering groceries to their door. But it is also creating a world of disempowered workers who have to labour in this on-demand world; the gig economy in which a working week is no more than a series of 'gigs' contracted out by the online dispensers of on-demand work. The case against the gig economy is that it bids down wages; it makes working lives episodic; it displaces risk from corporations on to ordinary people; and, furthermore, it is a source of growing stress. Gig work does not come with pensions, sick pay, holiday entitlement and parental leave, and perhaps most importantly a feeling of belonging to a team or organisation, the so-called 'physiological contract'. Gigs are one-to-one relationships between the contractor and the contractee; are easy to abuse and hard to monitor. There are workers in the global labour market, students, older workers and adults with childcare responsibilities seeking flexible working hours that fit around their lifestyle for which the gig economy presents real opportunities. However, for the mass of workers it is not great news, especially as, increasingly, it forces mainstream employers to compete on the same terms. Therefore for the workers in many industries, and in a range of jobs from professional to unskilled, the gig economy is slowly eroding full-time, tenured employment as many people know it.

The gig economy first developed outside the hospitality industry, but is slowly and steadily entering it. Therefore we do expect that workers in the hospitality industry will be more and more affected by its negative consequences. In the absence of a legislative system protecting the gig worker, and confronted with a weak response by the traditional labour unions, businesses have to take responsibility in ethically and sustainably handling the challenges presented by outsourced and gig work. To support hospitality businesses in this new and demanding task, we have reviewed in this chapter changing work practices and tools to address the new challenges at a global level. However, the main focus of the research and articles used reflect current employment practice in the US, the UK, and Northern Europe, as these economies are the first to move from a bureaucratic system to a more networked society. Our main message is that while business may take responsibility they should be supported on one side by more research on sustainable outsourcing of personnel and on the other by changes in labour market regulation to adapt to the new forms of recruitment and employment practice in this labour market. Hence trade unions need to reform and government legislation will need to be developed not only in the above mentioned countries but also worldwide to ensure fairer and sustainable employment practices in the future.

References

Aloisi, A. (2015) The rising of on-demand work, a case study research on a set of online platforms and apps, paper presented at the *IV Regulating for Decent Work Conference*, ILO, Geneva, 8-10 July. https://www.uu.nl/sites/default/files/iwse_2015.39_the_rising_of_on-demand_work.pdf. Accessed 31 January 2018.

Bagga, T. (2015) Jaypee takes the express-way to strategic HR: Outsourcing deal cedes control of toll employees, *Human Resource Management International Digest*, **23** (1), 18-20.

Baum, T. (2007) Human resources in tourism: still waiting for change, *Tourism Management*, **28** (6), 1383-1399.

Baum, T. (2015) Human resources in tourism: still waiting for change? – A 2015 reprise, *Tourism Management*, 50, 204-212.

Bedrijven Voor Elkaar (2018) *Bedrijven Voor Elkaar* (Business for each other). http://bedrijvenvoorelkaar.nl. Accessed 31 January 2018.

Bharma, R.S. (2012) Sustainable outsourcing: a practice survey and research opportunities, *International Journal of Sustainable Engineering*, **5** (4), 304 - 311

Brinkley, I. (2015) Ditch your assumptions about Uber and Airbnb: the 'gig economy' is no game-changer, *The Guardian*, 19th August.

Bergvall-Kåreborn, B. and Howcroft D. (2014) Amazon Mechanical Turk and the commodification of labour, *New Technology, Work and Employment*, **29** (3), 213-223.

CBS (2017) *Kwartaalmonitor Horeca, Tweede Kwartaal 2017* (Quarterly Hospitality Monitor, second quarter), Den Haag: CBS

Chan, E.S.W. (2011). Implementing environmental management systems in small and medium-sized hotels: Obstacles, *Journal of Hospitality & Tourism Research*, **35** (1), 3-23

Cherry, M. (2009) Working for (virtually) minimum wage: Applying the Fair Labor Standards Act in cyberspace, *Alabama Law Review*, **60** (5), 1077-1110.

CIPD (2017) *Resourcing and Talent Planning Survey*, June 2017, CIPD and Hays. www.cipd. co.uk/resourcingandtalentplanningsurvey. Accessed: 31 january 2018.

Costa Navarino (2018a) Sustainability web pages. https://www.costanavarino.com/sustainability-development/. Accessed 10 January 2018.

Costa Navarino (2018b) Economy web pages. https://www.costanavarino.com/economy/. Accessed 10 January 2018.

Costa Navarino (2018c) Society web pages. https://www.costanavarino.com/society/. Accessed 10 January 2018.

Davidson, M., McPhail, R. and Barry, S. (2011) Hospitality HRM: Past, present and the future, *International Journal of Contemporary Hospitality Management*, **23** (4), 498-516.

Dessler, G. (2013) *Human Resource Management*, 13th edition, Upper Saddle River: Pearson Education, publishing as Prentice Hall.

Elkington, J. (1997) *Cannibals with Forks: The Triple Bottom Line of the 21st Century Business*, Chichester: Capstone.

Eurofound (2013) *Self-employed or not self-employed? Working conditions of 'economically dependent workers'*, Background paper, Dublin: Eurofound.

Eurofound (2015) *New Forms of Employment*, Dublin: Eurofound.

Felstiner, A. (2011) Working the crowd: employment and labor law in the crowdsourcing industry, *Berkeley Journal of Employment and Labor Law*, **32** (1), 143-204.

Gilmore, S. and Williams, S. (2013) *Human Resource Management*, 2nd edition, Oxford: Oxford University Press.

Goudin, P. (2016) *The cost of non-Europe in the sharing economy: economic, social and legal challenges and opportunities. European Parliamentary Research Service*. www.europarl. europa.eu/RegData/etudes/STUD/2016/558777/EPRS_STU(2016)558777_EN.pdf. Accessed 31 January 2018.

Greenhouse, S. (2015) Uber: On the Road to Nowhere, *The American Prospect*, Winter 2016 http://prospect.org/article/road-nowhere-3. Accessed 31 January 2018.

Hiamey, S.E. and Amenumey, E. K. (2013) Exploring service outsourcing in 3–5 Star hotels in the Accra Metropolis of Ghana, *Tourism Management Perspectives*, **8** (2013) 9–17.

Hoque, F. (2015) How the rising gig economy is reshaping businesses, *Fast Company*, 22 September. https://www.fastcompany.com/3051315/the-gig-economy-is-going-global-heres-why-and-what-it-means. Accessed 31 January 2018.

Howe, J. (2006) The rise of crowdsourcing, *Wired Magazine*, Issue 14.06 (June), http://www. wired.com/2006/06/crowds/. Accessed 31 January 2018.

Joint Committee on Taxation (2007) Present Law and Background Relating to Worker Classification for Federal Tax Purposes, JCM-26-07, Washington, DC: Joint Committee on Taxation, U.S. Congress.

Kessler, S. (2015) The gig-economy won't last because it's being sued to death, Fast Company, 17 February. http://www.fastcompany.com/3042248/the-gig-economy-wont-last-because-its-being-sued-to-death. Accessed 31 January 2018.

Lashley, C. and Rowson, B. (2000) The wasted millions: staff turnover in licensed retailing. In: *CHME 9th Annual Hospitality Research Conference Proceedings*, CHME 9th Annual Hospitality Research Conference, Huddersfield: University of Huddersfield.

Lashley, C. (ed.) (2016) *The Routledge Handbook of Hospitality Studies*, London and New York: Routledge.

Lee, M.K., Kusbit, D., Metsky, E. and Dabbish, L. (2015) Working with machines: the impact of algorithmic and data-driven management on human workers, in *CHI '15 Proceedings of the 33rd Annual ACM Conference on Human Factors in Computing Systems*, Seoul, Republic of Korea — April 18 - 23, pp. 1603-1612

Manyika, J., Lund, S., Robinson, K., Valentino, J. and Dobbs, R. (2015) *Connecting talent with opportunity in the digital age*, McKinsey Global Institute. www.mckinsey.com/global-themes/employment-and-growth/connecting-talent-with-opportunity-in-the-digital-age. Accessed 31 January 2018.

NH Hotel Group (2015) *Code of Conduct*. https://www.nh-hotels.com/corporate/sites/default/files/files-rsc/ia-comp-eng-280616-cdec.pdf. Accessed 22 November 2017.

O'Conner, S. (2016) When your boss is an algorithm: In the gig economy, companies such as Uber and Deliveroo manage workers via their phones. But is this liberating or exploitative?, 8th September, *Weekend FT, Financial Times*: London. https://www.ft.com/content/88fdc58e-754f-11e6-b60a-de4532d5ea35. Accessed 31 January 2018.

Petersen, H. (2016) Gig economy – Will it reshape SMEs?, *Linkedin Pulse*, March 28th . https://www.linkedin.com/pulse/gig-economy-reshape-small-medium-enterprises-henrik-petersen. Accessed 1 April 2016.

Rogers, B. (2015) *Employment as a Legal Concept*, Temple University Legal Studies Research Paper No. 2015-33. http://ssrn.com/abstract=2641305 or http://dx.doi.org/10.2139/ssrn.2641305 Accessed 06 July 2017.

Rowson, B. and Lashley, C. (2012) Lifestyle entrepreneurs: Insights into Blackpool's sector, *Higher Learning Research Communications*, **2** (4), 54-70, http://dx.doi.org/10.18870/hlrc.v2i4.86 small hotel

Rowson, B., van Poppel, W. and Gehrels, S. (2016) Wasted millions: Revenue management in Dutch culinary restaurants, *Research in Hospitality Management*, **6** (2), 127-134. http://dx.doi.org/10.1080/22243534.2016.1253278

Said, C. (2015) Growing voices say gig workers need protections, benefits, *SFGate* (17 February. http://www.sfgate.com/business/article/Growing-voices-say-gigworkers-need-protections-6079992.php. Accessed 26 June 2017.

SPERA (2016) Freedom Economy Report, SPERA, *Business Reports*, July. https://spera.io/freedom-economy/. Accessed 31 January 2018.

SPERA (2017) Freedom Economy Report, 2017; Cyptocuriosity. SPERA, *Business Reports*, December. https://spera.io/freedom-economy. Accessed 10 January 2018.

13

Smith, R. and Leberstein, S. (2015) *Rights on Demand: Ensuring Workplace Standards and Worker Security in the On-Demand Economy,* New York: National Employment Law Project.

Singer, N. (2014) In the sharing economy, workers find both freedom and uncertainty', *The New York Times* (16 August). http://www.nytimes.com/2014/08/17/technology/in-the-sharing-economy-workers-find-both-freedom-and-uncertainty.html. Accessed 26 October 2017.

Taylor, F.W. (1911) *The Principles of Scientific Management,* New York and London: Harper & Brothers.

Taylor, S. (2010) *Resourcing and Talent Management,* 5th ed., London: Chartered Institute of Personnel and Development.

Taylor, M., Marsh, G., Nicol, D. and Broadbent, P. (2017) *Good Work: the Taylor Review of Modern Working Practices, Independent Report,* Department for Business, Energy and Industrial Strategy, UK Government (July). https://www.gov.uk/government/publications/good-work-the-taylor-review-of-modern-working-practices. Accessed 31 January 2018.

Torrington, D., Hall, L., Taylor, S. and Atkinson, C. (2011) *Human Resource Management,* 8th ed., Harlow: Pearson Education Limited.

UNUDHR (1948) *The Universal Declaration of Human Rights.* http://www.un.org/en/universal-declaration-human-rights/. Accessed 22 November 2017.

United Nations World Tourism Organisation (2016) *Tourism Highlights 2016 edition,* UNWTO. http://mkt.unwto.org/publication/unwto-tourism-highlights-2016-edition Accessed 12 June 2017.

Vinke, V., Wagner, M., Shofer, J. and Pietzonka, M. (2017) How digitalization, the Internet of Things, and New Work are shifting sustainability paradigms, in Legrand, W. (ed.), *Hotel Year Book 2018, Special Edition on Sustainable Hospitality,* s.p.: Wade and Company, pp. 78-79

Woktowalk (2017) *New Catering Service.* https://www.woktowalk.com. Accessed 8 January 2018.

14 The Rooms Division

Femke Vrenegoor

Learning goals

After studying this chapter, readers will have the ability to:

1 Define Rooms Division (RD) and describe its impact on profit, people and planet;

2 Describe the main sustainability challenges faced by the RD department regarding the impact of water, energy, waste and wellbeing on both guests and employees;

3 Provide examples of ways to address some of these challenges;

4 Identify good practices in sustainable RD.

Introduction

Depending on the organisational structure of the hotel, the Rooms Division department may or may not include reception, the laundry room, or even the guest service desk, as well as the housekeeping staff. For the sake of this chapter, we will focus on the hotel room itself, the choices that management can take to add value to the triple bottom line, and the behaviour of guests and employees in the physical hotel room.

According to Baloglu and Jones (2015: 237), "the industry's great challenge in energy conservation is the balance between maintaining gracious service and controlling costs". This statement can actually be applied to any kind of conservation efforts, be it in energy, water, waste or anything else. A balance needs to be struck between providing guests with the comfort they seek in a hotel, and reducing the negative impact on the environment due to the hotel's operations. The Rooms Division department has some typical sustainability challenges, which will be discussed in the remainder of this chapter.

We can broadly split the factors that drive the amount of resources consumed in a hotel into two categories, namely operations-centred factors and customer behaviour-centred factors (Zhang *et al.*, 2012). Both offer opportunities and challenges for any hotel. It could be argued that the first category may be easier to control by hotel management than the second, even though the attitude of guests is an important factor affecting the use of resources. Guests in general feel less morally obliged to behave in an environmentally sound manner when on holiday than when they are at home. At home they are more likely to engage in certain green practices (Baker *et al.*, 2013). This conclusion is challenged by other studies where it was found that most hotel guests state that they are aware of a hotel's conservation efforts, that they view these actions positively and that they are willing to participate in them (Millar and Baloglu, 2012; Cavagnaro and Melissen, 2018). A possible explanation for these mixed findings on the behaviour of guests may be that guests wish to stay in a 'green hotel', but that the conservation efforts should fall in the operations-centred category, and should not be too much effort for the guest. In sum, when looking at conservation challenges and opportunities in RD, it is essential to look at both operations and behaviour.

In this chapter, the impact of actions by hotel management, employees or guests aimed at reducing the environmental impact or adding value to it will be discussed. These actions have been grouped by elements related to water, energy, waste and wellbeing. As in the other chapters, challenges will be discussed first, followed by some best practices and, finally, solutions will be given for each area.

Main sustainability challenges

This section will focus on the guest's room. We present a description of sustainability challenges in four areas: water, energy, waste and wellbeing. These areas have been chosen because arguably they represent the main challenges that have to be addressed to manage RD sustainably. Facts and figures will be given about the magnitude of the problem, and the main points from current discussion in both academic journals and the hospitality industry itself will be covered.

Water

According to the World Wildlife Fund (WWF), managing water is recognised as "one of the key societal, environmental and economic challenges of the 21st century" (2015: 15). The growing concerns for the quantity and quality of global water even caused the World Economic Forum to move water from a top three ranking as the most important risk to global growth to the number 1 position (World Economic Forum, 2015). Millions of people are already living under water stress, and this number will only grow. According to Gössling *et al.* (2012), reported consumption of water in hotels varies in range from 84 to 2,000 litres per tourist per day, compared to an average household consumption of 468 litres per day per household in the Netherlands, and 1,219 litres per day per household in Australia (Grafton *et al.*, 2011). Though hotels may express the value of water only in financial terms, the above-mentioned statements show that hotels have an important role to play in the responsible management of water use in their properties, if not for their own well-being, then for the world at large.

Hotels are typically water-intensive businesses, as they need this resource to be able to deliver their services. Different sources, like the WWF and Gössling *et al.* (2012), show that the consumption of water in luxury hotels is much higher than that of average households. Within Europe the amount is double, and in other parts of the world much more than double the amount is used in households (Gössling *et al.*, 2012). This variation in consumption among hotels can be explained by looking at some of the factors that are taken into account when calculating these numbers. Some examples of these factors are the hotel's size in m², rating, regionality, seasonality, in-house or outsourced laundry facilities, and the age of the building. The size of the hotel in particular seems to be a determining factor for its total water consumption (Bohdanowicz and Martinac, 2007). The difference in water consumption between the different levels of luxury can be clearly seen when looking at the environmental footprint report of Accor (2011). It shows that the water usage at Accor's Formule 1 (a 1-star low-budget accommodation) is on average 189 litres per rented room, and at Sofitel (a 5-star luxury hotel) 1,556 litres per rented room. This makes sense, as the higher the level of luxury, the more services (like swimming pools, sauna, and restaurants) are offered to the guest. The difference in use of water due to geographical location is exemplified by comparing the litres of water per tourist per day used in Switzerland and in Egypt: 100 litres vs 400 litres respectively (Gössling *et al.*, 2012). Rankin and Rousseau (2006) report that water consumption in South African hotels is 30-40% higher in summer than in the cold season, while – within this percentage – the proportion of hot water consumed is lower. The effect of laundry can be seen when looking at the data found by Deng and Burnett (2002). They found that the average Water Use Index (WUI) for hotels with an in-house laundry is higher than that of hotels without one. The WUI is a figure that expresses the number of cubic metres (m³) of water used per square meter (m²) of gross floor area per year. The average WUI for a hotel with an in-house laundry is 5.10, and 3.64 for hotels without laundry facilities. In hotels with an in-house laundry, 47% of their total water usage is spent on this, and 30% of water usage on the guest rooms. If a hotel does not have a laundry, the water usage in the guest rooms amounts to 44% of the total water consumption. This way we see that the guest room percentage of the total water usage goes up significantly. This shows that when hotels outsource their laundry, in effect, they outsource (part of) their water consumption. If we look specifically at the division of how the water usage in guest rooms, we see that 45% of water is used in the sink, 33% by the shower and 22% by the toilet (Cobacho *et al.*, 2005). Besides the direct water consumption, there are also other factors indirectly affecting the amount of water needed in hotel rooms, such as cotton. A typical hotel room contains several cotton items, like towels, pillowcases, bed sheets, and curtains. According to the WWF (1999), it can take more than 20,000 litres of water to produce 1 kilogram of cotton. One bale of cotton (about 217 kilogram) can produce 249 bed sheets, or 1,256 pillowcases (National Cotton Council of America, n.d.). When you do the math, it quickly becomes clear how this impacts the amount of water needed per hotel room. Of course these are

14

only the water numbers, not taking into account the pesticides and insecticides needed in the production process. Table 14.1 summarises these numbers.

Table 14.1: Water usage in hotels

Description	Amount of water used	Source
Water usage for whole hotel	84-2,000 litres per day, per guest	Gössling et al, 2012
Formule 1, 1* budget hotel	189 litres per room per day	Accor, 2011
Sofitel, 5* luxury hotel	1,556 litres per room per day	Accor, 2011
Average Swiss hotel	100 litres per guest	Gössling et al, 2012
Average Egypt hotel	400 litres per guest	Gössling et al, 2012
Hotel with in-house laundry	5.10 WUI	Deng and Burnett, 2002
Hotel with outsourced laundry	3.64 WUI	Deng and Burnett, 2002

Energy

As with water, there are challenges related to the energy usage in hotel rooms. Non-green energy is created by burning fossil fuels which have a negative impact on the environment. It is estimated that per m² of floor area, a hotel produces 160-200 kg of the greenhouse gas CO_2; that it uses on average 200-400 kWh/m² of energy per year (Hotel Energy Solutions, 2011); and that an average of 3-70 kWh per occupied room per day is used, depending on size and other hotel features (Chan, 2009). The energy consumption of a hotel in one climate may be higher than if that same hotel was situated in another climate. A luxury hotel with a good sustainable energy performance uses less than 145 kWh/m² per year in a tropical climate, less than 150 kWh/m² per year in a moderate climate, and less than 220 kWh/m² per year in a Mediterranean climate (Kasim, 2007). The type of hotel matters, too. Accor's luxury 5-star brand Sofitel uses over seven times more energy per guest room per day than its budget option Formule 1 (98.3 kWh versus 13.4 kWh respectively) (Accor, 2011). Hotels consume energy round-the-clock for lighting and water heating, regardless of whether rooms are occupied or not (Kasim, 2007). According to Deng and Burnett (2000), the average hotel uses 32% of its total energy for air-conditioning, 28% for heating of water and spaces, 23% for small electrical appliances, 12% for lighting and 5% for elevators and escalators. Except for the last category, all elements are also used in-room by guests and/or employees. Their behaviour with regard to energy consumption therefore has a big impact. The above information already demonstrates the importance of managing a hotel's energy usage, more so when we realise that a significant percentage of the energy use is caused by loss and waste. This loss and waste is due to employee and guest behaviour related to the energy usage categoriesd mentioned here above. Therefore, it becomes clear that there is a large potential for reduction. According to Hotel Energy Solutions (2011), this saving potential is anywhere between 10 - 30%, depending on factors such as the size and age of the building, equipment installed, etc. Table 14.2 summarises these numbers.

Table 14.2: Energy usage in hotels

Description	Amount of water used	Source
Average CO_2 produced	160-200 kg / m²	Hotel Energy Solutions, 2011
Average energy use - hotel	200-400 kWh/m²	Hotel Energy Solutions, 2011
Average energy use - room	3-70 kWh per day	Chan, 2009
Energy usage - sustainable luxury hotel in tropical climate	< 145 kWh/m² per year	Kasim, 2007
Energy usage - sustainable luxury hotel in moderate climate	< 150 kWh/m²/per year	Kasim, 2007
Energy usage - sustainable luxury hotel in Mediterranean climate	< 220 kWh/m²/per year	Kasim, 2007
Formule 1, 1* budget hotel	13.4 kWh per room per day	Accor, 2011
Sofitel, 5* luxury hotel	98.3 kWh per room per day	Accor, 2011

Waste

In this part, product related solid and liquid waste will be discussed. Waste such as plastic water bottles and guest amenities is created before, during and after a guest's stay in a hotel room. A typical hotel guest produces more than 1 kg of waste per day (Bohdanowicz, 2005). A large hotel may create up to 8 tons (+/- 907 kilograms) of waste per day, of which 60% is recyclable (Potts *et al.*, 2002. This waste, such as guest amenity packaging, is inherent in the product that a hotel sells, though that does not mean there are no ways to reduce its impact. Among the luxuries of staying in a hotel, are the amenities that come with your booking as a guest. In the Rooms Division department, the most notable amenities are the toiletries provided in the bathroom. Traditionally, these are offered as individually packaged mini bottles of shampoo, conditioner, body lotion, etc. According to Kees Teer (GM Corendon Vitality Hotel Amsterdam, personal communication, 3 December, 2015), an average hotel uses 500,000-700,000 bottles of toiletries per year. If these are the typical toiletry bottles made from non-biodegradable plastic, they will take 450 years to dissolve (Watkins, 2010 as cited in Bobbett, 2010). Buckley and Araujo's study amongst hoteliers in Australia found that 70% of their sample provided toiletries to their guests, and that 94% of those hoteliers used non-refillable items of which a further 43% was thrown out without repurposing (1997). The problem with individually packaged toiletries is that it is almost impossible to refill them, in terms of time and hygiene. This means they are thrown away after use, thus contributing to an increased amount of waste which is not easily broken down. The higher the property rating, the more toiletries they provide. In part this is due to the property managers wishing to provide luxury amenities, but also due to hotel classification systems. The European Hotelstars Union classification system, for example, awards extra points to 1-4-star hotels for providing toiletries in mini bottles. It also gives bonus points for offering shampoo, shower gel, etc. Moreover, for a 5-star hotel it is a requirement that mini

14

bottles of toiletries are offered. According to Watkins (2010, as cited in Bobbett, 2010), the AAA diamond classification, a system used in North America, has similar demands, where 2-5 diamond properties are required to provide bottled or packaged toiletries. This forces high-end hotels to produce waste which could have been avoided, if some of the solutions described later on had been followed. Other factors contributing to waste in the RD department are amenities that are not fully finished, thus wasting whatever amount of product is left in the bottle and adding to the waste of amenties packaging material.

Wellbeing

Wellbeing, defined as "the state of being comfortable, healthy, or happy" (Oxford Dictionary), is a recent trend in the hospitality industry, although, depending on how you define it, you may argue that it has been around for years. In this case, we are looking at the wellbeing of both guests and employees, and both have specific challenges in terms of sustainability. Due to the human factor, most of these challenges relate to the social dimension of sustainability. To start off on a light note, we might mention a guest's health during their stay at a hotel. While on the road, it may be hard for hotel guests to maintain the healthy habits they have at home. Outside of their regular routine, they may face challenges in keeping up their workout regimen, and not succumbing to the temptation of eating unhealthy food at the breakfast buffet, for example. Furthermore, the air quality in the room due to air-conditioning or the chemical cleaning of the bed sheets and towels may affect them.

On a more serious note, another wellbeing topic to consider is human trafficking. Human trafficking can be split into several categories, where labour trafficking and sex trafficking are the types that may occur in the hospitality industry. Both are forms of forced labour. Though forced labour is mostly associated with second and third world countries, there is actually a medium risk of it occurring in first world countries as well (Maplecroft, 2011). Numbers for human trafficking are always estimates, as it is hard to measure this 'hidden' crime, and there are hardly any estimates available for the lodging industry. The International Labour Office (ILO) estimated in 2012 that, globally, there were about 20.9 million forced labourers, of which 90% were exploited by individuals or enterprises. Of that 90%, 22% were victims of forced sexual exploitation, and 68% victims of forced labour exploitation (ILO, 2012). The United Nations (UN) Global Report on Trafficking in Persons adds to this that 70% of detected trafficking victims are female, and of these, 21% are girls under the age of 18 (UN, 2014).

Anti-Slavery International states that "exploitation and forced labour mostly occur in industries that depend on casual and temporary labour, offer low-wages, predominantly subcontract, and where it is often hard to track supply chains" (Anti-Slavery International, 2016: 15). These characteristics are typical of, although not exclusive to, the hospitality industry. In another report by Anti-Slavery International (2008), it is mentioned that the vast majority of people trafficked to developed countries are migrant workers. Stereotypically you will find a high number of foreign employees in the housekeeping department, where hotels may not have 100% insight into the labour conditions of the room attendants if they are subcontracted employees. Language barriers, due to not (fully) speaking the local language, make it harder for such employees to defend their own rights, and to check what their rights are according to local labour laws. Furthermore, there might be a fear of being forced to leave the country due to not having permanent residency. In 2011, 5% of the potential victims of forced labour in the UK were employed in restaurants (Serious Organized Crime Agency, 2012).

Labour trafficking is defined as "A situation in the hospitality industry...where the victim is made to believe, through the use of force, fraud, or coercion that he or she cannot quit and has no other choice but to continue to work" (National Human Trafficking Resource Centre, n.d.). An example of this could be when an individual's passport is taken away by someone, who then forces this individual to work somewhere and hand over the money they earn to the person withholding the passport. Due to not having a passport, the individual cannot go back to his or her own country, and is unable to get any help from the authorities.

In broad lines, sex trafficking follows the same definition as labour trafficking, only in this case, the labour is of a sexual kind. Though the ILO estimated the global average percentage of sex trafficking to be 22% of total human trafficking, the UN reported that a number of 66% of detected trafficking victims in Europe and Central Asia were sexually exploited, 19% of whom were children (UN, 2014). A BEST (Businesses Ending Slavery & Trafficking) study, as cited in Sarkisian (2015), found that 63% of sex trafficking crimes took place in hotels or motels. Sex traffickers and their victims would also make use of hotel rooms for accommodation when moving from city to city as to avoid detection (Polaris Project, n.d.). One explanation for sex traffickers choosing to use hotels is the possibility to pay for the room in cash, allowing them to not leave a paper trail. In addition, apart from the check-in at reception, there is typically very little contact with guests once they have entered their room, making it hard(er) to detect these illicit practices.

Besides the challenges surrounding forced labour 'employees', there are also unfortunate challenges concerning legal labour in the housekeeping department. Typically, housekeeping staff gets very little time to clean a room. In 2016, the Netherlands faced outrage due to a number of hotel chains and outsourcing companies who paid their room attendants per room, rather than per hour, forcing them to work overtime to be able to finish the amount of rooms assigned. This can be defined as fraud, and in this case led to questions being asked in the Dutch house of representatives (NOS, 2016). Furthermore, research points out that employees working in the cleaning industry are more prone to physical injuries caused by strain and stress. Charles *et al.* (2009) found that respiratory and dermatological diseases were the most common physical issues among cleaners, which can be related to the fact that they work with cleaning agents, liquids and rubber latex. Other physical threats to cleaners were caused by handling broken

14

glass, and the risk of finding needles, for example between the bedsheets. In their research amongst Latina housekeeping staff in the US, Hsieh *et al.* (2015) found that 81% suffered skin irritations, 48% back and/or shoulder injuries, and 44% eye irritations. Krause *et al.* (2005) found that the injury rate among hotel cleaning workers exceeded the national service sector average. Burgel *et al.* (2010) found in their study amongst room cleaners, that 65% reported shoulder pain in the preceding four-week period. Besides the physical risks, employees working as cleaners also face psychological damage due to the highly repetitive work, low job status and lack of opportunities for promotion. These figures show that working in housekeeping might be one of the most physically and psychologically demanding, and at the same time lowest-paid and lowest-valued, jobs in the hospitality industry. However, it is hard to estimate the exact rates of absenteeism and illness in housekeeping, since i n cases where this service is outsourced, the number of employees and the pertaining absenteeism no longer appear on the records of the hotel itself, but on those of the outsourcing company (Sweers and de Graaff, 2013). If you are interested in more information on sustainability challenges connected to outsourcing, please refer to Chapter 13.

Best cases

Case 14.1: Please Disturb

The Dutch Hotel and Restaurant Association (KHN), AccorHotels, National police and the Public Prosecution Office, in cooperation with End Child Prostitution in Asian Tourism (ECPAT), commissioned a campaign to train hotel staff to recognise and act on the signals of human trafficking (including sex trafficking). This was started after recognising that the cooperation between police and hotels was not optimal. On the basis of the information shared by hotels, police officers were not always able to get a clear picture of the situation. This made it difficult for officers to determine how to approach the alarming situation, and whether it was necessary to visit the hotel immediately to take action. Furthermore, there was not a lot of communication regarding suspected victims and their pimps between hotels. To improve their understanding of the topic at hand, a few police officers did a 'mini-placement' at one of the AccorHotels.

The outcome of this cooperation was, at first, a sign recognition checklist for Front of House & Housekeeping staff members, that helped them recognise possible signs of human trafficking or illegal prostitution. Later on, this checklist served as the basis for a movie (made by Roel Simons, in corporation with Ibis Amsterdam Schiphol Airport) called *Please Disturb*, which was launched in 2013. The DVD has been sent to all hotels in the Netherlands for training purposes, and has been subtitled in various languages. The KHN also created awareness for this campaign at European level. In addition, the checklist and DVD were shared throughout the AccorHotels chain worldwide.

The movie explains that without the eyes and ears of a hotel staff member, a victim of human trafficking is completely on his or her own, and the exploitation will continue. In the video, tell-tale signs of human trafficking are depicted. An example is a reservation for one night that is made with a cash payment, and/or the fact that the guests' stay is extended one day at the time. These clues are gathered, and, when compiled, may cause a hotel to involve the police. The video shares personal experiences to create more awareness, and to help other hotels fight this crime by recognising it more adequately.

As a result of this task force, human trafficking calls to the police emergency room are now given priority, and police emergency room staff trained accordingly. The Dutch police now offers workshops on recognising the signs to hotel staff, and before big events they contact hotels to alert them. All these actions together, although not quantifiable in data, help reduce this modern form of slavery.

Even though some years have passed since the checklist and the movie were launched, at Hotel Ibis Amsterdam City West (part of the AccorHotels network), the movie is still part of the induction training for new employees. Refresher courses are given to existing employees to keep the topic current and relevant. In addition, employees are referred to an ECPAT website with instructions on how to deal with child sex tourism. Furthermore, when preparing an invitation to tender for outsourced cleaning, one of the requirements is that the cleaning company must become involved as well, and that they must train their staff on this 'Please Disturb' programme. Lastly, AccorHotels has a mandatory training programme for their hotels worldwide called 'WATCH', in which the hotel teams are trained to detect and respond to cases of sexual abuse or exploitation of minors in their hotels. This demonstrates AccorHotels' ongoing commitment to battling human trafficking.

The sign recognition card can be found here (Dutch website, but the links go to Dutch, English, Romanian and Polish signal cards):
https://www.khn.nl/nieuwsberichten/2015/10/khn-vraagt-gemeenten-om-meer-inzet-aanpak-illegale-prostitutie. Accessed 07 January 2018.

The movie can be found at:
http://www.roelsimons.nl/pleasedisturb/PLEASE_DISTURB.html

The ECPAT website with instructions on child sex tourism:
http://www.reportchildsextourism.org. Accessed 07 January 2018.

Sources:

Haan, R. (2015) Illegale prostitutie in hotels: Please disturb! [Illegal prostitution in hotels: Please disturb!], *Secondant*, 2 July 2015. http://www.ccv-secondant.nl/magazine/secondant-2-juli-2015/illegale-prostitutie-in-hotels-please-disturb/. Accessed 07 January 2018.

The author would like to thank AccorHotels for their support in writing this case.

14

Case 14.2: Cradle-to-cradle mattresses – Royal Auping

Royal Auping is the largest independent Dutch bed manufacturer, based in Deventer. In the Netherlands it is a well-known bed and mattress brand, holding a substantial market share in the private sector. Royal Auping is also gaining popularity in the business-to-business market, especially amongst hotels in the higher segment and/or those with CSR policies. In several European countries, including Belgium, Germany and Denmark, there is an increasing demand for their products. In 2016, they produced tens of thousands of mattresses for both the private and business markets.

This company realised that, in the Netherlands, over 1.2 million mattresses were incinerated after being discarded every year. This number of mattresses, when stacked on top of each other, equals 1,000 times the height of the Eiffel Tower. Therefore, Royal Auping decided in 2010 to redesign all their mattresses according to the cradle-to-cradle principle and to critically evaluate their entire value chain. This resulted in mattresses that only use materials that can either be reused in the technical chain to produce new goods or recycled organically without any negative impacts on nature. All their mattresses are cradle-to-cradle, like the Vivo, Adagio and the Cresto.

Their Auping Essential is the first bed in the world to receive a cradle-to-cradle certificate (Silver level), even winning an internationally renowned product design award by Red Dot Award: Design Concept in 2012. This bed is 100% recyclable without loss of quality of the materials, potentially even improving their quality.

To further reduce the impact of their business, they offer their customers the Auping Take Back System (ATBS). With this programme, customers can return their old mattress to Royal Auping so they can take care of recycling it, even if it is from another brand. The same goes for hotels: old mattresses can be handled by Royal Auping upon delivery of the new mattresses, which reduces the negative impact on the environment and prevents additional waste management costs for the hotel. Royal Auping's programme prevents wasting the mattress materials: 90% of the materials collected via the ATBS are recycled to make judo mats, amongst other things. This percentage of materials that are being recycled is much higher than that of other mattress brands.

Royal Auping realised that in terms of sustainability, it wouldn't be enough to just make a product that is cradle-to-cradle and durable due to its quality. Therefore, they decided to fully re-evaluate the way that they produce and ended up implementing almost 30 measures, like heat and cold storage, that led to a 90% reduction in the consumption of gas. They also moved their company in the city of Deventer in 2014, and went from having two locations in the same city to having all their facilities at the same location. On an annual basis, this saved enough kilometres in internal transport to go around the world more than once. Furthermore, they now only produce to order. This lean production means Royal Auping does not have any mattresses in stock, which may be considered a sustainability measure as well.

Royal Auping's critical evaluation of their waste streams led to the minimisation of their production waste, for example by creating throw pillows, called 'leavings' after the material it is made from. These are made out of strips of fabric remnants which are turned into a saleable product, which is also more sustainable for the environment. Examples and a further explanation can be found here: https://www.auping.com/en/leavings (Accessed on 07 January 2018).

Finally, Royal Auping is taking care of responsible and healthy working conditions for all stakeholders involved, from the supplier to the end-user. Upon moving their facility in 2014, they changed their management style from top-down to bottom-up. This means that now employees are not only responsible for delivering the right quality of output, but they also have the chance to organise their work environment to achieve the required quality. Employees who are interested, can get increased responsibilities on the job, like training new employees. The wishes of employees are incorporated in the daily operations where possible. Staff in the woodwork hall indicated, for example, that they preferred not to wear dust masks and safety glasses, as they found them bothersome. Therefore, Royal Auping installed sanding tables that vacuum the dust from below the workbench, and humidifiers were mounted to the ceilings which enabled practically immediate removal of dust in the air via water vapour.

Since producing in a sustainable manner requires their suppliers to change as well, Royal Auping tries to involve them in the production process where possible. All suppliers were asked to sign a code of conduct to adhere to the UN Global Compact human rights principles, such as parental leave, the right to organise themselves in unions, and so on.

Despite already being a responsible company, Royal Auping's goal is to take this even further and become a 100% cradle-to-cradle company by 2020.

The author would like to thank Royal Auping for their support in writing this case.

Tools to address the challenges

The best cases have hopefully given some inspiration about ways to address sustainability challenges in RD. In this section we will address other opportunities looking at the four areas that we identified above as crucial to the sustainable management of the guests' rooms: water, energy, waste and well-being.

Water

To save water in guest rooms (and public restrooms), many hotels have already taken basic water-saving measures such as the installation of low-flush toilets, and reduced flow taps in sinks and showers. These measures may be seen as easy to implement with a short-term return on investments (ROI). To explain: low-flush toilets save up to 5 litres of water per use, reduced flow taps save 8 litres of water per minute and aerated shower heads save 8 litres of water per minute (Styles *et al.*, 2015). Another simple cost and resource effective measure is a swift

14

response to water leakages of taps and toilets, by having housekeeping staff check for leakages while cleaning the rooms. According to ITP, a leaking toilet can lose up to 750 litres per day, and a leaking tap up to 70 litres per day (Kasim *et al.*, 2014). Preventing extended leakages can therefore save a lot of water and reduce the financial and environmental costs. Table 14.3 contains an overview of the ROI of some of these measures. It reflects the difference between an optimised and non-optimised performance.

Table 14.3: Water-saving solutions (Adapted by the author from: Styles, Schoenberger, Galvez-Martos, 2015).

Fitting	Non-optimised performance	Optimised performance	ROI
Low-flush bathroom toilets	9.5 litres water per flush	4.5 litres water per flush	Cost: € 70-150 Payback: 36-78 months
Retrofitted flow restrictor and aerator water taps	12 litres of water per minute	4 litres of water per minute	Cost: € 10 Payback: 4 months
Retrofitted flow restrictor and aerator showerhead	15 litres of water per minute	7 litres of water per minute	Cost: € 10 Payback: 2 months

Besides hotel employees, guests may be involved with water reduction efforts as well. Some hotels use a so-called shower coach, an hourglass usually set at 6 minutes, to make guest aware of how long they are showering. However, this measure may be less effective than less visible ones, such as water-saving showerheads, because this measure may be perceived by guests as impacting negatively on their indulging experience, an experience moreover for which they pay. Framing this in terms of behaviour, the hedonic and gain values of guests may conflict with more normative, pro-environmental values.

A similar challenge is presented by another well-established measure to reduce water consumption, namely, asking guests to reuse their towels and bed linen. Yet, there are ways to nudge guest towards reusing their towels that do not negatively affect their guest experience. For example, Goldstein *et al.*(2008) experimented with different messages on cards placed in the hotel's bathrooms, asking guests to reuse their towels. The overall message was the same: asking guests to reuse their towels, and to put their towel on the rack if they wanted to reuse it, or leave it on the floor if they wanted new towels. The only difference was that different phrasing was used per card, so as to address different personal values of guests. It turned out that the norm of reciprocity and the descriptive norm for pro-environmental action were the ones most effective in improving the reuse of towels by guests, leading to an increase from 16% to 49%. The most effective message, therefore, was one that encouraged hotel guests to identify with the sustainable behaviour of other hotel guests who had previously stayed in the same room, thereby activating their normative behaviour. This is the message they used (Goldstein *et al.*, 2008: 476):

JOIN YOUR FELLOW GUESTS IN HELPING TO SAVE THE ENVIRONMENT. In a study conducted in Fall 2003, 75% of the guests who stayed in this room participated in our new resource savings program by using their towels more than once. You can join your fellow guests in this program to help save the environment by reusing your towels during your stay.

There are also other ways to get guests to take part in pro-environmental behaviour. As we know from literature, hedonic and gain values easily dominate biospheric values in individuals. Some hotels, such as the Bovum Hotel in Berlin, have found a way to use hedonic values to promote biospheric behaviour. They ask guests to place a card on their bed if they wish to have their bed sheets changed. Guided by their hedonic values and a wish to avoid hassle, guests in general do not take the trouble of putting the card on their bed, as a result of which there is no need to change linen daily.

The above actions may have an effect on the hotel's water usage, regardless of whether the laundry takes place in-house or is outsourced, as in both cases it should be taken into account when calculating a hotel's water usage. On average, a regular hotel room produces 4 kg of laundry per day, and needs 10 litres of water per kilogram to wash this, whereas a hotel that has sustainability measures in place for its laundry equipment, and that uses the cards asking guests to reuse will produce about 2.8 kg of laundry per room and need 5 litres of water per kilogram of laundry (Styles *et al.*, 2015). Although the cost of laundry depends on many variables, such as whether the laundry facilities are in-house or outsourced, the number of hotel rooms and the occupancy rate, the energy efficiency of the laundry equipment, the cost of the washing detergent and so on, it is possible to give some indication of cost-savings. According to Styles *et al.* (2015), the annual cost-saving potential of reducing the usage of linen to the best practice of 2.8 kg of laundry per room, per day, may save a 100-room hotel € 8,219 annually. An example of the cost for replacing a towel for a small hotel with outsourced laundry is € 0.30-€ 0.46, depending on the type of towel to be replaced. This doesn't seem like a huge amount of money, but if you calculate it for the whole year, the cost-saving potential is remarkable.

A different solution to reduce the water usage in hotel rooms requires both the hotel's and the guest's participation. A hotel might use a rotating system for assigning rooms to bookings, allocating the rooms that have been unoccupied longest. The advantage of this is that housekeeping staff will not need to leave the water in the hotel room running for 2-5 minutes to avoid the risk of the Legionella bacteria in the taps, due to stagnant water. To achieve this, however, hotels must be equipped with a reservations system supportive of this policy. Even though this a hotel's reservation system might offer this feature, hoteliers might still choose to put pleasing guests before saving water: some hotels will only allocate less attractive rooms (for example lower floors with a less appealing view or noisier rooms close to the elevator) if they have to, due to the occupancy rates. A possible way to overcome the tension between sustainability and pampering guests is to

14

stipulate that the room that has stayed unoccupied the longest will be allocated unless the guest makes a special request with regard to the room's location (H. Jager, Stenden Hotel Quality and CSR Manager, personal communication, 30 January 2017).

Other more complex water-saving measures are, for example, the use of rain water, sea water or grey water for flushing the toilet. According to Kasim *et al.* (2014), using rainwater may reduce the usage of potable water by up to 55%. This, of course, will also help with reducing the utility costs. However, this measure will require more effort on behalf of the hotel to install, and has a longer pay-back period than measures such as water-saving taps. Research shows that, despite the investment paying off after a certain period of time, most hoteliers are not willing to go for sustainability efforts with a payback period longer than 3 years (Kasim *et al.*, 2014).

An indirect way for hotels to decrease their negative impact on the water usage earlier on in their supply chain, is to opt for Fairtrade and/or organic cotton for their bed linen, towels, and potentially also for curtains and their housekeeping staff work outfits. As stated before, it takes up to 10,000 litres of water to produce just one kilo of regular cotton, which is the equivalent of one t-shirt and one pair of jeans (WWF, 2016). WWF set up a programme, the 'Better Cotton Initiative', to help cotton farmers produce in a more sustainable way, which resulted in them using 20% less water, 20% less pesticides and 19% less chemical fertiliser, and in an increase in income of 29% in the case of Pakistani cotton farmers (WWF, 2016). To compare: organic cotton, which is rain-fed, uses 182 litres of water per kilogram of lint, whereas conventional cotton uses 2,120 litres of water to produce the same amount (Textile Exchange, 2016). Since Fairtrade cotton is still a niche market in the supply of cotton in general, it is often grown organically as well. By buying Fairtrade and/or organic cotton, value can be added to people and planet earlier on in the supply chain.

Energy

As with water, energy is a major contributor to the ecological footprint of a hotel, and offers a lot of reduction opportunities. Again, there are direct and indirect ways for a hotel to do so, where some actions will be easy (the so-called low-hanging fruit), and others require more resources and effort. An easy way to immediately save energy is by replacing all light bulbs with LED lights. Though results may vary, an LED light bulb typically uses 6 - 8 Watts, compared to 60 Watts for a conventional light bulb, thereby saving 75%-80% of energy. The lifespan for a conventional light bulb is typically around 1,000 hours, and that of an LED light around 25,000 hours (Greenhotelier, 2011; Energy Saver, n.d.a). Therefore, although LED lights have higher initial purchasing costs, the investment can be rapidly recouped, usually within 2 or 3 months. In addition, because LED lights use less energy, they produce less CO_2 emissions which, in turn, is better for the environment (see also Chapter 8).

Another relatively easy measure to install is a solar control window film. This is a film made of polyester that a hotel can stick to its windows. This film absorbs the heat from the sun and brings it to the outside surface of the glass, where it can be cooled off by air currents. It is a simple, low-cost solution that can be retrofitted to already existing hotels. The solar control window film can be used in warm climates, where radiation from the sun results in the need to cool rooms to make them comfortable. Depending on the current usage of energy to cool the rooms, the cost price of energy, and other variables, this measure saves about 155 kWh per room per year, and the investment for fitting the windows with a solar control window film like this can be earned back in 4 to 5 years (Chan *et al*, 2008).

Key card control systems are seen in hotel rooms more and more, although they are still not considered common. With this system, guests are required to insert their room key into a card slot, which will then activate the electricity in the room. This way, the heating and/or cooling systems, lights and other electrical appliances will only turn on when the guest is actually in the room. This measure is sometimes used in conjunction with light sensors in bathrooms. When the hotel is being built, it is easy to choose the key card control option, but retrofitting it to existing hotels might be more time and cost consuming. Existing hotels are therefore more likely to choose light sensors in the guest rooms when they want to improve their energy reduction measures in the room. However, some hoteliers may be hesitant to implement either of these solutions out of fear that they might reduce the guests' comfort during their stay. They might think, for example, that guests will not want to wait for their hotel room to cool/heat after checking in and/or (re)entering (Baloglu and Jones, 2015). Other research shows that guests are largely accepting of such measures, and that they appreciate their sustainable nature. Millar and Baloglu (2011) found that both business and leisure guests prefer a room with various sustainability attributes incorporated, of which one was the ability to control the power of their own room. It even showed that guests preferred the key card system over the light sensors, but would potentially accept both when present in their room.

Unfortunately, not all guests are equally concerned about the environment, and some may cheat the system because they feel they paid for the room already and do not want the energy saving solutions to negatively impact the comfort of their stay. In case of the key card control system, guests might ask for a second room key at reception which they leave inserted while out, or they might insert one of their own plastic cards, like a loyalty card from a shop. Like with the reuse of towels, experiments have been done to nudge hotel guests to show more sustainable behaviour in their hotel room with regard to energy usage. Via scenario research it was found that guests would react favourably on seeing their real-time energy consumption rate in-room, compared to that of others staying in the hotel. Seeing themselves using more or less energy, would increase their intention to conserve (more) energy, thus making it likely that this nudge would improve their behaviour (Chang *et al.*, 2016).

14

As a hotel will receive both guests who are intrinsically motivated to conserve energy, and guests who need an extrinsic motivation, it begs the question whether hotels should not take this choice out of the guests' hands entirely. As already proven, a large part of a hotel's energy consumption is unnecessary (Hotel Energy Solutions, 2010), and in part caused by carelessness on behalf of guests or employees. By leaving lights, heating/cooling running during the day, even when the room is not occupied, a lot of resources are wasted. A hotel could choose to control the climate centrally with minimal input from guests, by only allowing them to increase or decrease the in-room temperature by a few degrees. Furthermore, hotels could choose to insert a circuit break for the heating/cooling system once windows are opened, so as not to operate them simultaneously. These actions will decrease the energy consumption in the Rooms Division department, but one might also argue that it decreases guest comfort. It is up to the management of the hotel in that case to choose what best fits with their strategy.

Following the requirements for 4 and 5-star hotels, traditionally, hotel rooms are stocked with a minibar filled with drinks and snacks. However, for a lot of hotels this is actually a huge cost due to the time it takes employees to check and maintain the fridges, as well as the actual electricity used by the minibar. Of course, highly eco-efficient, AAA+ models exist nowadays, but a study by Rasmussen and Pedersen (2006) found that electricity costs for the minibar could account for up to 10% of a hotel's total electricity cost. Furthermore, it seems that, besides all the effort involved in maintaining the fridges, guests are less interested in consuming the pricy goods from the minibar when other cheaper alternatives are nearby. In urban areas, a guest can usually find a corner store or a bar. Some hotels now opt for removing the minibars from the room, and having a mini-market where guests can buy drinks and snacks in their reception area. Water taps and ice cube machines that guests can use free of charge can then be provided in the hotel corridors. Another option is that hotels replace the minibars with smaller fridges that are empty, allowing guests to store any food and drinks they have brought themselves. This might already save energy due to having a smaller area to cool. Further energy-saving could be achieved by providing minibars in the room, but switching them off and only turning them on again upon request. Another option would be to have fewer stocked fridges in storage, and to install these in guest rooms and turn them on upon request. Again, the challenge here is caused by hotel certifications systems. For example, the European Hotelstars Union classification system awards 2 points to hotels that have a fridge in their rooms, and 6 points to hotels with filled fridges. For 4-5 star hotels it is even mandatory to have fully stocked minibars in the rooms (Hotelstars.EU, 2015). In this case, no energy is saved, unless the minibar is turned off until the guest needs it.

Along with solar panels, installing heat pumps is one way to generate sustainable energy. A simple way to understand what a heat pump is, is to think of a reverse refrigerator. This system transfers heat from a source outside of the pump, such as the air, the ground or sewage, into its system to raise the temperature of water stored in a tank. This will then bring up the temperature of the water tank, which results in needing less energy to heat the water to the desired temperature, as it is already warmer (Energy Saver, n.d.b, and Chan *et al.*, 2013). According to Chan *et al.* (2013), heat pumps can save up to 30% of energy, as less electricity is needed for heating and/or cooling. One hotel reported a payback period of 1.2 years for the heat pump water system they acquired to warm their swimming pools (Greenhotelier, 2011). In this situation, regardless of how much energy the hotel needs, the system can be used without any negative environmental impact, as long as renewable energy is used.

Other ways to decrease the usage of air conditioners in a hotel room are installing ceiling fans (they use less electricity by comparison) and/or night ventilation to use the colder outside air to cool the inside.

For further insights please read Chapter 8.

Waste

Guests staying in a hotel room create waste. Research shows that most guests are willing to participate in waste separation efforts, but both business and leisure guests would prefer the bins to be outside of their room in the reception area (Millar and Baloglu, 2011). To make this an effective solution, it is important to provide bins that are 100% fool-proof. Colours, text and pictures should be used to inform guests on what should go in which bin. In essence, the hotel should make it easy for guests to show the right behaviour, because if it requires too much effort, the egoistic value of guarding one's time and energy will prevail. However, one could argue that only very biospherically motivated guests will take the waste from their room to the lobby to separate it there, rather than just throwing it in the bin in their room, which costs less effort (hedonic motivation).

There are also other types of waste from a guest room, that a guest doesn't necessarily have a choice in as it is pre-decided by the hotel, but which may affect their appreciation of the service of a hotel. As described earlier, the luxury of bathroom toiletries could challenge the sustainability of a hotel room. Luckily there are many options that can help reduce the negative impact of toiletries. These options can be divided into two categories: considerations with regard to packaging, and considerations with regard to content. When looking at the packaging, there are some options for a hotel to reduce the impact on the triple bottom line. If a hotel wishes to keep the mini toiletry bottles, there are brands offering biodegradable packaging for their products. Biodegradable plastic 'only' take nine years to decompose, rather than the 450 years for oil-based plastic (Watkins, 2010 as cited in Bobbett, 2010). A condition for this, though, is that bio-plastics do not end up in 'regular' landfill, as they need to be exposed to air, light and moisture to decompose. The best option for individually packaged amenity bottles would be using compostable plastic, which can be bio-degraded in just a matter of days. Another option would be to offer the toiletries in bulk, meaning either dispensers or pump bottles. These two options automatically reduce waste, as less plastic is used in bulk packaging than in individual bottles. It also allows the housekeeping

14

staff to spend somewhat less time in each room, as they will only need to check whether any product is left in the dispenser or pump bottle and they will only need to refill once every few days or weeks. Furthermore, this option will reduce the number of items to be stocked on a housekeeper's trolley, thereby potentially also helping reduce the challenge of lifting heavy equipment, as described in the Wellbeing section of this chapter. Dispensers and pump bottles are also preferable to individual bottles as they reduce the amount of plastic waste, even if it is biodegradable plastic. Lastly, these options prevent wasting the actual product, as partially used bottles and soaps are not thrown out. While hoteliers may be hesitant to provide dispenser or pump bottles in hotel bathrooms out of fear this will diminish the guests' feeling of luxury and pampering (Silano *et al.*, 1997), research shows that guests are supportive of sustainable actions such as refillable shampoo dispensers (Millar and Baloglu, 2011) and truly concerned with the amount of waste that individual amenities cause (Cavagnaro and Melissen, 2018). Another objection to the dispenser may be that it looks unattractive and cheap, but guest room amenity suppliers have caught on to the trend of sustainable toiletries and are now offering more design options for dispensers. It is even possible to have your hotel's brand or another name or picture on the dispenser (Cavagnaro, 2015). In Europe, using bulk packaging for soap and shampoo is already quite common, with 59% of hotels using them (AmEx, 2007 as quoted in Bobbett, 2010), but it still seems to be used less in the USA (22% in 2008, according to AH&LA, 2008).

Considering the toiletries' contents, there are again several options to choose from. A hotel can offer toiletries that are fair trade and/or certified organic. The Fairtrade products will make sure that the farmers producing the ingredients for the soap were paid a fair price and that no use was made of forced or bonded labour. Organic products will make sure that no pesticides and other harmful chemicals were used during the growth of the ingredients, and that these were produced in an environmentally sound manner. Additionally, it can be checked whether the product ingredients are all plant-based, rather than animal-based, as some soaps may contain tallow or other animal-derived ingredients. Choosing for plant-based products reduces the environmental impact, due to the fact that these products have a lower ecological and water footprint than animal-based products (Mekonnen and Hoekstra, 2010). Tallow is a by-product of meat slaughter, however, and it could be argued that using it in soap is sustainable, as it is not wasted this way. Finally, we must look at whether a product contains any chemicals that are harmful to people's health, like parabens and sulphates.

Some hotels repurpose the toiletries that are not used in full by donating them to charities, or by giving them to their employees. This makes sure at least that the product is not wasted, regardless of the sustainability of the packaging and/ or content. Another initiative to make new soap from hotel soaps that have not been fully used is 'Clean the World' (https://cleantheworld.org/). The newly made soap is then donated to charities such as the Red Cross and The Salvation Army.

Ideally, a hotel would choose to use either a dispenser or bottle pump made of biodegradable or recyclable plastic, containing fair trade and/or organic plant-based toxic free products. Since bulk packaging is cheaper than single packaging, the money saved could be used to buy a brand of higher quality and luxury. This way, the guest's need for pampering is met. An example of a hotel that tried to make the best possible choice is Scandic. It was the first hotel to use a completely recyclable and environmentally friendly system in their guest hotel rooms, leading to a reduction of the soap and shampoo used by 25 tonnes per year, and a reduction of packaging waste of 8.5 tonnes (Goodman, 2000). However, a requirement is that rating agencies accept those more responsible options of providing toiletries to guests. Forbes, for example, gives hotels more freedom to choose how they wish to provide toiletries to their guests. It does not specify *how* toiletries should be provided, just that they need to be there (Watkins, 2010 as cited in Bobbett, 2010).

The waste measures described above are the ones that are easily visible to guests. There are other solutions, however, that a hotel can take with regard to waste reduction in their rooms and that are less easily visible. This doesn't mean that they are less valuable. First, let's have a look at the floor of the guest room. A hotel has many choices in flooring for their bedrooms and hotel corridors. Many of these options are made from natural materials, such as cork, bamboo, wood, ceramic and marble. Depending on how they were produced, these may provide recyclable flooring options. In the context of this chapter, we will focus on one material, carpet tiles. Carpets can either be made from a natural material like wool, or from synthetic materials like polyester or nylon. The latter type of carpets are cheaper, and therefore more often used, but they are also harmful for the environment, as they need a lot of petroleum and energy to produce. An example of an innovative carpet company that already committed to environmentally sustainable production in 1994 is Interface. This company's ultimate goal is to eliminate any negative effects it has on the environment. In 15 years (1996 through 2011), it managed to reduce the following per production unit: energy use by 50%, greenhouse gas emission by 85%, water use by 89%, and landfill waste by 89%, leading to a reduced carbon footprint of 31% (Interface, n.d.). This already shows how this company manages to deliver more sustainable carpet tiles, but they add even more value by offering modular carpet tiles, rather than 'regular' carpet. When a room has carpet in it, some areas will wear out faster than others. For example, the doorway will typically be worn out first while the carpet around the outer walls still looks great. Furthermore, stains will occur at some point when rooms and corridors are used, and they don't always come out using a vacuum cleaner with a brush, or a special roller. Nowadays, more and more hotels use steamers to remove the stains, as this requires no chemicals. Some stains will remain, however. These modular carpet tiles allow hotels to replace only the areas in the carpet that are worn out or filthy, rather than replacing the whole carpet. This saves time, money and minimises waste. Another company that produces sustainable carpet is Desso. They have various carpet options, one

14

of which is a carpet tile, similar to the one described above. This company is the first carpet tile producer in the world to achieve Gold in the Cradle to Cradle certification (Desso, n.d.). They even offer clients to take back their carpets after they have been replaced, to take them apart and recycle the materials into new carpets. Besides reducing their environmental impact, they also try to add value to social aspects with things like fair-trade labelled products and the fact that they don't use child labour and take extra care of the health of their employees.

To continue, a typical guest room is equipped with a bed and bedside tables, a desk and a chair, lamps, art, and other fixtures. For all of these elements, a hotel should consider the impact on people and planet. Factors to consider when purchasing furniture for a hotel room are the materials from which it is made, the way it is produced, how and how far it was transported, and to what extent the product can be reused or recycled once it is no longer being used in a hotel room. This method of looking at the entire chain of production is also known as Life-Cycle Assessment (LCA). According to ISO (n.d.), LCA "addresses the environmental aspects and potential environmental impacts throughout a product's life cycle from raw material acquisition through production, use, end-of-life treatment, recycling and final disposal". As with the carpets, natural materials that are organically grown and fair trade certified are usually better than non-natural materials. Take wood, for example: taking its origins and production method into account, LCAs assess whether it is FSC certified, whether it came from the hotel's region or was imported from afar, whether it was produced using green energy and without using child or forced labour. In terms of use, things to take into account are whether it is safe and easy for the housekeeping staff to clean and/or move. Finally, LCAs look at whether the piece of furniture is durable, and whether it was constructed in such a manner that it can easily be taken apart and re-used or re-cycled at the end of its economic life. Ideally, the product should be cradle to cradle certified for the lowest impact to the environment. Once the item needs to be disposed of, it could sold so it has a second life, or donated it to charity. Unfortunately, there is no single formula for purchasing sustainable furniture, fixings and fittings to find the 'right' (i.e. most sustainable) option. A balance needs to be struck between adding value to people, planet and profit. Please see Chapters 8 and 15 for further explanation on this topic.

Let's explore one example in more depth, one that is arguably the most essential element in the room: the mattress. In general, hotel mattresses are replaced every 2-7 years. A double mattress represents about 79 kg of CO_2, requires over 6 cubic meters of landfill and takes more than 10 years to decompose. Looking at what a mattress is actually made from, it makes a lot of sense to recycle them, rather than to throw these resources away and let them go to waste (literally). The average mattress is made up of about 30% metal (usually steel), 38% cotton, 10% foam and 4% wool shoddy (Mattress Warehouse, n.d.). This makes at least 82% of the mattress recyclable, and a hotel's commitment to recycling their mattresses can have a positive impact on the environment. One hotel brand that has redesigned their mattress to take into account the materials' recyclability is Ibis by Accor. 60% of the foam core is made from fully recycled foam, and their box springs are made from FSC-certified wood. An example of a supplier of hotel mattresses that focuses on the sustainability of their product is Auping. They offer a cradle-to-cradle bed, more about which can be read in the mini-case provided in this chapter.

Wellbeing

The wellbeing of guests and employees is becoming increasingly important in today's world, where the pace of daily life is fast. It is often hard for travellers to maintain their healthy lifestyle on the road. Hotels may anticipate on this and make it easier for guests by providing in-room health facilities. For example: Intercontinental Even Hotels, located in the USA, provide in-room fitness zones where the guest can do chin ups on the clothing closet and crunches using the bed, and where resistance bands are provided in the hotel rooms as well. Besides providing in-room workout facilities, there are other things hotels could consider for their guests' wellbeing: Six Senses hotels, located in Europe, Asia, the Americas, the Middle East and Africa, uses purified water, for example. Purified air, antibacterial surfaces and anti-jetlag lights are all named as in-room wellbeing trends by the group director of Spa & Wellness at the Mandarin Oriental (2016). Furthermore, research shows that colours in a guest room affect the guests' emotional state. Cool colours, for example, reflect wellness better than warm colours, as cool colours are linked to calmness and coolness (Lee *et al.*, 2016).

Another, more serious, way to work on the wellbeing of your guests is to address sex trafficking, one of the forms of human trafficking. As described before, human trafficking is largely an unseen crime, and may be challenging to address. Nonetheless, there are things that hotels can do. Some examples of tangible and easy measures a hotel can take are installing cameras in the reception area and the corridors of the hotel rooms, and implementing a policy of not accepting cash payment for hotel rooms. Both will facilitate the detection of traffickers, as they provide facial recognition and a paper trail. In addition to this, and perhaps even more importantly, hotels should train their front office and housekeeping staff to recognise the signs of sex trafficking. Some typical signs the front office staff should look out for are guests trying to pay in cash, not wanting to provide identification, and not taking luggage with them to the room. For housekeeping staff, some things to keep an eye out for are the continuous use of the 'do not disturb' sign, frequently asking for additional towels, and different persons entering and leaving the hotel room. The tourism industry (of which the hospitality industry forms part) has initiated a code of conduct to prevent the sexual exploitation of children, and provides online resources to support hotels in their prevention efforts. It is called *The Code*, and hotels can join this effort to fulfil their social responsibility (http://www.thecode.org/, accessed 6 February 2018). In the best practice section, Accor's "Please Disturb" campaign is discussed. This is the same campaign that was presented here as a best case.

14

For the labour trafficking, there are also measures a hotel can take to protect their employees, where housekeeping staff in particular may be at a higher risk. Again, it is essential that hotels are able to recognise signs of staff being exploited. Some examples are signs of physical abuse, persons looking unkempt and mal-nourished, two or more employees having their salaries paid on the same bank account, employees who do not carry their own identification papers and so on. Just like with sex trafficking, providing training to recognise the signs is essential to fighting human trafficking.

Of course, forced labour will – hopefully – not frequently occur in your hotel. Some issues that housekeeping staff in particular face have been described earlier. To solve some of the physical and mental (stress) hazards, a hotel should make sure to address the three major problems relating to equipment and supplies, namely, heavy cleaning equipment, a lack of the right cleaning tools and supplies, and toxic cleaning chemicals (Hsieh *et al.*, 2015).

The first of these might not be easily solved (the equipment cannot just be made lighter), although training about how to work ergonomically could be offered to all housekeeping staff, and supervisors and managers should see to it that the cleaning staff apply these principles in their daily work. This will help decrease the high number of back injuries amongst cleaning staff, as reported earlier. The second element, a lack of the right cleaning equipment and supplies, can be solved more easily. Doing so will decrease the stress levels of room attendants, who already find it very challenging to clean the rooms in the stipulated time without having to look for cleaning supplies. For the third issue, the toxic cleaning chemicals, several ecologically certified cleaning products for hotels exist nowadays. Two well-known brands used in the hotel industry are Diversey (http://diverseysolutions.com/uk) and Ecolab (http://en-uk.ecolab.com/). Both offer cleaning solutions that are sustainable, certified, and contain fewer chemicals. In housekeeping, both offer a dispenser system from which concentrated cleaning product can be pumped into the room attendants' cleaning bottles, and then diluted with water. Besides being less harmful to the environment as it does not contain any harsh chemicals, this system also reduces plastic waste, as the concentrated cleaning agents can be shipped in smaller packaging than non-concentrated cleaning agents. One challenge with these cleaning agents is that the enzymes in the cleaning base only work on the day they are mixed from the pump dispenser. This means that if the needed quantity for cleaning is not correctly estimated, the remaining cleaning solution will need to be thrown out at the end of the day. A brand that solves this challenge is Tana. They have two-component spray bottles (one to be filled with water, and the other one is the cleaning product) which are mixed on the spot when using the product (wmprof.com/en/int/products_7/product_overview_level_1.html, accessed 6 February 2018). The fact that the product is pre-mixed, eliminates wasting the cleaning product. Another sustainable cleaning brand is Mother Nature Cleans (www.mothernature-cleans.com/). This brand uses only cold water and electricity to create ozone water, rendering the use of 'daily cleaning' materials superfluous. This again reduces the impact on the environment. Finally, all hotels have daily cleaning, and periodical cleaning. For the latter, hotels may wish to consider switching from cleaning as scheduled to cleaning on demand, which might occur less often.

Conclusion

As can be derived from this chapter, there are many challenges to consider in the Rooms Division department. Some of these challenges are strategic in nature, and others operational. Owners/managers, employees and guests all have their role to play in creating a low-impact hotel stay. The solutions presented in this chapter give a first insight into the main challenges related to water, energy, waste and well-being in the Rooms Division department. They are by no means exhaustive, and many more challenges and solutions could be presented. The author hopes that, after reading this chapter, readers will have a better appreciation of how value may be added in the operation of a hotel, and how even relatively simple measures can help a hotel become more sustainable.

Key readings

Bobbett, E. J. (2010) An investigation of sustainable environmental practices and consumer attitudes & behavior toward hotel bathroom amenities. *UNLV Theses, Dissertations, Professional Papers, and Capstones.* https://digitalscholarship.unlv.edu/cgi/viewcontent.cgi?article=1481&context=thesesdissertations. Accessed 1 September 2017.

Gössling, S., Peeters, P., Hall, C. M., Ceron, J. P., Dubois, G., Lehmann, L. V. and Scott, D. (2012) Tourism and water use: Supply, demand, and security. An international review, *Tourism Management*, **33** (1), 1-15.

Millar, M. and Baloglu, S. (2011) Hotel guests' preferences for green guest room attributes, *Cornell Hospitality Quarterly*, **52** (3), 302-311.

Styles, D., Schoenberger, H. and Galvez-Marto, J. L. (2015). Water management in the European hospitality sector: Best practice, performance benchmarks and improvement potential. *Tourism Management*, **46**, 187-202.

References

Accor (2011) *The Accor group's environmental footprint – First multi-criteria life-cycle analysis for an international hospitality group,* Accor Hotels. http://www.accorhotels.group/-/media/Corporate/Commitment/PDF-for-pages/Planet21Research/Empreinte/Empreinte-2011/2011_12_08_accor_empreinte_environnementale_dp_bd_en.pdf. Accessed 1 September 2017.

Anti-Slavery International (2008) *Arrested Development – Discrimination and slavery in the 21st century,* Anti-Slavery International. http://www.antislavery.org/wp-content/uploads/2017/01/arresteddevelopment.pdf. Accessed 1 September 2017.

14

Anti-Slavery International (2016) *Trafficking for Forced Labour in Europe – Report on a study in the UK, Ireland, the Czech Republic and Portugal*, Anti-Slavery International. http://www.antislavery.org/wp-content/uploads/2017/01/trafficking_for_fl_in_europe_4_country_report.pdf. Accessed 1 September 2017.

Baker, M. A., Davis, E. A. and Weaver, P. A. (2013) Eco-friendly attitudes, barriers to participation, and differences in behaviour at green hotels, *Cornell Hospitality Quarterly*, **55** (1), 89-99.

Baloglu, S. and Jones, T. (2015) Energy efficient initiatives at upscale and luxury U.S. lodging properties: utilization, awareness, and concerns, *Cornell Hospitality Quarterly*, **56** (3), 237-247.

Bobbett, E. J. (2010) An investigation of sustainable environmental practices and consumer attitudes & behavior toward hotel bathroom amenities. *UNLV Theses, Dissertations, Professional Papers, and Capstones*. https://digitalscholarship.unlv.edu/cgi/viewcontent.cgi?article=1481&context=thesesdissertations. Accessed 1 September 2017.

Bohdanowicz, P. (2005) European hoteliers' environmental attitudes: Greening the business, *Cornell Hotel and Restaurant Administration Quarterly*, **46** (2), 188-204.

Bohdanowicz, P. and Martinac, I. (2007) Determinants and benchmarking of resource consumption in hotels – Case study of Hilton international and Scandic in Europe, *Energy and Buildings*, **39** (1), 82–95.

Buckley, R. and Araujo, G. (1997) Environmental management performance in tourism accommodation, *Annals of Tourism Research*. **24** (2), 465-469.

Burgel, B. J. White, M. C., Gillen, M. and Krause, N. (2010) Psychosocial work factors and shoulder pain in hotel room cleaners, *American Journal of Industrial Medicine*, **53** (7), 743-756.

Cavagnaro, E. (2015) *CELTH Project 'Fully Sustainable Hotel Experience', Final Report*, Leeuwarden/Breda: Stenden/NHTV. http://www.stendenaihr.com/media/77/NL/algemeen/original/CELTH%20project%20Fully%20Sustainable%20Hotel%20Experience%20final%20report.2015-%281%29.pdf. Accessed 06 February 2018.

Cavagnaro, E., Melissen, F.W. and Düweke, A. (2018) The host-guest relationship is the key to sustainable hospitality: Lessons learned from a Dutch case study, *Hospitality & Society*, **8** (1), 23-44.

Chan, W. W. (2009) Environmental measures for hotels' environmental management systems: ISO 14001, *International Journal of Contemporary Hospitality Management*, **21** (5), 542-60.

Chan, W. W., Mak, L. M., Chen, Y. M., Wang, Y. H., Xie, H. R., Hou, G. Q. and Li, D. (2008) Energy saving and tourism sustainability: solar control window film in hotel rooms, *Journal of Sustainable Tourism*, **16** (5), 563-574

Chan, W. W., Yueng, S., Chan, E. and Li, D. (2013) Hotel heat pump hot water systems: impact assessment and analytic hierarchy process. *International Journal of Contemporary Hospitality Management*, **25** (3), 428 – 446.

Chang, H., Huh, C. and Lee, M. J. (2016). Would an energy conservation nudge in hotels encourage hotel guests to conserve?, *Cornell Hospitality Quarterly*, **57** (2), 172-183.

Charles, L. E., Loomis, D. and Demissie, Z. (2009) Occupational hazards experienced by cleaning workers and janitors: A review of the epidemiologic literature, *Work Journal*, **34** (1), 105-116.

Cobacho, R., Arregui, F., Parra, J.C. and Cabrera Jr., E. (2005) Improving efficiency in water use and conservation in Spanish hotels, *Water Science and Technology: Water supply,* **5** (3-4), 273–279.

Deng, S. and Burnett, J. (2002) Water use in hotels in Hong Kong, *Hospitality Management,* **21** (1), 57–66.

Desso (n.d.) *Cradle to cradle.* http://www.desso.nl/c2c-corporate-responsibility/cradle-to-cradle/. Accessed 1 September 2017.

Energy Saver (n.d.a). *How energy-efficient light bulbs compare with traditional incandescents.* https://energy.gov/energysaver/how-energy-efficient-light-bulbs-compare-traditional-incandescents. Accessed 1 September 2017.

Energy Saver (n.d.b). *Heat pump water heaters.* https://energy.gov/energysaver/heat-pump-water-heaters. Accessed 1 September 2017.

Goldstein, N. J., Cialdini, R. B. and Griskevicius, V. (2008) A room with a viewpoint: using social norms to motivate environmental conservation in hotels, *Journal of Consumer Research,* **35** (3), 472-482.

Goodman, A. (2000) Implementing sustainability in service operations at Scandic Hotels, *Interfaces,* **30** (3), 202-214.

Gössling, S., Peeters, P., Hall, C. M., Ceron, J. P., Dubois, G., Lehmann, L. V. and Scott, D. (2012) Tourism and water use: Supply, demand, and security. An international review, *Tourism Management,* **33** (1), 1-15.

Grafton, R. Q., Ward, M.B., To, H. and Kompas, T. (2011) Determinants of residential water consumption: Evidence and analysis from a 10-country household survey, *Water Resources Research,* **47** (8), 1-14.

Greenhotelier (2011). *Retrofit for the future.* http://www.greenhotelier.org/our-themes/retrofit-for-the-future/. Accessed 1 September 2017.

Hotel Energy Solutions (2011) *Analysis on energy use by european hotels: online survey and desk research.* http://hes.unwto.org/sites/all/files/docpdf/analysisonenergyusebyeuropeanhotelsonlinesurveyanddeskresearch2382011-1.pdf. Accessed 1 September 2017.

Hotelstars (2015) *Criteria 2015-2020,* https://www.hotelstars.eu/fileadmin/Dateien/PORTAL_HSU/Kriterienkataloge/EN_Hotelstars_Union-Criteria_2015-2020.pdf Accessed 1 September 2017

Hsieh, Y. C., Apostolopoulos, Y. and Sönmez, S. (2015) Work conditions and health and well-being of Latina hotel housekeepers, *Journal of Immigrant and Minority Health,* **18** (3), 568-581.

Interface (n.d.). Our Mission. http://www.interface.com/EU/en-GB/about/index/Mission-Zero-en_GB. Accessed 1 September 2017.

Kasim, A. (2007) Towards a wider adoption of environmental responsibility in the hotel sector, *International Journal of Hospitality & Tourism Administration,* **8** (2), 25-49.

Kasim, A., Gursoy, D., Okumus, F. and Wong, A. (2014) The importance of water management in hotels: a framework for sustainability through innovation, *Journal of Sustainable Tourism,* **22** (7), 1090-1107.

14

International Labour Office (2012) *ILO Global Estimate of Forced Labour – Results and methodology*. http://www.ilo.org/global/topics/forced-labour/publications/WCMS_182004/lang--en/index.htm. Accessed 1 September 2017.

International Organization for Standardization (n.d.). *ISO 14040:2006 (en) Environmental management — Life cycle assessment — Principles and framework*. https://www.iso.org/obp/ui/#iso:std:iso:14040:ed-2:v1:en. Accessed 1 September 2017.

Krause, N., Scherzer, T. and Rugulies, R. (2005) Physical workload, work intensification, and prevalence of pain in low wage workers: results from a participatory research project with hotel room cleaners in Las Vegas, *American Journal of Industrial Medicine*, **48** (5), 326-337.

Lee, A. H., Guillet, A. D and Law, R. (2016) Tourists' emotional wellness and hotel room colour, *Current Issues in Tourism*, **2016**, 1-7.

Maplecroft (2011) Risk calculators and dashboard. https://maplecroft.com/about/news/forced-labour.html. Accessed 1 September 2017.

Mattress Warehouse (n.d.). Mattress Recycling. http://www.mattresswarehouse.com/Mattress-Recycling. Accessed 1 September 2017.

Millar, M. and Baloglu, S. (2011) Hotel guests' preferences for green guest room attributes, *Cornell Hospitality Quarterly*, **52** (3), 302-311.

National Cotton Council of America (n.d.) *What can you make from a bale of cotton?* https://www.cotton.org/pubs/cottoncounts/what-can-you-make.cfm. Accessed 1 September 2017.

National Human Trafficking Resource Centre (n.d.). *Hospitality*. https://humantraffickinghotline.org/labor-trafficking-venuesindustries/hospitality-0. Accessed 1 September 2017.

NOS (2016). *Kamervragen na Rambam-uitzending over schoonmaak hotels*. Available from: http://nos.nl/artikel/2083289-kamervragen-na-rambam-uitzending-over-schoonmaak-hotels.html. Accessed 1 September 2017.

Polaris Project (n.d.). *Human trafficking in hotels and motels – victim and location indicators*. http://www.twolittlegirls.org/ufiles/Hotel%20and%20Motel%20Indicators%20AAG.pdf. Accessed 1 September 2017.

Potts, D., Christenbury, H. and Wolak, J. (2002) *Recycling for the hospitality industry – A guide for instituting recycling programs in hotel and motel properties*, Cooperative Extension Service, Clemson University. http://www.hcpcme.org/environment/hotel/hotelrecyclingguide.pdf. Accessed 1 September 2017.

Rankin, R. and Rousseau, P.G. (2006) Sanitary hot water consumption patterns in commercial and industrial sectors in South Africa: impact on heating system design, *Energy Conversion and Management*, **47** (6) 687–701.

Rasmussen, S. and Pedersen, H. (2006). *Electricity consumption of minibars*. http://www.elforsk.dk/elforskProjects/337-049/minibar.pdf. Accessed 1 September 2017.

Sarkisian, M. (2015) Adopting the code: Human trafficking and the hospitality industry, *Cornell Hospitality Report*, **15** (15), 3-10.

Silano, M., Meredith, S. and Jones, P. (1997) Environmental management in UK hotels: The role of employees as stakeholders, *Proceedings of the CHME 6th Annual Hospitality Research Conference*, CHME, n.p., 24-36.

Serious Organized Crime Agency (2012) *UKHTC: A Baseline Assessment in the Nature and Scale of Human Trafficking in 2011.* http://cdn.basw.co.uk/upload/basw_33454-4.pdf. Accessed 1 September 2017.

Styles, D., Schoenberger, H. and Galvez-Marto, J. L. (2015) Water management in the European hospitality sector: Best practice, performance benchmarks and improvement potential, *Tourism Management*, **46** (2015), 187-202.

Sweers, J., and de Graaff, I. (2013) *Hospitality Benchmark*, Amstelveen: KPMG Accountants N.V.

Textile Exchange (2016) *Material snapshot – organic cotton*, http://textileexchange.org/wp-content/uploads/2016/03/TE-Material-Snapshot_Organic-Cotton.pdf. Accessed 1 September 2017.

United Nations Office on Drugs and Crime (2014) *Global report on trafficking in persons 2014, Vienna: United Nations publications*, http://www.unodc.org/res/cld/bibliography/global-report-on-trafficking-in-persons_html/GLOTIP_2014_full_report.pdf. Accessed 1 September 2017

World Economic Forum (2015) *Global Risks 2015.* http://www3.weforum.org/docs/WEF_Global_Risks_2015_Report15.pdf. Accessed 1 September 2017.

WWF (1999) *The impact of cotton on fresh water resources and ecosystems – a preliminary synthesis.* http://wwf.panda.org/?3686/The-impact-of-cotton-on-fresh-water-resources-and-ecosystems. Accessed 1 September 2017.

WWF (2015) *From risk to resilience: Does your business know its water risk?.* Available from: http://assets.wwf.org.uk/downloads/wwf020_from_risk_to_resilience.pdf?. Accessed 1 September 2017.

WWF (2016) *Better cotton.* Available from: http://awsassets.panda.org/downloads/cotton_pakistan_2016_v2_hr_sp.pdf. Accessed 1 September 2017.

Zhang, J. J., Joglekar, N. R. and Verma, R. (2012) Exploring resource efficiency benchmarks for environmental sustainability in hotels, *Cornell Hospitality Quarterly*, **53** (3), 229-241.

14

15 The Food & Beverage Department:

At the heart of a sustainable hotel

Elena Cavagnaro

Learning goals

This chapter helps readers to understand and critically evaluate different measures to address sustainability issues in one of the core activities of a hotel: the offer of food and beverages. After studying this chapter, readers will have the ability to:

1 Define F&B and describe its impact on profit, people and planet;

2 Describe the main sustainability challenges the F&B department faces considering the space in which and the vessel on which food and beverages are served, food and beverages items purchased, and the relationship between host and guest;

3 Provide examples of ways to address some of these challenges;

4 Identify good practices in sustainable F&B.

Introduction

Alongside Rooms Division and Front Office, Food and Beverage (F&B) is one of the core operational departments within a hotel. Its purpose is to professionally manage food and drinks. From a hotel perspective, this department is responsible for satisfying the food and beverage needs of both hotel guests and casual guests. The F&B department is usually the largest department in a hotel, and deals with the purchasing of materials and products, their storage, retrieval, processing and serving. Serving can occur as part of room service, in bars and restaurants on the hotel premises, and in banquet and conference rooms.

F&B is a complex department where many activities take place, as can be deduced from the description provided above. Just to give an example, processing involves retrieving items from the storage rooms, cleaning and washing them, cutting and carving them, (pre-)cooking them, assembling them on a plate while ensuring that each order is promptly attended to. Each activity in the F&B department presents several specific sustainability challenges. One can easily imagine how much information needs to be conveyed in a chapter dedicated to sustainability and F&B. To structure the discussion, and following a suggestion by food designer Francesca Zampollo (personal communication, Belfast, 5 May 2016), this chapter groups F&B activities in four main categories: space, vessel, food and beverages, and person. 'Vessel' is the device used to serve food and drinks whilst 'space' refers to the physical environment, such as a bar or a restaurant, in which food and beverages are served. By 'person' we mean both the person enabling (host) and the person enjoying (guest) the food and drinks service.

For hotels with restaurants, the F&B department is generally the second-largest operating department on the premises and the second contributor to total revenues, after Rooms Division. Proper management of this department is undoubtedly crucial for a hotel's healthy financial balance and usually features during hotel management courses. As we will see in more detail in the next two sections, proper management is also needed to accommodate the impact of F&B on people and planet.

Main sustainability challenges

Like any other department in a hotel, the F&B department consumes materials, energy and water. Direct energy and water consumption is a challenge that the F&B department shares with other hotel departments, such as Room Division. Therefore, we will not enter into it here in any detail. A more distinctive challenge pertains to the choice of vessel on which food and drinks are served, and the arrangement of the space in which they are served. The most distinctive sustainability issues, though, occur during the purchasing and handling of the (raw) materials that will eventually constitute the food and beverages offer to guests. Therefore, the remainder of this section will first look at the physical environment or space in which the food is served, then at the food and beverages offer itself, and lastly at the vessels. A final note concerns the challenges with regard to hosts and guests.

Space

The space in which food and beverages are served consists of an outer shell (the building) and an inner shell (the restaurant, rooms or conference room). The sustainability challenges in connection with the construction of the outer shell have already been touched upon in Chapter 8 and will not be considered again here.

In designing the inner shell, the major sustainability challenges are connected with the choice of furniture, fixture and fittings (Legrand *et al.*, 2010). Similar to fitting out a hotel room, these challenges concern both the product used and the labour conditions under which the product was produced. Labour conditions vary greatly from country to country, and are under particular scrutiny in

15

countries that produce at low cost for the Western mass market. As an example, let us consider the production of natural stone, a material used for pavements and walls. A recent report examined the environmental and social impacts of natural stone production in the Chinese provinces of Fujian and Shandong (Bjurling *et al.*, 2008). The main people-related issues that emerged during the inspection were related to a lack of attention for the health and safety of workers in quarries and factories, wages under the legally required minimum and the absence of written employment contracts. Main environmental issues observed were a high water usage, the release of wastewater, the dumping of tailings and waste from broken stones, as well as a lack of restoration of exhausted quarries. Though the study concluded that at the time these environmental issues do not seem to have had any negative impact on the surrounding community, it also encouraged all parties involved, including the buyers and their clients on the European market, to join forces to improve the environmental and foremost the social impacts of the Chinese natural stone industry.

As can be seen from the example of natural stone, sustainability challenges occur all along the supply chain of products needed to fit out the space where food and beverages are served. In other words, to assess the environmental and social impacts of a product or service one needs to consider not only how an item is produced, but also how and how long it is used and the way it is discarded. In other words, a Life Cycle Assessment has to be done. It would be require too much detail here to provide a full Life Cycle Assessment of all materials that could possibly be used to furbish the F&B space, however, we will be able to give some general indications about the main impacts during usage, considering that the general concept of waste has already been discussed in the Introduction to this book. 'Usage' of products needed to fit out a restaurant space refers generally to the energy and water consumption of the equipment, to safety in handling the equipment, and to cleaning of the space. From a sustainability perspective, the main issue connected to cleaning is the use of chemical substances and the impact they may have on the natural environment on the one hand and human health on the other. For example, it has been found that exposure to spray cleaners, chlorine bleach and other disinfectants could cause asthma in cleaning workers (Zock *et al.*, 2010). Energy and water are used in the space where food is stored and pre-pared, namely the storage rooms and kitchen. Compared to food procurement, though, the amount of energy and water used in storage and cooking is minimal, namely 1.9% versus 95% (Baldwin, 2010). This is contra intuitive, yet it should be considered that the production of the procured food has a significant water and energy footprint. This means that the kitchen and storage space mainly consumes energy and water indirectly, i.e., through procurement. Food procurement will be investigated in more detail in the section on Food and Beverage below.

Food and beverage

To understand the social and environmental impact of food and beverage ingredients, a distinction is usually made between four main food service activities: procurement, storage, preparation (including cooking), and operational support (Baldwin, 2012). Procurement is the act of finding and buying from an external supplier those goods needed for the F&B department. Operational support refers to the space in which food is stored or prepared and will not be discussed here. This section centres on food procurement because, as noted previously, the main environmental impact of food and beverage lies in procurement and not in storage and preparation (Baldwin, 2012). The impact of procurement is indirect; it is a consequence of the land, water and energy used during the farming, producing, processing, including packaging, and transporting of the purchased food and beverages. Table 15.1 summarises and exemplifies some of those impacts.

When interpreting the table, it should be considered that biodiversity loss due to monoculture not only results in weaker ecosystems but also constitutes a loss of traditional varieties and thus, indirectly, of culinary possibilities. Looking into the future, some studies foresee a situation in which *real* products are so expensive that they are kept for the exclusive enjoyment of a rich minority whilst the majority eats only surrogate food and pills (Yeoman and McMahon-Beattie, 2016). Though this may seem an improbable scenario, chefs are already confronted with declining availability of certain ingredients, such as tuna fish and eel.

Looking at Table 15.1, it should also be considered that not all types of food have the same impact on the environment. Different studies conclude that meat and poultry have the highest impact, followed by milk and dairy products. Fruit and vegetable, cereals and bread have a much lower impact (see, e.g., Foster *et al.*, 2006). To illustrate this point, Table 15.2 shows the CO_2 emissions and the water footprint of different types of meat as found in two authoritative studies. There are several studies in which the environmental impact of food and beverage items is calculated. These studies, however, are not always comparable due to the use of different methodologies.

15

Table 15.1: Summary of environmental and social impacts of food and beverages

Impact	Example	Main source(s)
Farming and Production		
Climate change	Greenhouse gasses emitted due to forest clearance (CO_2); livestock and rice (methane); and fertilisers (nitrous oxide)	Turenne and Baldwin, 2012
Biodiversity loss	Decreasing crop variety; decreasing fish stocks (17% overexploited; 7% depleted)	FAO, 2010 FAO, 2011b
Land degradation	Increased soil salinity through wrong irrigation; loss of soil quality due to poor farming; erosion and desertification. 30 % of the total global land area is degraded; about three billion people live in degraded lands	Oldeman *et al.*, 1991 (GLASOD;) Nkonya *et al.* (eds.), 2016
Water pollution and depletion	Increasing groundwater pollution by agrochemicals (fertilisers, pesticides, antibiotics) and manure; 70% of water worldwide is used in agriculture; worldwide 20% more groundwater is pumped up than can be naturally replenished; 1.4 billion people are confronted with water scarcity	FAO, 2015; Lundqvist *et al.*, 2015
Air pollution	Chemical compounds (fertiliser, pesticides); see also under Climate change	Turenne and Baldwin, 2012
Food lost and waste	Losses during agricultural production (e.g., mechanical damage and spillage) and post-harvest handling (e.g., wrong storage and careless transport)	FAO (2011)
Health issues	Inhalation of silicate; contact with chemical compounds (fertiliser; pesticides)	Turenne and Baldwin, 2012
Unfair labour practices	Seasonal and low-pay work (e.g., 30% of US farm workers have total family income below the poverty line, i.e., below $19.790); child and forced labour	NAWS, 2001-2002; ILO, 2010
Processing		
Energy and water use	Food processing accounts for 16% of total energy in the food cycle and 25% of total water consumption worldwide	Turenne and Baldwin, 2012
Water pollution	Wastewaters contain high concentrations of suspended solids and soluble organics such as carbohydrates, proteins and lipids	Hansen and Yeol Cheong, 2013
Food waste	In developed countries 7% of food is wasted during processing; in developing countries 40% of food losses occur during post-harvest handling and processing	Turenne and Baldwin, 2012 FAO, 2011
Packaging	Packaging can prevent food losses but accounts for almost 2/3 of total packaging waste by volume. It consists mostly of fossil fuel based products such as plastic.	Williams and Wikström, 2011; Turenne and Baldwin, 2012
Unfair labour practices	Low pay and unsafe working conditions in, e.g., US abattoirs	Schlosser, 2001
Transportation		
Air pollution and climate change	Green House Gas emissions	Gössling *et al.*, 2011

Table 15.2: CO_2 emissions and the water footprint of different types of meat (adapted from Scarborough *et al.*, 2014 and Mekonnen and Hoekstra, 2012)

Food category	CO_2 emissions (kgCO$_2$/kg)	Global average water footprint (l/ton)
Bovine meat	68.8	15,400,000
Sheep meat	-	10,400,000
Pig meat	-	6,000,000
Goat meat	64.2	5,500,000
Offal	35.9	-
Poultry meat	5.4	4,300,000
Fish (sea)	5.4	-

Alongside the impact of meat on the natural environment, it should be also considered that the way livestock is raised in most (Western) countries threatens animal welfare. For example, chickens are selected to grow quickly and mostly in their breasts (the part that Western consumers prefer). As a consequence, a chicken's legs cannot support its full weight and the chicken literally collapses. Moreover, raising animals, such as pigs and chickens, in packed groups increases their aggressive behaviour towards each other. Chickens then tend to peck each other, and pigs bite their mother and other pigs – unless chickens' beaks are trimmed and piglets' teeth are cut. Boars (male pigs) are often castrated to keep their meat from tasting gamey, which customers might not like. This procedure has caused public outrage in Europe, leading to new regulations. For example, in 2012 the European Union prohibited castration without anaesthesia and announced plans to prohibit castration completely by 2018 (EU, 2010). Beak trimming in layer hens will be prohibited in the Netherlands by September 2018 (Dijksma, 2013).

Bottled beverages come with significant environmental and social costs. It has been reckoned, for example, that a can of diet soda requires 2,100 calories (a measure of energy) to be produced (Pimentel *et al.*, 2008) and that producing bottled water requires 2,000 times the energy cost of producing tap water (Gleick and Cooley, 2009). The same study estimates that "the annual consumption of bottled water in the US in 2007 required an energy input equivalent to between 32 and 54 million barrels of oil or a third of a per cent of total US primary energy consumption" and that "roughly three times this amount was required to satisfy global bottled water demand" (Gleick and Cooley, 2009: 6). One third of a per cent of US oil consumption may not seem much, but to put this into perspective, imagine that one quarter of each bottle of water is filled with oil; that oil is what it takes to make the bottle. It has also been reckoned that a typical sugar-containing soft drink takes 170 to 310 litres of water per 0.5-litre bottle (Ercin *et al.*, 2011). Some bottled beverage factories are located in areas where water supply is already scarce, and therefore bottled beverage production negatively affects local water supply and adds to the environmental as well as social costs.

15

Last but not least, food waste is a major issue all along the food chain. It is true that most food waste is generated either on the land or during transport in low-income countries and at home in high-income countries. Even so, the hospitality industry has its share of responsibility. It has been reckoned that in the UK 920,000 tonnes of food are wasted in the hospitality and food service sector annually and that 75% of this waste is avoidable (Parfitt *et al.*, 2013). Considering the environmental impact of food production and the existence – even in high-income countries – of undernourished people, food wastage is a serious environmental and social issue. Moreover, what is wasted has been paid for; therefore, reducing food waste is also a sensible measure from a financial perspective.

Food waste occurs when food intended for human consumption is not used as such. This definition not only accommodates non-avoidable food waste, such as mussel shells, but also considers the whole food chain, making, for example, a restaurant that uses pre-packaged potatoes co-responsible for the food loss that occurred during cutting and trimming at the pre-packaging station. Besides the distinction between avoidable and non-avoidable food waste, a distinction is usually made between pre-consumer and post-consumer food waste. Pre-consumer food waste consists of leftovers from the production process in the kitchen that is thrown away before the dish reaches the table. Post-consumer food waste consists of leftovers that are returned to the kitchen after the consumer has finished eating (see Table 15.3).

Table 15.3: Typologies of food waste in restaurants and catering, with examples (Cavagnaro and de Kruif, 2014).

	Avoidable	**Non-Avoidable**
Pre-consumer	Garnishes Usable leftovers from the kitchen	Non-usable leftovers from the kitchen
Post-consumer	Returned to the kitchen, e.g., portion too big	Returned to the kitchen, such as meat bones or fish skin

A recent study in the United Arab Emirates has shown that (avoidable) preparation waste ranges from 5% to 15% of total food prepared, and post-consumer waste from 11% to an astonishing 58% in the case of a buffet lunch (Pirani and Arafat, 2016). These figures are not unique; similar ones have been found in a Dutch study on caterers (Soethoudt, 2012).

Observing the amount and complexity of issues illustrated above, it can safely be concluded that food and beverages procurement and preparation represents an area full of opportunities for a more sustainable approach to hospitality.

Vessel

Food and beverages are normally served using a vessel, such as plates and glasses, and are set on tables often covered by cloths. This section briefly describes the environmental and social impacts of these materials, starting with tablecloths.

Tablecloths and napkins are usually made of cotton or, in upscale restaurants, of linen. The environmental and social impacts of cotton are well researched, usually in the context of the clothing industry. Social issues are similar to the ones presented above in the case of natural stone processing, but may also include child labour. The environmental impact of cotton is mostly caused by the enormous amount of water and insecticide needed to grow this delicate crop. In the further processing of cotton, such as dyeing and bleaching, water, energy and chemicals play a major role. It has been reckoned that cotton farming is responsible for 25% of worldwide use of pesticides, whilst cotton takes up only 2.4% of the world's arable land. The same report states that it can take more than 20,000 litres of water to produce 1kg of cotton, equivalent to a single T-shirt and pair of jeans (WWF, 1999). These data are not widely known. This can be explained by considering that most cotton farming and processing occurs in developing countries, whereas the main consumers of cotton products live in developed countries. A study, for example, concluded that more than 80% of the water footprint of cotton consumed in the EU25 region is located outside Europe, and particularly in India and Uzbekistan (Chapagain *et al.*, 2006). As a consequence, the negative impact of cotton on the planet and on people is not very visible to the majority of consumers. Unfortunately, there are no proper systems in place to ensure that consumers pay the price for the negative impacts that cotton production and processing have in other parts of the world. Sadly, in the case of cotton, out of sight also means out of mind.

Glass manufacturing is an energy intensive process. Consequently, the main environmental impact of glass is due to emissions of gasses such as CO_2 that are generated by the use of fossil fuels. Other environmental issues during production are water pollution, the use of non-renewable natural raw materials such as sand and minerals, the production of solid waste, and emission of volatile organic compounds (Wintour, 2015). The production of dinnerware, such as cups and plates, has environmental challenges similar to the production of glass. Transportation should be added to these issues. In fact, margins on tableware are high enough to cover transportation costs from low-wage countries (Wintour, 2015). Europe, and in particular Germany, is a main producer on the dinnerware market, although it still imports almost half of its tableware from developing countries and in particular from China (CBI Ministry of Foreign Affairs, n.d.). During use, the main environmental costs are in the energy and water needed for washing and sanitation. The older and the less efficient a washing machine is, the higher its environmental impact is. This issue should therefore be taken into account when deciding on (new) equipment (see Chapter 8 for more information on equipment). Lastly, similar social challenges are encountered in the production of tableware and glass as in the production of other goods, ranging from fair pay for workers to their working conditions (Wintour, 2015).

15

Person: hosts and guests

Offering food and drink is an traditional and archetypal way of showing hospitality to strangers and thus making them feel welcome. This tradition requires that guests be liberally treated with the best the house has to offer. With the enormous possibilities of modern production, storage and transportation the offer of food and drink has changed dramatically. Hosts are now able to serve their guests a vast array of local and non-local, seasonal and non-seasonal food and beverages. The only limitation to the offer seems to be the price that the guest is prepared to pay. Hosts are convinced that guests expect a wide offer of products as an essential component of their guest experience and are therefore unwilling to restrict the offer for the benefit of a more sustainable approach. Evidence from studies inside and outside the hospitality industry shows that citizens have an increasing awareness for sustainability related themes, and an increased willingness to buy sustainable products. However, when push comes to shove, and consumers have to decide between different options, this intention does not always translate into a sustainable choice. This intention-behaviour gap seems to confirm the host's disbelief that guests would appreciate a sustainable food and beverage offer if this comes at the expense of their comfort or curtails their power of choice (Melissen *et al.*, 2015).

Best cases

Case 15.1: Fair Trade

Matthias Olthaar

Offering customer value requires hotels to source certain products globally. This is not only due to cost-competitive considerations, but also because certain food and beverage products can only grow in certain areas. Think of cocoa. The main ingredient of chocolate can only grow within ten degrees of the equator. By far most cocoa comes from West Africa. The labour and income conditions of farmers and labourers in producing countries may vary significantly from those in consuming countries. Cocoa production in West Africa allegedly even involves forms of forced labour. A luxury product produced with the intent to give pleasure to its consumers such as chocolate (the nutritional value is very low) can get a bittersweet taste considering the way cocoa is produced. Organizations such as the Fair Trade Labelling Organization (FLO), UTZ and others find such practices unacceptable and introduced certification schemes for products produced according to their standards for fair trade. The main aim of these certifying bodies is to improve the working and income conditions of farmers and labourers in developing countries. Fair trade certification schemes have not been unequivocally successful (Olthaar, 2009). In this case two factors are discussed: 1) conflicting fair trade institutions and 2) challenging bargaining positions.

Concerning the first factor, the FLO struggles with its intent to make the supply chains they certify entirely transparent and traceable. In the case of chocolate this means that this intent should allow the organization to guarantee consumers that the cocoa used in certified chocolate bars actually comes from certified farmers. FLO does not feel much for a so-called 'green energy'-solution in which beans inside bars cannot be traced back to certified farmers, but the consumption of these bars contributes to supporting certified farmers. This solution is similar to the way that green energy is sold: consumers of green energy do not solely get green energy in their houses but rather a blend of green and grey energy, like any household. However, purchasing green energy contributes to the growth of green energy. Making the supply chain transparent and cocoa traceable results in various costly problems: 1) all certified cocoa has to be stored and labelled separately from non-certified cocoa, 2) upon arrival at two factories in the supply chain (the first for making cocoa butter, the second for making chocolate) the factories need to clean their machines, pumps, and pipelines to ensure that there is no more uncertified cocoa in the factories, 3) companies may charge higher profit margins for certified produce and there is no method to control certain practices, and 4) each and every company in the supply chain needs to become certified (Olthaar, 2009).

Concerning the second factor a challenge is that many large firms are not interested in certifying primary producers. At times they claim to do so, but upon closer inspection the contrary may be true. Consider a public-private partnership (PPP) between large European commodity traders and manufacturers and the government of a European country. The PPP was set up to help coffee farmers in Ethiopia to produce and market organic coffee beans. At the time the PPP was initiated, no grades and standards existed for organic coffee at the Ethiopia Commodity Exchange (ECX). All coffee has to be traded via the ECX according to Ethiopian law. One of the goals of the PPP was to lobby for a standard for organic coffee on the ECX such that farmers could sell organic produce. While this may seem interesting at first glance because organic farm production is good for the health of the farmer and the farm land and also generally implies a price premium, the intended standard did not prove so interesting for farmers at all upon closer inspection. Ethiopian coffees are normally sold at above world market prices for Arabica and Robusta coffee. Ethiopian coffee prices are higher because Ethiopia produces many single-origin speciality coffees such as Sidamo, Harar, Jimma, Limu and Yirgacheffe. The unique tastes of these heterogeneous specialty coffees result in higher market prices. However, the PPP did not intend to make an organic standard for all speciality coffees but rather one organic standard for all organic Ethiopian coffee. In this way all speciality coffees are blended into a homogeneous product (personal communication). Anyone slightly familiar with the economic laws of supply and demand understands that this homogenization results in lower prices. The various sources of power of different actors in the global commodity trade make it difficult to pursue better positions and improved working and income conditions of primary producers in developing countries.

Despite above there is no reason to be overly pessimistic. Social entrepreneurs exist that aim to trade differently. These small firms, sometimes even still start-ups, do business differently. Examples include Tony's Chocolonely, Divine Chocolate, Madécasse, Moyee

15

Coffee and Good African Coffee. Tony's Chocolonely decided to engage in direct relationships with cocoa cooperatives in Ghana and Ivory Coast. A higher price is paid to these farmers and investment plans for business development of the cocoa cooperatives are being developed. Divine Chocolate is a British company 44% owned by cocoa cooperative Kuapa Kokoo in Ghana. Both chocolate firms do not actually produce chocolate in the country of origin because of technical challenges resulting from, among other things, high temperatures. However, through the arrangements made they do give farmers indirect access to the final consumer markets. Madécasse is one of the few companies actually manufacturing the chocolate in the country of origin (Madagascar), despite the challenges involved. Though successful, Madécasse chocolate is sold at above-average market prices. Moyee Coffee and Good African Coffee both set up processing facilities in the countries of origin (Ethiopia and Uganda respectively) such that value addition takes place in these countries. The chocolate bars and coffee are now sold in Europe and the United States.

'Fair trade' is not a pleonasm. However, within the dynamics of our bargaining society interesting new initiatives emerge that may lead to new societal norms. According to the Norm Life Cycle model, norms develop in three phases: the norm first emerges, after which it spreads, and then finally internalises. 'Norm-entrepreneurs' are motivated by altruism, empathy, idealism, and commitment in the first phase. When many larger companies adopt a norm because of legitimacy and reputational motives, the spreading takes place. Internalisation takes place if the norm is accepted at large as minimal standard (Knorringa, 2007). Through these initiatives hotels are offered food and beverage alternatives that provide its guests next to nutrition, taste, health, and convenience, also novelty, status, and ethics. All these aspects together maximize customer value.

Effective fair trade initiatives can be recognized as follows:

■ Identify whether a certified company is only certified for marketing reasons or also for the purpose of ethical trade. In case of the latter, companies often do more than what is required from the certification scheme, such as sharing ownership of the firm with farmers.

■ Identify where in the supply chain value is added. In other words, identify whether the processing of the produce takes place in countries of origin or in industrialized countries. A distinction can be made between processing for semi-finished products and processing for finished products.

■ Request the supply chain codes of conduct, if they exist, and identify whether: 1) codes are developed jointly by supply chain firms, or by powerful firms individually; 2) whether or not the codes are specific; 3) what the level of compliance of powerful firms is; and 4), what the likelihood of implementation of the codes is. Codes of conduct, if implemented, explain what firms do to act not just legally correct, but in a legitimate way as well (Van Tulder *et al.*, 2009).

Case 15.2: Food of the future

Lennart Buchholz and Elena Cavagnaro

The World population is expected to reach 9 billion people in 2050. To feed this number of people food production will almost need to double, resulting in an even greater pressure on the agricultural system and the natural environment. Scarcity of farm land, nutrients, water, fish and other natural resources and services are already visible, and are predicted to increase in the future also due to the consequence of climate change. Demand for food in general and for meat in particular is, in fact, already steeply increasing thanks to the economic development and changing diets in countries such as China. These developments confront policy makers, scientists and businesses with a pressing question: how to guarantee sufficient food for all people now – worldwide nearly 1 billion people still suffer from hunger – and in the future. Promoting urban farming, increasing crop yields in developing countries and reducing food waste all along the supply chain are some of the answers given to this pressing question. Yet, particularly to cope with the increasing demand for meat, new sources of animal proteins will need to be exploited. Edible insects may become a successful alternative for meat on our plates both at home and out of home (Huis *et al.*, 2013).

Insects are often perceived as a nuisance; yet they do not only perform essential functions for humankind such as pollination, but are also part of the traditional diet of at least 2 billion people (Huis *et al.*, 2013), though the majority of people worldwide, particularly in Western societies, consider eating insects as a rather disgusting practice. Notwithstanding the widespread refusal of edible insects, the tide is changing. Nowadays edible insects may be bought on Amazon.com and from specialized wholesalers such as EatGrub in the UK (www.eatgrub.co.uk, accessed on 31 January 2018). In 2015 one large Dutch supermarket chain started selling burger, schnitzels and nuggets containing about 16% of Lesser mealworm flour (Huis, 2016). Cookbooks, such as *The Insect Cookbook* by Huis, Gurp and Dicke in 2014, have been published and restaurants, such as Grub Kitchen in Pembrokeshire (UK) under the lead of head chef Andy Holcroft, are experimenting with insect-based menus (http://www.grubkitchen.co.uk/the-restaurant/, accessed on 31 January 2018).

Yet why should we consider eating insects instead of traditional meat such as beef and poultry? The answer lies in the benefits for the economies of many a country, the environment and for human health.

In economic terms, the advantages of edible insects are their diversity and variety. They can be found in forests, uncultivated land, agricultural fields or water bodies. Many different kinds of insects can count as edible and all over the world people may be able to grow and harvest local insects. A whole new business market could help developing countries to stabilize their economies with the production and export of edible insects. Countries such as Thailand, Vietnam and South Africa already support the mass rearing of insects (Huis *et al.*, 2013). Additionally, if not used for direct human consumption, insects can potentially also be used as feed for other animals.

15

From an environmental perspective, insects have a high food conversion rate: in other words they need less food per gram protein. Moreover, a larger portion of an insects' meat can be eaten compared to traditional livestock. It has, for example, been estimated that up to 80% of a cricket is edible compared with 55% for chicken and pigs and 40% for cows. This means that crickets are twice as efficient in converting feed to meat as chicken, at least four times more efficient than pigs, and 12 times more efficient than cattle (Huis *et al.*, 2013). Finally, if properly managed, insect production releases far less greenhouse gasses than rearing traditional livestock (Oonincx *et al.*, 2010).

Opponents of eatable insects question whether insects are a nutritious and healthy food source. Research has shown that, even though the nutritional value of insects varies per species, insects are highly nutritious and are a healthy food source with high fat, protein and mineral content. For example, the composition of unsaturated omega-3 in meal-worms is comparable with that in fish and higher than in cattle and pigs (Huis *et al.*, 2013). Insects, if handled hygienically and properly cooked, have be found to be as safe as meat (Feng *et al.*, 2017; Huis, 2016).

Another often heard critique of edible insects is that their taste and texture is not appetizing. The choice of food is largely a matter of personal preferences and habits, yet – as noted above – it should be rememberd that insects have been and are consumed by billions of people in countries as diverse as China (Feng *et al.*, 2017), Japan (Mitsuhashi, 2005) and Mexico (Ramos Elorduy, 1997). Moreover, attitudes towards food items may change; what has been considered in the past as non-edible (e.g. potatoes in the 16th century) is now staple food. Without doubt, although it may need extensive convincing, the common prejudice against edible insects can be changed (Pliner and Salvy, 2006).

Concluding, we may state that, while accepting insects as a source of food is an essential component of a more sustainable human diet, the majority of consumers are still reluctant to try them. To change consumers' mentality it is essential to turn edible insects into palatable dishes. Restaurants may seize the opportunity and take the lead in this process of change towards a more sustainable food pattern by sensitizing their guests toward the benefits of eating insects, including benefits for their personal health, and by letting guests taste some carefully chosen and designed dishes.

Case 15.3: Feldmilla and a sustainable food supply chain

Silvana Signori

Feldmilla.designhotel is a small, elegant and sustainable hotel in Val Pusteria, one of the most beautiful valleys in the mountains of northern Italy. Run by two generations of the Leimegger family (Elisabeth and Pepi, first, and now their daughters Karin and Ruth), the hotel has always been characterized by its considerable attention to sustainability. This commitment became even stronger when the management passed to the two daughters. In fact, when the daughters decided to take over the running of the hotel, they had to decide which direction they intended to move in and how to characterize their activity:

"It was up to us to define our path. Thanks to an external consultant, we realized in what direction we wanted to go: sustainability and renewable energy was our decision for the future!" (Ruth Leimegger, Campo Tures, 6 September 2015, personal communication).

This intention is clearly stated in their own words:

Our nature. Our home. What makes us proud. We protect and preserve it as a matter of course. A matter of honor. For this reason, clean electricity from our own hydropower plant is what flows through the veins of the feldmilla.designhotel. And heat from the biomass heating plant. This is why we support climate protection projects. It's why everything in our kitchen is regional, seasonal and ecological. Conserving resources and respecting nature. Simply because it makes us feel good. And because it makes people happy being surrounded by lovely things, Mother Nature is also our favorite designer. Wood. Stone. Earthy tones. Clear, pure design. Individual pieces, made to measure. Style and sustainability - no contradiction. (www.feldmilla.com, last accessed on 22 August 2017)

An important step was the decision, taken in 2011, to calculate the Corporate Carbon Footprint (CCF). Feldmilla was in a privileged position as the hotel already had a green and renewable energy source from a hydropower plant (a fondness for environmentally friendly energy runs in the family, in fact, guests can still have breakfast next to the old 'family' hydroelectric turbine dating from 1939). Surprisingly, the CCF showed that the greatest impact on Feldmilla's carbon footprint was made by food procurement. They realized that daily purchases of products like meat, fish, milk, eggs and vegetables, had a strong influence on their total score. They decided to change their policy. "[They] are convinced of the fact that sustainability and a respectful way of dealing with nature have to start with the shopping list" (www.feldmilla.com, last accessed on 22 August 2017).

Feldmilla gradually changed the menu, reducing the use of beef but maintaining other kinds of meat with a lower carbon impact, replacing seafish with local freshwater fish like trout and char, and serving local eggs and speciality cheeses made in the traditional way.

Furthermore, besides special menus for vegetarians and vegans, they introduced the "Feldmilla's veggie day", a day on which all the guests can opt for a full vegetarian menu with a low carbon impact.

An important change also involved the procurement system. They realized that their main fruit and vegetable supplier was located in Padua, about 300 km. from Campo Tures, the village were Feldmilla is situated. Every week, potatoes, carrots, salad, etc. were transported by van from wherever to Padua and then on to Campo Tures. The transport impinged heavily (too much!) on Feldmilla's carbon footprint. Therefore, they decided to shift to seasonal products and, where possible, regional products.

It was one of the hardest decisions to be put into practice. It was not easy to find a local farmer willing to produce all the products we needed. They usually grow only one product. (Ruth Leimegger, Campo Tures, 5 September 2015, personal communication)

15

In regions like Alto Adige, where the natural landscape is the major resource, farmers usually prefer monoculture. The Leimegger looked for and contacted various farmers from their own village, but they were not willing to change their practices. After quite a long search, they finally found a young farmer working only 8 kilometres from the hotel. He started to introduce new crops (like carrots, for example) and the hotel guarantees to procure its weekly supplies from him.

> Of course, not all vegetables (and even more so fruit) can grow in Alto Adige (like tomatoes, for example) but, most of the vegetables served now come from this local producer. Once a week we go and pick up what we need for the whole week. Eggs are also purchased from a local organic producer, 1 kilometre from the hotel. (Ruth Leimegger, Campo Tures, 5 September 2015, personal communication)

The Leimegger family believes in the importance of every day practices: small changes that slowly improve CO_2 parameters. For example, for them water is a precious commodity: they consciously take care of their mountain spring water. This means that the melted ice from the sparkling wine coolers is not simply poured away, but used to water the flowers. The total amount of water saved is only 20 litres per day, but the gesture is repeated every day. Moreover, in each room's minibar they offer "fresh mountain spring water from the Valle Aurina, decanted into glass bottles. Pure, sustainable and healthy" (www.feldmilla.com, last accessed on 22 August 2017).

Some decisions were not easy to take, sometimes collaborators did not share the same opinion as the owners, like reducing the quantity of food available at buffets in order to reduce food waste. However, with a constant willingness to share ideas, values and meanings and a strong and open dialogue, day after day, a lot of small, but important changes were made. A crucial role was played by the kitchen and the willingness of the chefs to find a balance between values and taste, tradition and innovation. Essential ingredients were "a pinch of passion and a shot of innovative spirit" (www.feldmilla.com, last accessed on 22 August 2017).

(This case was written thanks to the willingness and kindness of Ruth Leimegger who, during a pleasant holiday at Feldmilla in September 2015, dedicated a lot of time to assuaging my curiosity about their commitment towards sustainability).

Tools to address the challenges

This section presents and discusses a number of possibilities for addressing the challenges identified earlier. It follows the same structure, by looking briefly at the space in which the food and beverages are offered, then discussing at more length food and beverage items themselves and considering the vessels on which they are served. The section concludes with some considerations regarding the people involved – the hosts and guests.

Space

In the space where food and beverages are served, the major sustainability challenges are connected with the choice of furniture, fixtures and fittings. The best option when looking for a sustainable choice for these items is to refer to national and international certification schemes (Legrand *et al.*, 2010). For example, certified wood should be preferred to uncertified wood. A certification such as that of the Forest Stewardship Council (FSC) FSC guarantees that the wood is harvested from forests that are sustainably managed. In a sustainably managed forest, for example, new trees are planted to replace the trees that are harvested and safety measures are in place to protect workers.

Certification schemes undoubtedly differ, and some are considered more stringent than others. When choosing between different certification options, one should consider that from an environmental perspective the ultimate aim is to achieve zero-waste, as it has been explained in the Introduction to this book. To achieve zero-waste it is essential that no waste is produced throughout the economic life of a product, including the moment it is discarded. Cradle-to-cradle certification testifies that the materials of which a product is made can be either reused without loss of quality or returned to the natural environment without any damage. Cradle-to-cradle certification is currently the most stringent environmental certification and should, if possible, be preferred above other forms of certification.

People-related issues, such as fair pay and safe labour conditions, are addressed by specific certification schemes. The world's largest and most renowned certification scheme is the Fair Trade mark issued by Fair Trade International. Fair Trade certified products guarantee that a 'fair price' has been paid to the producer, i.e., a price that assures a decent livelihood for the farmer and his family. A 'fair price' is often higher than the market price, and this is one of the reasons why Fair Trade certified goods are usually more expensive than uncertified goods. The focus of Fair Trade is on food and precious metals, and not on fittings or decorations. Even so, national programmes for the certification of home decorations and apparel are starting to develop. The USA Fair Trade organisation (http://fairtradeusa.org/certification/producers/apparel) and the Dutch based Handed-by (http://www.handedby.nl) launched similar programmes, and more may be expected in the near future.

A difficult issue arises when considering non-certified products from local, small producers. Supporting local employment is surely a praiseworthy sustainable measure; and yet to be more fully sustainable the buyer should also in this case check that the production is carried out in a socially and environmentally sustainable way.

Whatever the decision taken about the use of certification schemes, it is essential that the space is aligned with the overall sustainability vision of the organisation and with its F&B concept. Offering, for example, local and organic produce in a space fitted with sustainable but non-locally sourced tables and chairs may

15

seem contradictory and may bring guests to doubt the authenticity of the whole concept, unless these choices are clearly explained to them as resulting from the overall sustainable stance of the organisation that may, for example, try to achieve a positive sustainable impact both at home and far from home.

Food and beverage

The best way to appreciate the richness and complexity of sustainable food and beverage management is to refer back to Table 15.1 and the vast array of issues presented by food and beverage procurement. The debate on the most sustainable solution for issues such as biodiversity loss, land degradation, water pollution and unfair labour practices has not yet reached a definitive conclusion, and following this debate may be daunting for those restaurateurs who are looking for practical advice on how to implement sustainability in their premises. From a F&B managerial perspective, what are needed are basic guidelines that reflect the environmental, social and economic dimension of sustainability and take into account the knowledge developed so far on the most sustainable solution.

In the book entitled *Five Ingredients for Better, Fresher, Healthier and More Just Food* Albert Kooy, executive chef at Wannee restaurant in The Netherlands (http://www.restaurantwannee.nl), offers what at present are the best practical guidelines for people who wish to opt for sustainable F&B. Kooy labels these five 'ingredients' as culture, health, nature, and quality and profit (see Table 15.4). Let's briefly consider them one by one.

The *culture* ingredient calls for respect for the culinary tradition of the region in which the restaurant is situated. Respecting the regional culinary tradition means first to choose local and seasonal products. We indeed need to remember that the wide availability of non-seasonal, non-local ingredients is a very recent phenomenon limited to high-income countries. Second, respect can be shown by creating new dishes in line with the regional culinary heritage. The aim of the 'culture' ingredient, however, is not to fix a culinary tradition to a specific moment in time. It is rather to give guests a sense of the place that they are visiting or where they are living when they taste a dish.

Regional and *local* are broad concepts. In practice, people tend to consider 'local' to be open grown food from a specific climate area or food that is produced within well-defined spatial limits such as 100 miles, or around 160 kilometres (Schulp, 2015; see also Chapter 9). It is important to recognise that locally sourced food may support the local culinary culture and local farmer, but is not by definition environmentally sustainable. Food labelled as local may still have been produced with the use of chemical fertilisers and pesticides. It might, moreover, cause higher CO_2 emissions than non-locally sourced food due to inefficient transportation. For example, when Kooy started applying his principles he needed to source food from a large number of different suppliers, so that instead of one transport every few days by the national wholesaler, several small vans rolled up to the back door of his restaurant every day. Transport issues should be as much as possible addressed (see Chapter 11 for suggestions). Yet, as long as these are not solved, it is important to insist on the social component when opting for local ingredients, and this is the support given to local traditions and local farmers. It is, finally, widely recognised that not all ingredients can or should be sourced locally. Even from quite a broad regional perspective, by considering Europe, for example, as a region, coffee, tea, chocolate and several spices cannot be produced 'locally'. Moreover, some economies (for historic reasons that are too complex to explain briefly here) depend heavily on the export of agricultural products to high-income countries. If you wish more information on this issue, you may start by reading the section on Colonialism in Cavagnaro and Curiel's book *The Three Levels of Sustainability* (2012: 54-56). For the scope of this chapter it will suffice to notice that resorting to complete self-sufficiency would severely damage these economies, and thus counteract on a global scale any sustainable effect achieved on a local scale. As a rule of thumb, Albert Kooy proposes to use 80% local and 20% imported ingredients.

Summing up, as a component of sustainable F&B, culture touches both on the social (culinary heritage, local) and on the environmental (seasonal, open grown) dimension of food sustainability.

The second and third ingredients for sustainable restaurants – *health* and *nature* – are related: health refers to our personal wellbeing and safety whilst nature focuses on Earth's 'health' and integrity. Our own and Earth's health are best served by reconsidering the role that meat and vegetables play in our daily diet and in a standard (Western) restaurant menu on the one hand, and reducing portions on the other (Tukker *et al.*, 2009). Typically, meat is the most important dish component with some vegetables as a garnish. A healthy human diet requires exactly the opposite. Considering that a full vegetarian or even vegan menu might be a bridge too far for many guests and hosts, Albert Kooy suggests creating dishes using the ratio of 80% vegetables and 20% meat as a rule of thumb. The choice of placing vegetables at the centre of a dish has an immediate, positive impact also on the planet because, as explained above, meat production has a significant, negative impact on Earth's resources (Fotouhinia Yepes, 2015). Finally, looking at the relative costs of meat and vegetables, this choice may become the most rational also from a financial point of view. Similar positive outcomes for our guests' and our planet's health are achieved by reducing portions. Restaurant portions often greatly exceed the daily calories we need, and lead either to overeating or to avoidable waste. What is not wasted does not need to be produced, transported and bought, and so reducing portions is a sustainable choice environmentally and financially. By reducing waste, resources can be freed up and used to buy organic food and beverages, even though they are more expensive than non-organic ones.

Research has shown the health risks connected to excessively high consumption of salt (Lang *et al.*, 2011) and sugar (Khan and Sievenpieper, 2016). To indulge people's desire for sweet and salty food, salt and sugar are often overused (such as sugar in jam) or added when they are not needed (such as sugar in mayonnaise).

15

Albert Kooy's health principle requires an appropriate use of salt and sugar. Along the same lines, and avoiding unnecessary and potentially harmful substances, fresh ingredients should substitute pre-packaged ingredients as often as possible (Pollan, 2009). Finally, where meat is concerned, the whole animal should be used – including 'odd bits' such as the head and offal. This way, restaurateurs can realise a positive outcome for both the planet and the profit dimensions of sustainability, because they will not waste any part of an environmentally and financially costly resource.

The fourth ingredient for a sustainable F&B proposition is *quality*. Opting for quality as a guideline in the choice of food and beverages means showing respect for the products and for the people who produce them, wherever they live, by paying a fair price for their produce.

The last ingredient of sustainable F&B is *profit*. Of course, profit is needed for a business to survive. Yet sustainable profit in F&B is achieved by applying the other four principles, and therefore it means focusing exclusively on the survival of one's own business but creating value for all stakeholders including suppliers, guests, the Earth and the business itself.

Table 15.4: A. Kooy's five ingredients and the three dimensions of sustainability

Ingredient	Key principles	Sustainability dimension
Culture	Culinary heritage; local; seasonal; open-grown	Social; environmental
Health	80-20 ratio; no unnecessary ingredients; smaller portions	Social; financial
Nature	80-20 ratio; no waste	Environmental
Quality	Respect for products and producers (fair trade)	Social
Profit	Profit for all stakeholders	Financial; social

Vessel

Certification schemes can also help in addressing the sustainability issues of vessels, such as china, glass and table linen. For example, Fair Trade certified table linen is becoming more available, and more affordable. Even though organic cotton represents less than 1% of total cotton production, in the last few years an increase in demand has driven a steep increase in production, but still outstrips it (Textile Exchange, 2015). It will therefore take some time before organic cotton is an easily available and affordable choice for hoteliers. Interestingly, companies offering organic and fair trade linen to hoteliers such as the Dutch Blycolin (http://www.blycolin.com/home.html) signal an increase in requests particularly from more exclusive properties (Personal communication, Utrecht, April 2014).

Glass and plastic can be separated from other waste and recycled. This option, though, is not available in all countries and, even if it is available, not all glass and plastic are handled and recycled separately. Moreover, recycling still costs a vast amount of water and energy. Therefore, the first step to take here is to try to prevent and reduce glass and china waste, and use sustainable options in place of plastic as often as possible (Baldwin, 2012).

The issue of reusable versus disposable plates has been addressed in several studies. The choice between reusable or disposable plates and containers is a complex one because it involves calculating the relative environmental impacts of at least water consumption, wastewater generation, air pollution, solid waste disposal and energy usage throughout the life cycle of the product. Not all Life Cycle Assessment studies reach the same conclusion, but it is safe to say that most disposable plates excel in some respects, and reusable plates excel in other respects (Broca, 2008). A similar conclusion has been reached for the use of traditional plastic versus the use of bio-based plastic, which is plastic made not out of oil but out of biodegradable materials such as corn starch (Hottle et al., 2013). Therefore, deciding between reusable and disposable plates, and between plastic and bio-plastic should be done carefully and communicated to guests as discreetly and transparently as possible. As in the case of the space, the choice may be based on opportunities derived from the geographic location of the outlet, and should be aligned with its overall vision on sustainability. In any case, when opting for reusable vessels, they should be handled with care so as to prolong their usable life, washed as energy efficiently and water efficiently as possible, reused when possible and properly disposed of when other options are exhausted (such as donating incomplete or out-dated but still usable dishware to charity).

Lastly, it should be noted that the offer of sustainable vessels is developing rapidly. Companies such as the Dutch Bixxs with its YuuNaa collection propose plates and cups made of bamboo, a material considered to be environmentally friendly because it is a fast grower and does not require the use of chemicals (http://www.bixxs.com/en/brands/yuunaa.html). Bamboo tableware still needs to be washed efficiently and properly disposed of to be fully environmentally friendly. Narayana Peesapaty, an entrepreneur from Hyderabad in the Indian province of Andhra Pradesh, has gone a step further in tackling the waste issue by developing edible cutlery made of flour and sorghum blended with rice and wheat (http://www.bakeys.com). Along a similar line, product design student Ari Jónsson from the Iceland Academy of the Arts has created a biodegradable bottle made of red algae powder and water. The bottle will keep its shape as long as it is full of water, but will begin to decompose as soon as it is empty. The bottle was exhibited at the 2016 Reykjavik festival DesignMarch and is not yet in production. These rapid developments require an inquisitive attitude from hospitality professionals to be able to choose the most suitable and sustainable vessel option.

Person: hosts and guests

The implementation of sustainable measures such as those discussed previously has consequences for the people involved, both hosts and guests.

For the hosts, training will probably be needed in at least three different directions: improving the knowledge of F&B related sustainability issues among staff; enhancing cooking techniques; and improving employees' communication skills.

15

In kitchens often the best-trained people, such as chefs, focus on meat preparation. Moreover, many restaurants use pre-cooked food and ready-to-cook ingredients. Cooks may therefore have lost their skills to work with fresh ingredients. Training, therefore, may be needed such as in preparing vegetables and dressing *odd cuts* of meat. For restaurants that wish to go even further, and use only sustainable energy sources to cook, training will be needed in planning differently (e.g. prepare dishes during the day when sun energy supply is high) and in using techniques that make possible to prepare ingredients quickly (such as chopping) or with a minimal source of warmth for a longer time (such as the Italian technique of cooking beans in a glass jar, a *'fiasco'*, that was left in a corner of the fireplace under warm ash overnight to give fresh cooked beans in the morning). Restaurant CIRCL in Amsterdam, for example, works this way (https://circl.nl/restaurant/).

A better communication techniques to help guests in deciding in favour of a more sustainable option are needed because, though concern for the environment in general and animal welfare in particular has gained public attention in recent years, and though people seem more conscious of the effect of a bad diet on their health, the majority of guests does not yet translate these concerns into actions, neither in their daily life nor when dining out. Through well-designed communication, guests could be nudged towards more sustainable choices without negatively affecting their guest experience. For example, a series of experiments in the Netherlands has proven that guests not only tend to go for a vegetarian option when it is presented as the chef's choice but also judge it to be fresher and less expensive than other choices on the menu (Schuttelaar, n.d.). Another experiment shows that guests do not notice a reduction of the meat portion size by 12.5% when it is accompanied by more vegetables than in the original portion (Reinders *et al.*, 2017). However, further reduction of the meat portion size will indeed be noticed and requires proper explanation of the F&B concept (on the website, on the menu and by the personnel) before guests can understand and accept it (personal communication A. Kooy, Leeuwarden, June 2015). Another often-wasted food is vegetables and potatoes served as side dishes. Research has shown that guests feel less responsible for eating these dishes when they are offered as a standard accompaniment to the main course. Here, too, smaller portions could be a solution, and waiters can be instructed to inform guests that they can always order more of the side dishes, free of charge. Lastly, in an effort to reduce food waste from buffets, studies have shown that unobtrusive interventions such as smaller plates, more slender glasses, smaller serving cutlery, a buffet lay out where salads come first, could reduce post-consumer food waste by 20% (Wansink and Hanks, 2013; Kallbekken and Saelen, 2013). Here, too, an invitation to serve oneself as many times as one wishes could help guests to overcome the embarrassment of returning to the buffet table more than once, and thus help them to pile less on their plate the first time around.

A final note on guests' expectation is due. Though as has been observed above, guests not always translate their concern for people and the planet into action, it is also true that times are changing. A recent study carried out among international hotel guests in the Netherlands has shown that guests are more interested in sustainable development and have a much broader perspective on this societal challenge than would be expected considering previous studies. Moreover, guests are particularly aware of food related issues and expect the hotel to take responsibility. Specifically, most guests expect that hotels fight food waste and offer a wide range of local, seasonal and organic products. Some guests went even further and expected the hotel to grow its own food and to respect animal welfare (Cavagnaro *et al.*, 2018)

Conclusion

F&B is one of the most complex and visible hotel departments. It therefore offers a vast array of opportunities to demonstrate the hotel's commitment to sustainability. This chapter discussed opportunities in three main areas, i.e., the fitting out of the space where food and beverages are served, the choice of vessel on which they are served, and the selection of items actually served to guests. Moreover, F&B offers the opportunity to engage the personnel in the sustainability challenge by relying upon and enhancing their professional skills. Lastly, it offers the opportunity to cater for emerging guests' needs for sustainable food and to involve guests as well through skilful communication of the hotel's F&B choices.

Further readings

Cavagnaro, E. (2015). Sustainable restaurant concepts, in Sloan, P. and Legrand, W. (eds.), *Handbook of Sustainable Food, Beverages and Gastronomy*, London: Routledge, pp.245-2.

Sloan, P. and Legrand, W. (eds.) (2015) *Handbook of Sustainable Food, Beverages and Gastronomy*, London: Routledge.

On bio-based vs. oil-based plastic:

Song, R.J, Murphy, R., Narayan, R. and Davies, G.B.H. (2009) Biodegradable and compostable alternatives to conventional plastics, *Philosophical Transactions of the Royal Society B*, **364** (1526) 2127-2139. http://rstb.royalsocietypublishing.org/content/364/1526/2127. Accessed 31 January 2018.

References

Baldwin, C. (2012) *Greening Food and Beverage Services, A Green Seal™ Guide to Transforming the Industry*, Lansing (Michigan): American Hotel and Lodging Educational Institute

Bjurling, K., Weyzig, F. and Wong, S. (2008) *Improving the working conditions at Chinese natural stone companies*, SL: SwedWatch and SOMO. http://www.somo.nl/publications-en/Publication_2459. Accessed 31 January 2018.

Broca, M (2008) A comparative analysis of the environmental impacts of ceramic plates and biodegradable plates (made of corn starch) using Life Cycle Analysis, Major report submitted for the partial fulfillment of MSc. in Environmental Studies, Department of Natural Resources TERI University. http://sustainability. tufts.edu/wp-content/uploads/LifeCycleAnalysisPlasticPlatevsCeramic.pdf. Accessed 19 March 2018.

Cavagnaro, E. and De Kruijf, E. (2014) Food waste, in Cavagnaro, E. (ed.) *Profiles in the Hospitality Industry* (EHMA), Leeuwarden: Stenden, pp. 87-99.

Cavagnaro,E. and Curiel, G.H. (2012) *The Three Levels of Sustainability*, Greenleaf Publishing

Cavagnaro, E., Melissen, F.W. and Düweke, A. (2018) The host-guest relationship is the key to sustainable hospitality: Lessons learned from a Dutch case study, *Hospitality & Society*, **8** (1), 23-44.

CBI Ministry of Foreign Affairs (n. d.) *CBI Product Factsheet: ceramic dinnerware in Europe, Practical market insight in your product*, The Hague: Ministry of Foreign Affairs, https://www.cbi.eu/sites/default/files/market_information/researches/product-factsheet-dinnerware-europe-home-decoration-textiles-2014.pdf. Accessed 31 January 2018.

Chapagain, A.K., Hoekstra, A.Y., Savenije, H.H.G. and Gautam, R. (2006) The water footprint of cotton consumption: An assessment of the impact of worldwide consumption of cotton products on the water resources in the cotton producing countries, *Ecological Economics*, **60** (1), pp. 186-203

Dijksma, S.A.M. (2013) *Brief aan de Tweede Kamer over ingrepen bij pluimvee*, The Hague: Ministry of Economic Affairs. https://www.rijksoverheid.nl/documenten/kamerstukken/2013/06/09/ingrepen-bij-pluimvee. Accessed 31 January 2018.

Ercin, A.E., Aldaya, M.M. and Hoekstra, A.Y. (2011) Corporate water footprint accounting and impact assessment: The case of the water footprint of a sugar-containing carbonated beverage, *Water Resources Management*, **25** (2), 721-741.

European Union (2010) *European declaration on pig castration 20_2*. ec.europa.eu/food/animals/docs/aw_prac_farm_pigs_cast-alt_declaration_en.pdf. Accessed 31 January 2018.

FAO (2010) *The Second Report on the State of the World's Plant Genetic Resources for Food and Agriculture*. FAO: Rome

FAO (2011) *Global food losses and food waste – Extent, causes and prevention,* Rome: FAO, 7 http://www.fao.org/docrep/014/mb060e/mb060e00.pdf. Accessed 31 January 2018.

FAO (2011b) *Review of the state of world marine fishery resources*, FAP Fisheries and Aquaculture Technical paper nr 569, Rome: FAO, http://www.fao.org/docrep/015/i2389e/i2389e.pdf. Accessed 31 January 2018.

FAO (2015) *Groundwater governance a call for action: A shared global vision for 2030*, FAO: Rome, http://www.fao.org/fileadmin/user_upload/groundwatergovernance/docs/general/GWG_VISION.pdf. Accessed 31 January 2018.

Feng, Y., Chen, X.M., Zhao, M., He, Z., Sun, L., Wang, C.Y. and Ding, W.F. (2017) Edible insects in China: Utilization and prospects, *Insect Science*, doi:10.1111/1744-7917.12449

Foster, C., Green, K., Bleda, M., Dewick, P., Evans, B., Flynn A. and Mylan, J. (2006) *Environmental Impacts of Food Production and Consumption: A report to the Department for Environment, Food and Rural Affairs,* London: Manchester Business School Defra, http://randd.defra.gov.uk/Document.aspx?Document=EV02007_4601_FRP.pdf. Accessed 31 January 2018.

Fotouhinia Yepes, M. (2015) Vegetarianism for public health and for the environment: major F&B implications, in Sloan, P. and Legrand, W. (eds.), *Handbook of Sustainable*

Food, Beverages and Gastronomy, London: Routledge, pp. 113-119.

Gleick, P.H. and Cooley, H.S. (2009) Energy implications of bottled water, *Environmental Research Letters*, 4, 1-6, doi:10.1088/1748-9326/4/1/014009

Gössling, S., Garrod, B., Aall, C., Hille, J., and Peeters, P. (2011) Food management in tourism. Reducing tourism's carbon 'foodprint', *Tourism Management*, **32** (3), 534-543.

Hansen, C.L. and Yeol Cheong, D. (2013) Agricultural waste management in food processing, in Kutz, M. (ed.) *Handbook of Farm, Dairy and Food Machinery Engineering*, 2nd ed., Amsterdam: Elsevier, pp. 619-666

Hottle, T. A., Landis, A. E. and Bilec, M.M. (2013) Sustainability assessments of bio-based polymers, *Polymer Degradation and Stability*, **98**, 1898-1907

Huis, van, A. (2016) Edible insects are the future?, *Proceedings of the Nutrition Society*, **75** (3), 294-305. doi:10.1017/S0029665116000069

Huis, van, A., Gurp, H.V. and Dicke, M. (2014) *The Insect Cookbook*, New York: Columbia University Press.

Huis, van, A., Itterbeeck, J., Klunder, H., Mertens, E., Halloran, A., Muir, G. and Vantomme, P. (2013) *Edible insects: future prospects for food and feed security*, Rome: Food and Agricultural Organization of the United Nation

ILO (2010) *Accelerating action against child labour – Global Report under the follow-up to the ILO Declaration on Fundamental Principles and Rights at Work*, Geneva: ILO (International Labour Organisation). http://www.ilo.org/global/publications/ilo-bookstore/order-online/books/WCMS_127688/lang--en/index.htm. Accessed 31 January 2018.

Kallbekken, S. and Saelen, A. (2013) 'Nudging' hotel guests to reduce food waste as a win–win environmental measure, *Economic Letters*, **119**, 325–327

Khan, T. A. and Sievenpiper, J. L. (2016) Controversies about sugars: results from systematic reviews and meta-analyses on obesity, cardiometabolic disease and diabetes, *European Journal of Nutrition*, **55** (Suppl 2), 25–43. http://doi.org/10.1007/s00394-016-1345-3

Knorringa, P. (2007) *Asian Drivers and the Future of Responsible Production and Consumption – Exploring a Research Question and Hypotheses for Further Research.* Working Paper No. 442, Institute of Social Studies, Erasmus University (Rotterdam) https://ideas.repec.org/p/ems/euriss/18752.html. Accessed on 31 January 2018.

Kooy, A. (2013) *5 ingrediënten voor beter, verser, gezonder en eerlijker eten (Five ingredients for better, fresher, healthier and fairer food'*, Zutphen: KMuitgevers.

Lang, T., Dibb, S. and Reddy, S. (2011) *Looking back, looking forward, Sustainability and UK food policy 2000-2011*, S.L.: Sustainable Development Commission.

Legrand, W., Sloan, P., Simons-Kaufmann, C. and Fleischer, S. (2010) A review of restaurant sustainable indicators, in Chen, J. S. (ed.) *Advances in Hospitality and Leisure, Volume 6*, Bingley: Emerald Group Publishing Ltd, pp.167-183

Lundqvist, J., Grönwall, J. and Jägerskog, A. (2015) *Water, food security and human dignity – a nutrition perspective*, Stockholm: Ministry of Enterprise and Innovation, Swedish FAO Committee. http://www.government.se/contentassets/5ef425430d2f49cea3ebc4a55e8127e5/water-food-security-and-human-dignity. Accessed 31 January 2018.

Mekonnen, M.M. and Hoekstra, A.Y. (2012) A global assessment of the water footprint of farm animals, *Ecosystems*, **15**, 401–415, DOI: 10.1007/s10021-011-9517-8

15

Melissen, F., Cavagnaro, E., Damen, M. and Düweke, A. (2015) Is the hotel industry prepared to face the challenge of sustainable development?, *Journal of Vacation Marketing*, **22** (3) 227-238, DOI: 10.1177/1356766715618997

Mitsuhashi, J. (2005) Edible insects in Japan, in Paoletti, M.G. (ed.) *Ecological Implications of Minilivestock: Role of rodents, frogs, snails, and insects for sustainable development*, New Hampshire, USA: Science Publishers, pp. 251–262

Nkonya, E., Mirzabaev, A. and von Braun, J. (eds.) (2016) *Economics of Land Degradation and Improvement – A Global Assessment for Sustainable Development*, Heidelberg: SpringerOpen, DOI 10.1007/978-3-319-19168-3_1, http://www.commonland. com/_doc/5091_699899401.pdf. Accessed 31 January 2018.

NAWS (2001-2002) *Findings from the National Agricultural Workers Survey (NAWS) 2001 – 2002 A Demographic and Employment Profile of United States Farm Workers*, https://www. doleta.gov/agworker/report9/toc.cfm. Accessed 31 January 2018.

Oldeman, L.R., Hakkeling, R.T.A. and Sombroek, W.G. (1991) *World Map of the Status of Human-Induced Soil Degradation: an explanatory note*, Wageningen: International Soil Reference and Information Centre; Nairobi: United Nations Environment Programme. -I11. Global Assessment of Soil Degradation GLASOD.

Olthaar, M. (2009) *Can Tony's Factory Change the World?– A study of the opportunities of a small downstream company to promote upgrading of upstream companies in global agricultural value chains*. MIMEO, Master Thesis in the Global Business and Stakeholder Management Series, Rotterdam: Erasmus University.

Oonincx, D.G.,Van Itterbeeck, J., Heetkamp, M.J.W., van den Brand, H., van Loon, J.J.A. and van Huis, A. (2010) An exploration on greenhouse gas and ammonia production by insect species suitable for animal or human consumption, *PLoS One*, **5** (12):e14445. doi: 10.1371/journal.pone.0014445, https://www.ncbi.nlm.nih.gov/pubmed/21206900. Accessed 31 January 2018.

Parfitt, J., Eatherley, D., Hawkins, R. and Prowse, G. (2013) *Waste in the UK Hospitality and Food Service Sector* (Technical Report No. HFS001-00 6). UK: Waste and Resources Action Programme (WRAP).

Pimentel, D., Williamson, S, Alexander, C.E., Gonzalez-Pagan, O., Kontak C. and Mulkey, S.E. (2008) Reducing energy inputs in the US food system, *Human Ecology*, **36** (4), 459-471

Pirani, S.I., Arafat, H.A. (2016) Reduction of food waste generation in the hospitality industry, *Journal of Cleaner Production*, **132**, 129-135.

Pliner , P. and Salvy, S.J. (2006) Food neophobia in humans, in R. Shepherd and M. Raats, (eds.) *The Psychology of Food Choice*, Wallingford, CABI Publishing, pp. 75–92.

Pollan, M. (2009) *In Defence of Food*, London: Penguin.

Ramos-Elorduy, B. J. (1997) The importance of edible insects in the nutrition and economy of people of the rural areas of Mexico, *Ecology of Food and Nutrition*, **36** (5), 347–366. doi: 10.1080/03670244.1997.9991524.

Reinders, M. J., Huitink, M., Dijkstra, S. C., Maaskant, A. J. and Heijnen, J. (2017) Menu-engineering in restaurants - adapting portion sizes on plates to enhance vegetable consumption: a real-life experiment, *International Journal of Behavioral Nutrition and Physical Activity*, **14** (1), 41, http://doi.org/10.1186/s12966-017-0496-9.

Scarborough, P., Appleby, P.N., Mizdrak, A., Briggs, A.D.M., Travis, R.C., Bradbury, K.E. and Key, T.J. (2014) Dietary greenhouse gas emissions of meat-eaters, fish-eaters, vegetarians and vegans in the UK, *Climatic Change*, **125** (2) 179-192. doi:10.1007/s10584-014-1169-1.

Schlosser, E. (2001) *Fast Food Nation: the Dark Side of the All-American Meal*, New York: Houghton Mifflin.

Schulp, J.A. (2015) Reducing the food miles: locavorism and seasonal eating, in Sloan, P. and Legrand, W. (eds.), *Handbook of Sustainable Food, Beverages and Gastronomy*, London: Routledge, pp. 120-125.

Schuttelaar en partners (s.d.), *Helpt 'Nudgen' bij een gezonde en duurzame keuze? (Does 'nudgen' help making a healthy and sustainable choice/)*, The Hague: Schuttelaar en partners.

Soethoudt, H. (2012) *Reductie voedselverspilling in Nederlandse cateringsector (Reducing food waste in the Dutch catering industry)*, Wageningen: Wageningen UR Food & Biobased Research.

Textile Exchange (2015) *2014 Organic Cotton Market Report, Overview*, US: Textile Exchange.

Tukker, A., Bausch-Goldbohm, S., Verheijden, M., de Koning, A., Kleijn, R., Wolf, O. and Pérez Domíngues, I. (2009) *Environmental Impacts of Diet Changes in the EU*, Seville: European Commission Joint Research Centre Institute for Prospective Technological Studies.

Turenne, J. and Baldwin, C. (2010) Food, in Baldwin, C. (2012) *Greening Food and Beverage Services, A Green Seal™ Guide to Transforming the Industry*, Lansing (Michigan): American Hotel and Lodging Educational Institute, pp. 19-55.

Van Tulder, R., Van Wijk, J. and Kolk, A. (2009) From chain liability to chain responsibility, *Journal of Business Ethics*, **85** (2), 399-412

Wansink, B. and Hanks, A.S. (2013) Slim by design: serving healthy foods first in buffet lines improves overall meal selection, *PLoS ONE*, **8** (10): e77055. doi:10.1371/journal.pone.0077055.

Williams, H. and Wikström, F. (2011) Environmental impact of packaging and food losses in a life cycle perspective: a comparative analysis of five food items, *Journal of Cleaner Production*, **19** (1) 43–48. doi:http://dx.doi.org/10.1016/j.jclepro.2010.08.008.

Wintour, N. (2015) *The glass industry: recent trends and changes in working conditions and employment relations, Working paper (WP) 310*, Geneva: International Labour Office, Sectoral Policies Department, http://www.ilo.org/wcmsp5/groups/public/---ed_dialogue/---sector/documents/publication/wcms_442086.pdf. Accessed 31 January 2018.

WWF (1999) *The impact of cotton on fresh water resources and ecosystems, Background paper*, Zurich: WWF, http://wwf.panda.org/about_our_earth/about_freshwater/freshwater_problems/thirsty_crops/cotton/. Accessed 31 January 2018.

Yeoman, I. and McMahon-Beattie, U. (2016) The future of food tourism, *Journal of Tourism Futures*, **2** (1), 95 - 98

Zock, J.-P., Vizcaya, D. and Le Moual, N. (2010) Update on asthma and cleaners, *Current Opinion in Allergy and Clinical Immunology*, **10** (2), 114–120. http://doi.org/10.1097/ACI.0b013e32833733fe.

15

16 Conclusion

Elena Cavagnaro

It is difficult to write a conclusion to a book dedicated to sustainability in hospitality. In fact as long as the hospitality and tourism industry is not fully engaged in the transition towards sustainability, one cannot speak of a 'conclusion'. It is therefore more appropriate to remind ourselves here that sustainability requires a paradigm shift in the way we look at the economy; in the way we understand our responsibilities as professionals; and in the way we look at ourselves and others. Paradigms can be regarded as lens or viewpoints through which we look at the world. Therefore, paradigms are not a perfect representation of the world and may change if people perceive that another paradigm describes reality more accurately. In this case a paradigm shift occurs. When a paradigm shift happens people not only see the reality differently (because they look from a new paradigm or viewpoint) but will also act differently. A typical example of a paradigm shift can be found in astronomy. For centuries it was believed that the earth stood still at the centre of the solar system while the sun, the planets and all stars rotated around it. In the 16th century, first as an hypothesis to render the calculation of the planets' orbits more easily, then as a better representation of reality, the sun was considered as the focus around which our planet and its neighbours rotate. Even later, it was understood that the whole solar system is located in the periphery of the Milk Way galaxy and shares its movement through space. The transition from a 'business as usual', or mainstream, model to sustainability constitutes a paradigm shift. This shifts, as stated above, affects the way we think and act in our economy; our businesses and among ourselves.

I will explain this statement briefly starting with the mainstream paradigm on the economy. This paradigm states that the economy can grow forever because the natural environment is an endless source of raw materials and an unlimited sink for waste. In this view, if a resource becomes difficult to get or too costly to dig, technology will solve our problems by finding new materials that can substitute the old one. Technology will also help if waste becomes a problem, or pollution hits in.

The mainstream paradigm was seriously shaken when people, on Christmas Eve 1968, were confronted for the first time with an image of planet earth from space. Our planet was shown rising from the moon surface, on a background of black nothing. If you have never seen this iconic picture you can do so by following this link: https://www.nasa.gov/multimedia/imagegallery/image_feature_1249.html (accessed on 27 February 2018).

The image, known as Earthrise, made immediately evident that the Earth is limited. To sustain itself on the long run we should, therefore, understand these limits and learn how to operate inside them. From linear, the economy should become circular. Technology, therefore, should not attempt to transform resources into good and services as quickly and cheaply as possible, in the assumption that when a resource is gone another will be found. On the contrary, it should care for materials and aspire at lengthening their life as much as possible. Technology in the sustainability paradigm is not cradle-to-grave, but circular and cradle-to-cradle. Moreover, because resources are limited, this paradigm also calls for fairness and equity in sharing resources, among people living now and among the present and future generation.

Let us go back to the mainstream paradigm and ask how managers are supposed to behave in it. In this scenario, hospitality professionals should not worry about reducing their energy or water use; taking care for less polluting forms of transport; sourcing locally and the like. In fact there is nothing to worry about because, whatever may happen, technology will help. Managers are encouraged to take care of their business solely, to let it grow and generate a return on investment for the owner or financer. In fact, in this paradigm, managers have no other responsibility than towards their shareholders, provided that they obey the country's law and regulations.

Managers' responsibilities are understood quite differently in the sustainability paradigm. Because natural resources and services are limited and should be shared equitably, and because hospitality and tourism (as we have shown all along this book) consume a vast amount of resources, managers have the responsibility to operate their business so that the least possible resources are consumed and when possible resources are restored, while benefitting as many people (guests and employees) as possible. The manager's responsibility is not only towards shareholders, but also towards all stakeholders, that is all people affected by the operations of a manager's organisation.

Let us look now at paradigms about people. In hospitality settings 'people' are hosts and guests. Hospitality, we should not forget, is the art of making people feel welcome and at ease even if they are away from home. It is in hosts' nature to wish to be hospitable towards their guests. Hospitality, though, is in the eyes of the beholder. In other words it is the guest who decides whether he (or she) has been properly welcomed. Hosts have to guess at the best of their capabilities which are guests' wishes so that she (or he) can feel properly welcomed. It is here that paradigms come into play. There is a widespread perception among hosts that guests' main desire is to enjoy their stay, to be pampered, and to get the highest benefits (such as a spacious room) at the lowest costs. In hosts' minds,

16

therefore, guests are moved by hedonic and gain values. Guests, hosts say, are not interested and not willing to support the hotel's sustainability efforts if these come at the expense of their hospitality experience. Interestingly though, when hosts think about their most hospitable experience, they tell stories of intimacy with the host and the host's family, of caring for the local people and enjoying the beauty of natural environments (Melissen *et al.*, 2016). Hosts (in their role as guests) see themselves as moved by other values than enjoyment and gain. They attribute to themselves values of care for others and for the wider environment. Hosts seem therefore to hold a different paradigm when they consider their guests and when they consider themselves as guests.

What about the guests themselves? In our research we found a similar picture, but then the other way round. Guests do not deny their wish to enjoy hospitality. Yet they also claim that their hospitality experience is affected when they see that their hosts do not care for other people, such as hotel's employees, or the natural environment. Some guests expressed openly their doubts that hosts truly intend to care for the natural environment, and claimed that if hosts go only half way guests will do even less (Cavagnaro, Melissen and Düweke, 2018).

If we combine the results of our research on hosts and our research on guests we could draw one of these two conclusions: either the paradigm that hosts have of guests and guests of hosts is not correct; or the paradigm that hosts have of themselves (as guests) and guests have of themselves is not correct. In other words, either hosts and guests are only interested in their own benefits, or hosts and guests are able and willing to take other people's and nature's interests into account. Which of these two paradigms is nearest to reality? Our take, on the basis of ample research (see e.g. Steg *et al.*, 2014), is that people have the capacity to care for themselves, others and nature; and that therefore the second paradigm is the one nearest to reality.

Yet, someone may object, it may be true of people in general but not for tourists and guests. The reasoning goes that tourists and guests are engaged in hedonic activities, that is activities that they undertake for the sake of their personal enjoyment and happiness. Even more strongly, tourism is considered to be by definition a hedonic experience (Kim *et al.*, 2012). Therefore, even if in general people may feel obliged to care for others and nature, as tourists and guests they are immerse in an environment that strengthen their desire for relaxation, fun and enjoyment. Hedonic values then become dominant, and crowd out any concern for other people or nature. This vision on tourism is in strong contrast with the transformative power that is attributed to it by organisations such as the World Tourism Organisation of the United Nations (UNWTO, 2016). Several academic studies have also concluded that travelling befits people in many ways, and not only because it generate a short-lived sense of happiness (Gössling, 2018). By bringing people in touch with other cultures and with the beauty of nature, these studies contend, tourism has the capacity to sensitize people to the need of protecting our cultural heritage and nature. So we are left again with the question:

which of these two paradigms is nearest to reality? A final answer to this is not yet possible. However, recent research suggests that at least young tourists are not only seeking fun and enjoyment. Alongside escapism and relaxation, the avowed motives speak of inner development and personal growth through the encounter with other people (Cavagnaro, Staffieri and Postma, 2018). In another study, moreover, it has been shown that tourism in general, and not a specific tourism experience such as eco-tourism, has the capacity to let people feel changed, not only in the way they look at themselves and other, but also in the way they look at nature (Cavagnaro and Staffieri, 2016). These results need to be probed further, yet they indicate that tourists are not by definition only looking for untroubled enjoyment. The message of all we know about people in general and tourism in particular is that hosts might wish to reconsider their paradigm of guests as interested in only their own benefit.

If you have already read Chapter 2, you may have recognized that the sustainability paradigm we present here is the same as the Three Levels of Sustainability illustrated there. You may also have recognized in the discussion above the sustainability principles of not harming and doing good. If you wish to dig deeper into these notions, please go back to Chapter 2 and the literature quoted there.

What we wish to stress here, in conclusion, is that all along this book we have shown that it is possible to manage hospitality and tourism more sustainably. Even stronger, though the best cases presented in each chapter of the book we have shown that there are businesses already acting from the sustainability paradigm, businesses that have designed and operate a business model that stays inside the limit of our planet while benefiting people. At the end of this book, but not of the quest for a more environmentally sustainable and socially equitable development, we encourage you to follow their steps, create new sustainable business models in tourism and hospitality and behave as a true Guest on Earth.

References

Cavagnaro, E. and Staffieri, S. (2016) Change as a benefit from travelling: for 'me', for 'me & you' or for 'all'? - A case study among students studying in the Netherlands', in Lira, S., Mano, A., Pinheiro, C. and Amoêda, R. (eds.) *Tourism 2016, Proceedings of the International Conference on Global Tourism and Sustainability*, Lagos, Portugal, 14-16 October, Barcelos: Green Lines Institute for Sustainable Development, pp.115-124 (ISBN 978-989-8734-18-1)

Cavagnaro, E., Melissen, F.W. and Düweke, A. (2018) The host-guest relationship is the key to sustainable hospitality: Lessons learned from a Dutch case study, *Hospitality & Society*, **8** (1) 23-44.

Cavagnaro, E., Staffieri, S. and Postma, A. (2108) Understanding millennials' tourism experience: values and meaning to travel as a key for identifying target clusters for youth (sustainable) tourism, *Journal of Tourism Futures*, https:// doi.org/10.1108/ JTF-12-2017-0058.

16

Gössling, S. (2018) Tourism, tourist learning and sustainability: an exploratory discussion of complexities, problems and opportunities, *Journal of Sustainable Tourism*, **26** (2) 292-306

Kim, J-H., Ritchie, J.R.B. and McCormick, B. (2012) Development of a scale to measure memorable tourism experiences, *Journal of Travel Research*, **51** (1) 12-25.

Melissen, F., Cavagnaro, E., Damen, M. and Düweke, A. (2016) Is the hotel industry prepared to face the challenge of sustainable development?, *Journal of Vacation Marketing*, **22** (3) 227-238

Steg, L., Bolderdijk, J. W., Keizer, K. and Perlaviciute, G. (2014) An integrated framework for encouraging pro-environmental behaviour: The role of values, situational factors and goals, *Journal of Environmental Psychology*, **38**, 104-115.

UNWTO (2016) *Affiliate Members Global Report, Volume fourteen – The Transformative Power of Tourism a paradigm shift towards a more responsible traveller*, Madrid: UNWTO. http://cf.cdn.unwto.org/sites/all/files/pdf/global_report_transformative_power_tourism_v5.compressed_2.pdf. Accessed on 28 February 2018.

Index

accreditation systems 129
algorithmic management 231
  and control of behaviour 241–242
algorithms 63-65, 71, 90, 91, 231, 241-242
all-inclusive holidays 54
Anderson, R. 110
aviation industry self-regulation 43

bamboo tableware 293
behaviour, 54, 55, 218
  and technology 114
  online 90
big data 64
billboard effect 80
biodiversity 277
biofuels 39
bookingchannels 68–69
bottled water, environmental impact 279
BREEAM green building accreditation
        124–125, 129
building materials
  bio-based 132
  life-cycle phases 121
  passports 125–126
buildings 118–144
  accreditation systems 120–121
  clean energy generation 134
  cradle-to-cradle approach 136
  end-of-use issues 136
  energy consumption and design 134
  environmental impacts 121–122
  equipment sustainability challenges 122–123
  financing 123, 127, 139
  incentives for sustainability 140
  regenerative or restorative 119
  sustainability and Material Passport 125–126
buyer-supplier relationships 171, 178–179

carbon-offsetting schemes 41
CASBEE green building accreditation 130
cases
  Alpine Pearls 35, 56
  Association of Christian hotels 57
  Bad Hofgastein 194
  Bilderberg 234–235
  BlaBlaCar 36
  BookDifferent 97
  BREEAM certificate 124
  Costa Navarino (Greece) 235–237
  cradle-to-cradle production 256
  edible cutlery 112
  employees' customer journey 212
  employees from local community 235–237
  environmentally friendly logistics 194
  Eurostar 177
  Fairmont Hotels 175
  Fair Trade 282
  Feldmilla 286
  financing 126–128
  Fogo Island Inn 157
  halal food logistics 193
  Healthy Kansas Hospitals 158
  Hilton Universal City 126–128
  holidays by train 36
  horsemeat scandal 176
  hotel and impact of TPIs 75
  hotel reservation systems 72
  inclusion project 211
  insects as food 285
  labour rights 233–234
  light as a service 111
  Material Passports 125
  Meliá Roma Aurelia Antica 211
  NH Hotel Group and labour rights 233–234
  Online Travel Agency 97
  outsourcing 234–235

PACE 126–128
Philips 111
Please Disturb 254
Royal Auping mattresses 256
safeguarding guest data 72
social approach to transport services 194
social initiatives 212
Spier, Stellenbosch (South Africa) 194
sustainable food supply chain 286
The Madaster Foundation 125
Travellers café Viavia Jogja 212
TripAdvisor GreenLeaders Program 98
Van der Valk hotel chain 124
certification schemes 289
circular economy 39–40, 114
clean energy generation, new buildings 134
climate change 2, 29
  hotel sector's contribution 120
CO2 emissions 189
  and meat production 279
  and tourism activities 32
  reduction 196–197
competitive advantage 21
croncrete, reuse and recycling potential 132
confirmation bias and web personalisation 100
cookies 65, 91
corporate outsourcing 225
Corporate Social Responsibility (CSR) 79, 179
cost reduction 13
cotton 260
  environmental impact 281
  water usage 249
cradle-to-cradle technology 113–115
cradle-to-grave technology 111
crowd work 227
culinary tradition 290
customer supply chain 174–175
cyber ethics 66–67

data analysis, profit opportunities 90
data brokerage 90
data collection and handling 64–71
  security issues 78–80
data mining 90
data privacy legislation 78
data storage and privacy 67

destination
  behaviour of tourists 54
  distribution of guests 50–61
  distribution of wealth 55
digital fingerprint 65
digital marketing and guest journey 63
dimensions of sustainability, economic, social
    and environmental 14–17
distribution 27
  of guests at the destination 50–61
distribution channels
  definition 87
  management 80, 88
district heating system 136
diversity 209–210
  embracing 213
domestic tourism 33
Ducker, Peter 15
eco-efficiency 6, 7
economic dimension, principle 17
economic leakage 56
Electronic Customer Relationship
    Management (eCRM) 95
employees
  critical importance 208–211
  discrimination 210
  diversity 210, 213
  engagement 208, 213–216
  health issues 253
  housekeeping 253
  organizational culture 216–218
  recruitment and retention 223
  well being 208, 215–16
  See also outsourcing, gig economy
employment practices 209, 213, 222
  flexibility 223
  and globalization 225, 240
  See also human resource management
energy
  key card control 261
  reduction 6, 260–262
  usage in hotel rooms 250
  consumption 120, 134
environmental certification 197–198
environmental dimension, principle 19–20
ethically produced goods 173
ethics 18
  and information 66–67

and international purchasing 173
avoiding harm 18
do good 18
cyber ethics 66
examples
    Amazon 231
    Bennu 101
    Bilderberg 6
    BookDifferent 100
    Conscious Hotels 7
    Eat With 161
    freon and ozone layer damage 108
    G Adventures 8
    GreenHotelWorld 100
    GreenLeaders Program 101
    Hilton sustainable seafood project 176
    I Amsterdam 12
    incandescent light bulbs 109
    Meliá Hotels 5
    Radisson Blu Hotel 6
    Trolltunga 55
    Uber 227, 232

Fair Trade certification 289
farm-to-plate 159
farm-to-table 159
    and slow food 160
filter bubble 93, 100
    and web personalisation 93–95
financing
    for green buildings 139
    PACE (Property Assessed Clean Energy) 127
    sustainable buildings 123
fixture and fittings, sustainable production
    issues 275–276
flooring, more sustainable options 265
food and beverage 274–299
    environmental impact of production
        277–279
    'Five Ingredients' 290–292
    healthy diet 291
    local sourcing 290
    reducing waste 294
    serving vessels 280–281
food miles 152
food waste in restaurants and catering 280
food zone model 165
forced labour 252

Forest Stewardship Council certification 289
fossil fuels 39
fuels, alternative 38–39

General Data Protection Regulation (GDPR)
    78
gig economy 221–246, 227–231
    and globalisation 240–241
    organisations, platforms and apps 228
    people employed 228–229
glass and heat gain/loss 133
globalisation
    and labour market 225–226
    impact on employees 226
globalisation and the gig economy 240–241
global sourcing compared to international
    purchasing 179
global warming 5
    See also climate change and greenhouse gas
        emissions
goods ethical production 173
green building programmes 119
    financing 123
greenhouse gas emissions 29, 36, 38, 135, 191,
    198
guest journey
    definition 63-64
    digital marketing 63
    lowering the influence of TPIs 98–99
    steered by TPI 91
    Third-Party Internet sites 84–104
guest profiles, TPI sites 65

heating systems, sustainable options 135
heat pumps 135
hospitality, defined 1
hospitality industry, HR management 209
hospitality providers
    responsibility for guests 53
hotel chains, potential for impact 4
hotels
    energy consumption 120, 123
    water use for cleaning 138
hotel supply chain 170
housekeeping staff
    healthier working conditions 268
See also employees

human resource management
  for highly engaged workforces 213–216
  in the hospitality industry 209
  in tourism 222
  return on investment 239–240
  outsourcing 224
human trafficking 252
  cases 254

incentives, 58
information and privacy 62–83
insulation, sustainable options 133
Internet Distribution System (IDS) 85
ISO 14001, environmental management 197

key cards, sustainability issues 137

labour market
  flexibility 223
  globalisation 225–226
labour trafficking 268
LEED green building certification 119, 127, 131
life-cycle analysis 196, 198
local
  abuse of term 156
  cuisine 149
  defining by distance 164–165
  definitions 152
  foods
    advantages 148–150
    and customs 160
    and seasonal 155
    habits and preferences of guests 155
  logistics and multiplier effect 30-31, 195–196
  purchasing 147–168
    and local food consumption 162
    and waste management 153
    imact on international suppliers 173
    negative impacts on other countries 154
    paradigm shift 163
  suppliers, cooperative 164
logistics 187
loyalty programmes 52, 99

marketing budget and TPIs 72
market segments and TPIs 80
mattresses, recycling possibilities 266
meaningfulness in work 216

meat production, environmental impact 279
minibar, energy costs 262
motivations 15
multiplier effect 1, 56, 163, 195–196

nature sensitive sites, protecting 55
networks, local and virtual 181
NH Hotel Group, cases 233–234
nutrients, technological and biological 113

obsolesce and sustainability 109
offshoring 224, 238–239
Online Travel Agencies (OTAs) 85
organizational culture 216–218
operations 205, 231–233, 247–248
outsourcing 221–246, 234, 238–239

PACE financing 127
package deals 52
packaging
  and local purchasing 153
  recycling 197
  toiletries 263
Paris climate agreement 2, 38
Pariser, E 94
pay-per-click advertising 71
persona concept 91
personal data use by TPIs for marketing 91–92
Porter, Michael 20
Porter's value chain 20–22
predictive analytics 66
privacy and personal data 62–83, 88–89
privacy leak 66
profit, people and the planet 14
Property Management System
  and personal data 67
Property Management Systems 85
pull technology 92
purchasing
  and supply chain management 170
  core activities 171
  defined 150
  problems of small-scale suppliers 162
  single source 189
  sustainable in international context 169–185
  sustainable vs green, 174
  traditional v. sustainable 150–151

purchasing locally 147–168
 See also local purchasing
push technology 92

rebound effect 114
recycling, problems of mixed materials 110
reservation horizon 84
restaurant space, sustainability issues 276
revenues, increasing - limitations 12
Rooms Division 247–273

scientific management 230–232
Search Engine Marketing 71, 81, 88
Search Engine Optimization 81
search engines and TPI sites 71
seasonal products 155
security
 of data 66, 78
sex trafficking 253, 267
Shorefast label 158
slow food 161
smartphones 95
 breaches of privacy 95
 signs of changing attitudes 101
social dimension, basic principles 17–18
social licence to operate 3
social media
 accounts and data sharing 65
 impact on hotel marketing 87–88
social responsibility 207–220
solar panels 134
staff, *see* employees
stakeholders 8, 53–54, 58–59, 171–172
 importance of relationship management 180
supply chain
 customers 174–175
 logistic 186–187
 motives for sustainability 190
 of tourism, defined 186
supply chain management
 social impact 192
supply chains 169–170
 international 169
 lack of transparency in international 176
 local vs global, 189–190, 195–196, 199
 potential for corruption 173
 typical hotel 170
surveillance capitalism 90

sustainability
 and resources 148
 as a business opportunity 7
 definition 2
 dimensions 2
 stances:
  business opportunity 7
  compliance 4
  stewardship 4-7
  transformation and innovation 8-9
 why hotels engage 3–5
sustainability education and level of
  commitment 180
sustainability initiatives, enhancing employee
  engagement 215
sustainable development, social dimension
  208–220
Sustainable Hospitality Value Chain 11–26
 origins 22
sustainable purchasing 169–185
sustainable, responsible and impact investing
  (SRI) 140
sustainable transport, at a destination 56
sustainable value,
 defined 148
 creation 11–16,

tableware, reusable versus disposable 293
Taylorism 230
Taylorism on steroids 232
technology 107–117
 beneficial developments 108–109
 cradle-to-cradle 20, 23, 113, 256, 289
 cradle-to-grave 110
 definition 107
 effects on human behaviour 114
 planned obsolescence 109
 sustainability focussed 114
think global, act local 147
Third-Party Internet sites 62–83
 business models 68
 commission costs 70
 definition 63
 guest journey 84–104
 marketing expenses 71
 pre-set filters on searches 93
 use of social media data 89
 websites, reasons for success 89

Three Levels of Sustainability framework 22
toiletries
  and waste 251
  organic & fair trade 264
tourism
  global value 31
  supply chain, definition 186
  transformative power 85
  transformative power, negated? 94
tourism marketing, impact of World Wide
    Web 86–90
tourism multiplier effect 163
tourist mobility 29–49
  behavioural change to mitigate 40–42
  dilemmas 33–34
  environmental impact 30
  policy changes to mitigate 42–45
  use of technology to mitigate 38–40
TPIs *see* Third-Party Internet sites
transportation
  and local purchasing 151–154
  and international purchasing 154
  and tourism mobility 29–50
  carbon-offsetting 197
  defined 30
  hidden costs 196
  of goods 186–204
  sustainability issues 31, 151, 188-193
  ways to reduce costs 188
triple bottom line 237

value chain
  defined 20
  Porter's 20–22
  See also sustainable hospitality value chain
value creation 187
  and decreasing costs 13-14
  and increasing revenues 12-13
  and sustainability 14
  definition 12
  principles of 17

visitor management 54
  incentives 58
  information provision 58
  local collaboration 59
  non-promotion 59
  packages 59
visitor management techniques 58–60

wage slaves 233–234
waste
  and purchasing 153-154, 162
  created by guests 251
  reduction in guest rooms 263
  waste management 153
  zero waste 19, 289
water
  consumption in hotels 138, 248–250
  saving 257–258
  usage for laundry 249, 259
water consumption
  guest behaviour 258
water stress 248
wearables 95–96
  breaches of privacy 95
Web 1.0, hotel marketing 87
Web 2.0 87, 92
Web 3.0 86–88, 101
web personalisation 93
wellbeing, guests and staff 252–254
whole life-cycle costing 198
wind turbines 134
wood, sustainability issues 133
wood pellet heating systems 135
work with meaning 215
World Wide Web, effect on tourism marketing
    86–90

zero waste principle 19